RAILWAYMEN AND REVOLUTION

RAILWAYMEN
AND REVOLUTION

Russia, 1905

HENRY REICHMAN

UNIVERSITY OF CALIFORNIA PRESS
BERKELEY   LOS ANGELES   LONDON

University of California Press
Berkeley and Los Angeles, California

University of California Press, Ltd.
London, England

Library of Congress Cataloging-in-Publication Data
Reichman, Henry, 1947-
  Railwaymen and revolution.

  Bibliography: p.
  Includes index.
    1. Railroads—Soviet Union—Employees—History.
2. Soviet Union—History—Revolution of 1905. I. Title.
HD8039.R12S827 1987   331.7'61385'0947   86-7084
ISBN 0-520-05716-3 (alk. paper)

Printed in the United States of America

1   2   3   4   5   6   7   8   9

To my parents
for their patience, support, and love

Contents

List of Tables   ix

Acknowledgments   xi

Note on Dates and Transliteration   xiii

Abbreviations   xv

Introduction   1

Part One: Railroads and Railroad Labor in the Tsarist System

1. Railroad Development and Labor Policy   15
2. Railroad Labor: Recruitment, Composition, Structure   41
3. Railroad Labor: Wages, Hours, Conditions   71
4. The Railwayman's Life   98

Part Two: Railroad Workers in Revolution

5. First Assaults and the Time of Petitioning   123
6. The All-Russian Union of Railroad Employees and
    Workers   159
7. The Pension Congress and the October Strike   186
8. The Rush to Organize   224
9. The December Strike and Armed Uprisings   259
10. Repression and Retreat   291

Contents

Conclusion   307

Bibliography of Sources Cited   313

Index   329

Tables

1. Number of Railroad Personnel by Department, 1905   51
2. Number of Railroad Personnel by Job Category, 1905   52
3. Earnings of Permanent Staff by Department   75
4. Salaries of Selected Permanent Staff Positions   76
5. Average Annual Salary of Railroad Employees, 1885–1905   86
6. Average Annual Salaries of Railroad Pension Fund Participants by Department, 1899–1905   88

Acknowledgments

This book was written in two stages. Between 1973 and 1977 I researched and wrote a doctoral dissertation on this subject at the University of California at Berkeley. In 1981 I resumed research in the Soviet Union, and in subsequent years I entirely rewrote the original manuscript. During both periods my greatest debt by far has been to Professor Reginald Zelnik, who, first as advisor and then as mentor and friend, more than any other individual encouraged and guided my scholarly work. Without his steady support, assistance, and advice this project could have never been completed. We have not always agreed—about history and life—Lut I have learned through hard experience to place great value on his counsel. His careful reading of both incarnations of this work saved me from more than a few mistakes; those that remain undoubtedly testify to my need to learn more from experience.

I want to thank Diane Koenker, William Rosenberg, and Allan Wildman for their helpful readings of the manuscript. Gerald Surh's thoughtful comments on a paper based on the penultimate draft also helped refine my arguments. Janet Rabinowitch read the manuscript and provided needed advice at a key juncture. Gerald Feldman and George Breslauer served on my dissertation committee, and some of their suggestions have survived into the final version. In the Soviet Union Professor Irina M. Pushkareva was kind enough to meet with me on short notice, and even kinder to share her knowledge of archives and other sources on Russian railroad labor.

During my graduate training I was supported by a University of California Special Career Fellowship. The International Research

and Exchanges Board (IREX) supported my travel to the Soviet
Union in 1981–82. A Memphis State University Faculty Research
Grant assisted the final preparation of the manuscript. I am grate-
ful as well to the archivists and librarians at the state historical archives in Leningrad and Moscow; the Lenin Library in Moscow;
the Library of the Academy of Sciences in Leningrad; the libraries
of the University of California at Berkeley and Columbia University; and the Library of the Hoover Institution on War, Revolution
and Peace, where research for this project was carried out. I also
want to thank Daniel Field, editor of the *Russian Review*, for permission to use material from my article "Tsarist Labor Policy and
the Railroads, 1885–1914."

Too many people contributed to this book indirectly to thank
them all individually, but I would like to single out three whose
help entailed a kind of sacrifice. Judith F. Krug of the American
Library Association lost an assistant to this project, but she offered
work, encouragement, and friendship when all three were hard
to find. For Raymond Lotta, my return to teaching and research
meant a rift in our common commitment to social change, if not in
our friendship. His broad-ranging intellect and iconoclastic spirit
continue to remind me which questions are truly important, and
his unique understanding of revolutionary change informs the pages
that follow.

Finally, my work on this book demanded the greatest sacrifices
from my wife, Susan Hutcher. But she was there at the start, and
she is there at the finish, and that's all that matters to me.

Note on Dates and
Transliteration

All dates are according to the Old Style (Julian) calendar used in tsarist Russia, which was thirteen days behind the Western (Gregorian) calendar in the twentieth century. Transliteration follows the Library of Congress system, although names and places that are well known are presented in their more familiar English forms. Names of railroad lines that in Russian appear in the adjectival form have been translated as English nouns (e.g., Nikolaevskaia = Nicholas, Moskovsko-Kazanskaia = Moscow-Kazan). In a few cases where translation yields awkward English, the Russian name has been transliterated without the adjectival ending (e.g., Vladikavkazkaia = Vladikavkaz).

Abbreviations

The following abbreviations are used in the notes:

Bir. ved.	*Birzhevye vedomosti*
Privol. kr.	*Privolzhskii krai*
Statistika	Ministerstvo putei soobshcheniia. Pensionnaia kassa. *Statistika sluzhashchikh na kazennykh zheleznykh dorog uchastnikov pensionnykh kassy*
TsGAOR	Tsentral'nyi Gosudarstvennyi Arkhiv Oktiabr'skoi Revoliutsii (Central State Archive of the October Revolution)
TsGIA	Tsentral'nyi Gosudarstvennyi Istoricheskii Arkhiv (Central State Historical Archive)
Vech. poch.	*Vecherniaia pochta*
VMPS	*Vestnik ministerstva putei soobshcheniia*
Vrach-san otchet	Ministerstvo putei soobshcheniia. Vrachebno-sanitarnaia chast'. *Otchet o vrachebno-sanitarnom sostoianii eksploatiruemykh zheleznykh dorog*
ZhD	*Zheleznodorozhnoe delo*
Zhel.	*Zheleznodorozhnik*
ZhN	*Zheleznodorozhnaia nedelia*

Introduction

On the tortuous journey to the Bolshevik October, the first Russian revolution of 1905 was a fateful crossroads. It was not simply that 1905 was, as Lenin put it, a "dress rehearsal" for the more decisive confrontation twelve years later.[1] Rather, the events and outcome of 1905 redefined the terms of the struggle. This first revolution shattered the fragile oppositional spirit that seemed to bring together noblemen and peasants, industrialists and workers, Marxist Social Democrats and reformist *zemstvo* activists, if not always in a common movement with mutually accepted demands, then in a briefly shared ethos of "liberation," and it left in its wake an explosive realignment of political and social forces.

To be sure, conflicting trends within the opposition were already defined before the tsar's troops fired on the St. Petersburg workers that Bloody Sunday in January 1905, but these retained a somewhat scholastic aura. If various oppositional elements and their intelligentsia representatives posed differing visions of both the road forward and the future goal, such differences were founded as much on the assumed interests of perceived agents of change as on the real ones of the political actors themselves. Only in the fiery crucible of revolution were still often nascent theoretical debates joined to, and ultimately transformed by, the more fundamental, if equally complex, class and social cleavages of a rapidly changing and highly volatile society. In 1905 emerging economic and social conflicts ruptured old loyalties and invalidated old programs, and

1. V. I. Lenin, "Left-Wing Communism: An Infantile Disorder," in *Collected Works* (Moscow, 1961–66), vol. 31, p. 27.

political disagreements in turn helped crystallize deep-rooted economic and social distinctions.

One product of 1905 was a dramatic change in the role of the working class. Recent research has underlined the heterogeneity of the proletariat and the complexity of its social structure.[2] Throughout 1905 the working class remained politically diverse, and its political divisions reflected and interpenetrated with a host of geographic, professional, cultural, and other structural distinctions. To a very real degree, however, as the revolution unfolded, workers began through complex struggle to develop a unique and defining political vision of their own, a very genuine, if still nascent, consciousness of class. This emerging consciousness was highly immoderate in its approach to both political and economic grievances and fundamentally hostile to privileged society in both its tsarist and bourgeois garb. The class consciousness of 1905 was forged not only out of the varied circumstances of the workers' own lives, but from their manifold interaction with other social classes and strata under the guidance of competing representatives of the intelligentsia, who at once sought to articulate the workers' own incipient values and aspirations and to impose upon their activities more universalist goals and strivings. Most important, the development of proletarian political consciousness and of a distinctly working-class political culture were products of complex struggles internal to the emerging proletariat.

To most of its theoreticians the 1905 revolution was a "bourgeois revolution" aimed at the overthrow of tsarism and the establishment of a democratic republic. Yet the revolution was distinguished from

2. Works that broaden our picture of the prerevolutionary Russian working class to include artisan sectors, women, and others not so readily integrated into the traditional emphasis on the large factory inherited from Soviet (and prerevolutionary) studies include Robert Eugene Johnson, *Peasant and Proletarian: The Working Class of Moscow in the Late Nineteenth Century* (New Brunswick, N.J., 1979); Victoria E. Bonnell, *Roots of Rebellion: Workers' Politics and Organizations in St. Petersburg and Moscow, 1900–1914* (Berkeley and Los Angeles, 1983) and Rose L. Glickman, *Russian Factory Women: Workplace and Society, 1880–1914* (Berkeley and Los Angeles, 1984). A very illuminating picture of the complex diversity of the working-class experience in tsarist Russia is offered by the memoirs and other documents collected by Bonnell in *The Russian Worker: Life and Labor Under the Tsarist Regime* (Berkeley and Los Angeles, 1983). Soviet scholars have also begun to lay greater stress on the diversity of the proletarian experience in Russia. See Iu. I. Kir'ianov, *Zhiznennyi uroven' rabochikh Rossii* (Moscow, 1979).

previous revolutions in that, as Lenin put it, "it was a bourgeois-democratic revolution in its social content, but a proletarian revolution in its methods of struggle." The story of 1905 is the story of the strike movement of that year. This movement displayed both an economic and a political character, and at decisive moments these complementary aspects merged to determine the consciousness of the participating workers. "There can be no doubt that only this very close tie between the two forms of strike gave the movement its great power," Lenin concluded.[3]

The principal political demands of the workers were never specifically class demands reflecting the proletarian struggle for socialism.[4] They were instead general democratic demands for elementary rights, "demands which will not destroy capitalism but, on the contrary, bring it within the framework of Europeanism, and free it of barbarism, savagery, corruption and other 'Russian' survivals of serfdom."[5] The key demands directly challenged the state edifice of tsarism, calling for a constituent assembly, for "four tail"— general, equal, direct, and secret—suffrage, and for a democratic republic and political freedom. Such issues were jointly raised by oppositional society as a whole, but different political forces and social classes supported them for their own reasons, and each could give them a distinctive coloration.

In the political struggle the working class could choose between two alternative paths of action. Workers could support the political movement initiated and led by more educated strata of the opposition, subordinating their own perceived interests to this movement and its program; or they could strive to play an independent political role and seek to lead the political struggle for democracy in their own way. As is well known, this latter course was the path

3. V. I. Lenin, "Lecture on the 1905 Revolution," in *Collected Works*, vol. 23, p. 238.

4. Here and elsewhere in this study the term "political demand" is used mainly to indicate those demands aimed primarily at influencing affairs of state or acts of government. An economic demand is generally one that has as its goal the improvement of the worker's economic position, mainly with respect to the place of employment. However, as the discussion makes clear, many working-class demands related to factory issues could also have a real impact on government insofar as they called into question fundamental relations of power in society. In certain situations, such demands should also be labeled political.

5. V. I. Lenin, "The Socialist Party and Non-Party Revolutionism," in *Collected Works*, vol. 10, p. 77.

encouraged by the Bolsheviks, but debate over the independent role of the proletariat and its political representatives was not confined to Marxist intellectuals. As workers entered political activity in 1905, the question of their relation to other political forces became very real to them and was greatly affected by their broader social relations and economic interests. Tsarist statisticians distinguished political from economic strikes, but this division was not always meaningful. The economic strike movement could represent a political force in its own right, though perhaps only latently. For it was in the economic struggle that large numbers of Russian workers first came into battle *as a class*, distinct from other oppositional forces, and in this setting they began to define a politics of their own.

This can be seen when the demands raised by workers in 1905 are examined. Usually those demands categorized as "political," including civil and political liberties, a democratic republic, and a constitution, were part and parcel of the program generally endorsed by liberals and socialists, workers, and some reformist gentry alike. But the workers also raised demands of their own, which were not without political significance and impact. The struggle for political liberty both pushed forward and was itself advanced by the even broader spontaneous movement for a better material life. Workers demanded shorter hours, higher wages, pension funds, and health-care benefits. They also called for an end to harassment and brutality by foremen and for respect on the job and in society. They demanded the right to participate in hiring and firing and in setting piece rates. Such demands very often revealed a deep-seated hostility to the class divisions fundamental to both tsarism and capitalism, and, by implication at least, could reflect nascent political motives as deeply as endorsement of the broader demands of the democratic program. This was especially true as worker demands for participation and control of the work process found expression in calls for political participation and control and vice versa.[6]

6. Anthony Giddens has pointed out that "any sort of extension of industrial conflict into the area of control poses a threat to the institutional separation of economic and political conflict which is a fundamental basis of the capitalist state—because it serves to bring into the open the connections between political power in the polity as such, and the broader 'political' subordination of the working class within the economic order" (*The Class Structure of the Advanced Societies* [New York, 1975], p. 206).

Economic demands could themselves also become politicized when workers raised them in a coordinated national fashion. General adoption of such a demand in virtually every strike program indicated that many workers saw the issue as soluble only on a national scale, through political action of some sort. Such was the case with the demand for the eight-hour day. Moreover, even the most basic economic strikes were rendered political through confrontations with the tsarist police and troops who tried to suppress them. Raising the demand to free those arrested in a strike was a simple, but sometimes significant, political step. It could bring workers into sharp, often violent, confrontation with the government.

This is not to argue that proletarian political consciousness grew spontaneously out of the economic struggle. Workers did not simply gravitate to politics in order to achieve economic goals. The development of political consciousness took place together with a deepening of the workers' economic struggle. What workers increasingly brought to political life from their economic battles was a unique sense of self-identity and a militant combativeness forged there, which distinguished them from other oppositional strata. Moreover, it is inadequate simply to trace the political awakening of the workers; the politics to which they awakened must also be defined. There was no preordained path to radicalism that moved smoothly from economic rebellion to revolutionary socialism by way of some liberal halfway house. The most radical elements among the workers were not those who only supported the political demands of the day, or even those who were among the first of their comrades to do so, but those who *combined* oppositional politics with the fight workers had already begun for material betterment and, more important, for dignity as a class in the plants and in society. In doing so, they helped redefine political issues.

This book is about the development of political activity and the emergence of class consciousness in 1905 among one group of workers, the railwaymen. Given the important role of the railroad system in Russian industrialization and the extraordinary part played by railroad labor in the revolutionary process, it is remarkable that this segment of the labor force has garnered limited attention.[7] In 1905 railroad workers had the highest strike propensity of

7. Despite the undeniable centrality of the railroads to the industrialization process in Europe and North America, railroad workers have been somewhat neglected by labor historians. Some useful studies are: on Britain, Peter Kingsford,

any industrial group. The railroad lines served as important avenues of communication for all strikers; at times they were "the channels along which the strike epidemic spreads."[8] In both the October and December general strikes railroad labor proved pivotal.

Yet the great variety of skills and incomes, socialization of work, and geographic situation within the railroad work force made railroad workers as much a highly differentiated microcosm of the working class as a significant and distinct occupational category in their own right. From the big-city machinist in a state railroad workshop to the lonely switchman on a country spur and the almost haughty engine-driver mounted high in his cab, who might feel toward "his" locomotive as a cavalry officer might toward his horse, widely varied workers joined in the common enterprise of moving passengers and freight across the vast expanse of European and Asiatic Russia. Even the word "railwayman" held a different meaning for different strata. Significantly, common usage often lumped together the technical and administrative intelligentsia that ran the railroads with those who were hired by them. To the former, to be a "railwayman" meant to be part of a privileged and bureaucratized profession. To ordinary railroad labor, however, the term denoted membership in another kind of industrial family.

To the overwhelming majority of blue- and white-collar railroad workers and employees the notion of "professional" life was essentially synonymous with industrial life—that is to say, with the world of railroad service in general. Among railroad workers, political consciousness developed not only in the whirlwind of broader national, and especially urban, developments, but also in the course of their professional mobilization as railroad workers. In this study the term *professional* is used in a specific sense. The Russian term

---

Victorian Railwaymen: The Emergence and Growth of Railway Labor, 1830–1870 (London, 1970); on France, Guy Chaumel, *Histoire des cheminots et de leurs syndicats* (Paris, 1948); and on the United States, Walter Licht, *Working for the Railroad: The Organization of Work in the Nineteenth Century* (Princeton, N.J., 1983). Although Western scholars have begun expanding the scope of their study of Russian labor, railroad workers have still been investigated only in passing. William G. Rosenberg, however, has begun an important study of railwaymen in 1917 and immediately after. See his "The Democratization of Russia's Railroads in 1917," *American Historical Review* 86 (1981): 983–1008. Among Soviet historians the expert is Irina M. Pushkareva, whose *Zheleznodorozhniki Rossii v burzhuazno-demokraticheskikh revoliutsiiakh* (Moscow, 1975) is a good introduction.

8. Leon Trotsky, *1905*, trans. Anya Bostock (New York, 1972), p. 81.

professional'nyi soiuz, or *profsoiuz,* is usually translated as "trade union." This is generally accurate, but with respect to the railroads the term *professional'nyi* carried added significance, uneasily combining the images evoked by both the English terms *trade* and *profession.* Many "trades" or "crafts" were involved in the railroad economy; hence the idea that railroad workers could be united into one "professional" group was replete with quasi-syndicalist implications. More important, however, the professional concept in Russian railroading implied hostility to political notions of class. The professional mobilization of Russian railroad workers was not simply the mobilization by trade of an occupational category within the working class. It was, rather, the mobilization of proletarian elements together with, and usually under the leadership of, middle-class professionals, mainly railroad engineers and administrators. Such mobilization was thus marked by a sharp and highly complex internal conflict, pitting the influence of the administrative and managerial elite, important sections of which functioned within the liberal movement, against that of more radical elements who, in the end, found their strongest support among the most classically "proletarian" and industrial sectors of the railroad work force, especially skilled blue-collar metalworkers.

The many thorny questions in social theory that surround the notion of class consciousness lie beyond the scope of this introduction, but use of such a controversial term demands at least minimal definition. I understand class consciousness in a generally Marxist sense to mean a mainly political state of mind common to a social group and determined principally—but not directly or exclusively—by that group's relationship to the means of production. I would stress, however, that proletarian class consciousness, though not the same as revolutionary activism, and certainly not identical with Marxism itself, can develop only in the context of class struggle. While consciousness may ultimately be a product of socioeconomic position, it is still, as E. P. Thompson has stressed, something that "happens."

Class consciousness is perforce *political* consciousness and presupposes, first, a rudimentary definition of social position and political goals vis-à-vis other social classes and strata, and, second, recognition of the antagonistic relationship between the working class on one side and the employing class and its political representatives on the other. If class consciousness does not presuppose a fully articulated political theory, it does imply the emergence of an implicit political culture and a vision of the political transformation of social and economic relations. As will be clear from the body of this work, I do not believe class consciousness can arise spontaneously from the experience of the working class alone. The proletarian political consciousness of 1905 was very much a product of working-class interaction with other classes and social groups and, in particular, with revolutionary socialism—principally, in the case of the railroad workers, with Bolshevik Social Democracy.

The relationship between professional mobilization, frequently manifested in trade union activity, and the development of broader political consciousness posed a vexing problem for the revolutionaries. It was largely the more privileged and least classically "proletarian" elements of railroad labor, in particular the administrative section of the work force, that responded most readily to mobilization on a professional basis. Professional mobilization and trade unionist activity were certainly not spontaneous among railwaymen in the sense that these can be said to have flowed naturally from the struggle of the workers themselves. To a certain extent, in fact, trade unionism and the posing of professional identity at least partly in opposition to class consciousness were products of the influence in the railroad world of the administrative hierarchy. White-collar railwaymen were the first to enter the political arena, and their activism was an essential lever in the subsequent radicalization of the blue-collar rank and file. Yet the politics they frequently espoused—no matter how revolutionary in the context of 1905—were in essence professional and trade unionist and by no means the more Marxian politics of class, either theoretically or, more important, in their basic spirit and vision. The strongest supporters of professional mobilization and trade unionism among railroad workers essentially sought to subordinate emerging proletarian consciousness to professional interest, and, ultimately, to bourgeois liberal democracy.

By contrast, professional identity was much weaker among more industrial and "proletarian" segments of the railroad work force, especially in the workshops and depots. Such workers—and, it should be stressed, these were highly skilled, educated, and self-conscious strata, and not simply the unskilled mass—were initially less influential, and their mobilization occurred first in the context of rather narrow economic battles. But as they became more political the parameters of their vision tended to extend beyond the sphere of railroading in a very different spirit. Before the general strike of October 1905, the dominant trend in the mobilization of railroad workers was that represented most forcefully by the leadership of the All-Russian Railroad Union and other liberals. After the strike, however, this leadership was challenged with increasing force by more radical elements arising from among the more industrial sectors of railroad labor, whose positions were most frequently and clearly articulated by revolutionary Bolsheviks and radical members of the Socialist Revolutionary Party. The massive repression on the railroads cut down the first emerging shoots of proletarian consciousness, but nonetheless by the end of the year two rival tendencies could be distinguished, and their confrontation defined the movement's internal dynamic.

The principal task of this study is to recount and analyze the interrelations between economic and political struggle and between professional mobilization and class consciousness among railroad workers in 1905, the basic arguments concerning which have just been summarized in a cursory fashion. A second, almost equally important, goal is, however, to illuminate the formation, social structure, and life of a hitherto underinvestigated, but critical, segment of the prerevolutionary Russian working class. Study of the railroad workers serves to further undermine two classic opposing stereotypes of the Russian workers, according to which the prerevolutionary proletariat was either a fully developed and "mature" industrial class, firmly united behind Bolshevik leadership almost from the start, or a volatile mass of rootless peasant recruits subject to easy manipulation by revolutionary intellectuals. Empirical studies have already revealed the variety of working-class experience in Russia, and, rather than suggesting that social dislocation led to revolutionary violence, they have indicated that the most rebellious were often the least uprooted, conclusions further confirmed by this investigation of the railwaymen. But the railroad workers likewise provide little comfort to those who, on the basis of local and partial studies, have sought eclectically to combine these two fading paradigms by presenting the persistence of rural ties as precisely the basis for class organization and maturity.[9]

The experience of the railroad workers confirms that proletarian consciousness and revolutionary activity developed not only under the influence of the village and the revolutionary intelligentsia but through regular and varied contact with professional and white-collar groups who transmitted their political dissatisfaction to the workers even as workers were beginning to define their own politics in good measure in opposition to that of allies in the middle strata. Moreover, although it is often assumed that radicalism originated in the economic and political centers of St. Petersburg and Moscow, moving from there to the periphery, the experience of railroad workers in 1905 suggests that the extremism of workers in the provinces may have done nearly as much to spark rebellion among workers in the capitals as vice versa.

The study is divided into two parts. Part I offers a detailed sketch of the railroad work force and its situation on the eve of the first Russian revolution. Following a brief survey of the development of railroading in tsarist Russia, chapter 1 surveys the nature of railroad labor relations and the emergence of a growing recognition of the need for labor reform in the first years of the twentieth century. Chapter 2 analyzes the recruitment, structure and composition of railroad labor, emphasizing its extreme occupational and social heterogeneity, its ties—and lack of ties—to the peasantry

9. Interpretations that identify working-class radicalism with the disruptive or alienating effects of industrialization on recently proletarianized peasants have found considerable resonance in literature on Russia, as in Theodore H. Von Laue, "Russian Labor Between Field and Factory," *California Slavic Studies* 3 (1964): 33–66, and "Russian Peasants in the Factory, 1892–1904," *Journal of Economic History* 21, no. 1 (1961): 61–80. Recent studies, however, confirm the important role played by such "stabilizing" factors as skill, literacy, and prolonged urban tenure in the radicalization process. See Bonnell, *Roots of Rebellion*, and Diane Koenker, "Collective Action and Collective Violence in the Russian Labor Movement," *Slavic Review* 41, no. 3 (1982): 443–48, and *Moscow Workers and the 1917 Revolution* (Princeton, N.J., 1981). Johnson, *Peasant and Proletarian*, postulates a new version of the peasant in the factory thesis, arguing that pre-industrial and rural customs and habits survived in the urban factory environment and it was precisely these survivals, rather than either the disruptions or the new forms of social integration associated with industrialization and urbanization, that enabled workers to mount effective revolts. Johnson's work applies to an earlier period, however, and despite the originality of his research the general applicability of his thesis is questionable.

and the land, and, most important, the links between the railroad proletariat and the intelligentsia through the medium of white-collar and professional staff. In chapter 3 the railwaymen's economic position is discussed, with emphasis placed on the relative deterioration of that position in the decade before 1905. Finally, chapter 4 treats the everyday lives of railwaymen, their family situations, health, literacy, housing, and prerevolutionary organization, emphasizing the emergence of an urbanized core of relatively educated and self-conscious workers.

Part II offers a basically chronological account of the railroad workers' participation in the events of the failed revolution. The focus is on European Russia, especially Moscow, St. Petersburg, and the south. The movement in tsarist Poland is brought into the narrative only insofar as events there had an impact on Russia proper, since, for obvious reasons, the Polish struggle unfolded according to a very different dynamic. The highly explosive and chaotic movement of railroad workers in Siberia and Asiatic Russia lies beyond the narrative's scope. The book concludes with a brief account of events in the wake of the revolution and a final summation.

Part One

Railroads and Railroad Labor in the Tsarist System

The railroad is like a leaven, which creates a cultural fermentation among the population. Even if it passed through an absolutely wild people along its way, it would raise them in a short time to the level prerequisite for its operation.

Count Sergei Iu. Witte

One

Railroad Development and
Labor Policy

Railroad construction "was the essential condition of industrial development" in tsarist Russia. The expanding railroad network gave a terrific boost to trade, opening new markets to Russian industry. It laid the basis for the growth of new industrial regions, especially in the south. Construction of railroad lines and manufacture of railroad equipment provided the chief domestic market for the young iron and steel industry.[1]

The bulk of Russian railroad building took place during the last third of the nineteenth century, chiefly during the boom years of 1866–77, when Mikhail Reutern was minister of finance, and 1891–99, under Sergei Witte. As elsewhere in Europe, the first rail transport systems developed during the eighteenth century in coal mining. Although the primitive vehicles employed in the mines provided a training ground for the first engine-drivers and stokers, these lines were not themselves proper railroads.[2] The first genuine

1. Roger Portal, "The Industrialization of Russia," in *The Cambridge Economic History of Europe* (Cambridge, 1966), vol. 6, pt. 2, p. 813. Also: "Railways were as important to Russia as a stable currency. Without them [the] Russian economy (not to speak of Russian military power) could hardly develop" (Theodore H. Von Laue, *Sergei Witte and the Industrialization of Russia* [New York, 1963], p. 12). See also M. I. Tugan-Baranovsky, *The Russian Factory in the Nineteenth Century* (Homewood, Ill., 1970), pp. 270, 274, 292.

2. J. N. Westwood, *A History of Russian Railways* (London, 1964), pp. 20–21. The term *zheleznaia doroga* (railroad) first appeared in Russian at the beginning of the nineteenth century in reference to England and rapidly entered general usage. The adjectival and other derivative forms such as *zheleznodorozhnik* entered the language in the 1860s. S. D. Lediaeva, *Istoriia zheleznodorozhnoi leksiki v Russkom iazyke XIX veka* (Kishinev, 1973), pp. 8–23.

railroad was the largely symbolic Tsarskoe Selo line, just sixteen miles long, which was opened in 1838 to connect the suburban palaces of the imperial family to St. Petersburg. This was followed in the 1840s by construction of the St. Petersburg–Moscow road, christened the Nicholas Railroad after Tsar Nicholas I, who somewhat reluctantly presided over the introduction of rail transportation. By 1855, at the close of Nicholas's reign, however, Russia could still claim but 570 miles of track.[3]

From 1866 to 1900 the network grew tenfold; only in the United States was the pace of growth faster. Until the mid 1870s most lines were built first to serve the needs of Moscow and the central industrial region, and then to join grain-producing areas to Baltic and Black Sea ports. After this other cities and towns entered the system according to their economic importance or, at times, political influence. The 1880s, a period of relatively sluggish growth, saw construction of important connecting lines, especially in the Ukraine and the Caucasus. During the construction boom of the 1890s the railroads were extended to frontier regions, partly for military motives; many branch lines were built; and the important Ukrainian network was filled out to a more adequate density. On the eve of the 1905 revolution there were 31,623 miles (54,280 versts) of track on thirty-three major state and private railroads in European and Asiatic Russia.[4]

Accompanying this expansion was the tremendous and virtually uncontrolled growth of the labor force, which far outstripped increases in track mileage and freight and passenger traffic. Between 1860 and 1905 the number of railroad workers multiplied 67.7 times. In the decade preceding 1905 the work force more than doubled. During the boom years of the 1890s the number of workers employed in railroading rose by an average of 30,610 each year. Yet, between 1900 and 1905, when new construction ebbed and increases in freight and passenger volume slowed owing to a depressed

3. N. A. Kislinskii, *Nasha zheleznodorozhnaia politika po dokumentam arkhiva komiteta ministrov* (St. Petersburg, 1902), vol. 1, p. 49. On the start of Russian railroading, see Richard Mowbray Haywood, *The Beginnings of Railway Development in Russia in the Reign of Nicholas I, 1835–1842* (Durham, N.C., 1969), and, for a Soviet view, A. M. Solov'eva, *Zheleznodorozhnyi transport Rossii vo vtoroi polovine XIX v.* (Moscow, 1975), pp. 16–80.

4. Ministerstvo putei soobshcheniia, Otdel statistiki, *Statisticheskii sbornik*, no. 89 (St. Petersburg, 1907), table i.

economy, the average yearly growth actually *rose* to 39,360. In 1870 there were 70,100 workers and employees on Russian railroads, 10.4 for every mile of track. By 1890 there were 248,300, and by 1900, 554,400, or 19.9 per mile. In 1905, 751,197 workers and employees were employed in railroading, 23.5 for every railroad mile.[5] In 1902, among the slightly more than half of all workers covered by the railroad pension fund, less than a fifth could claim more than a decade of service, and 57.6 percent had worked fewer than five years. The average length of railroad employment among fund contributors was but 5.8 years.[6]

The hub of the railroad network was Moscow. By the twentieth century, nine major lines converged on the old capital, and three state and two private roads were headquartered there. From Moscow rail lines radiated outward like the spokes of a giant wheel, connecting with lesser regional junctions. Among the more important Moscow lines were the state-owned Moscow-Kursk and Moscow-Brest roads and the private Moscow-Kazan and Moscow-Kiev-Voronezh lines. Three roads, the Moscow-Iaroslavl-Archangel, the Nicholas Railroad from St. Petersburg, and the Kazan line, all terminated at downtown Kalanchevskaia Square. By 1905 at least 12,000 railroad workers and employees were stationed in Moscow: some 3,000 were attached to the administrative headquarters of separate roads, and more than 9,000 labored in repair workshops, depots, and freight and passenger stations.[7] Moscow was the gateway to the matrix of lines that covered the breadbaskets of the Ukraine, the Volga, the Black Sea littoral, and the Kuban, as well as the industrial areas of New Russia. Through these roads, Moscow was joined to lines in the Urals, Central Asia, the Caucasus, and

5. A. G. Rashin, *Formirovanie rabochego klassa Rossii* (Moscow, 1958), p. 117; S. G. Strumilin, "Zheleznodorozhnyi transport," *Izbrannye proizvedeniia* (Moscow, 1964), vol. 1, p. 398; *Statisticheskii sbornik*, no. 89, table i.

6. *Statistika*, 1903, p. 18.

7. Approximate figures for St. Petersburg and Moscow were obtained by combining from different sources totals for railroad repair workshops and central administrative offices. See *Statisticheskii sbornik*, no. 89, table xii, and TsGIA, f. 273, op. 12, d. 527, ll. 7–9. Also I. M. Pushkareva, *Zheleznodorozhniki Rossii v burzhuazno-demokraticheskikh revoliutsiiakh* (Moscow, 1975), p. 45. At the turn of the century, the Moscow city census counted 21,281 skilled and unskilled railroad workers, excluding those employed in workshops. By contrast, the figure for St. Petersburg was 5,389. *Perepis' Moskvy*, pp. 160–61; *Sankt Peterburg po perepisi*, pp. 88–93, 156–61.

Siberia. It was mainly through Moscow that the agricultural sur-
pluses of the black earth regions were transported to northern industrial centers and industrial products in turn distributed to the
country.

Although just six lines terminated in St. Petersburg, and only
four, including the Nicholas Railroad, were headquartered there,
by virtue of its larger repair facilities the capital could claim more
than 13,000 railroad workers. Yet, for reasons of geography, St.
Petersburg could not rival Moscow as a railroad center. The St.
Petersburg terminus was the key regional junction of the north-
west, serving the rapidly expanding industry of the capital and
functioning as the country's main link to the Baltic provinces and
Poland, but connections to the Russian heartland went overwhelmingly through Moscow. A direct line from St. Petersburg to the
Ukraine was only completed in 1904.

Among provincial railroads, the most important were the southern roads, built for strategic considerations, to facilitate grain transport, and, later, to serve industry. These included the state-owned
South West Railroad, headquartered in Kiev and built for military
transport and the export of Ukrainian agricultural products. It was
the largest system in the national network, and among the first to
prove economically profitable. Also of importance in the south
were the state Kursk-Kharkov-Sevastopol and Catherine Railroads
and the private South East line. Other provincial roads linked the
imperial heartland to areas on the periphery. These included the
important private Vladikavkaz Railroad in the grain-rich northern
Caucasus, the Transcaucasian Railroad, and, of course, the Siberian line, as well as the private Riazan-Ural Railroad and lesser
roads to the east, and to the west, the Libau-Romny and Riga-Orel
Railroads in Belorussia and the Baltic provinces, and the Polish
lines. After Moscow and St. Petersburg the largest centers of railroad employment were Kharkov, Ekaterinoslav, Krasnoiarsk, Tiflis,
and Rostov-on-Don. Concentrations of railroad labor in Saratov,
Kiev, Riga, and Voronezh were also volatile in 1905.

Although railroad construction stimulated economic growth, strategic considerations were initially more important to railroad building
than profitability. Close links were early established between rail-

roading and the military. Defeat in the Crimean War signaled the need not only for industry but also for a strategic railroad system capable of moving troops and military equipment to potential war zones. In the first years of railroad operation, especially on the Nicholas Railroad, workers were frequently recruited from the lower military ranks, serving in military labor units under the command of army officers. In 1859, after the regime decided to emphasize private investment and management, assignment of army units to railroad service ceased, although military labor could be found on the Nicholas line as late as 1868 and the armed forces retained special railroad units, which were employed as strikebreakers among other things.[8]

In 1857 the government drew up preliminary plans for an integrated railroad network, based on "private industry, our own as well as foreign."[9] Efforts by the Russian government to mobilize foreign and domestic capital through the Main Society of Russian Railroads, however, were not immediately successful. Faced with peasant unrest, financial difficulties, the Polish uprising of 1863, and a huge and inefficient army, tsarism hardly presented a rosy fiscal picture. The government sought to build a few lines of its own to prove its case, but construction took off only when the state offered to guarantee the investments of those willing to build lines authorized by the 1868 state plan.[10] In effect, new railroads were funded jointly by private capital and the state treasury, but were handed over to the private interests for operation. Shrewd operators saw in railroad construction opportunities to turn quick profits at the government's expense. By 1880 only about thirty-eight miles of railroad remained under direct state control, yet the government still held the great majority of private debentures. According to one estimate, in 1883, 90 percent of total capital invested in private railroads could be traced, directly or indirectly, to the state treasury. Under such conditions private managers often found it more

8. TsGAOR, f. 6865, d. 49, ll. 6–10, 20. At first, military railroad units were attached to each sapper battalion, but in 1886 special railroad battalions were organized. P. A. Zaionchkovskii, *Samoderzhavie i Russkaia armiia na rubezhe XIX–XX stoletii* (Moscow, 1973), p. 142.

9. *Polnoe sobranie zakonov, vtoroe sobranie*, no. 31448.

10. Kislinskii, vol. 1, pp. 69–70, 338; Westwood, pp. 40–43.

advantageous to take a loss than turn a profit, thereby placing a substantial drain on state finances.[11]

Involvement of foreign capital in railroad construction and management combined with shortages of skilled domestic labor to make foreign workers especially important in the initial staffing of the railroads and in the training of Russian workers, especially engine-drivers. When the Tsarskoe Selo line opened in 1838, English drivers ran the trains. They and other foreign personnel received higher wages in Russia than in their homelands, along with lodging. They were soon replaced, however, with Russians put under military command. Later, as service expanded, Germans and Austrians became prominent as engine-drivers, conductors, and stationmasters.[12] In the years when foreign investment was greatest, recruitment of foreign staff could reach ridiculous extremes. On one line, connecting Odessa and Balta, which was run by a German firm, passengers complained "that all the officials employed on the line are Germans, most of whom are unacquainted with the Russian language, and not able to make themselves understood by the natives." Here timetables and tickets were even printed in German.[13]

In the repair shops and depots, use of foreign labor accorded with the pattern in the metal industry. Especially during the crucial period of construction and starting up of production, Belgian, French, or German workers were employed, mainly in southern workshops. In the 1840s American craftsmen came to St. Petersburg to help train Russian workers and engine-drivers and assist in converting the Alexander workshops into the first Russian locomotive factory and repair facility. Well into the twentieth century, locomotives were still imported from Britain and Germany, and with them arrived foreign mechanics who helped with their assembly and supervised their initial operation.[14] The great expense of foreign labor and the serious antagonisms the presence of foreigners could create among the Russian workers combined with the Rus-

11. Strumilin, p. 400; Solov'eva, pp. 116–17; Westwood, pp. 75–76; Von Laue, *Witte*, p. 14.

12. Haywood, pp. 143–44.

13. Westwood, p. 51.

14. Ibid., pp. 32, 92. On foreign metalworkers, see John P. McKay, *Pioneers for Profit* (Chicago, 1970), pp. 255–59.

sifying policies of the tsarist state, however, to insure that foreigners never counted for more than a small part of the railroad work force and that their use was a temporary expedient. Even foreign foremen and highly skilled technicians, who remained important in private industry until 1905, were relatively rare on the railroads after about 1890.

The initial spurt of construction also saw the emergence of a group of often unscrupulous, but dynamic, financiers and railroad magnates, analogous perhaps to the American railroad robber barons of the same era. Of mixed social background, these Russians, Poles, Jews, and Germans worked closely with large banks and the Ministry of Finance. Among the more notable were Samuel Poliakov, who organized construction of much of the southern network, and the Polish Jew turned Catholic Jan Bloch, under whose aegis on the South West Railroad the future finance ministers I. A. Vyshnegradskii and Witte gained experience in railroad management. These "railroad kings," as they were often called, were complemented by the emergence of a generation of technically able, but frequently corrupt and cliquish, railroad engineers, mainly Russians, under the Ministry of Communications.[15]

Several factors joined in the late 1870s to cause the government to abandon its commitment to private control of railroading, which in practice was largely foreign. The negligent and frequently wasteful practices of the private firms were coming under increasing public scrutiny. When added to the deficit of skilled labor and still inadequate capacity, such practices could create serious difficulties in both finance and traffic management. In 1873, for instance, export grain piled up outside Odessa and nearly a fifth of it spoiled. The Ministry of Finance was also concerned about the effects on its economic plans of the high and totally chaotic freight rates set by the private companies. The inefficiency and inadequacy of the railroads were most clearly spotlighted by their "terrible disorder," to quote Witte, during the Turkish War of 1877.[16] The war and subse-

15. Solov'eva, pp. 103–4; Von Laue, *Witte*, pp. 14, 45–46; Westwood, pp. 70–74; I. F. Gindin, *Gosudarstvennyi bank i ekonomicheskaia politika tsarskogo pravitel'stva, 1861–1892* (Moscow, 1960), p. 44.

16. Solov'eva, pp. 95–118; Westwood, p. 86; S. I. Witte, *Vospominaniia* (Moscow, 1960), vol. 1, p. 105.

quent diplomatic defeat at the Congress of Berlin did more than reveal that the railroads were inadequate from the military point of view. Pan-Slav agitation and Russia's weakened diplomatic position stirred resentment against domination of railroading by foreign capital and the prevalence of non-Russian managers. Moreover, the war resulted in a sharp drop in exports, while imports rose. Sales of government-guaranteed railroad bonds plummeted.

In 1876, then, a government commission headed by Count Baranov, which included among its members Witte, was appointed to review railroad policy. The commission sat until 1884, producing a general charter for the railroads, which was published in 1885. By that time, at the commission's instigation and under the leadership of Finance Minister N. K. Bunge, the government had already begun to purchase railroads from private investors. The first lines so obtained—including some of strategic significance but limited economic worth—were the least profitable and held the greatest debt to the government. Later profitable lines such as the South West Railroad were also taken over, although the state did not operate railroads principally to make money from them, but to insure strategic security and encourage economic growth. By 1890 about a quarter of the country's trackage was directly owned and operated by the government. The Baranov Commission also strengthened the regime's legal powers over private railroads, mandating, among other things, that representatives of the ministries of Finance and Communications sit on the boards of all railroad firms. The commission established a unified state and private railroad network for the first time. Rolling stock was standardized and could now be interchanged, and traffic on different lines could be coordinated.

During the next decade, the pace of state acquisition accelerated, and there was a tremendous boom in new construction. The new roads were mostly built, financed, and directly managed by the state, although development of some secondary lines was still entrusted to the private sector. Between 1890 and 1900 the government paid more than 120 million rubles annually for railroad construction, derived mostly from domestic sources. By 1898, 55 percent of total track was state-owned and run and the government roads employed more than two-thirds of the railroad work force. In 1901 the state lines carried 69 percent of the freight and 71.8 percent of the passengers. In 1905 some 21,744 of 31,623 miles of track were in government hands and 74 percent of all railroad workers were employed by the state.[17]

The transfer of railroads to the government and the reorganization of the system by the Baranov Commission resolved some of the difficulties associated with the era of private enterprise. Despite heavily subsidized freight tariffs, the drain on the treasury slowed. Managerial inefficiency continued to plague both state and private roads well into the twentieth century, however. Equipment was regularly permitted to deteriorate, with little maintenance, and sometimes important apparatus, even entire trains, could turn up as "lost," compounding chronic shortages of boxcars. When famine hit the country in 1891–92, the railroads were not much better prepared than they had been to supply the troops in 1877. The Voronezh junction proved incapable of carrying the flow of grain from the Kuban to the famine regions, and shipments backed up on the Vladikavkaz Railroad. By late August 1891, 7,481 boxcars were stuck in stations in the northern Caucasus and the Don basin. Colonel A. A. von Vendrikh, an expert on traffic management dispatched to deal with the chaos, discovered one station where a valuable turntable had been totally forgotten, the rails leading to it being covered with junk. Stymied by official incompetence, Vendrikh wrote that "management was entirely without direction. . . . Every stationmaster gave orders on his own, striving somehow to get rid of the trains at his station, paying no attention to the consequences."[18]

In fact, greater state involvement probably exacerbated inefficiency, as the railroads became embroiled in the bureaucratic bickering of the late tsarist period. Railroad management became a form of state service, and managers, especially at the highest levels, often took on the corrupt and obsequious characteristics of many tsarist bureaucrats. For the coordination of railroad affairs, the Baranov Commission had recommended an autonomous Railroad Council to end the dominance of the Ministry of Communica-

17. Petr Liashchenko, *Istoriia narodnogo khoziastva Rossii* (Leningrad, 1948), vol. 2, p. 155; Westwood, p. 76; *Statisticheskii sbornik*, no. 89, table i; L. E. Mints, "Statistika chislennosti i sostava rabochei sily na zheleznodorozhnom transporte v Rossii," in Akademiia nauk SSSR, *Ocherki po istorii statistiki SSSR (sbornik tretii)* (Moscow, 1960), p. 120.

18. Richard G. Robbins, Jr., *Famine in Russia, 1891–1892* (New York, 1975), pp. 76–94; Westwood, pp. 165–66.

tions and the consequent overemphasis on technical matters in which it excelled. But in the final charter approved by the government the Council for Railroad Affairs was a relatively inconsequential body under the very ministry whose influence it was supposed to undercut. After 1885 railroad administration was divided among three departments, but each was subordinate to the Committee of Ministers, which could decide disputes between government roads and private companies and took a keen interest in railroad policy. The railroad building program was directed by the Railroad Department of the Ministry of Finance; an interdepartmental tariff committee regulated freight and passenger rates; and the Office of State Control inspected the accounts of individual roads.[19]

The Ministry of Communications, which was charged with both the technical operation and the financial management of the state railroads and with supervision of private lines, remained the single most important government body concerned with railroad management. Under the ministry, after an 1899 reorganization, responsibility for railroad operations, including labor relations, lay with the Administration of Railroads, to which were subordinate the directors of each state line, who were themselves assisted by councils formed of representatives of each of the three departments concerned, Communications, Finance, and State Control.[20] The Ministry of Communications brought to its task a fine technical tradi-

19. Westwood, pp. 82–83; Solov'eva, pp. 261–70; Von Laue, *Witte*, p. 78. Rivalry between the ministries could become both intense and petty. A 1907 report of the Duma budget commission bemoaned "the complete anarchy in the activity of separate ministries, pursuing in railroad matters each its own goal and often in a state of mutual enmity where there should be agreement and mutual aid" (quoted in Westwood, p. 145). The War Ministry also maintained a strong interest in railroad affairs, lobbying continually for the construction of new strategic lines (see Zaionchkovskii, pp. 86, 89–90, 127, 148).

20. According to its May 3, 1899, reorganization, the Ministry of Communications was headed by its minister, who was responsible for several sections and departments. The Administration of Railroads was headed by its director, who chaired the Committee for the Administration of Railroads, on which sat delegates from all its subordinate units and from the Ministries of Finance, Internal Affairs, Agriculture, and State Properties, and from the Office of State Control. Under the Administration of Railroads there were three departments, technical, operational, and economic; the administration chancellery; and three sections, public health, juridical, and accounting. Operations inspectors and certain engineers functioned under the director. The railroad pension committee was also under the Administration of Railroads. See *VMPS*, June 5, 1899, pp. 255–65.

tion, but it was not overflowing with talent, and much of its work was characterized by bureaucratism and inertia. "[On the railroads] one encounters a really developed and capable individual who stands above the vulgar ranks only as a rarity," wrote one observer, echoing an oft-heard theme. "The engineers, men with the highest educational qualifications who in the majority of instances were trained in the spiritual and intellectual centers of the country, rarely bring to their places of service anything besides a modest desire to advance their careers." The majority of railroad officials limited their activity to passive enforcement of often contradictory and irrational regulations.[21]

This is not to argue, of course, that positive qualities were wholly absent. There was a long-standing reformist tradition in the ministry that vainly sought to rationalize and systematize railroad management. This was, after all, a ministry intimately involved with the modernization of Russia's economy; its cliquishness was more that of the professional-bureaucratic than the nobiliary elite. By the turn of the century, reformist and critical voices could be heard from various sectors of railroad management, but the critique of bureaucratic inertia and careerist corruption offered by such men was itself marked by timid caution and bureaucratic obfuscation. Like so many tsarist bureaucrats, the dedication of some railroad officials to rational management proved more difficult for them to implement than to declare. The ministry, moreover, applied to railroad management the Russifying policies of the last tsars, which tended further to close the ranks of railroad officialdom and technical staff to capable outsiders. As the state gained control of the railroads, foreign personnel were dismissed, as were the

21. *Zhel.*, September 28, 1903, pp. 4–5. See also *Zhel.*, April 18, 1905, p. 4; ZhN, September 10, 1899, p. 563; and Witte, *Vospominaniia*, vol. 1, p. 87. With respect to inefficiency and corruption on lower levels a caution must be raised that the image of the corrupt and bungling local careerist was a favorite distortion of those in the major cities who, for their own reasons and sometimes without basis, chose to look down on provincial officials. See George L. Yaney, *The Systematization of Russian Government* (Urbana, Ill., 1973), pp. 100–101. It seems likely, however, that the image was more or less accurate with respect to railroad engineers, even if big-city prejudices hid from view some capable administrators. The railroad press printed considerable material sent directly from the provinces, including reprints from provincial newspapers and letters, all of which tended to support the image of official mediocrity.

many qualified Jews and Poles who had earlier played a disproportionately large role in the system.[22]

Such measures were accompanied by revivals of the military element in railroad affairs, which intensified with the expansion of
state control. Some officials of the Ministry of Communications and
railroad engineers held military rank and dreamed of running the
roads as they would a regiment, their attitudes mixing congenially
with the cliquish bureaucratism of many civilian engineers. A number of ministry programs were inspired by military practice, and
references to the "railroad army" were common among railroad
officials and in the press. On many roads, preference in hiring was
given to demobilized veterans. During the Turkish War, a quasi-
military command structure was introduced on several southern
roads, culminating in 1880 in the promulgation of rules whereby
uniformed railroad employees were obliged to salute not only
members of the imperial family and high government officials but
their immediate superiors as well.[23]

The Ministry of Communications never formulated a consistent labor policy. Before 1905 it responded to problems on an essentially
ad hoc and ineffective basis, and during and after that fateful year it
relied increasingly on repression to maintain labor "peace." It
might be thought that in its capacity as an employer the tsarist
state could have found opportunities to practice the benevolent paternalism it so often preached. But administration of the state railroads—and of most private lines, which were regulated by the
state—could claim neither the rationality of efficient capitalist
management nor the "patriarchy" of an idealized past. In 1902 one
writer compared the Ministry of Communications to a family "consisting only of older sons—the engineers. As for the younger sons,
all the remaining employees, the ministry does not recognize them

22. Witte, *Vospominaniia*, vol. 1, p. 144; Westwood, p. 162.
23. TsGAOR, f. 6865, d. 45, l. 12. On the "railroad army," see, for example,
ZhN, September 28, 1902, pp. 588–89. On the preferential hiring of soldiers, see
E. M. Mil'man, "Formirovanie kadrov zheleznodorozhnogo proletariata Urala vo
vtoroi polovine XIX veka," in *Iz istorii rabochego klassa Urala. Sbornik statei*
(Perm, 1961), p. 219. The military influence on railroading was not confined to
Russia. See Frank McKenna, "Victorian Railway Workers," *History Workshop
Journal* 1 (1976): 28, and Margot B. Stein, "The Meaning of Skill: The Case of the
French Engine-Drivers, 1837–1917," *Politics and Society* 8, no. 3–4 (1978): 406.

as its own flesh and blood. For them, there is no parental embrace; at best, they are stepsons, given neither kindnesses nor attention."[24] With its myriad petty satrapies and the sway of systematic corruption and arbitrary rule, the structure of railroad authority resembled most the decaying hierarchy of the Russian countryside. There were elements in the railroad bureaucracy who recognized this, but their efforts at change were doomed to failure.

Before 1905 the legal status of most railroad workers was difficult to determine. The labor legislation of the 1880s, limited as it was, at first applied only partially to their situation. In 1882 a law governing child labor and providing for factory inspectors was enacted. In 1886 a comprehensive set of rules covering relations between employers and employees was promulgated. This legislation pertained mainly to factories and hence most wage workers in railroading remained uncovered. But beyond this the 1882 law specifically exempted state-owned enterprises, including the state railroad repair and maintenance workshops, from the inspection system. Under the 1886 law, workshops of state or private railroads could be placed under inspection only by special order. In 1887 the St. Petersburg shops of the Nicholas Railroad were made subject to inspection, and in 1895 those of the Brest and Iaroslavl roads were too. In 1893 the Ministry of Finance ordered those factory boards charged with inspecting railroad shops and depots to include in their ranks representatives of railroad management. Private railroad operators, however, resisted incorporation into a system from which their state counterparts were largely exempt. Consequently, in 1896, the State Council ruled that all roads, state and private, were outside the inspection system, leaving railroad managers themselves to regulate hours and conditions of labor with guidance from the Ministry of Communications.[25] Although the ministry frequently adopted guidelines patterned after legislation applicable to workers in private industry, exemption of the railroad system from factory legislation and, in particular, from supervision by the fac-

24. *ZhN*, September 28, 1902, p. 589.
25. TsGIA, f. 273, op. 12, d. 46, l. 511; *VMPS*, April 8, 1896, p. 295. On the factory inspectorate, see Theodore H. Von Laue, "Factory Inspection Under the 'Witte System': 1892–1903." *American Slavic and East European Review* 19 (1960): 347–62.

tory inspectorate deprived railroad workers of the benefits, however limited, of a mediating authority to which they might appeal
for assistance in conflicts with management.

The General Charter of 1885 mandated drawing up a separate
charter for railroad labor defining the rights and responsibilities of
each category of railroad work uniformly for all lines, but this task
was essentially ignored for fifteen years. Instead, most lines set
their own rules and standards, while the ministry spewed forth a
seemingly unending torrent of highly specific, confusing, and often
contradictory—or nearly impracticable—administrative orders
and directives. By the century's turn, railroad labor policy was defined by a maze of temporary regulations and ad hoc decrees, heavily supplemented by unwritten rules of "common practice."[26] Conditions and regulations differed sharply from line to line. No two
roads could claim a common wage structure and even definitions of
tasks were not uniform. The situation was no better on the private
roads. In February 1905 employees on the Moscow-Kazan Railroad
complained that labor relations were still formally governed by a
twenty-year-old charter. The situation was further complicated by
the rapid growth of the work force and the increasing complexity of
railroad labor, as well as by the transfer of private lines to the state
and the reorganizations this could entail.[27]

Where the ministry did set standards or guidelines, these were
regularly breached.[28] In 1891 the ministry ordered every railroad
workshop to issue a pay-book to its workers. In addition to space
for recording wage payments and fines, these were to include rules
and regulations set according to guidelines established by the ministry delineating the worker's rights and obligations, including such
rules of factory order as starting and finishing times, schedule of

26. V. Dmitriev, "Byt sluzhashchikh i rabochikh na zheleznykh dorogakh,"
Sovremennyi mir, 1912, no. 1: 282; V. Romanov, "Dvizhenie sredi sluzhashchikh i
rabochikh Russkikh zheleznykh dorog v 1905 godu," *Obrazovanie*, 1906, no. 10,
26; *Zhel.*, 88, February 2, 1905, pp. 1–2.

27. TsGIA, f. 273, op. 12, d. 328, l. 77. The changeover from private to state
ownership occasioned several disturbances in railroad workshops during the
1890s, several of which are mentioned in chapter 5.

28. Actually, this was not so unusual. In reality, George Yaney points out that
"many of the statutes of Russian law were not enforceable legal rules but exhorta-
tions to behave or work according to this or that ideal" (Yaney, p. 21). These words
are certainly appropriate to the labor regulations of the Ministry of Communications. See Romanov, p. 26.

holidays, overtime rules, and provisions governing entitlement to railroad housing or other benefits. Few pay-books, however, lived up to the mandate. Within a few years nearly all were out of date, and most paid only perfunctory attention to the guidelines, which were hopelessly vague to begin with. There was a wide variance from line to line, and even among workshops on the same road. In 1903 provincial authorities complained that the pay-book of the Vladikavkaz Railroad shops in Rostov-on-Don contained none of the information required by the ministry, offered "no rules of internal order," and stood in consistent violation of labor legislation applicable to industrial enterprises.[29]

Ineffective, too, were orders limiting the number of hours to be worked. As will be discussed further in chapter 3, service shifts of up to twenty-four hours were not unheard of among switchmen, locomotive crews, and conductors, which was of concern to the ministry in light of the alarming incidence of railroad accidents, often attributed to overtired personnel.[30] As early as 1876 the Baranov Commission considered regulating labor time in railroading, but failed to establish norms. In 1877 the hours of locomotive crews were limited, but the restrictions were relaxed somewhat two years later. In 1890 24-hour service was forbidden for switchmen and signalmen, and the following year the rules for locomotive crews were strengthened. Conductors' hours were regulated in 1893. These limits were very modest, with considerable flexibility granted local managers. Yet it was commonly assumed that few lines followed the prescribed norms. The ministry found it necessary to repeat its directives, albeit in modified forms, in 1896, 1897, 1898, 1900, and 1902.[31]

It should not, however, be assumed that the record was entirely negative. In 1888 the State Council ordered private railroads to es-

29. TsGIA, f. 273, op. 12, d. 354, l. 26; d. 46, ll. 512–15; TsGAOR, f. 6865, d. 70, ll. 273–76.

30. That the ministry's concern was with the accident rate and not the workers' welfare is clear from its internal correspondence. TsGIA, f. 273, op. 12, d. 107, passim, espec. ll. 1, 411.

31. TsGIA, f. 273, op. 12, d. 107, ll. 1–2; TsGAOR, f. 6865, d. 49, l. 24; *ZhN*, May 18, 1902, pp. 283–85; *VMPS*, December 21, 1896, p. 1396; S. L. Tregubov, *Opyt izucheniia v sanitarnom otnoshenii byta zheleznodorozhnykh sluzhashchikh v predelakh Kursko-Kharkovo-Sevastopol'skogo zh. d.* (Kharkov, 1904), p. 23; *ZhD*, 1898, 30–31, p. 396.

tablish pension funds for their permanent work force. In 1894 these merged with state railroad pension funds to form a central fund. Within two years there was an investment of over five million rubles, and by 1906 membership stood at nearly 400,000. Many lower-level line and station employees and most workers in the repair shops were, however, exempt from coverage. During 1905 the fund became the target of bitter criticism as a speculative plaything for privileged interests that offered few tangible benefits to its members.[32]

In 1894 the ministry established its public health section, modeled, it would seem, after the military health care system. This was in many respects an ambitious effort in health care delivery, probably superior to the primitive care sometimes offered in private industry. Within a few years a rudimentary network of railroad hospitals, clinics, first aid, and midwife stations had been set up. By 1905 the service was handling more than three and a half million patient visits annually. Yet here, too, there was persistent and vocal criticism of both the quality of care offered and its availability.[33]

Institutions and programs offering benefits to railroad employees were sometimes established by the directors of individual lines. Probably the least paternalistic of these were the consumer cooperatives, which frequently involved a significant segment of the workers, especially at provincial junctions, where goods were often difficult to obtain or expensive. In every case, however, these mutual aid groups were initiated and directed by higher management. A number of lines established libraries and reading rooms or presented lectures, theatricals, and other programs aimed at promoting "sobriety."[34]

The South West Railroad was especially noted for both the extent and quality of its efforts under the leadership of the road's energetic director, Klavdii S. Nemeshaev. Appointed in 1896, Nemeshaev quickly established a national reputation as an imaginative reformer and opponent of railroad "pocket despots." Under his

32. *VMPS*, June 22, 1896, pp. 644–45. For more on the pension fund, see chapter 7. Criticisms of its operation are summarized in TsGAOR, f. 6865, d. 29a, ll. 20–21.

33. *VMPS*, June 8, 1896, pp. 581–82; *Vrach-san otchet*, 1905, pp. 266–73. For more on the public health section, see chapter 4.

34. For more on cooperatives, libraries, reading rooms, and "sobriety" programs, see chapter 4.

aegis a program of evening study for workers was launched and a commission studied and offered creative solutions to the railroad housing crisis. Perhaps his most interesting innovation in labor relations was the institution of "courts of honor" in which elected representatives of the engine-drivers sat in judgment on their colleagues accused of disciplinary infractions. As early as 1897 Nemeshaev submitted to the ministry a draft charter for railroad labor, which received lavish praise in the railroad press, although nothing came of it.[35] Nemeshaev was an exception, however, and his innovative projects served but a fraction of the work force. Moreover, the paternalism that stood behind the overwhelming majority of such efforts, as well as the paucity and weakness of uniform rules and regulations defining the rights and responsibilities of railroad labor, left almost no room for worker initiative. To most railwaymen the capricious paternalism of some railroad directors was simply another side to an arbitrary despotism under which they labored. Nemeshaev himself earned the sarcastic sobriquet "little papa" after he addressed striking employees in January 1905 as "my children."[36]

On the railroads arbitrary authority and petty tyranny were the real operative principles behind ostensibly paternalistic labor relations. To be sure, the railroad industry in all countries tends toward an authoritarian mode of operation owing to the complex division of labor and the pressure to maintain schedules and observe safety routines. In Russia, however, this tendency combined with political autocracy and the lack, especially on the railroads, of mediating institutions, creating an especially arbitrary command structure. "It is difficult to find a sphere of labor so penetrated by the demoralizing influence of our old regime," wrote the All-Russian Railroad Union leader V. Romanov in 1906.[37] With some exaggeration, a for-

35. TsGIA, f. 1162, op. 6, d. 357, ll. 87–105; *Zhel.*, September 28, 1903, p. 4; *ZhN*, April 9, 1899, pp. 211–13, 222; *ZhD*, 1904, 25–26, p. 297. On Nemeshaev's proposed charter, see *ZhN*, May 21, 1899, pp. 311–12; May 28, 1899, pp. 390–92; June 11, 1899, pp. 360–63.

36. TsGAOR, f. 6865, d. 31, l. 8.

37. Romanov, 1906, no. 10, p. 26. On the authoritarian organization of railroading elsewhere, see, for example, McKenna, p. 26. Walter Licht, *Working For the Railroad: The Organization of Work in the Nineteenth Century* (Princeton, N.J., 1983), pp. 111–12, notes, however, that in the United States, as in tsarist Russia, arbitrariness and inconsistency were also products of the decentralized nature of disciplinary authority and the lack of formal grievance procedures.

mer clerk on the Riazan-Ural Railroad drew an analogy with the patriarchal relations of the pre-emancipation village:

The legal position of the railroad worker, especially the manual worker, the man of the repair shops, the conductor, in short, of the lower strata, was such that there was not the slightest distinction from the position of the serf. The difference was only that it was not the landlord who ruled over these railroad nobodies, but the railroad big shots, all sorts of officials, backed by the gendarme's fist. Repressions rained down as if from a horn of plenty. The arbitrariness of their rule defies description. Firings and fines, simply at the whim of this or that "Mr. Director," were interminable. . . . Tyranny was the very system of management.[38]

"In the railroad world, the director is tsar and god," wrote a pamphleteer in 1906, echoing the very words used by one manager to subordinates just two years before.[39] Official authority could extend even to the private lives and leisure time of railroad staff. Early in 1905 workers on the Moscow-Vindau-Rybinsk Railroad demanded removal of the line's assistant director, whom they charged with forcing workers to repair his apartment and clean his clothes. On one road in the late 1890s the director forbade workers and nearby residents to hang laundry in places visible to passing trains so as to avoid offering passengers a "motley and unattractive" view. When train greasemen on another line petitioned for a redress of their grievances, the director dismissed them haughtily, wondering with open contempt, "Do greasemen have rights? What kind of rights could they have?"[40]

Such abuses were not the sole preserve of higher officials. "He fails to grab only who does not want," went a common saying on the railroads. It was normal, for example, for a stationmaster or road

38. I. S. Sokolov, *1905 god na Riazansko-Ural'skoi zheleznoi doroge* (Saratov, 1925), p. 16. A comparison to the pre-emancipation village was also made in *Zhel.*, 57, June 29, 1904, p. 3. *ZhN*, December 8, 1902, p. 751 referred to officials and the majority of workers as "two hostile camps between which there could be no thought of comradely relations."

39. A. N. [pseud.], "Chto nuzhno zheleznodorozhnikam," p. 5. Two copies of this pamphlet are in TsGIA, f. 273, op. 12, d. 468, ll. 25–58. In 1904 a protest by four assistant engine-drivers against 24-hour work assignments drew the wrath of their director, who immediately labeled their complaint a strike. "How dare you talk like this to me! How dare you cause trouble!" he was reported to have declared. "After all, I am your tsar! I am your god!" (*Zhel.*, 56, June 22, 1904, pp. 19–20).

40. TsGIA, f. 273, op. 12, d. 343, ll. 153–56; TsGAOR, f. 6865, d. 29a, l. 92; *ZhN*, September 10, 1899, p. 563.

foreman to order a switchman or track repairman to milk his cows, feed his horses, hoe his cucumber patch, carry water to his kitchen, or chop his wood, even after a twelve-to-fourteen-hour shift. A chief clerk might force subordinates to overcharge shippers so that he might pocket the excess. On one road a worker unloading grain ripped the sole from his shoe and, after putting on his bast sandals, was fired by the stationmaster for damaging railroad property with his feet.[41] The authority of the railroad director could be so extensive and personalized that official wives often tyrannized subordinates alongside their husbands. "These 'madames' played no small role in the organization and management of the work force," one memoirist recalled. "Since the creation of the world, not a single soldier has been subject to as many officers as in this dismal railroad gloom," went a line from an 1896 railroading tale.[42]

It was not simply to arbitrary commands that workers might object, but also to the very attitudes and language of their superiors. In 1905 one of the principal demands of striking railwaymen was for "courteous treatment" by officials and foremen. But before the revolution the railroad press was already filled with complaints about foul or impolite language and even physical assaults. In 1903 one article complained that "crudeness in personal relations has spread to all strata of service personnel. Rudeness is experienced in little things, such as the failure to respond to the bow of a subordinate [that such gestures were even deemed necessary is, of course, itself revealing—on one southern road office employees were required to stand at their posts and bow at the entrance of senior personnel], or to shake his hand." Indeed, the article contended, insults were "the ordinary seasoning of railroad service conversation."[43] In 1905 workers at the Vilna freight station of the St. Petersburg–Warsaw Railroad charged that the stationmaster related to them "as [he would] to animals. We never hear from him a single kind or friendly word, but always at every step vulgar cursing and such expressions as are used only with cattle or morons."[44]

41. Romanov, 1906, no. 10, pp. 26–27; TsGAOR, f. 6865, d. 29a, ll. 19–20; Westwood, p. 161.

42. TsGAOR, f. 6865, d. 45, l. 27; d. 35, l. 77. According to ZhN, November 24, 1902, p. 720, arbitrary authority was related to a pervasive departmentalism in which each department functioned as a "state within a state."

43. Zhel., 18, September 28, 1903, pp. 3–4.

44. ZhN, December 8, 1902, p. 751; TsGIA, f. 273, op. 12, d. 295, l. 15.

Railroad officials commonly addressed subordinates with the familiar "thou" (*ty*), normally reserved at that time for intimates, children, and animals, despite continued decrees on some lines against this practice.[45]

The fundamental repressiveness of railroad labor relations was confirmed by the extensive activities of the railroad police. A special railroad gendarmery was established as early as 1867, and by 1905 nearly 8,000 policemen, or slightly more than one gendarme for every 100 railroad employees, stood guard over the Russian railroad network. This was over 3,000 more police than there were staff employed in the entire public health section. By comparison, the regular norm for the number of policemen per inhabitant was about 1:500, and in 1898 the Ministry of Internal Affairs proposed a ratio of one policeman to every 250 factory workers. Though the function of the railroad police was ostensibly to protect railroad property, freight, and passengers, few doubted that their main purpose was to prevent labor unrest. Although there was liaison with the Ministry of Communications, the railroad gendarmery was under the Ministry of Internal Affairs. On most lines the chief officer held a veto over all hiring and could order a worker fired without explanation.[46]

By the century's turn the railroads became subject to a new round of public criticism, and a growing recognition emerged within some railroad circles of the need for a more systematic and reformed labor policy and for improvements in the working and living conditions of railwaymen. Throughout the last third of the nineteenth century, the Russian railroads were rarely profitable enough to finance interest payments on debentures guaranteed by the state treasury. Although the situation improved somewhat during the 1890s, after 1900 increasing losses were experienced, necessitating ever-larger disbursements from treasury accounts. While state expenditures approximately tripled overall between 1882 and 1903, expenditures by the Ministry of Communications increased by

45. *ZhN*, June 16, 1901, p. 381; *Zhel.*, 23, November 2, 1903, pp. 13–14; *ZhD*, 42, October 10, 1905, p. 472.

46. *Vrach-san otchet*, 1905, p. 16; M. K. Dymkov and D. Ia. Lipovetskii, eds., *1905 god na Kazanke. Sbornik* (Moscow, 1925), p. 33. TsGAOR, f. 6865, d. 35, ll. 80–81; Theodore H. Von Laue, "Tsarist Labor Policy, 1895–1903," *Journal of Modern History* 34 (1962): 137.

1,084 percent.[47] At the same time, observers could hardly ignore several clear signs of deteriorating service. The backlogs of freight characteristic of railroad operations during the 1870s and the 1891–92 famine were again common by the turn of the century: it was estimated that during the years 1900 to 1904 the continuous backlog averaged 50,000 carloads annually. Moreover, the average weight of freight trains did not increase, despite the introduction of more powerful locomotives.[48]

Another shocking indication of poor management was the marked rise in the accident rate, which the railroad press often attributed to overworked and poorly motivated personnel.[49] The initial inefficiency and disorganization of the railroads were strikingly revealed by such events as the monstrous 1875 Telegul crash on the South West Railroad, in which a troop train derailed into a ravine during a blizzard and some hundred soldiers were killed after a track crew repairing the line had retired to a hut to drink tea without replacing the rail they had removed, posting warning signals, or informing nearby stations. Nevertheless, during the 1880s, the overall accident rate was not especially high, being only a fraction of the American rate. As traffic density multiplied and train speeds increased, however, the number of accidents also catapulted upward with alarming speed.

Where in 1880, 455 people were killed and 979 injured on the railroads, by 1900 the grim statistics had skyrocketed to 1,448 dead and 7,707 injured, of whom 539 and 5,926 respectively were railroad workers. Expressed as casualties per million train-kilometers, the rate more than doubled from 14.4 in 1880 to 30.8 in 1900. In 1905, 13,005 people, including 8,445 workers, were killed or injured in railroad accidents, a casualty rate of 35.7. In 1891, 4.98 out of every 1,000 railroad workers were involved in traffic accidents. Just four years later this figure had more than doubled to 10.88, and in 1905 it stood at 11.25.[50] Significantly, the private railroads could uniformly boast a better safety record than the state lines.

47. Zaionchkovskii, p. 82.
48. Westwood, pp. 129, 132.
49. For examples, *ZhN*, January 15, 1899, pp. 22–24; January 22, 1899, pp. 37–40.
50. Strumilin, p. 413. These figures include all deaths on the railroads, even suicides, and hence tend to exaggerate the extent of the carnage. Accidents involving passengers were much fewer. For more on accidents involving workers, see chapter 3.

The highest accident rates were to be found on the new Siberian and Trans-Baikal Railroads, but older lines, including the Moscow-Brest, Kursk-Kharkov-Sevastopol, and Nicholas Railroads could also merit the name "bone-breaker" used by railwaymen to designate roads with especially bad records.[51]

Managerial and administrative difficulties were both reflected and exacerbated by the uncontrolled expansion of the labor force and resultant low productivity. During the boom years rapid growth and chronic labor fluidity could be tolerated without undue cost. But by 1898 the burden of chaotic expansion began to affect productivity levels and, ultimately, profitability. Between 1892 and 1898 the productivity of railroad labor rose steadily from 78.5 ton-kilometers per worker to a high of 91.2 ton-kilometers per worker. Yet over the next decade the figures essentially stagnated, dropping to a low of 85.0 ton-kilometers per worker in 1902. On the Nicholas Railroad, which, despite its high accident rate, was still thought to be one of the more efficiently run lines and a pacesetter for the entire network, freight traffic increased by some 14 percent from 1896 to 1904, while the number of workers rose by a whopping 50 percent.[52]

Railroad managers and critics alike often pointed with special alarm to the high rate of labor turnover.[53] Even as the labor force grew by leaps and bounds, a significant number of workers left each year. This only aggravated productivity problems by magnifying still further the inexperience and instability of the work force. Widely cited and quite revealing were the annual reports of the railroad pension fund, which showed, for instance, that 21.7 percent of all fund participants left railroad employment in 1895. By 1902 the effects of the economic crisis had lowered the rate to 15.8 percent. This was much higher than the often-cited figure for the German railroads of 5.1 percent, but compared favorably with the

51. On the accident records of the separate state and private railroads in 1905, see *Statisticheskii sbornik*, no. 89, tables x, xi.

52. Strumilin, p. 409; Westwood, p. 130.

53. For examples, *ZhN*, March 10, 1900, pp. 147–51; I. I. Rikhter, *Lichnyi sostav Russkikh zheleznykh dorog* (St. Petersburg, 1900); Tregubov, p. 12. A 1903 publication of the Administration of Railroads, "On Changes in and Additions to the Charter of the Pension Fund for Employees on State Railroads," p. 93, also took note of the turnover rate, acknowledging that it indicated both the "low attraction of railroad service" and "the extremely poor quality of those entering it." See also TsGIA, f. 273, op. 12, d. 407, l. 42.

less frequently mentioned situation in the United States, where, according to one historian, turnover "reached staggering proportions." In Russia slightly more than half of all those hired in 1901 and 1902 were no longer at their jobs at the start of 1903. Moreover, the percentage of those leaving who did so at their own volition rather than owing to retirement, illness, death, or dismissal rose from 59 percent in 1897 to 69.6 percent in 1902. "The railroad employee considers his position a temporary lodging, and himself an occasional transient," wrote one contemporary.[54]

Turnover was greatest on the recently constructed Asian roads and on those lines nearest to developing areas with alternative opportunities in industry. Fluidity was lower on lines known for relatively efficient management, in places where wages were exceptionally high, and in Poland. On all lines, however, turnover was most extensive among lower-paid and unskilled workers. In 1902 the average annual salary of railroad pension fund contributors was 361 rubles. Among those earning more than that amount 11.5 percent left railroad service, but among those earning less the figure was 18 percent. Turnover was especially high among laborers, switchmen, and track watchmen, all of whom were leaving at rates above 20 percent annually. According to the pension fund manager A. D. Pokotilov, in most years more than half of all newly hired switchmen did not complete a full year.[55]

To be sure, much of the problem could be attributed on the one hand to the transitional semi-peasant character of many Russian workers and on the other to the general tightness of the skilled labor market. Still, a growing number of railroad officials concluded, if a stable work force was to be achieved, and productivity and service thus improved, employment would have to be rendered more attractive. Efforts would have to be made to better the workers' material lot, and the rights and responsibilities of railroad labor would have to be more clearly defined. In 1898 Aleksandr Radtsig, a respected official on the Kharkov-Nikolaev Railroad known for his concern with such matters, proposed using pension fund capital to finance improvements in housing and called for stricter enforcement of regulatory provisions on overtime. Two years later the

54. *Statistika*, 1896, p. 28; 1903, pp. 15, 18, 28; *Zhel.*, December 14, 1904, p. 4. On the United States, see Licht, pp. 73–78.
55. *Statistika*, 1903, pp. 14–15, 32–34, 59–60; *ZhN*, March 10, 1900, p. 150; TsGIA, f. 273, op. 12, d. 925, l. 193.

prominent railroad engineer I. I. Rikhter published an influential book on railroad labor in which he offered drafts of a uniform charter and disciplinary code that drew on Nemeshaev's earlier project. Rikhter's writings won considerable praise, and in 1900 a national conference of railroad directors called for the rapid development and adoption of a labor charter, as well as other measures designed to improve conditions. Several suggestions were also made to create a specific agency within the ministry to deal solely with labor and personnel concerns. Voices within the Ministry of Internal Affairs called for creating a special railroad factory inspectorate.[56]

In this discussion a very important role was played by the railroad press. In addition to the official publications of the Ministry of Communications, such as its weekly *Vestnik*, several independent professional publications sought an audience of railroad engineers and officials, and even white-collar and skilled railroad workers. *Zheleznodorozhnoe delo* began publication in 1882 as an organ of the Imperial Russian Technical Society, carrying articles on railroad policy and labor conditions in addition to technical pieces. More important was *Zheleznodorozhnaia nedelia*, which first appeared in 1899. Its popularity grew rapidly, largely, it would seem, because it dared to criticize the ministry and offer outlets for reform-minded officials to voice their ideas. In 1902, however, the ministry approved *Zheleznodorozhnaia nedelia* for placement in waiting rooms and employee lounges, which apparently led many to think the journal enjoyed official support. The editors later pointed to this as a cause of a decline in circulation that caused the paper to fold in May 1903.

But the gap left by the failure of *Zheleznodorozhnaia nedelia* was quickly filled by another publication, destined to become the voice not only of railroad reform but in 1905, if a bit reluctantly, of railroad revolution. The journal was *Zheleznodorozhnik*, a lively St. Petersburg-based weekly, which soon after its first issue in the summer of 1903 became the most significant publication on railroad affairs in Russia and an outlet for railroad officials and employees impatient with inefficient management and repressive labor policies. Though *Zheleznodorozhnik* moderated its critical

56. *ZhD*, 1898, 13–14, pp. 157–60; 30–31, pp. 393–97; Rikhter, *Lichnyi sostav;* VMPS, March 17, 1901, pp. 152–54; *ZhN*, June 9, 1901, pp. 363–64; August 4, 1901, pp. 480–82; TsGIA, f. 273, op. 12, d. 46, ll. 506–16.

tone somewhat in deference to the government's war with Japan, which the editors supported, during 1905 its pages grew ever more strident in their criticism of the ministry and increasingly adventurous politically. Neither *Zheleznodorozhnaia nedelia* nor *Zheleznodorozhnik* were political journals, but they offered reform proposals that reflected oppositional concerns.[57]

The Ministry of Communications was slow to respond to calls for change. Part of the problem was the minister himself, Prince Mikhail I. Khilkov. Scion of an old princely family, Khilkov left for the United States after the serf emancipation, where he went into railroading, rising through the ranks to become an experienced engine-driver. Returning to Russia some ten years later, he entered state service and worked on the Moscow-Riazan road, where he became a favorite of the tsaritsa Maria Fedorovna. In 1895, after a brief stint as minister of railroads in Bulgaria, he was named to head the Ministry of Communications. According to Witte, Khilkov was technically experienced, but "naive"; he was never a true statesman, "remaining for his entire life more the chief engine-driver than the minister." Khilkov usually delegated problems of labor management to his subordinate, the director of the Administration of Railroads, Petr N. Dumitrashko, a competent, if colorless, bureaucrat who lacked the political muscle and will to steer a program of reform through the bureaucracy.[58]

Khilkov released a report on the need to "preserve the safety and regularity of railroad movement" by improving the economic and legal position of railroad workers and employees on January 26, 1901. According to the report, railroad workers' lack of rights made it difficult for the roads to keep experienced workers, and this led to unacceptable losses. Khilkov ordered the ministry to revive discussion of the labor charter first mandated fifteen years earlier by the Baranov Commission.[59] Privy Councillor S. N. Iastrzhembskii was appointed to chair a commission of railroad engineers, bureaucrats, and economists to draft the long-projected document, whose goal was to systematize the maze of railroad labor policy and for-

57. On *Zheleznodorozhnik* and its influence, see the memoir of its editor, P. S. Solomko, TsGAOR, f. 6865, d. 44.

58. On Khilkov, see *Al'manakh sovremennykh Russkikh gosudarstvennykh deiatelei* (St. Petersburg, 1897), pp. 186–90; TsGIA, f. 1162, op. 6, d. 585, ll. 80–108; Witte, *Vospominaniia*, vol. 2, pp. 22, 553. On Dumitrashko, see TsGIA, f. 1162, op. 6, d. 188, ll. 63–76.

59. TsGAOR, f. 6865, d. 29a, l. 14.

mally define the rights and responsibilities of the varied categories of railroad labor. The commission had before it drafts by Nemeshaev and Rikhter, but it was slightly more than two years before it could offer its own version.

This proposal, submitted on May 15, 1902, divided all railroad employees into officials and workers.[60] The latter, defined as those involved in "lower forms of physical labor" with no direct link to traffic safety, included the great majority of railroad employees. The charter applied to "officials" only, and thus completely failed to address the problems in labor relations about which there was growing concern. It simply defined and systematized the recruitment, training, and service of members of the engineering corps and a limited range of white-collar managers, remaining silent not only about most manual labor but even about some technical and administrative positions. To be sure, the commission recognized "the necessity of raising the authority of railroad employees in the eyes of the public by granting some of them rights of state service," but this group was so narrow that the problems of the great majority were effectively ignored.

Largely for this reason, the draft charter came under substantial criticism, in light of which Dumitrashko assembled a new commission under the ministry's chancellery.[61] But the chancellery archives offer no evidence that this body ever took up its task. For three years the railroad press bemoaned the unexplained shelving of the charter, but even so by 1905 no progress could be reported. Basic documents governing employment on the state railroad system were not produced by the Ministry of Communications until early 1906, and these were not formally approved by the government until 1907.[62] On the eve of the 1905 revolution labor policy continued without direction. The legal status and position of most railroad workers and employees and their rights and responsibilities of employment lacked any formal or generally applicable definition.

60. For the text of the commission draft and its explanatory note, see TsGIA, f. 229, op. 4, d. 925, ll. 1–16, 17–46.
61. On the criticisms of the commission draft, see TsGIA, f. 229, op. 4, d. 925, ll. 170–200.
62. *Zhel.*, 6, July 6, 1903, p. 1. For more on the history of the labor charter and railroad labor policy generally, see Henry Reichman, "Tsarist Labor Policy and the Railroads, 1885–1914." *Russian Review* 42, no. 1 (1983): 51–72.

Two

Railroad Labor: Recruitment, Composition, Structure

Administrative tyranny and the accompanying rift between the privileged ranks of the railroad elite and the great majority of workers and employees tended to vitiate the formation of rigidly defined hierarchies. Otherwise disparate occupational and social groups were commonly victimized by arbitrary rule and thus could readily be drawn together in mutual hostility to superiors. Yet such rule tended also to reflect and perpetuate the atomization of railroad labor and its subordination to prevailing patterns of authority. The polarity in the railroad "family" between the privileged "older sons" of the engineering corps and the unacknowledged "stepsons" of labor was mediated by and perceived through an array of additional polarities. To individual workers the composition of the elite could take on different configurations depending on the angle from which it was perceived.

If, moreover, the position and legal status of railroad labor remained ill-defined, this was in some measure a consequence of the extraordinary diversity of railroad occupations and of the social heterogeneity of the work force. Railwaymen were differentiated by variations in sex, nationality, age, social origin, and family relations, as well as by occupation and distinctions in mode of hiring, income, and working conditions. The various divisions—between skilled and unskilled, white-collar and blue-collar, train crew and station staff, high-paid and low-paid, the urbanized and those retaining ties to the land—were by no means coterminous; workers could be separated along any of several distinct, and at times conflicting, axes.

Sources on the number of women employed in railroading vary, but all indicate that at the start of the twentieth century the work force was overwhelmingly male. The 1897 census listed 12,462 women and 162,784 men on the railroads, which would make women 7.1 percent of the total, although the definition of railroad employment used was limited and imprecise. In 1905 *Zheleznodorozhnoe delo* reported that almost 22,000 women were employed on the state lines, which was just 3.5 percent of the total work force and 7.5 percent of permanent staff. According to this report, female labor was most common on the Baltic Railroad, where it amounted to 15.9 percent of permanent staff, and least prevalent on the Nicholas Railroad, where women accounted for only 4 percent of staff employees.[1] Although several ministry circulars encouraged hiring more women, there are indications that use of female labor may actually have declined somewhat in the decade preceding 1905. In 1895, 13.6 percent of pension fund participants were women; by 1903 the figure had dipped to 9 percent.[2] The decline may, however, be partly attributed to the gradual extension of fund coverage to segments of the work force in which women were less frequently found. Still, the pension figures exaggerate the participation of women, since the exclusively male workers in the repair and maintenance shops were largely denied pension rights.

Women were employed almost entirely either in white-collar office work as clerks and ticket cashiers or in track maintenance as road and crossing guards. Women also served as telegraph operators, numbering some 8 percent of all telegraphists in 1902, very often in senior positions. Where in 1902 the average male telegraph operator had been employed for just under 4 years, female operators had served an average of 6.3 years; this was the only area of work in which women were more experienced than men.[3] No women were employed in train operations as engine-drivers or conductors, in the workshops and depots, or—outside the public health sec-

1. E. E. Kruze, *Polozhenie rabochego klassa Rossii v 1900–1914 gg.* (Leningrad, 1976), p. 103; ZhD, 9–10, 1905, p. 112.

2. *Statistika*, 1903, p. 62.

3. Ibid., pp. 48–49.

tion—in posts of administrative responsibility. In 1900 the ministry granted roads permission to hire women as stationmasters, but
the number of females in these positions remained insignificant.
Largely because of their concentration in unskilled and low-paying
work, women's salaries averaged less than half those of male railroad
workers.[4]

By nationality most railwaymen were Russian.[5] Even on lines
serving non-Russian areas of the empire, ethnic Russians—or, to a
lesser extent, Ukrainians—were dominant, especially in permanent staff and skilled positions. Russians were attracted to railroad
work on the empire's periphery by relatively higher wages and access to benefits such as subsidized housing and railroad schools. In
the Caucasus most workers initially hired in the Tiflis workshops of
the Transcaucasian Railroad were skilled Russians from older railroad centers, but by 1900, 44 percent were Georgians, with a smat-
tering of Armenians. Still, the work force did not reflect the ethnic
balance of the region; managerial and many higher white-collar
positions were filled by Russians, as were certain skilled manual
jobs. Railroad office employees in Tiflis were required to take hu-
miliating Russian language competency exams. In the northern
Caucasus an Ossetian engine-driver recalled his arrest at the Mineral Waters station of the Vladikavkaz Railroad for speaking his
native tongue with other strikers. "Who gave you permission to
speak this dog's language?" asked the chief railroad gendarme.[6]

In the Belorussian, Polish, and Baltic provinces, Jews, Poles, and
Lithuanians were victims of systematic discrimination. As already
noted, when the state took over private railroads large numbers of
Jews and Poles were dismissed from managerial posts. Similar dismissals took place among skilled and other workers, though these
were sometimes limited by the availability of qualified Russian
hirees. In 1894 the ministry ordered the Libau-Romny Railroad to

4. *Zhel.*, 58, July 6, 1904, pp. 3–5; *Statistika*, 1903, p. 60.
5. I. M. Pushkareva, *Zheleznodorozhniki Rossii v burzhuazno-demokraticheskikh revoliutsiiakh* (Moscow, 1975), p. 42. An informal review of lists of railwaymen arrested or fired for revolutionary activity in late 1905 shows a prepon-
derance of Russian names, even on lines running through minority areas.
6. E. V. Khoshtaria, *Ocherki sotsial'no-ekonomicheskoi istorii Gruzii* (Tbilisi,
1974), p. 195; *Rabochee dvizhenie v Rossii v XIX veke: Sbornik dokumentov i materialov* (Moscow, 1958), vol. 3, pt. 1, p. 479; I. Kh. Danilov and P. G. Sdobnev,
eds., *Zheleznodorozhniki v 1905 godu* (Moscow, 1940), p. 8; TsGAOR, f. 6865,
d. 70, l. 176.

limit the percentage of Catholic engine-drivers to 33 percent on one section and 40 percent on another. The road's managers apparently could not do without skilled Polish and Lithuanian drivers, however, for the brunt of discrimination fell on younger assistants: in 1905 half of all chief engine-drivers were still Catholics, but only 13 percent of their assistants professed the Roman faith. In that year the director of the Libau-Romny Railroad requested permission to increase the quota for heterodox engine-drivers to 60 percent, since the limitations were a source of discontent and could not be fully implemented.[7]

With respect to recruitment and social origin of railroad labor, Soviet historians of the 1920s emphasized the peasant component of the work force, and the majority of railwaymen were indeed ultimately recruited from the villages and carried peasant passports.[8] A recent Soviet study of railroad lines in the Ukraine in the 1890s has concluded that from 36.7 to 63.9 percent of the workers were "proletarianized peasants," and a similar investigation of Belorussian roads numbers recruits from the villages at between 81 and 94 percent of the total, about a third of whom maintained rural land holdings.[9] Not only was seasonal migration traditional in many regions, but a significant portion of young male workers might labor for several years in "permanent" positions while their families remained in the village, to which the workers themselves ultimately returned. High rates of railroad labor turnover, especially in the lower ranks, also suggest that such "nomadism" was not unheard of in railroading.

Even among those without land and with established urban ties, village relationships of a social or cultural nature could be naggingly persistent. Robert E. Johnson's study of Moscow factory workers has revealed how village life and habits could be reproduced in the urban factory environment, in part through the abid-

7. TsGIA, f. 273, op. 12, d. 330, ll. 29–30.
8. For example, an unpublished essay by a Soviet historian of the 1920s states: "A significant percent of railwaymen were in fact peasants, only yesterday resident on the land, today torn away from it and thrust onto the railroads" (TsGAOR, f. 6865, d. 29a, l. 86).
9. E. F. Belinskii, "Formirovanie zheleznodorozhnogo proletariata na Ukraine vo vtoroi polovine XIX v.," Kandidat diss., Kiev, 1965, pp. 8–9; V. A. Titok, "Formirovanie i revoliutsionnaia bor'ba zheleznodorozhnogo proletariata Belorussii vo vtoroi polovine XIX v.–nachale XX veka," Kandidat diss., Minsk, 1966, p. 11.

ing influence of regional ties and loyalties both in recruitment of new workers and in the lives of veteran urban dwellers.[10] Although the sources remain inadequate for us to be able to draw conclusions on the extent of such ties in railroading, there are some indications that in certain strata these did play a part. Where possible, railroads recruited unskilled and even skilled workers from villages along the right of way. In lists of railwaymen arrested for revolutionary activity in 1905, groups of arrestees whose passports indicated a common origin in a single village can sometimes be found.[11]

The "peasant" component of railroad labor should not be exaggerated, however, as contemporary Soviet researchers are quick to stress. The extreme diversity of railroad tasks, the very complexity of railroad operations, and the unique combinations of mental and skilled manual labor required by many railroad occupations dictated the development of a modern urbanized core within the work force. Many white-collar and skilled railroad workers, including those of relatively low economic stature, were recruited not from the peasantry but from more privileged and urban estates (*sosloviia*). At one station, 40 percent of employees involved in traffic movement and telegraph operation came from the gentry and the *meshchanstvo*, the lower urban estate of petty shopkeepers, artisans, and the like sometimes deceptively labeled petty bourgeois; another 9 percent were former merchants. On the Belorussian railroads, some 20 percent of all clerks and accountants and 17 percent of stationmasters were gentry, while 50 percent of the telegraph operators, 40 percent of the engine-drivers, and 30 percent of accountants, cashiers, and clerks came from the *meshchanstvo*.[12]

In 1895 railroad engineer I. I. Rikhter cited figures indicating that 63 percent of railroad employees were officially peasants, 24

10. Robert E. Johnson, *Peasant and Proletarian: The Working Class of Moscow in the Late Nineteenth Century* (New Brunswick, N.J., 1979), especially pp. 67–79. See also Victoria E. Bonnell, *The Russian Worker: Life and Labor Under the Tsarist Regime* (Berkeley and Los Angeles, 1983), pp. 14–17.

11. For example, a group of six telegraph operators of the Moscow-Kazan Railroad in Moscow arrested in January 1906: two were of *meshchanstvo* background and the others peasants, but all were registered from the same town in Riazan *guberniia* and several had relatives employed in railroading elsewhere (TsGAOR, f. 6865, d. 194, ll. 66–79).

12. Pushkareva, *Zheleznodorozhniki*, p. 43; Titok, p. 11. In the Urals many railwaymen were recruited from the region's decaying mining and metal industry (see E. M. Mil'man, "Formirovanie kadrov zheleznodorozhnogo proletariata Urala

percent *meshchane*, and 8 percent gentry. According to Rikhter, however, only 25 percent of railroad hirees worked in agriculture before entering railroad service; another 27 percent, mainly, no doubt, sons of peasants, entered railroading directly from the military (another sign of the strong military influence in railroad life); 7 percent from the state civil service; 17 percent from private trade or industry; and 2 percent from the handicraft trades. The remaining railroad recruits entered employment after completing railroad technical school or directly from dependence on their parents. These statistics, however, were based on a narrow, and probably disproportionate, sample of those eligible to participate in the still infant pension fund, and they likely underestimate the peasant element.[13]

Although many who held peasant passports no doubt continued to maintain links to their native villages, perhaps an equal number had abandoned such ties. A 1902 article on "The Passport Question on the Railroads" in *Zheleznodorozhnaia nedelia* estimated that as many as 90 percent of all railroad workers and employees held peasant passports, but at least 40 percent could not even claim a single relative, much less a plot of land, in their "home" villages. Thus:

> Fifty percent of such peasants by no means merit this label. They are, in fact, "peasants" who have *never* [emphasis in original] lived in the countryside and grew up instead in the cities; even peasants whose grandfathers ruptured all ties with the village and became permanent urban dwellers. . . . This 50 percent, more developed and intelligent, feels more strongly its lack of rights.[14]

Yet the bounds of these groups were not so readily circumscribed. Even within those segments of the work force where "peasant" labor was most concentrated, urbanization and proletarianization could also be quite advanced. As I. M. Pushkareva has pointed out, among the skilled metalworkers of the repair and

vo vtoroi polovine XIX veka," *Iz istorii rabochego klassa Urala. Sbornik statei.* [Perm, 1961], pp. 215–16). For a useful discussion of the role of the *sosloviia*, or estates, in the social structure of late imperial Russia, see Gregory L. Freeze, "The *Soslovie* (Estate) Paradigm and Russian Social History," *American Historical Review* 91 (1986): 11–36.

13. I. I. Rikhter, "Zheleznodorozhnaia psikhologiia," *ZhD,* 25–26, 1895, p. 224. This was a book-length work serialized in *ZhD,* 1895, 25–26 through 47–48.

14. *ZhN,* September 22, 1902, p. 571; September 28, 1902, p. 589.

maintenance workshops the "peasant" component could not have been very much larger—and may well have been smaller—than in the metalworking industry in general, where by 1905, according to the studies of the Soviet historical demographer A. G. Rashin, only about one in four craftsmen held land in the countryside.[15] Even rural track repair gangs, in which peasant labor unquestionably predominated, included in their ranks road foremen and others recruited from railroad construction crews, who over the years had been molded into the nucleus of a permanent semiskilled force.

The point is simply to stress the difficulty of generalizing, one way or the other, about the social position of railroad workers solely on the basis of the urban-rural nexus; the real situation was far more complex and stratified than simplistic class or estate labels would indicate. There were in railroad life a number of workers whose recent recruitment or long-standing rural ties surely left the "stamp of the village" on their behavior and thought, although it should be recognized that in many regions the rural environment was itself changing rapidly. At least an equal number, and probably more, were full-fledged members of a developing urbanized working class, with few, if any, rural ties. This, of course, hardly meant that a "Chinese wall" separated urbanized from country workers. In between, most Russian workers were, at least psychologically, in transit from village to city. On the railroads "peasant" and proletarian elements could both be found in a variety of occupational situations and economic conditions.

For administrative purposes workers and employees on each railroad line were usually divided into four departments. These were the Administrative Department (*sluzhba upravleniia*), the Department of Engines and Rolling Stock (*sluzhba tiagi i podvizhnogo sostava*), the Department of Traffic Management (*sluzhba dvizheniia*), and the Department of Track Maintenance and Construction (*sluzhba puti i stroenii*).[16] This structure did not fully conform to the division of labor, but was related to it.

15. Pushkareva, *Zheleznodorozhniki*, p. 40; A. G. Rashin, *Formirovanie rabochego klassa v Rossii* (Moscow, 1958), p. 576.
16. Although most railroad lines followed the four department division, some were divided five or even six or seven ways. For statistical purposes, the public health section divided the labor force into nine departments: management, repair, station, train, depot-train, workshops, telegraph, medical, and gendarmery.

The Administrative Department, the smallest of the four, was charged with railroad management, although managerial personnel and white-collar employees could also be found in each of the other departments. On most railroads the department's overwhelmingly white-collar staff of clerks, accountants, and petty officials was divided among the central administrative offices (generally situated at or near the line's main workshops and largest freight yard) and smaller local offices and stations. In addition, the doctors, nurses, and other employees of the public health section and employees of railroad schools were under this department, which in 1905 included 56,481 employees, or 7.5 percent of all those employed on the Russian railroads.

The Department of Engines and Rolling Stock was in charge of maintenance, repair, and operation of locomotives, boxcars, and passenger carriages. The greatest number of workers in this department were in the repair and maintenance shops, situated every 100 to 300 miles along major trunk lines. The largest such shops employed a minimum of 500 skilled and unskilled workers, and petty repair facilities and depots could hire several hundred. In 1900 there were a total of 70 major workshops and 445 locomotive depots in the Russian railroad system.[17] Attached to the depots were the locomotive crews, including engine-drivers, their assistants, and stokers, as well as various blue-collar service workers, including greasemen, whose job it was to keep the bearings and moveable parts of the rolling stock lubricated, couplers, train handlers, and their assistants. In 1905, 223,634 workers, 29.8 percent of the total, worked in this department, including 164,067, 21.8 percent of all railwaymen, in the workshops.

Operation of the train system was the responsibility of the Department of Traffic Management. Workers in this department were employed in all large and small stations and at switching posts throughout the railroad network. They included switchmen, who controlled the movement of trains, attending to the switching mechanisms both at larger stations and isolated track connections, signalmen, ticket agents, and much of the station staff, including stationmasters, customs-house employees and freight handlers. Conductors and other members of train crews—but not locomotive

17. M. S. Volin et al., eds., *Rabochii klass Rossii ot zarozhdeniia do nachala XX v.* (Moscow, 1983), p. 178.

cabmen—were also under this department. On several roads there was a separate Telegraph Department, but where this did not exist, telegraph operators were counted here. In 1905 there were 202,561 workers employed in this department, 27 percent of all workers and employees. This included some 24,921 employed in the railroad telegraph service.

Finally, the Department of Track Maintenance and Construction included track and crossing guards, road and bridge foremen, and construction and repair crews assigned to the upkeep of track, bridges, and rights-of-way. This was especially important in Russia, where severe weather conditions took a heavy toll on track. These workers were often recruited from the unskilled ranks of the local peasantry, frequently on a seasonal basis, but some, as already mentioned, were at least semiskilled and permanently employed in railroad work. This was the largest department, employing 268,511 men and women, or 35.7 percent of the railroad work force in 1905.

In all departments workers were hired on a permanent, temporary, or daily basis. This division reflected certain technical and economic particularities of railroading, but also the managerial compulsion to keep the work force arbitrarily divided. Permanent staff workers amounted to just over half of all railroad labor in 1905, down from slightly more than 70 percent in 1885, but their distribution by department and job category was uneven. Among the permanent staff were manual workers and office employees, administrators and laborers, skilled and unskilled, including the occupants of both highly paid and relatively low-paying positions. Permanent status did not, therefore, of itself denote privilege. This was nonetheless the more stable half of the labor force, however, and it enjoyed certain benefits denied temporaries and dailies, including vacations, rights to complimentary railroad transport, to railroad housing or housing subsidies, to uniforms, and, after an initial probationary period, to participation in the pension fund. According to rules adopted for railroad workshops by the ministry in the 1890s and printed in shop pay-books, shop workers with staff status—a decided minority—enjoyed seniority over all nonstaff workers and could be fired only by the railroad administration and not simply by the director of the workshop.[18]

18. TsGIA, f. 273, op. 12, d. 347, l. 102.

Temporary workers, who in 1905 accounted for just 5.6 percent of all employees, were hired, mainly in construction, to work on specific projects or for a designated period. In 1905 daily workers accounted for just over 40 percent of the work force, up from 25.2 percent two decades earlier. In theory, dailies included recent hirees whose status was still probationary or who were employed as needed on a day-to-day basis, with limited benefits betokening a peripheral role in railroad operations. In practice, there were genuine dailies and "permanent dailies," the latter including the overwhelming majority of both skilled and unskilled metalworkers in the repair shops and depots. These were in reality permanent full-time workers—often highly skilled and, in key respects, economically privileged—who were paid a daily wage and/or by piece rate, as opposed to the monthly or even annual salaries received by permanent staff. Such dailies lacked, however, many of the rights and privileges accorded staff. Employment of dailies was concentrated in the Department of Engines and Rolling Stock, in which 65.9 percent of all workers were dailies in 1905, including the great majority of skilled and unskilled workshop hands, and in the Department of Track Maintenance and Construction, in which 50.1 percent were dailies, mainly in repair crews. Together these two departments accounted for 91.4 percent of all daily workers (see Table 1).

If, however, railroad labor is classified not by administrative categories, as above, but according to the technical, economic, and social division of labor, four broad groupings, which correlate only partially with the four departments of railroad administration, can be distinguished. These involved workers and employees in (1) administrative work and communications; (2) industrial labor; (3) railroad operations; and (4) track repair, maintenance, and construction. Although this division was by no means clearly delineated either formally or in everyday practice, and several categories of railroad labor straddle its borders, this basic differentiation proved more determinative of variations and conflicts in political and strike behavior than did administrative divisions, though, to be sure, hardly in a linear or mechanical way. In 1905 the administrative and communications personnel on the one hand and the industrial-type workers of the repair and maintenance shops on the other were the two most important elements of the railroad work-

TABLE 1.   *Number of Railroad Personnel by Department, 1905*

	Permanent		Temporary		Daily		Total	
Department	Number	%	Number	%	Number	%	Number	%
Administration	39,496	69.9	6,059	10.7	10,926	19.4	56,481	7.5
Engines and Rolling Stock	69,641	31.1	6,659	3.0	147,334	65.9	223,634	29.8
Traffic Management	169,845	83.8	16,986	8.4	15,730	7.8	202,561	27.0
Track Maintenance	121,241	45.2	12,806	4.7	134,474	50.1	268,511	35.7
All Departments	400,223	53.3	42,510	5.6	308,464	41.1	751,197	100.0

Source: Ministerstvo Putei Soobshcheniia. Otdel statistiki i kartografii. *Statisticheskii sbornik*, no. 89, St. Petersburg, 1907, table xii.

ers' movement. The response of the highly differentiated operative personnel was more complex and varied, and the track repair and maintenance workers, whose isolation and rural ties were greatest, formed in the main a passive rearguard.

The remainder of this chapter treats the role played in the railroad economy by each of these groupings, and by key job classifications within them, and discusses distinctions in recruitment and composition. The working and living conditions peculiar to specific categories are left mainly to the more general discussions of economic position and everyday life in chapters 3 and 4. (Table 2 presents a quantitative portrait of these groupings and component categories.)

Administration and Communications

There has to date been no comprehensive study of white-collar work in tsarist Russia.[19] As a result, little is known of what distinguished

19. The only substantial work was done in the 1920s. See A. M. Gudvan, *Ocherki po istorii dvizheniia sluzhashchikh v Rossii* (Moscow, 1925), and D. Antoshkin, *Ocherk dvizheniia sluzhashchikh v Rossii (so vtoroi poloviny XIX v.)* (Moscow, 1921).

TABLE 2. *Number of Railroad Personnel by Job Category, 1905*

	Number	Percentage Total
Higher management and railroad engineers[a]	10,710	1.4
I. *Administrative work and communications*		
Accountants, clerks, and other office personnel[b,c]	39,142	5.2
Administrative department	24,163	
Other departments	14,979	
Public Health Section[d]	4,514	0.6
Doctors	711	
Nurses	1,613	
Midwives	341	
Stationmasters and assistants[c]	13,568	1.8
Telegraph operators[b]	24,921	3.3
Total	82,145	10.9
II. *Industrial labor*		
Workshops and depots[c]	164,067	21.8
Skilled	120,464	
Unskilled	43,603	
Skilled craftsmen in other departments[a]	84,124	11.2
Total	248,191	33.0
III. *Railroad operations*		
Locomotive crews[b]	34,241	4.6
Conductors[b]	44,865	6.0
Couplers and train handlers[b]	9,484	1.3
Greasemen[c]	8,741	1.2
Signalmen[a]	1,612	0.2
Switchmen[b]	38,066	5.1
Cashiers, ticket agents and other white-collar station personnel[a,c]	36,027	4.8
Porters, doormen, cleaning staff and other blue-collar station service personnel[a,d]	25,091	3.3
Total	198,127	26.5

	Number	Percentage Total
IV. *Maintenance and construction*		
Road and bridge foremen[a]	4,015	0.5
Track and crossing watchmen[b]	57,838	7.7
Repair and construction crews[b,c]	150,171	20.0
Total	212,024	28.2
Total All Personnel	751,197	100.0

Sources: Where more than one symbol is given, the figure was derived from a combination of two sources. [a] I. M. Pushkareva, *Zheleznodorozhniki Rossii v burzhuazno-demokraticheskikh revoliutsiiakh* (Moscow, 1975), p. 51; [b] *Statisticheskii sbornik,* no. 89, table xii; [c] TsGAOR, f. 6865, d. 28b, 11. 1–2; [d] *Vrach-san otchet,* 1905, pp. 16, 20–21; [e] TsGIA, f. 273, op. 12, d. 407, 1. 89.

office employees (*sluzhashchie*) from their blue-collar brethren, from social groups above them in the status hierarchy, and from white-collar labor in western Europe. To be sure, the collar line is everywhere a product of the structure and function of production and distribution in industrial societies. Hence, outside the specific national context, certain characteristic features of white-collar work are universal. White-collar employees are involved in commercial, administrative, financial, legal, and coordinating functions. Their tasks are frequently less routinized, harder to measure, and more concerned with information than materials than those of manual laborers. The very structure of white-collar work requires greater continuity between ranks. Authority may far more frequently be delegated in the office than on the shop floor, and the office hierarchy will therefore generally be more gradated than that of the factory, although at the turn of the century the historical trend was toward the differentiation of an increasingly subordinate and "proletarianized" stratum of clerks at the bottom of the white-collar world. Yet the line of demarcation between the collars can hardly be said to be everywhere the same. In all societies complicated and particular historical processes have specified not only whether a given occupation is considered blue- or white-collar, but also whether the collar distinction itself is of greater or lesser social, cultural, and political bearing.[20]

In Russia the white-collar work force, including white-collar railroad workers, developed in the interstices between three larger overlapping social groups: the state bureaucracy, the intelligentsia, and the industrial working class. It remains, however, entirely unclear whether white-collar workers distinguished themselves as unique and separate from these larger categories or if, instead, their "loyalties" were to one or more of them. Soviet historians have discussed white-collar workers as members of the intelligentsia—defined broadly as those who work with their minds—and certainly the proportion of educated men and women among them was not insignificant.[21] More than a few university graduates found work at the middle levels of railroad administration, and no doubt a number of local stationmasters and commercial agents, not to mention railroad doctors, identified with the concerns of the liberal or even radical urban intelligentsia, or had relatives or acquaintances in the *zemstvo* "third element." In railroad administration the top managerial ranks were occupied by men whose status and outlook were those of the state bureaucracy, but many could also be said to belong to the intelligentsia. Especially among the reform-minded, quite a few could sympathize with the grievances of subordinates and often shared common concerns with them, in general exercising considerable ideological and political influence in their lives.[22]

Though the line separating those white-collar employees who worked for the railroads from those who ran them could be hazy, it was nonetheless real. Tyrannical behavior toward subordinates and obsequious toadying before superiors were as common to railroad offices as they were to the entire bureaucratic order. "Oppressed and deprived of individuality, we feared everything," recalled one provincial railroad clerk. "To just walk by the boss's office made us

20. Jürgen Kocka, *White-Collar Workers in America, 1890–1940* (London, 1980), pp. 6–16, offers a fascinating discussion of the collar line that questions traditional assumptions. My discussion owes much to Kocka.

21. L. K. Erman, *Intelligentsiia v pervoi Russkoi revoliutsii* (Moscow, 1966), pp. 24–25; A. V. Ushakov, *Revoliutsionnoe dvizhenie demokraticheskoi intelligentsii v Rossii, 1895–1904* (Moscow, 1976), p. 104.

22. TsGAOR, f. 6865, d. 30, ll. 15–16.

quiver to our souls with fear."[23] Few, if any, white-collar railroad employees came from the countryside, and many looked down on even skilled and highly paid industrial workers as urban extensions of the benighted village. Yet for the great majority incomes and working conditions were not much better, and at times could be significantly worse, than those of skilled blue-collar labor, even though railroad clerks were thought to earn more and work in better conditions than their state office counterparts.[24] Although by 1905 white-collar workers in Russia could clearly distinguish their situations and backgrounds from those of more classically proletarian elements, they were themselves, in a formal sense, also hired labor, and there was neither structural nor historical reason for them to make the collar distinction determinative of political or social behavior.

There were, moreover, clear distinctions between administrative employees in major railroad centers and those at smaller stations. One former administrator on the Moscow-Kursk Railroad labeled relations between the men of the administrative centers and those on the lines "clearly antagonistic."[25] Employees at large junctions, especially Moscow, were at the nerve centers of the railroad network, with access to a functioning web of communications and authority that placed them in a unique position to exercise leadership over a professionally based movement, and, of course, they were closer as well to urban political and social trends. On the lines, administrative and communications personnel were more isolated, but by virtue of the authority and knowledge of railroad operations they commanded, they could often play a determining role in local mobilization.

Central Office Employees

The central railroad offices brought together significant concentrations of white-collar workers. The largest, the Kiev administration

23. *1905 vo vospominaniiakh ego uchastnikov* (Rostov-on-Don, 1925), p. 5.

24. According to one railroad publication, employees in railroad administration earned two or three times what equivalent *chinovniki* received in state offices (*ZhN*, July 21, 1900, p. 452).

25. *1905 god na Moskovsko-kurskoi-nizhegorodskoi i muromskoi zh. d.* (Moscow, 1931), p. 61.

of the South West Railroad, employed a staff of 2,326 in 1905, and several other offices employed more than 500.[26] These included comparatively small groups of highly paid administrators and legal officers, modestly situated accountants, and a large staff of secretarial personnel and clerks. If a few white-collar staff carried to the offices some of the worldly concerns of the oppositional intelligentsia, before 1905, according to the memoir of one clerk, "The majority had degenerated into narrow bureaucrats, with no outside interests and shunning any life beyond railroad service and their own domestic shells." In the offices of the Vladikavkaz Railroad, another clerk later recalled, "Each lived his own life; there was no social existence, not even the pretense of one." Separated from the workers "by the exterior sheen of petty privilege," before 1905 office employees were largely ignored by agitators, rarely read newspapers, and were generally thought to be "politically unconscious." Still, crowded working conditions, inadequate salaries, and continual browbeating by superiors provided fertile soil for dissatisfaction, which could combine with intelligentsia ties into a potentially explosive mix. As early as 1900 *Zheleznodorozhnaia nedelia* warned that the situation of clerks in central offices, especially in the two capitals, was "not only extremely abnormal, but even shockingly unjust" and "immeasurably worse than the situation of junior line staff."[27]

Stationmasters

As the representative of railroad management, the stationmaster symbolized official authority. Yet, outside a few major terminals, stationmasters and especially their assistants stood only slightly above the workers they commanded, and could share common grievances with them. "What is a stationmaster?" asked *Zheleznodorozhnik* in mid 1904. "If this is a member of the intelligentsia, then how can he and his family exist on just 45–50 rubles a month? If this is just an ordinary laborer, then how can he be the representative of management?"[28] Although stationmaster positions were open to all applicants who could pass a qualifying examination,

26. TsGIA, f. 273, op. 12, d. 345, l. 79.
27. TsGAOR, f. 6865, d. 34, l. 3; *1905 vo vospominaniiakh ego uchastnikov*, p. 6; ZhN, March 31, 1900, p. 199.
28. *Zhel.*, 61, July 27, 1904, p. 3.

most were recruited from the ranks of lower employees, especially telegraph operators. A typical career pattern included eight to ten years' work in the telegraph department and five to six years as an assistant stationmaster before responsibility for a station was granted. A station assignment, however, depended in the end on the candidate's willingness and ability to kowtow before, and often bribe, those in charge of appointments.[29]

The stationmaster's life was inextricably joined to that of his station and his administrative tasks were extremely burdensome. One stationmaster called himself "the chief agent, responsible for everything and everyone." Being a stationmaster demanded extensive knowledge of railroad operation and the maze of complex bureaucratic rules and regulations that governed it. The position thus called for a "phenomenal memory. . . . In a word, the stationmaster must know—and I do not exaggerate—as many as 6,000 printed sheets."[30] The stationmaster was obliged to greet each arriving passenger train personally, which on the busier lines frequently meant he could never get an uninterrupted night's rest. Although in theory entitled to a month's vacation every three years, staff shortages made such breaks a rare exception in the lives of many stationmasters and their assistants. Largely as a product of such conditions, most stationmasters came to be characterized by an "apathetic indifference" to everything outside the narrow world of their stations.[31]

Telegraph Operators

Two characteristics of railroad telegraph personnel were repeatedly remarked upon by contemporaries: their extreme youth and, in apparent contradiction to this, their abnormally poor health. The latter, to be discussed in chapter 4, was attributable partly to difficult working and living conditions and partly to the often dissolute

29. S. L. Tregubov, *Opyt izucheniia v sanitarnom otnoshenii byta zheleznodorozhnykh sluzhashchikh v predelakh Kursko-Kharkovo-Sevastopol'skogo zh. d.* (Kharkov, 1904), p. 50; *Novoe vremia*, 10542, July 9, 1905; *Zhel.*, 75, November 2, 1904, p. 19.

30. *Novoe vremia*, 10542, July 9, 1905. This article and a sequel are also in TsGIA, f. 273, op. 12, d. 335, ll. 97–98.

31. TsGAOR, f. 6865, d. 49, l. 29, and Tregubov, p. 48; *Novoe vremia*, 10544, July 11, 1905; *Zhel.*, 9, July 27, 1903, p. 5.

life-style of many of these young workers.[32] More than 80 percent of railwaymen were between the ages of twenty and forty, compared to just 55 percent among all male workers, but railroad telegraph operators were by and large significantly younger, with 63 percent twenty-five or younger.[33] Though junior operators were "very young people, poverty-stricken and only semiliterate, often lacking even an elementary knowledge of arithmetic," by virtue of their early start, those who stayed the course in railroading often emerged with extensive practical knowledge of railroad affairs, qualifying many as stationmasters.[34] The telegraph department was considered the "sick sister" among all branches of railroad service; funding was low and even higher telegraph administrators received salaries noticeably below their counterparts in other departments. This combination of excitable and easily aroused youth with the practical grasp of railroad affairs and strategic position in communications of more senior telegraph employees who were frequently underpaid would make this group especially volatile.

Industrial Labor

Workshops and Depots

The skilled metal craftsmen (*masterovye*) of the workshops (along with blue-collar craftsmen in the depots and other departments) were the most segregated grouping within the railroad work force. To be sure, this was by far the largest and most cohesive bloc of workers in railroading, and by virtue of this alone they represented, insofar as they also *acted* cohesively, a pole to which more disparate groupings could be attracted. But these workers, whose situation was most recognizably industrial, were separated from their fellow railwaymen both administratively, since they were largely denied the rights and benefits of permanent staff, and structurally, owing to their differing pattern of recruitment and work and their physical isolation from actual train operations.[35]

32. *ZhD*, 1902, 34–35, pp. 329–32; *ZhN*, August 25, 1901, pp. 529–30; Tregubov, pp. 50–53.
33. *Statistika*, 1897, pp. 63–64; *ZhD*, 34–35, 1902, p. 329.
34. *ZhN*, September 1, 1901, p. 546.
35. "Understanding that the workshops represented for them an Achilles heel, the railroad bureaucracy strived to completely isolate them from the remaining

While the workshops specialized in repair and servicing of locomotives and rolling stock, they of necessity employed workers
whose skills were of broader utility in the machine-building and
metal-working fields, less railwaymen than metalworkers employed
by the railroads.

As metalworkers, however, they were part of a relatively well-
heeled stratum of the industrial working class, a self-defined labor
aristocracy.[36] Although there was considerable variation between
trades and skill levels, wages in the metal industry were well above
the general industrial average and metalworkers worked shorter
days and fewer days per year than those in other nonseasonal industries. For the sons of unskilled textile and other workers a
future in the metal trades was something to aspire to; the sons of
metalworkers themselves were attracted to higher technical education and a career in engineering.[37]

The high status of the metal trades was in part a function of the
shortage of skilled labor in tsarist Russia, especially during the
rapid industrial expansion of the 1890s. Even in the capitals, where
the number of skilled hands was greatest, metalworkers could still
move freely from job to job without inordinate fears of unemployment. On the railroads this shortage was especially severe outside the major industrial centers. Shops in cities such as Odessa,
Rostov-on-Don, Kiev, and Tiflis, as well as most smaller depots and
repair facilities in provincial towns, could face chronic recruitment
difficulties.[38] New blood continued to pour into the metal industry

---

line elements, and the 'special' care they gave to this deepened the antagonism
between the workshops and the other line employees. But the very character of
railroad technology was such that the workshops were a supplementary element of
the railroad economy and therefore an interruption of activity in the workshops
could influence the functioning of the road itself only in specially exceptional instances" (V. Romanov, "Dvizhenie sredi sluzhashchikh i rabochikh Russkikh zh. d.
v 1905 g.," *Obrazovanie* 1906, no. 10: 33).

36. See, for example, the statement of the St. Petersburg metalworker Alexei
Buzinov in Bonnell, *Russian Worker*, p. 11. On metalworkers, see Heather Hogan,
"Labor and Management in Conflict: The St. Petersburg Metal Working Industry,
1900–1914," Ph.D. diss., University of Michigan, 1979.

37. TsGIA, f. 273, op. 12, d. 46, l. 591.

38. "In provincial cities, especially nonindustrial ones such as Vitebsk—and
there are many like this—there is no local contingent of mechanics outside the
railroad shops" (*ZhD*, 23–24, 1896, p. 179). In the Urals railroad repair shops

in the two decades before 1905, but by the turn of the century a skilled hereditary work force had emerged. Especially in the south, railroad metalworkers could be highly mobile, traveling from city to city and from workshop to workshop, going wherever employment was most attractive.[39] In railroading, metalworkers were increasingly recruited from the sons of experienced craftsmen and from other less skilled ranks of the railroad work force.

One thing that distinguished railroad shops from the rest of the metal industry was their larger size and high degree of concentration. In 1904 St. Petersburg metal shops averaged 346 workers each, whereas many railroad workshops employed thousands, and all more than 500. Even many secondary provincial railroad facilities stood above the average for St. Petersburg metal shops. Yet within these giant enterprises the work force could be as divided by both social status and the division of labor as in railroading as a whole. Large and medium railroad repair operations were conglomerations of shops, each responsible for a specific production process. In these workshops were boilermakers, smithys, foundrymen, carpenters, and machinists, each with their assistants and apprentices. A complex status system, with relatively wide—and often unfathomably intricate—variations in wages and working conditions, divided these groups from, and at times against, one another.[40]

---

competed with local industry for skilled labor. The administration of the Motovilikh metal plant complained in the 1880s that competition for skilled craftsmen with the Perm railroad shops drove up wages. This was, however, a temporary problem; by 1900 wages on the Ural railroads were, as elsewhere, on a par with, or well below, those in the metal industry (Mil'man, pp. 216, 221–22).

39. In a police report concerning strikes in the Tiflis shops of the Transcaucasian Railroad in 1888 is the following: "Over a thousand craftsmen are in the shops, mainly Russian, who have been in Rostov, Odessa, Sevastopol, and other populated points where there are big workshops" (*Rabochee dvizhenie v Rossii v XIX veke. Sbornik dokumentov i materialov* [Moscow and Leningrad, 1950–63], vol. 3, pt. 1, p. 479).

40. The St. Petersburg figure is from Gerald Surh, "St. Petersburg Workers in 1905," Ph.D. diss., University of California, Berkeley, 1979, p. 79. For statistics on numbers of workers employed in individual workshops on the railroads, see TsGIA, f. 273, op. 12, d. 430, ll. 21–83, and Pushkareva, *Zheleznodorozhniki*, p. 46. On the division of larger metalworking plants, including railroad shops, into smaller units and the importance of this to the workers see Victoria E. Bonnell, *Roots of Rebellion: Workers' Politics and Organizations in St. Petersburg and Moscow, 1900–1914* (Berkeley and Los Angeles, 1983), pp. 63–64.

Because in this period the level of mechanization was not high and much work was still effectively done by hand, in most shops work was carried out in comparatively small groups, often numbering just twelve to eighteen men, according to a scheme inherited from the pre-industrial *artel* system. The arrangement at the Konotop workshops of the Moscow-Kiev-Voronezh Railroad may be taken as typical.[41] Here workers labored in "brigades" of several skilled workers, assistants, and apprentices headed by a *brigadir* or *master*, whose task it was to apportion and assign jobs and distribute pay. In larger brigades he could be assisted by several *montera* or *desiatniki* who functioned as his foremen. The *brigadir* was himself both shop foreman and master craftsman; the managerial functions he exercised had been assumed in part on the basis of experience and skill, and did not necessarily stand in contradiction to direct involvement in the work. In the Odessa workshops of the South West Railroad it was reported that only three of twenty *mastera* were railroad engineers; the remainder were veteran "*praktiki*" with over thirty years' experience.[42]

As Gerald Surh has suggested for St. Petersburg metalworkers, this mode of organization—the segregation and internal cohesion of work groups and the authority of the *mastera*—tended both to restrain metalworkers from hasty participation in strikes and, later, to facilitate their effective mobilization.[43] Yet as the system grew, especially in the larger railroad workshops, and as more lines came under state management, the independence and status of the brigade were eroded. At the workshops of the Nicholas Railroad in St. Petersburg in the second half of the 1890s, the number of workers assigned to each *desiatnik* doubled. By the eve of the 1905 revolution, it was extremely rare for a *master* to truly "represent" his brigade; more often than not he had become a target of their wrath.[44]

This was not yet the move to Taylorism that some investigators have detected in parts of the metal industry on the eve of World

41. Ivan Maruta, *Ocherki po istorii revoliutsionnogo professional'nogo dvizheniia na Moskovsko-kievo-voronezhskoi zh. d.* (Kursk, 1925), pp. 15–16. See also TsGIA, f. 273, op. 12, d. 46, l. 576.

42. TsGIA, f. 273, op. 12, d. 46, l. 572.

43. Surh, pp. 82–83, 252–53.

44. *ZhN*, April 7, 1900, p. 217. Dissatisfaction with *mastera* was evidenced by the great number of shops that demanded "courteous treatment" from them in 1905. See TsGIA, f. 273, op. 12, d. 328, l. 88, and chapter 5.

War I; instead it was closer to the erosion of an early industrial work order that, as David Montgomery has shown, energized protest among American craftsmen of the Gilded Age. Still, by 1905 some railroad managers were already speaking of the need for *Amerikanizm*, or the "American system," by which was meant not necessarily Taylorism per se, but a variety of incentive schemes aimed at increasing efficiency through tighter shop organization and authority, an important development consistent with international trends in the organization of factory labor.[45]

Status distinctions, not only between skilled and unskilled, but among those of different training, background, experience, and age, could also divide railroad metalworkers. The rapid growth of the labor force in the decades before 1905 must surely have strained traditional shop relations and exacerbated status distinctions, since, at least in railroading, there is no sign it was accompanied by significant technical developments. As work expanded and new and younger men entered the shops, foremen grew increasingly distant from those they led, and some older, more experienced workers could be drawn paradoxically closer to management even as their own positions deteriorated with the breakdown of previous, more fraternal patterns of work. This breakdown was a general phenomenon in the metal trades, but may well have been most advanced in the railroad shops, if only as a function of their size.

Pivotal among the new recruits were younger *skilled* workers, often second- or even third-generation urban dwellers and fre-

45. On Russian "Taylorism," see Heather Hogan, "Industrial Rationalization and the Roots of Labor Militance in the St. Petersburg Metalworking Industry, 1901–1914," *Russian Review* 42, no. 2 (1983): 163–90. Hogan is incorrect in identifying the phrase "American system" exclusively with Taylorism. The term was applied to a range of incentive systems by railroad managers as early as 1903, before Taylor's ideas had been widely propagated, even in the United States. On the changing organization of work under industrial capitalism in the United States and Europe and the movement for worker control of production connected to this, see especially David Montgomery, *Workers' Control in America* (New York, 1979), pp. 9–31, and James E. Cronin and Carmen Sirianni, eds., *Work, Community and Power* (Philadelphia, 1983); and, with specific reference to American railroad workshops, Shelton Stromquist, "Enginemen and Shopmen: Technological Change and the Organization of Labor in an Era of Railroad Expansion," *Labor History* 24, no. 4 (1983): 485–99. On *Amerikanizm* generally, see Hans Rogger, "*Amerikanizm* and the Economic Development of Russia," *Comparative Studies in Society and History* 23, no. 3 (1981): 382–420.

quently from railroading families. Only marginally respectful of the eroding traditional work order, they were no doubt impatient with their lowly positions in the labor hierarchy and could look with disdain on the accomplishments of older workers. So, for instance, S. F. Vasil'chenko, one of the leaders of the 1902 Rostov general strike and the son of a railroad switchman, recalled entering the workshops at the age of sixteen and encountering older men earning as much as four rubles daily, enough even to own a house, but thinking only that despite this they were still "but slaves."[46]

During 1905 the Ministry of Communications surveyed railroad directors about the advisability of extending staff status to experienced senior workers in the shops and depots as a means of pacification. To gauge the feasibility of such a measure, the ministry requested information on the numbers of workers in the Department of Engines and Rolling Stock who were already counted among permanent staff, as well as the numbers of those serving more than five and more than ten years, to whom such status might be extended. Unfortunately, responses were not received from several important roads, including most of those headquartered in Moscow, but the survey results are nonetheless revealing: of 77,570 workers in the Department of Engines and Rolling Stock on seventeen state lines responding, 7,113 had been employed for over a decade and another 13,238 between five and ten years, a total of just 26.2 percent with more than five years' experience. The numbers were significantly greater, though, in the central workshops, partly because many newer workers there had already served their apprenticeship at smaller line facilities, and there was considerable variation from road to road. Still, in most shops almost half the work force had been employed for less than five years and, in most cases, fewer than a third for more than ten.[47]

No direct correlation can be drawn between the size of the veteran work force and strike propensity in 1905 or the years preceding, but this is not the point. What was most significant, perhaps,

46. I. Kh. Danilov and P. G. Sdobnev, eds., *Zheleznodorozhniki v 1905 godu* (Moscow, 1940), p. 58.

47. TsGIA, f. 273, op. 12, d. 430. From the information submitted, the ministry concluded that extending staff benefits to those with five years' seniority would prove too costly, but that ten-year veterans might be accommodated.

was the division between old and young itself and not its proportions. The rapid erosion of older modes of work organization in the
entire metal industry, which could only have been most advanced
in the giant railroad shops, affected all workers, no matter what
their levels of skill and experience. If the new workers brought to
the shops the dissatisfactions of urbanized and mobile proletarian
youth, veteran workers could also turn rebellious in response to
the decay of an accustomed job situation and threatened losses in
perceived status, real or potential. This was, then, a volatile combination, especially in the railroad context where mediating institutions such as the factory inspectorate and a clearly delineated
labor policy were absent.

Railroad Operations

The administrative employees and the industrial workers of the
shops and depots were the two socialized poles within the railroad
proletariat, one white-collar, the other blue. Those in railroad operations were more fragmented and variegated. There were divisions between the more urban and socialized situation of station
employees and that of workers on the lines; between employees
who served on the trains and those who assisted from without;
between those whose role in the division of labor was technically
defined, such as greasemen and couplers, and those, such as ticket
agents and cashiers, whose position was a creation of the money
economy. Outside major urban centers and towns, especially among
the lower ranks, operations personnel tended to merge with the
semi-peasant track maintenance force. Despite their common participation in railway operations, each category of operative personnel was most often isolated from other railwaymen both by the
specificity of tasks and by barriers more social in nature; these
were most often men who worked alone or in very small groups,
whose world could thus be frustratingly narrow. It is not surprising, then, that the social position and ultimate professional and political behavior of operative personnel varied greatly, with most in
the end linking their interests with one of the more concentrated
and cohesive groupings. In 1905 only engine-drivers played a very
visible role.

Engine-drivers

The locomotive engine-drivers were the blue-collar aristocrats of railroad labor. Surviving photographs show no grimy Russian Casey Joneses, but proper middle-class gentlemen, complete with starched collars. The chief of the railroad police at the Mineral Waters station of the Vladikavkaz Railroad remarked that "the wives and daughters [of engine-drivers] can be seen strolling in silk dresses and bonnets . . . and each of them has several gold or silver baubles with stones; in their homes it is no rarity to find a piano. . . . On holidays their husbands are dressed in the most respectable coats and dinner jackets with pocket watch and derby hat."[48] Engine-drivers were older and more experienced than the average railwayman.[49]

The driver's job encouraged attitudes of independence and autonomy. His work combined supervisory functions with manual labor and involved considerable responsibility. Working in relative isolation, the engine-driver and his assistant cabmen formed a distinct and at times clannish subcommunity within railroading. A close relationship almost always developed between the engine-driver and his machine, which not only put the cabmen in opposition to sabotage, but could create a broader psychological barrier between them and other workers. During railroad strikes Russian engine-drivers and stokers sometimes found themselves in physical conflict with men from the workshops and depots attempting to prevent train movement by watering fireboxes or removing essential mechanisms.[50]

Yet, as Wolfgang Schivelbusch points out, "because a train runs on a predetermined line, an engine-driver can never aspire to the social role of a 'captain on dry land.'" His position is rather "that of an industrial worker, an operator of a machine," and his working world one of coal, smoke, and the ceaseless grinding of gears and

48. TsGAOR, f. 6865, d. 70, l. 49. A photograph of the militant engine-driver Ukhtomskii, leader of the All-Russian Railroad Union and martyr of the December insurrection in Moscow, dressed formally and with neatly waxed handlebar mustache is in V. Vladimirov, *Karatel'naia ekspeditsiia* (Moscow, 1906), p. 79.

49. Tregubov, p. 60.

50. On the close relationship between the nineteenth-century driver and his engine, the literature on France is most revealing. See François Caron, "Essai

clanking of wheels on track over long hours of exhausting service.[51] Drivers could also spend a significant amount of time in shops and depots tending to the upkeep of their locomotives. Hence, it is hardly surprising that, although the first generation of engine-drivers was recruited from the military, the lower gentry, and the urban estates, by the turn of the century a majority came from the blue-collar ranks of skilled depot and shop craftsmen, a career pattern that provided a very important link between railroad industrial labor and actual train operations. Moreover, the situation of engine-drivers was rapidly changing by 1905. As the length of runs grew and the machinery became more specialized, drivers found their tasks defined more narrowly in terms of train movement. The knowledge and skill demanded of drivers were both diminishing and increasingly different from those of metal craftsmen.[52] Although engine-drivers' salaries remained higher than those of other skilled workers, in the decade before 1905 their economic and social status was widely perceived to be in decline; real incomes were falling, work loads increasing and the prestige of the position waning as the social background of those occupying it broadened.[53]

The decline was evident despite a long-standing shortage of drivers, which worsened as the job's attractiveness ebbed. In theory, the shortage was to be alleviated by the railroad technical schools, which trained new drivers recruited mainly from among the sons of railroad employees. But the training system could not

d'analyse historique d'une psychologie du travail: Les Mécaniciens et chauffeurs de locomotives du reseau du Nord de 1850 a 1910," *Le Mouvement social* 50 (1965): 3–40; Margot Stein, "The Meaning of Skill: The Case of the French Engine-Drivers, 1837–1917," *Politics and Society*, 8 (1978): 407–9; and, for an evocative portrait in fiction, Emile Zola, *La Bête humaine*, trans. L. Tancock (New York, 1977). In the United States, "pioneer drivers guarded their machines as prized and personal possessions" (Walter Licht, *Working For the Railroad: The Organization of Work in the Nineteenth Century* [Princeton, N.J., 1983], p. 161).

51. Wolfgang Schivelbusch, *The Railway Journey: Trains and Travel in the 19th Century*, trans. Anselm Hollo (New York, 1979), p. 38.

52. Similar changes were occurring in other countries. See Stein, "Meaning of Skill," and Stromquist, "Enginemen and Shopmen."

53. *ZhN*, July 30, 1899, pp. 473–75; January 21, 1900, pp. 37–39; February 17, 1901, pp. 102–5; *VMPS*, March 24, 1901, 12, p. 162. *ZhN*, June 16, 1901, p. 381, reported increasing complaints among engine-drivers of rude forms of address by superiors.

keep up with demand. On the South West Railroad two such academies graduated forty qualified drivers each year, but only twenty to twenty-five entered service on the road, the others accepting posts on newer lines in Siberia and elsewhere. Since the road lost an estimated hundred drivers each year to death, retirement, or transfer to newer lines, the shortfalls had to be made up by recruitment from among skilled mechanics. And the South West Railroad was in unusually good shape; on some other lines drivers had to be recruited from the ranks of unqualified, even semiliterate, greasemen and stokers.[54] The shortage was worst on the newer roads, since these had to fill a full component from scratch, but as they grabbed drivers from older lines, including large numbers of assistants, who could in this way hasten their promotion, the old roads also suffered. The result could be remarkable turnover rates. It was estimated, for example, that newer drivers on the Nicholas Railroad lasted just seven to fourteen months.[55]

Conductors

Conductors and their apprentices, the brakemen, were among the most socially isolated operations workers, with relatively modest pay and demanding working conditions. Although they were formally part of the Department of Traffic Management, no special administrative structure supervised their activity. This did not mean, however, that conductors enjoyed more freedom from official abuse than other workers—precisely the opposite: the conductor, who spent nearly all his time on the road, was subject to the conflicting whims and demands of every stationmaster and depot director he might encounter. The situation of freight conductors was most difficult, since their hours were longer and more irregular, but passenger conductors were subject to abuse not only from officials but from the traveling public too, which held these men in low esteem, owing in part to their role in the widespread venality for which Russian railroads were famous. Although passenger conductors often posed as models of taste and respectability, both passenger

54. *ZhN*, February 19, 1899, p. 103; February 17, 1901, p. 102.
55. *VMPS*, March 24, 1901, 12, p. 162.

and freight conductors regularly supplemented their incomes with bribes from those they permitted to ride as "rabbits"—that is, without a ticket, or in a class to which they were not entitled—and thus became vulnerable targets of ridicule in the press and popular literature.[56]

Switchmen

The position of the switchman was "surrounded by a special halo" of great responsibility for road safety, yet also looked down upon as boring, monotonous work fit mainly for the lowest ranks. "No matter what happens, the switchman is always at fault," went a saying so common among railwaymen that it was adopted by the general populace as a universal lament for the plight of the scapegoat.[57] Outside the largest stations switchmen lived and worked in a situation similar to that of the line watchmen and track repair crews. They were generally recruited either from among demobilized army men or from the ranks of the largely peasant repair and construction gangs. On some roads, mainly east of the Volga and in the Ukraine, a switching post was accompanied by a grant of land along the railroad right-of-way, where the switchman might supplement his meager wage with near-subsistence farming. At the close of the nineteenth century centralized switching apparatus began to be introduced, which eliminated many switching personnel and improved safety records at larger junctions. At such stations, a new breed of switchman, more technically capable and responsible, began to emerge, but on the eve of 1905 only 10 percent of all switching had been automated.[58]

Track Maintenance and Construction

The Department of Track Maintenance and Construction was the largest of the four departments, but the workers who served in it

---

56. TsGAOR, f. 6865, d. 35, l. 128; *ZhN*, May 12, 1900, p. 298. For an example of the portrayal of conductors in literature, see the excerpt from Alexander Kuprin's novel *The Pit* in Westwood, p. 165. On conductors in the United States, see Licht, pp. 92, 234.

57. *ZhD*, 35–36, 1896, p. 317; TsGIA, f. 273, op. 12, d. 468, l. 27.

58. Tregubov, pp. 54–56; *ZhD*, 37–38, 1896, p. 334.

worked in the least socialized situations, were the least urbanized, and retained the most ties to traditional society. According to one memoir recorded in the 1920s, only a handful of station repair and maintenance staff were "strictly proletarian"; the majority were peasants, "benighted and unconscious people," many of whom did railroad work only seasonally.[59] The largest group in the department were members of repair and construction crews recruited mainly from the young men of the poorest peasant families. They worked—often in a traditional *artel*—under road foremen appointed by the railroads from experienced repair workers. Sometimes the road foreman could be an elder of the *artel*, although this became less frequent as more modern forms of labor organization emerged. The road foreman was "the right arm of the [line] section chief," but in status he did not always stand much above those he commanded and was often looked down upon by officials, especially younger engineers, "not as a working man, but as a soulless being automatically subservient to the official will."[60] Although track repair and construction were largely seasonal, workers still labored in all kinds of weather. They were housed in dark, dirty, crowded, and insect-ridden barracks, often little more than primitive shacks built of old railroad ties, provided by the foremen.[61]

   The permanent core of the track maintenance department were the road and crossing guards. These workers, too, were generally recruited from nearby villages, usually from landless elements, although on roads traveling through sparsely populated regions they and other track maintenance workers could be coaxed from considerable distances and, because of this, enjoyed somewhat better conditions. Most repair crews consisted of young males, who were often single, but the track and crossing watchmen were almost always married. Often a couple lived in a one-room hut provided by the road, with the husband walking guard duty along several miles of track and the wife supervising one or more crossings. Like the switchmen, whose situation in some rural areas and at smaller stations was not too dissimilar, the track and crossing guards were frequently entitled to farm a small section of railroad land, though

59. TsGAOR, f. 6865, d. 120, l. 63.
60. *ZhN*, February 5, 1899, pp. 74–75; January 6, 1901, p. 10.
61. Tregubov, pp. 35–43, describes the abominable living conditions in these barracks on the Kursk-Kharkov-Sevastopol Railroad.

this was usually good only for simple gardening and potatoes.[62] At small town and village stations, stationmasters, chief telegraph operators, and other senior staff also frequently engaged in agrarian pursuits. Whether such activity was a supplement to railroad work or vice versa is difficult to say.

62. Ibid., pp. 43–48; *Zhel.*, 39, February 22, 1904, pp. 3–5.

Three

Railroad Labor: Wages, Hours, Conditions

Most citizens of turn-of-the-century Russia held a positive image of railroad work. Railroading was thought to be overflowing with opportunity, if only owing to the rapid expansion of the work force, and the economic position of railwaymen was deemed enviable. As the former director of the South West Railroad, P. Andreev, wrote in 1900:

No other department can claim as many institutions devoted to improving the lives of its employees as on the railroads: pension funds offering basic insurance of which officials in other departments don't even dream; schools, hospitals, orphanages, affordable cafeterias, libraries, consumer societies—all aimed at bettering the lives of railroad employees. . . . [And] can anyone deny that salaries on the railroads are disproportionately higher than anywhere else?[1]

Such, however, was not the view of most railwaymen. In the decade preceding 1905 complaints of inadequate pay, long hours, and harsh working conditions were endemic. It would be difficult to exaggerate the extent to which the pages of the railroad press were filled with vivid exposures of railroad poverty and an accompanying lack of official concern. No railroad group, it seemed, was satisfied with its economic lot, no matter how privileged its position relative to the population as a whole, or even to other railwaymen. Andreev's voice was a lonely one, and his article, critics charged, was subjective, self-serving, and based solely on the ex-

1. *ZhN*, July 21, 1900, p. 452.

ceptional experience of the South West Railroad, the merits of which he exaggerated. One critic pointed out that a comparison of daily wages in the workshops of the South West Railroad with those in private industry offered by Andreev was invalid, since the rates cited for railroad work were for 1898 while those for industry came from an 1893 study. In reality, wages in railroad shops probably lagged behind incomes in the private metalworking industry.[2]

Clearly, the reality of the railroad worker's economic position was ambiguous: just as railroad work itself varied greatly, so, too, incomes and conditions differed substantially by position, level of skill, seniority, and region. The economic heterogeneity of railroad labor both compounded and confounded structural patterns of differentiation, simultaneously widening some cleavages and narrowing others. At the top of the salary hierarchy stood a small number of highly paid managers and engineers; at the bottom, a large number of junior staff, switchmen, and road maintenance crews whose standard of living was well below that of most urban skilled workers. In between there was considerable and complex gradation, but a substantial group of employees, engine-drivers, and skilled craftsmen received salaries and privileges well above industrial norms.

As industry developed and railroad employment expanded, however, polarization increased. In the early decades of railroad development skilled and administrative staff were in short supply, especially in less industrially developed regions, which pushed salaries and benefits upward. As profitability stagnated, however, it proved increasingly difficult, and also less essential and desirable, to maintain a rapidly expanding *and* highly paid work force. By the turn of the century, average railroad incomes were not significantly higher than in the metal industry. Especially with the onset of economic crisis in 1900, but beginning before this, the economic position of railwaymen, and of the more privileged among them in particular, began to deteriorate, both absolutely and, even more so, relative to other sectors of the industrial economy. The decline was, to be sure, not uniform, and some railwaymen even gained a bit. Yet it

2. Andreev's critics responded in *ZhN*, September 1 and 8, 1900, pp. 549–52 and 567–68. The article continued a piece on engine-drivers in *ZhN*, February 19, 1899, pp. 102–12, and February 26, 1899, pp. 115–19. These also provoked a critical response on March 26 and May 14, 1899.

was widespread enough for the complaints of the more poorly situated to merge with those of the relatively better paid, who saw previous gains come under attack.

In 1897 the average annual salary for railroad work was 317.20 rubles. By 1900 this had increased to 328.60, and by 1904 to 343.60. The year 1905 saw a big jump to 360.80 rubles, owing largely to gains won in strikes.[3] These numbers compare favorably to averages reported by Soviet scholars of 187 rubles in 1897 and 207 rubles in 1900 for all factory workers, and are roughly on a par with estimated prevailing wages of 282 rubles in 1897 and 338 rubles in 1900 in the metal industry, although, significantly, railwaymen fell behind metalworkers during this period.[4] These railroad statistics, however, are merely crude averages, derived by dividing the total wage bill (including bonuses and housing subsidies) by the number of workers, which tells very little about the actual situation, since the ratio between the highest and lowest salaries was as great as twenty-five to one.[5]

Precise information on prevailing salaries of differing categories of railroad labor is, unfortunately, difficult to assemble and assess, owing principally to the incredible intricacy of the salary and wage structure. On the South West Railroad, for instance, there were 207 different wage scales for permanent staff positions. In addition, on every line there was the distinction between salaried permanent staff, paid annually or monthly, and shop craftsmen, who received a daily wage and, increasingly in the first years of the century, payments based on various piece-rate schemes. Some permanent staff could also receive performance bonuses—engine-drivers were the prime example—or housing and uniform subsidies. Since each line recorded wages according to its own system, there was a large margin for error in reported averages. General conclusions are possible nonetheless.[6]

3. S. G. Strumilin, "Zheleznodorozhnyi transport," *Izbrannye proizvedeniia,* vol. 1 (Moscow, 1964), p. 412.

4. This may be due to lack of precision in the statistics. On wages of factory workers, see Iu. I. Kir'ianov, *Zhiznennyi uroven' rabochikh Rossii* (Moscow, 1979), p. 104.

5. J. N. Westwood, *A History of Russian Railways* (London, 1964), p. 161.

6. The starting point for wage statistics is I. M. Pushkareva, "Zarabotnaia plata zheleznodorozhnikov nakanune revoliutsii 1905–1907 gg.," *Istoriia SSSR,* 1957,

With respect first to permanent staff, according to the calculations of I. M. Pushkareva, based on information from twenty-three state railroad lines on the eve of 1905, 6.7 percent of permanent staff earned less than 120 rubles annually, 51.5 percent between 120 and 360 rubles, 28.1 percent between 360 and 720 rubles, 11.2 percent between 720 and 1,200 rubles, and 2.5 percent, officials and high management, over 1,200 rubles per year. (Since most daily and temporary workers probably fell within the 120–360-ruble bracket, the percentage of the total in this category was probably higher. Pushkareva's decision to add *all* such workers to this group, thereby increasing the share of the bracket to 74.1 percent seems arbitrary, however, and has not been followed here. As will be seen, a significant number of craftsmen probably fell in the next higher bracket.)[7] Excluding the Siberian, Trans-Baikal and Warsaw-Vienna Railroads, where salaries were unusually high, this distribution was more or less consistent among all lines, although average salaries for specific positions could differ greatly between roads. A 1905 press account distinguished seven income brackets on the Nicholas Railroad. Here, 7.5 percent of permanent staff received more than 600 rubles per year, 6.8 percent between 500 and 600 rubles, 9.9 percent between 400 and 500 rubles, 18.3 percent between 300 and 400 rubles, 17.1 percent between 200 and 300 rubles, 28.9 percent, the largest group, between 100 and 200 rubles, and 11.6 percent less than a hundred rubles annually.[8]

There was significant variation in the salary structure of permanent staff by department (Table 3) and job classification (Table 4). The salary hierarchy of permanent staff in the Administrative De-

---

no. 3: 159–73. Unfortunately, in addition to other weaknesses (discussed later in the text and in note 13 below) Pushkareva does not present average salaries by position. The major sources for such averages are Ministerstvo putei soobshcheniia, Otdel Statistiki, *Statisticheskii sbornik*, no. 89 (St. Petersburg, 1907), and *Statistika*. These are not consistent, however, and in places the discrepancy is significant. It is probably best explained by variations in both the definition of salary and of who holds what position, in addition to inconsistent reporting. A third source of salary figures is an unpublished table of average salaries by department and position from 1894 through 1913 compiled in the 1920s by Soviet historians in TsGAOR, f. 6865, d. 28b, ll. 1–2. Although no source is given for these figures, they are basically consistent with the reports in *Statistika*.

    7. Pushkareva, "Zarabotnaia plata," p. 162.
    8. *Bir. ved.*, 8679, February 19, 1905, p. 2. Figures total 100.1 percent owing to rounding.

TABLE 3.   *Earnings of Permanent Staff by Department*

Distribution, 1905[a]

Department	Less Than 120 R	120– 360	360– 720	720– 1200	More Than 1200	1904 Annual Average[b]
Administration	1.1%	17.8%	57.6%	14.2%	9.3%	625 R
Engines and Rolling Stock	0.6	56.9	30.4	5.9	6.2	491 R
Traffic Management	1.4	58.5	29.0	7.9	3.2	328 R
Telegraph	4.5	37.3	54.9	2.4	0.9	327 R
Maintenance and Construction	18.4	70.2	9.3	1.0	1.1	211 R
All Departments	6.7%	51.5%	28.1%	11.2%	2.5%	355 R

Sources: [a] I. M. Pushkareva, "Zarabotnaia plata zheleznodorozhnikov nakanune revoliutsii 1905–1907 gg.," *Istoriia SSSR*, 1957, no. 3:169–75; [b] TsGAOR, f. 6865, d. 28b, ll. 1–2.

partment was skewed above the norm and that of the Department of Track Maintenance and Construction substantially below it. In general, white-collar employees, including telegraph operators and stationmasters, received higher than average salaries, as did engine-drivers; conductors, greasemen, couplers, and other more or less skilled operations personnel stood toward the middle of the income hierarchy; and switchmen and track maintenance staff were near the bottom.

Variations were not, however, uniform geographically or proportionately similar on all roads. In industrialized and more urbanized locales railroads could more readily attract skilled personnel, but unskilled line labor might command relatively higher wages than in agrarian regions. In 1905, according to ministry statistics, the average wage of track and crossing guards ranged from a low of just 83 rubles per year on the South East Railroad to highs of 182 rubles on the Warsaw-Vienna Railroad and 168 rubles on the Transcaucasian Railroad, excluding the Siberian roads where, owing to the sparse population, such workers received as much as triple the national average. The average pay of engine-drivers (including some bonuses and again excluding Siberia) ranged from a high of 1,111 rubles on the Moscow-Kiev-Voronezh Railroad to a low of 651

TABLE 4. *Salaries of Selected Permanent Staff Positions*

Position	Salary Range[a]	1905 Average Annual Salary[b]
Administration & Communications		
Railroad doctor	1200–1800 R	—
Accountant	480–1500	725 R[c]
Clerk	240–780	
Stationmaster	720–2400	[875] 576
Asst. Stationmaster	300–840	[517]
Telegraph operator	300–780	327
Operations		
Engine-driver	360–720	699 (882)
Conductor	168–540	338 (391)
Coupler	240–680	315 (359)
Greaseman	180–240	321
Signalman	216–360	254
Switchman	120–420	182 (204)
Maintenance & Construction		
Road and bridge foreman	480–900	550
Track and crossing guard	120–420	142 (121)
Repair worker	180–300	—

Sources: [a]Approximate salary ranges were determined by combining information from the "Salary Table of the South West Railroad" in TsGIA, f. 273, op. 12, d. 345, 11. 175–78, with the national ranges in M. B. [M. Bogdanov], *Ocherki po istorii zheleznodorozhnykh zabastovok v Rossii* (Moscow, 1906), pp. 5–7, and partial figures for the Transcaucasian Railroad in TsGIA, f. 273, op. 12, d. 226, 11. 458–59, and the Moscow-Brest Railroad in TsGIA, f. 273, op. 12, d. 343, 11. 33–36, to indicate the broadest range. These ranges generally include both junior and senior positions within a specialty, although in the formal listings these were frequently given separately. [b]Annual average salaries are taken from pension fund materials in TsGAOR, f. 6865, d. 28b, 11. 1–2, except figures in parentheses from *Statisticheskii sbornik*, no. 89, table xii, and figures in brackets for stationmasters and their assistants, which are averages for the Transcaucasian Railroad only. For a discussion of the discrepancies between these sources, see note 6 above. [c]The average annual salary given for accountants and clerks is actually the figure for all white-collar permanent employees of the Administrative Department, since specific averages for separate white-collar occupations could not be found.

rubles on the St. Petersburg–Warsaw line. There was somewhat less variation, though, among conductors, couplers, and switchmen. On the Transcaucasian Railroad, the wage structure was transformed by national distinctions, as largely Russian enginedrivers received an average salary 23 percent above the empire norm for that position, but largely Georgian and Armenian conductors earned 22.2 percent less than the norm for that post.[9]

The extensive differentiation of the railroad salary structure reinforced occupational divisions among the workers, whether or not this was the conscious intent of management. Yet the very complexity of the salary hierarchy could also paradoxically tend to blur structural divisions by reinforcing other distinctions within each occupational group according to age, skill level, and experience or seniority. Different kinds of workers were paid at different scales, but within each scale there could be quite a distance from bottom to top. So, for instance, salaries of stationmasters ranged from 300 rubles annually for some assistants to as high as 1,500 rubles for directors of first-class stations. (Masters of the major Moscow, St. Petersburg, and a few other big city terminals were appointed from the engineer corps and paid as top managers, often earning as much as 2,400 rubles.) Salaries of simple clerks ranged from 240 to 600 rubles.[10] On the South West Railroad, a switchman at a basic hand switch was paid between 180 and 240 rubles, while a senior switchman at a major junction could get between 360 and 420 rubles. Overall, those with greater seniority and experience not surprisingly earned considerably more than others.[11] In those job categories where salary distinctions were greatest, workers were likely to be more concerned about the gap separating those at the bottom of the scale from those at the top than about the differences between the salary scale to which they were subject and scales in other spheres of railroading. Office employees earning 500 to 600 rubles, a hefty salary when compared to many operations personnel, were likely to be more conscious, for instance, of the less favorable comparison of their incomes with those of senior white-collar staff receiving thousands of rubles each year.

9. *Statisticheskii sbornik*, no. 89, table xii.

10. M. B. [M. Bogdanov], *Ocherki po istorii zheleznodorozhnykh zabastovok v Rossii* (Moscow, 1906), pp. 5–7.

11. TsGIA, f. 273, op. 12, d. 345, ll. 175–78; *Statistika*, 1903, p. 57.

Especially in the white-collar section of the work force, relatively low-paying posts might be stepping stones for junior personnel to advance upward, which could in turn moderate some tensions while exacerbating others. In the largest department of the central administration of the South West Railroad, for example, if a 1,200-ruble annual salary is taken as the dividing line between managerial incomes and employee salaries, 43 managers with an average salary of 1,927 rubles confronted 832 employees with an average salary of just 405 rubles. In this latter group, however, were joined 656 employees earning under 600 rubles, whose salaries averaged 347 rubles, and a smaller middle group of 176 employees earning between 600 and 1,200 rubles, whose average salary was 723 rubles. This latter group formed a kind of white-collar aristocracy; as such they were an important determinant of administrative hegemony. Yet because many had likely risen from below, but were barred from further advancement, they could also make common cause with, and exercise considerable influence over, the group below them in opposition to management.[12]

The overwhelming majority of craftsmen in the depots and workshops were paid by day and piece rates, which deepened the segregation of railroad industrial labor and tended to lower the status of such workers in the eyes of others in railroading. Statistical comparison with salaried staff is therefore awkward, a problem aggravated by a dearth of sources on workshop and depot wages. Railroad shops were exempt from the factory inspectors' reports, and the ministry did not keep systematic data. Payment systems varied greatly among different roads and the wage structure of a single facility might be as complicated as that of an entire road, with considerable breakdown by craft, level of skill, seniority, and performance.

It is nevertheless likely that the average annual income of shop and depot craftsmen was in the vicinity of the average for all railwaymen, even higher than average for some, though there are general indications that the basic wage level in the railroad repair shops was below the norm for other metalworkers, sometimes significantly so. Given the shortage of skilled labor, the difference could not, however, have been very great for comparably qualified workers. In part, the difference may have been attributable to par-

12. Ibid., l. 113.

ticularities of railroad locomotive and rolling stock repair, which may have demanded a somewhat different, and less costly, assortment of skills than other sectors of the metal industry.

According to ministry figures, in 1905 daily workers in the Department of Engines and Rolling Stock averaged 21 rubles per month (252 rubles per year) on the state railroads and a ruble less per month on private lines, almost 100 rubles per year below the national average for the metal trades. These figures are certainly too low and of limited utility, however, since as a gross average they not only disguise regional and craft differences, but also include the wages of semiskilled workers at minor rural facilities and genuine as well as so-called "permanent dailies."[13] In 1904 the average annual income in St. Petersburg metal plants was 471 rubles.[14] Yet at the main locomotive shops of the Nicholas Railroad the highest monthly wage in the assembly shop was reported to be 26–27 rubles, or 312–324 rubles per year, and that in the blacksmith shop around 22–23 rubles. The plant average for skilled labor was just 20 rubles per month.[15] In Moscow the average annual wage in the metal industry in 1901 was 309 rubles. At the Moscow workshops of the Moscow-Brest Railroad, however, the minimum wage of skilled craftsmen was just 18.75 rubles per month, or 225 rubles per year, according to an internal survey conducted by management after the February 1905 strike.[16]

It is impossible, however, to draw very useful conclusions from comparison of day rates alone, since by the turn of the century increasing numbers of shops supplemented the daily wage with various piece rate systems.[17] In the St. Petersburg shops of the Nicholas line workers could earn an average supplement of almost 80 percent of the daily rate through piece wages. Added to the monthly

13. *Statisticheskii sbornik*, no. 89, table xii. Pushkareva, "Zarabotnaia plata," p. 163, argues that these averages *over*estimate wages in the shops, citing various *minimum* shop norms and some illustrative material from the revolutionary press, and ignoring the share of wages contributed by piece rates. According to Pushkareva, only the most senior craftsmen earned more than 360 rubles. Given prevailing rates in metalworking, however, this seems incredible. Indeed, on some lines, if bonuses are included, the *average* wage was higher than this.
14. Kir'ianov, p. 114.
15. TsGIA, f. 273, op. 12, d. 316, l. 27.
16. Kir'ianov, p. 126; TsGIA, f. 273, op. 12, d. 343, ll. 33–34.
17. *ZhN*, July 14, 1900, p. 443.

average of 20 rubles in these shops, this yields an average annual income of 432 rubles, just 39 rubles below the St. Petersburg metal industry norm, but still considerably lower than the average in other large metal plants such as the Putilov works.[18] On the Kursk-Kharkov-Sevastopol Railroad daily rates stood above the average for the southern metal industry, but the railroad shops were more poorly equipped than most industrial plants, which were generally newer. As a result, workers found it difficult to earn more than 60 percent of their daily rate through piece rates, while those in private plants received on the average double this amount.[19]

Toward the end of 1903, A. A. Pavlovskii, a railroad engineer, submitted a lengthy report to the Administration of Railroads on the "labor question" in fifteen railroad workshops he had toured during the year.[20] Pavlovskii devoted special attention to the question of piece rates, applauding the arrangement used at the Ekaterinoslav workshops of the Catherine Railroad and the Kiev and Odessa shops of the South West Railroad, where piece-rate bonuses were paid on a regular monthly basis with no limit to the amount a worker might receive. Under this arrangement, Kiev workers earned piece-rate incomes ranging between 32 and 80 percent of their daily rate; as already noted, in St. Petersburg they could earn almost 80 percent. Many shop managers were concerned that an unlimited bonus system of this type would raise costs prohibitively, but "from a comparison of average monthly wages of various categories of skilled and unskilled workers," Pavlovskii concluded that total pay under the system was "far from excessive."[21]

In other shops the arrangement was frequently less generous and more informal. In the Tula workshops of the Moscow-Kursk Railroad and the Nizhnedneprovsk shops of the Catherine Railroad, Pavlovskii found no official written rates, with piece-work arrangements concluded informally by agreement between individual brigades and management on a job-by-job basis.[22] In the Dvinsk

18. TsGIA, f. 273, op. 12, d. 46, l. 571.

19. TsGAOR, f. 6865, d. 45, ll. 58–59.

20. TsGIA, f. 273, op. 12, d. 46, ll. 569–94. The report covered workshops in Tula, St. Petersburg, Dvinsk, Kiev, Warsaw, Odessa, Ekaterinoslav, Nikolaev, Nizhnedneprovsk, Rostov-on-Don, Saratov, Tambov, Kozlov, Penza, and Konotop. Pavlovskii also visited the Aleksandrovsk shops of the Kursk-Kharkov-Sevastopol Railroad, about which he wrote less confidentially in *ZhD*, 1904, 9, p. 80.

21. TsGIA, f. 273, op. 12, d. 46, ll. 578, 570–73.

22. Ibid., ll. 570, 573.

locomotive shops of the Riga-Orel Railroad, a brigade was given a time limit to finish an engine; if the deadline was met, a bonus of half the day rate for the work period was awarded. The incentive dropped if the job took longer. Significantly, here, and probably in most other shops, the incentive went to the brigade, not the individual worker, and was divided as its members—or, maybe, the *brigadir*—saw fit. Similar arrangements at the Nikolaev shops of the Kharkov-Nikolaev Railroad earned workers bonuses of between 35 and 50 percent of the day rate, and at the Kozlov shops of the Riazan-Ural Railroad between 50 and 60 percent.[23]

There was again significant variation by craft and skill level. In general, turners were thought to be among the most highly paid shop workers, and hammermen among the lowest. But the pattern was by no means uniform and could vary by locality or even year to year. In many shops workers could not predict what their wages would be, and two men could be paid at different rates for the same work.

Relatively complete wage statistics by shop and craft could be located only for the Tiflis workshops of the Transcaucasian Railroad for the month of May in each of three years, 1903, 1904, and 1905. These cannot be taken as indicative of either the size or precise proportional distribution of wages nationally, but they do offer some idea of the extent of variation by craft and shop.

Since in 1905 pay was lower than during the previous two years owing to closure of the shops by strikes, it will be most useful to look at 1904. In that year the average monthly wage for the entire facility was 36.46 rubles, of which a whopping 85.4 percent came from piece-rate payments. On an annual basis this monthly rate would convert to about 438 rubles, but since incomes were likely to be lower in winter, when much work was still done outdoors, that figure is probably high. Average shop incomes ranged from a high of 40.50 rubles in the forge to a low of 31.24 rubles in the assembly shop, but since each shop included men of varied skills in differing proportions, there was greater deviation by craft. Average monthly income by craft went from a high of 53.18 rubles for turners and 52.57 rubles for smithys, 45.9 and 44.2 percent above the shop average respectively, to a low of 25.64 rubles for hammermen,

23. Ibid., ll. 571, 573, 576.

which was nearly 30 percent below the shop average. Assistants received 24.71 rubles, about 5 rubles higher than in each of the adjacent years; unskilled laborers averaged 22.73 rubles; and apprentices got a meager 9.41 rubles per month.[24]

Both in and out of the shops railroad workers could receive an assortment of bonus payments and subsidies. In 1903 the railroads paid an estimated 11.7 million rubles in supplementary payments (not including piece rates), which amounted to 5 percent of the total wage bill.[25] This was unevenly distributed, however. A significant portion of the work force, principally permanent staff, were entitled to housing supplied by the roads, or, if such was not available, to rent subsidies. Conductors and other uniformed employees received allowances for uniform purchase and cleaning. Permanent staff and some craftsmen were entitled to limited free train transportation, a privilege sometimes also enjoyed by their families.

The housing subsidy had its origin in the early efforts of private entrepreneurs to house construction and repair crews, switching personnel, and others posted to isolated junctions, as well as to attract relatively scarce engine-drivers and white-collar officials to provincial service. Up to the 1890s housing was provided on state railroads only to workers in the Department of Track Maintenance, mainly in the form of primitive barracks, and to management. In 1888, however, in recognition of the severe housing difficulties faced both by many urban railwaymen and by those on the lines, the ministry adopted a series of complicated rules and regulations to govern granting of apartments or rent subsidies. By 1900 nearly half of all switchmen received housing support and on many lines the practice was extended to engine-drivers and conductors. In 1903 nearly half of all permanent staff on state roads were eligible for housing benefits. In that year, on twenty-three state lines (excluding the Moscow-Iaroslavl-Archangel Railroad), 137,398 employees received housing support, with 102,800 placed in shelter provided by the roads and 34,598 granted subsidies.[26]

24. Ivan Maruta, *Ocherki po istorii revoliutsionnogo professional'nogo dvizheniia na Moskovsko-Kievo-Voronezhskoi zh. d.* (Kursk, 1925), pp. 16–17; *Vestnik Zakavkazkikh zh. d.*, August 2, 1905, 15, pp. 10–12, in TsGIA, f. 273, op. 8, d. 180, ll. 140–41.

25. Strumilin, p. 407.

26. TsGAOR, f. 6865, d. 49, ll. 36–40; *Zhel.*, 46, April 11, 1904, pp. 10–11.

Expenditure on employee housing varied considerably among individual roads, ranging from just 13 rubles to 171 rubles per verst of track.[27] It was widely thought that private railroads offered more extensive programs than the state lines, but there was such variation by region and job category that meaningful comparison is impossible. Still, differences between lines could be striking: in 1905 the private Vladikavkaz Railroad offered housing support to 97 percent of its telegraph operators, while the nearby state Catherine Railroad offered such support to just 22 percent of its telegraphists.[28] On the Nicholas Railroad the size of the subsidy was considered "insufficient to obtain a residence in the vicinity of one's place of employment." On that line, of 2,500 locomotive crewmen entitled to support, just 311, or 12.6 percent, actually received it. The size of the subsidy payments varied according to job category, ranging from 16 to 17 percent of salary for station personnel to nearly a third of salary for some engine-drivers.[29]

Railwaymen were subject to various deductions and fines, which could substantially affect their actual incomes. All permanent staff who were members of the pension fund were assessed 6 percent of their regular salary (matched by a 3 percent payment by management) and an additional 10 percent of all bonus income.[30] Fines for absence, tardiness, and rule-breaking were also supposed to be paid into the pension fund. In 1903, according to one contemporary estimate, nine out of every ten railroad workers were fined at least once.[31] Although an 1886 law decreed that fines in both private industry and state workshops could not exceed a third of a single worker's monthly wage or a quarter of the wage of a married worker, on the Moscow-Kazan Railroad it was estimated that in the

27. TsGAOR, f. 6865, d. 49, ll. 36–40; *Zhel.*, 46, April 11, 1904, pp. 10–11.

28. TsGIA, f. 273, op. 12, d. 373, l. 195.

29. *VMPS*, March 24, 1901, p. 162; TsGIA, f. 273, op. 12, d. 328, ll. 161–65; *ZhN*, February 19, 1899, p. 103.

30. Rostov, "Zheleznodorozhniki v pervoi revoliutsii," *Proletariat v revoliutsii 1905–1907 gg.* (Moscow, 1930), pp. 127–28.

31. I. M. Pushkareva, *Zheleznodorozhniki Rossii v burzhuazno-demokraticheskikh revoliutsiiakh* (Moscow, 1975), p. 57. Fining was also common on the railroads in Victorian England, but notably absent in the United States. See Peter Kingsford, *Victorian Railwaymen: The Emergence and Growth of Railway Labor, 1830–1870* (London, 1970), pp. 22–27, and Walter Licht, *Working For the Railroad: The Organization of Work in the Nineteenth Century* (Princeton, N.J., 1983), pp. 118–19.

lower ranks fines could take an *average* of a third and up to half of monthly salary. On the Riazan-Ural Railroad, one official was said to have regularly and systematically fined each switchman for various petty offenses until the total collected reached the legal limit. The arbitrariness with which fines were assessed meant that for one and the same offense one worker might be fined fifty kopeks and another two rubles.[32]

Subsidies and bonuses, as well as fines, played an especially key role in the income of engine-drivers. On the South West Railroad basic annual salaries of engine-drivers ranged from 300 to 540 rubles without housing, and for assistant drivers from 240 to 300 rubles. This was modified, however, by a complex system of bonuses, incentive payments, fines, and deductions based on norms for distance traveled, overtime, fuel and grease economy, schedule maintenance, and repair expenses. Supplementary payments could push actual incomes as high as 1,200 to 1,600 rubles and sometimes 1,800 or even 2,000 rubles per year. In 1897 the average total income of engine-drivers on the South West Railroad was computed at 1,544.92 rubles per year, and that of assistant engine-drivers at 559.27 rubles.[33]

In the decade leading to 1905 changes in the incentive system and increasing fines for late train arrivals significantly diminished the actual incomes of most cabmen. On the Kursk-Kharkov-Sevastopol Railroad in 1894, taking bonuses and fines into account, the majority of engine-drivers received between 1,500 and 1,800 rubles annually; by 1901 they were lucky, it was said, to manage 1,200. The decline was entirely attributable to changes in the fuel economy and schedule maintenance norms. An 1894 reorganization of the bonus system, allegedly implemented to "rationalize" a confusing arrangement, disguised an actual cut. In 1896 a further change resulted in an average drop in driver income of 100 rubles. In 1898 the road began to purchase lower-quality coal, greater quantities of which had to be burned, thereby rendering consumption norms virtually unattainable; by the turn of the century the fuel economy bonus had all but disappeared. At the same time, denser traffic caused growing numbers of delayed arrivals, making

    32. M. K. Dymkov and D. Ia. Lipovetskii, *1905 god na Kazanke. Sbornik* (Moscow, 1925), p. 28; *Zhel.*, 66, August 31, 1904, p. 14; Maruta, p. 18; Push-kareva, *Zheleznodorozhniki*, p. 57.
    33. *ZhN*, February 19, 1899, p. 103; February 26, 1899, p. 115.

it ever more difficult to keep to schedule and increasing fines on tardy crews. One "old engine-driver" concluded that he actually earned less as a Class I driver in 1900 than he had as a Class III novice fifteen years earlier. The driver estimated that his actual income had declined from 135 to 100 rubles per month.[34]

The declining incomes of engine-drivers are but one example of an overall deterioration in the economic position of railroad workers and employees. According to ministry statistics, the average annual salary on the railroads between 1885 and 1901 remained essentially stable, averaging slightly less than 330 rubles, with a slight dip below 320 rubles in the mid 1890s. The year 1902, however, saw a big leap in the average salary to 343 rubles, and another large jump occurred in 1905. These statistics are deceptive, however. For one thing, earnings did not keep pace with other industries, especially the metal industry. For another, a not-inconsiderable portion of the 1902 increase may be owing to the opening in that year of the Siberian and Trans-Baikal Railroads, where wages consistently stood 50 percent or more above national averages. Railwaymen who moved from older lines to the new roads won significant pay hikes, the more so if, like many, they also moved up in rank. In 1904 and 1905 the war with Japan drastically increased Siberian traffic, and as a result large numbers of railroad workers were specially drafted for work there at the inflated Asian rates.

More important, the gross average salary increase did not match the rate of inflation. During the 1880s and early 1890s railroad workers benefited from declining grain prices. According to the calculations of S. G. Strumilin, between 1885 and 1895 real wages in railroading rose by about 18 percent, even though the nominal annual salary dropped a bit. The opposite was the case during the next decade. According to Strumilin's figures, real wages dropped sharply from 1895 to 1898, and then, despite significant nominal increases, remained essentially constant through 1905 (Table 5).[35]

The effects of inflation, however, were probably greater than Strumilin's figures indicate. Price increases were largest in the industrial cities, where most railroad workshops and central offices were located. In Moscow a meeting of factory inspectors concluded

34. *ZhN*, February 17, 1901, p. 103; *ZhN*, January 21, 1900, pp. 38–39.
35. Strumilin, p. 412.

TABLE 5.   *Average Annual Salary of Railroad Workers and Employees, 1885–1905*

Year	Annual Salary		Real Annual Salary	
	Rubles	Percent	1905 Rubles	Percent
1885	329.3	100	368.2	100
1890	328.2	100	394.0	107
1895	319.4	97	434.5	118
1897	317.2	97	371.9	101
1898	328.6	100	349.8	95
1899	328.1	100	353.5	96
1900	328.6	100	364.5	99
1901	328.6	100	357.2	97
1902	343.0	104	364.5	99
1903	345.9	105	375.6	102
1904	343.6	104	362.8	98
1905	360.8	110	360.8	98

Source: S. G. Strumilin, "Zheleznodorozhnyi transport," *Izbrannye proizvedeniia*, vol. 1 (Moscow, 1964), p. 412.

that between 1897 and 1903 the inflation rate had reached 14 to 15 percent, but the newspaper *Russkie vedomosti* reported inflation in prices of selected food items ranging from 25 to 60 percent. Another study cited an overall inflation rate for the region served by the Moscow-Kiev-Voronezh Railroad of 15.4 percent during the first half decade of the twentieth century, with the price of bread rising by over 20 percent.[36] "Under the inflationary conditions of urban life in general and of St. Petersburg in particular, the meager salary of employees is totally inadequate," striking employees on the Baltic Railroad declared in 1905. Representatives of the employees of the Samara-Zlatoust Railroad submitted a lengthy list comparing prices of essential commodities in 1895 and 1905, which revealed sometimes extraordinary increases. Inflation, they wrote, "has been especially bad during the past two to three years, when

36. *Russkie vedomosti*, February 13, 1905; Maruta, p. 14.

Samara has been turned into a semi-military city." In an official report on the February 1905 strike of office workers on the South West Railroad, line director Nemeshaev noted that in Kiev inflation had rendered the economic situation of lower employees "by no means easy, and often even impossible."[37]

The income trajectory of the first years of the twentieth century was not uniform for all job categories. Available averages for participants in the pension fund suggest that even if inflation is not taken into account, many salaries actually declined between 1899 and 1905 (Table 6). Pay increases were to be found only among the low-paid and semi-proletarian workers in the Department of Track Maintenance and among poorly paid switchmen and signalmen in the Department of Traffic Management, although these were hardly very large, exceeding the inflation rate only among track watchmen and repair crew members, and then but slightly. Increases for switchmen, moreover, may simply have reflected the increasing proportion of senior skilled switching personnel as switching operations were centralized and automated. The greatest declines in both nominal and real incomes were in the Administrative Department and the Department of Engines and Rolling Stock, with a drop in real incomes in both departments of well over 10 percent. These figures indicate not only an overall pattern of stagnation, but also that it was precisely railwaymen in the most highly paid and prestigious sectors, as well as the most socialized and urban situations, with the greatest potential influence over other workers and the best access to existing networks of communications and authority, whose positions were most threatened. Although those whose salaries rose a bit were no doubt the workers in greatest need, they were also the least capable of professional mobilization.

Unfortunately, the pension fund statistics cannot reveal the path taken by incomes in the workshops. A pattern of deterioration can nonetheless also be adduced for these workers. Since the average annual salary of pension fund participants remained essentially stable between 1899 and 1905—and actually dropped from 354 to 353 rubles—it can be conjectured that the bulk of the reported overall increase of these years went to workers paid by the day who

37. TsGIA, f. 273, op. 12, d. 313, l. 43; d. 364, l. 77; d. 345, l. 15. On inflation see also d. 322, ll. 144–45; d. 343, l. 27; d. 373, l. 50; and d. 295, ll. 13–14.

TABLE 6. *Average Annual Salaries of Railroad Pension Fund Participants by Department, 1899–1905*

Department and Category	1899– 1900 Average	1904–5 Average	1904–5 as % of 1899–1900	1904–5 as % of 1899–1900 (real)
Administrative				
Officials and employees	777 R	722 R	92.9%	86.4%
Dept. total	668	616	92.2	85.7
Engines and Rolling Stock				
Locomotive crews	710	691	97.3	90.5
Greasemen	318	321	100.9	93.8
Dept. total	510	484	94.9	88.3
Traffic Management				
Stationmasters	571	572	100.2	93.2
Conductors	333	340	102.1	95.0
Telegraph operators	324	332	102.5	95.3
Couplers	307	314	102.3	95.1
Signalmen	243	256	105.3	97.9
Switchmen	174	184	106.1	98.7
Dept. total	326	329	100.9	93.8
Track Maintenance				
Road foremen	546	550	100.7	93.6
Track and crossing guards	132	143	108.3	100.7
Repair crews (permanent)	166	183	110.2	102.5
Dept. total	201	209	104.0	96.7
All Pension Fund	354	353	99.7	92.7

Source: TsGAOR, f. 6865, d. 28b, ll. 1–2.

were outside the fund, including most shop craftsmen. Yet it can hardly be assumed that incomes were uniformly rising in the shops. It is quite possible, if not likely, that the pattern seen among pension fund members, in which lower-paid workers gained while higher-paid workers lost, was repeated among the dailies, which would mean shop craftsmen advanced the least, if they won anything, and the bulk of the apparent increase went to dailies and temporaries in track maintenance. Moreover, since most workshops were located in the inflation-plagued urban areas, it is also likely that these workers suffered even more than other railwaymen from rising prices.

Even if workshop incomes did rise a bit absolutely, this was surely overshadowed by their relative decline when compared to other metalworking establishments. In the context of increasingly polarized work relations within the shops, wage gains were won only through greater reliance on overtime and demanding piece rates. Judging from memoir literature, press accounts, and demands raised in strikes before and during 1905 (see chapter 5), railroad metalworkers were increasingly dissatisfied with both prevailing incomes and conditions and saw their status rapidly eroding. Following the 1903 strike at the Konotop shops of the Moscow-Kiev-Voronezh Railroad, a commission determined that shop wages had declined by an average of 3 to 5 percent since 1899. As the Old Bolshevik Sergei Alliluyev recalled, in the Tiflis shops of the Trans-caucasian Railroad basic daily "wages decreased by about 40 to 50 percent" in the 1890s. "To secure a minimum living wage, every workman had to put in fifty working days a month. In other words, one had to stay for a further five or six hours at overtime."[38]

In all spheres of railroading hours and working conditions were long and difficult. The demands on stationmasters have been mentioned, but hours and conditions could also be trying in the central offices; as traffic expanded, so too did paperwork. Twelve-hour and even longer shifts were by no means unusual for clerks, and especially telegraph operators, although, formally at least, ministry directives limited the number of continuous hours the latter could work to twelve (and to eight at the busier posts.)[39] Offices were frequently overcrowded, with inadequate heat and light and poor ventilation.[40] At busy stations telegraph operators spent long hours

38. Maruta, p. 15; D. Tutaev, ed., *The Alliluyev Memoirs* (London, 1968), p. 31.

39. Maruta, p. 17; S. L. Tregubov, *Opyt izucheniia v sanitarnom otnoshenii byta zheleznodorozhnykh sluzhashchikh v predelakh Kursko-Kharkovo-Sevastopol'skogo zh. d.* (Kharkov, 1904), p. 80; *ZhD*, 1902, 34–35, p. 331.

40. *ZhN*, March 31, 1900, pp. 198–99; TsGIA, f. 273, op. 8, d. 126, ll. 101–2; d. 138, l. 73.

hunched over their apparatus, often without break, the work illuminated by the harsh glare of a single gas or electric light. At more isolated stations the loneliness and boredom of a long shift were compounded by dreary surroundings. Telegraph operators complained frequently of headaches and vision problems.[41]

In the workshops the 1891 ministry rules established a work day of ten hours plus a lunch break of an hour and a half in winter and an hour and a quarter in summer. In most shops the official work day did range between ten and eleven hours, but in general "almost permanent" overtime rendered the ten-hour day a "simple illusion."[42] According to Alliluyev, in the Tiflis shops "a number of men stood for as long as eighteen hours" and others "did not leave the shops for weeks on end and slept beside their machines." At the Moscow shops of the Moscow-Kazan Railroad workers complained that long hours left little time to tend to even the most basic necessities.[43]

But the long day in the shops was balanced somewhat by a work schedule that included an inordinate number of holidays. The workshops generally ran on a six-day week and ministry rules designated 31 official holidays for a work year of just 282 days; on most lines the year was even shorter.[44] An 1893 article in *Zheleznodorozhnoe delo* complained that the average Russian railroad workshops were closed for 46 separate holidays annually, leaving a work year of 267 days, which, from the management point of view, compared poorly to the situation in the United States, where there were only 7 holidays and a work year of 306 days. In 1905 railroad officials were not averse to decreasing the number of hours worked each day if the number of holidays could also be cut, although here they ran into another obstacle, since in the eyes of many tsarist bu-

41. Tregubov, p. 52; Maruta, p. 20; *ZhD*, 1902, 34–35, pp. 329–32.

42. TsGIA, f. 273, op. 12, d. 347, l. 106; *ZhD*, 1897, 6–7, p. 51. See also Tregubov, pp. 40, 81; Maruta, p. 17; K. A. Pazhitnov, *Polozhenie rabochego klassa v Rossii*, vol. 2 (St. Petersburg, 1906), pp. 37–40.

43. Tutaev, ed., p. 31. I. Kh. Danilov and P. G. Sdobnev, eds., *Zheleznodorozhniki v 1905 godu* (Moscow, 1940), p. 8, says the work day in the Tiflis shops was generally thirteen to fourteen hours. On the complaints of the Moscow-Kazan craftsmen, see Kir'ianov, p. 85.

44. TsGIA, f. 273, op. 12, d. 347, ll. 106–7; d. 46, ll. 549–50; d. 373, l. 282; *ZhD*, 1897, 5, p. 33.

reaucrats work on imperial name days or minor saints' days was an affront to Orthodoxy and the autocratic principle.[45]

Conditions of labor in the workshops were probably somewhat worse than in the metal industry as a whole, since it was widely thought that railroad shops were poorly equipped. On the Moscow-Kazan Railroad workers often supplied their own tools. On the Kursk-Kharkov-Sevastopol Railroad steam hammers had been installed in only two departments.[46] There was also considerable variation between cities and lines. "Alongside the palatial workshops that have been built in Petersburg, Prushkovo, Nizhnedneprovsk, Tambov, and Ekaterinoslav exist such slums as in Warsaw, Penza, Saratov, Kiev, and elsewhere," reported Pavlovskii. "In some workshops they have hot and cold showers, in others they have to work in winter under an open sky, and inside it is dark and cold. . . . In some shops they dispense tea, in others not even water."[47] In most shops at least some work, usually carriage repair, took place outdoors in freight yards or under a plain wooden roof open at the sides to the elements. Indoors workers complained of stale and dirty air, filled with smoke and coal dust, and of inadequate lighting, and railroad doctors usually validated the accusations.[48] Shopmen also complained of headaches caused by incessant noise, and, especially in summer, of unbearable heat. At the Konotop facility of the Moscow-Kiev-Voronezh Railroad, temperatures in the forge were said to reach as high as 140° F.[49]

The continuous, yet irregular, nature of railroad traffic imposed the most serious demands on operations personnel. Where traffic was sporadic, scheduling difficulties compelled train crews and station personnel to work overly long or highly irregular shifts, and the situation was worst in those positions upon which safety most

45. *ZhD*, 1893, 41–42, p. 395; *Zhel.*, 136, January 27, 1906, p. 8. The comparison with the United States was not entirely fair, since employment on American roads was "irregular and uncertain"; American shop workers generally worked a ten- or eleven-hour day (Licht, pp. 165, 175).

46. TsGAOR, f. 6865, d. 45, l. 58; Dymkov and Lipovetskii, p. 29; Tregubov, p. 82. See also Maruta, p. 19.

47. TsGIA, f. 273, op. 12, d. 46, l. 590.

48. For graphic descriptions of these conditions, see Danilov and Sdobnev, p. 57; *ZhD*, 1897, 3–4, pp. 18–23; Dymkov and Lipovetskii, p. 29.

49. M. B. [M. Bogdanov], p. 13; Tregubov, p. 82; Maruta, p. 20.

depended. Concerned by the spiraling accident rate, the ministry began to impose limits in the 1890s, though, as already noted, these were not especially strict and on many lines seem to have functioned more as recommended standards. According to rules adopted in 1897 and 1898, switchmen and signalmen were prohibited from working 24-hour duty. At stations with continuous switching, shifts were limited to 8 hours on and 8 off, with a 24-hour rest period every third day.[50] At the average station, however, four switching personnel were responsible for two posts, each taking a 12-hour shift, and at isolated posts a solitary switchman could be forced to attend a switch at irregular hours throughout the day, often sheltered from winter storms and summer sun by only a ramshackle wooden hut. Sometimes a switchman or crossing guard awaiting passage of a delayed train, unable to stay awake, would lay down across the rails to sleep, expecting to be awakened by the vibrations of the approaching train. According to the railroad press, this practice was by no means unusual, but at least one who wrote about it narrowly escaped death, awakening only at the final second, in time to sprawl flat between the rails as the train passed over him.[51]

The hours of train and locomotive crews were more difficult to regulate, since service was subject to the vagaries of scheduling. It was not thought unusual for conductors to spend as much as two-thirds of their lives on the road. It was not until 1893 that continuous duty by conductors was limited to 18 hours (24 under special circumstances and with the minister's permission) to be followed by mandatory rest time of "no less than a third the preceding service time." According to these regulations, the number of hours on duty and off were to be equivalent within a defined period of no more than six days, with at least half of all rest at the conductor's station of residence. Because passenger schedules were more exact than the movement of freight, passenger conductors were more likely to work within these limits. On the Kursk-Kharkov-Sevastopol Railroad most passenger conductors worked from 6 to 14 hours and then rested from 7 to 15 hours at a distant station before making the return trip, followed by 24 to 60 hours at home. Freight crews

50. TsGIA, f. 273, op. 12, d. 107, l. 23.
51. *ZhN*, January 14, 1900, pp. 23–25. See also TsGAOR, f. 6865, d. 120, l. 191; *Zhel.*, 117, August 30, 1905, p. 8, and Rostov, *Zheleznodorozhniki*, p. 13.

generally worked irregular schedules and were compelled to ride unheated boxcars in winter. Frequently they could grab just 3 or 4 hours' sleep between shifts, and it was not unusual, at least on this line, for them to spend as many as twenty sleepless nights a month.[52]

Since locomotive crews were most responsible for train operation and safety, and as a relatively privileged group often in short supply could demand better treatment, their hours were more strictly regulated. Yet the shortage of qualified engine-drivers also put considerable pressure on managers to lengthen their shifts, and as incomes fell toward the end of the 1890s, some drivers were probably eager to take on overtime assignments. According to ministry regulations, locomotive crews were to be guaranteed rest periods of no less than 8 uninterrupted hours in each 24-hour period and no less than 120 hours in each ten-day stretch. Continuous duty was not to exceed 12 hours, including the time trains were stopped in stations.[53]

How closely were these standards actually adhered to? The record is not precisely clear, but contemporaries believed violations were widespread. When, in 1899, Andreev wrote in *Zheleznodorozhnaia nedelia* that the "largest part" of complaints by engine-drivers of extensive overwork and 24-hour shifts were "no more than a powerful exaggeration," the editors felt obliged to interject a note to the effect that although violations of work-time norms might be rare on the South West Railroad, that line was unusual; on other roads violations were more the rule than the exception.[54]

Yet there is limited evidence to suggest that Andreev might have been as close to the truth as those who corrected him. September 1903 work schedules on the Kursk-Kharkov-Sevastopol Railroad indicated that freight drivers were on duty 45.7 percent of their time and off 54.3 percent, while passenger drivers were on duty 42 percent and off 58 percent of the time, although these figures did not take into account delays, which were very common in freight runs.[55] In the early 1900s the Administration of Railroads often collected the work schedules of locomotive crews involved in train

52. TsGIA, f. 273, op. 12, d. 107, l. 21; Tregubov, pp. 72–73.
53. TsGIA, f. 273, op. 12, d. 107, l. 34.
54. *ZhN*, February 26, 1899, p. 116.
55. Tregubov, p. 62.

collisions to determine if the accident had been caused by overwork. Sixteen such schedules were found in the administration archive among materials on railroad accidents on the Moscow-Kursk,
Kursk-Kharkov-Sevastopol, and Transcaucasian Railroads. Although
it might be assumed that violations would be more likely in the
schedules of those involved in collisions, in fact there were only
two minimal violations among the sixteen schedules. The drivers
in the sample averaged slightly more than 160 hours of rest every
ten days, including a little more than 126 hours at their home stations and an average of a bit less than two full days off. None of the
sixteen drivers averaged more than the 120-hour work limit and
most considerably less. The two violations were duty periods of
more than 12 continuous hours (13 and 14 hours) on the Transcaucasian Railroad.[56] To be sure, the evidence provided by such a
limited sample is hardly conclusive, especially given the very real
possibility of falsification by local managers, but it would not be too
surprising if violations were not quite so extensive as contemporaries assumed, since for all job categories the limits had been derived from prevailing practice and were far from being exceptionally restrictive.

Even if the majority of train and locomotive crew members
worked within official standards, however, this by no means de-
tracted from the rigors of their labor. On most lines locomotive
cabs were not fully enclosed, and railroad doctors pointed to the
adverse effects of the constant contrast between the heat of the engine and the cold winter air.[57] Medical personnel were also critical,
as were crew members, of the service facilities provided for rest
breaks at stations away from home. Although these varied considerably among lines, most were overcrowded and dirty. On the
Catherine Railroad facilities for conductors included a small unheated sleeping room with plain wooden cots for each crew and a
kitchen, washroom, toilet, and laundry.[58] This was exceptional;
elsewhere locomotive and train crews were most often put up in
common "service rooms." At one station on the Moscow-Kiev-
Voronezh Railroad there were complaints that the facilities for lo-

56. TsGIA, f. 273, op. 12, d. 300, ll. 118–19, 129, 183, 189–90, 257, 372;
d. 301, ll. 22–23, 94–95, 107–8, 137; d. 304, ll. 86, 89.
57. Tregubov, p. 61; *Zhel.*, 30, December 21, 1903, p. 20.
58. Ibid., pp. 156–61; TsGIA, f. 273, op. 8, d. 126, ll. 15–16.

comotive crews were "worse than a barracks." Here engine-drivers could find but "one big room in perpetual turmoil" where "cooking odors merged with locomotive soot" and wet laundry to create an atmosphere hardly conducive to rest. On the Riga-Orel Railroad old boxcars sometimes served as rest facilities.[59] One driver on the Moscow-Kursk Railroad later recalled that locomotive crews "could only dream of a normal life" and that working conditions were particularly upsetting for younger men.[60]

Railroad doctors contended that railroading was exceeded in physical danger only by military combat. Nearly every railroad administration had an office to deal with the often pathetic efforts of maimed and crippled railwaymen to receive financial compensation.[61] In 1904 the rate of work-related accidents was four times greater than in industrial enterprises.[62] According to official ministry figures, between 1903 and 1907, 3,509 railroad workers were killed in accidents and another 42,940 injured, or an average of 702 killed—about 1 in every 1,000 workers—and 8,588—1 in 85—injured each year.[63] Yet these statistics underestimated the problem, since many lines did not report all incidents. Between 1903 and 1907 the public health section reported a total of 3,689 deaths and 405,590 injuries owing to accidents, of which 28,958 were considered serious, or an average of 738 deaths and 81,118 injuries, 5,720 of them serious, each year. During these years physical trauma was exceeded only by digestive disorders as a subject for medical treatment among railwaymen, with the number of cases handled by the public health section averaging 32.4 percent of the total work force each year and rising steadily.[64]

Although, not surprisingly, the greatest number of deaths took place as a consequence of train operations, the incidence of trauma reported by the public health section was highest among workers

59. *ZhN*, May 26, 1900, p. 332; TsGIA, f. 273, op. 8, d. 138, l. 73.

60. *1905 god na Moskovsko-kursko-nizhegorodskoi i muromskoi zh. d.* (Moscow, 1931), p. 92.

61. *Protokoly zasedaniia 4-go soveshchaniia s'ezda zheleznodorozhnykh vrachei* (St. Petersburg, 1911), p. 583; *Zhel.*, 34, January 18, 1904, pp. 3–4.

62. Pazhitnov, vol. 2, p. 165.

63. Strumilin, p. 413. By way of comparison, the U.S. Interstate Commerce Commission reported that for the year ending June 30, 1889, 1,972 railwaymen had been killed on the job and 20,028 reported injured, or one out of every 357 employees killed and one in 35 injured (Licht, p. 190).

64. *Vrach-san otchet*, 1903–7.

in the repair shops. Between 1903 and 1907 the number of trauma cases in the workshops averaged 56 percent of the work force, increasing steadily from one year to the next at a rate higher than the overall increase in traumas. The rate for locomotive crews was next highest at 43.5 percent, followed by train crews at 32.8 percent, and then station personnel at 26.6 percent.[65] Contemporary observers attributed the disastrously high rates of work-related injury to poorly trained and underqualified personnel. By the turn of the century, many reform-minded railroad officials pointed to the accident rate as another persuasive argument for improving the status of railroad labor.[66] Yet, at least in the workshops, the problem was probably as much a function of poor equipment and overburdened facilities combined with overtime and the increasing role played by piece rates in wage determination.[67]

Beginning in the mid 1890s, then, railroad workers found their still fragile economic position declining, and those who had previously benefited most from the prosperous railroad economy were, perhaps, the biggest losers. Railroad managers faced a conundrum insoluble within the confines of their industry. To improve service and increase profitability it was essential to improve the caliber of work, which meant, most believed, rationalizing and raising the status of railroad labor, especially among the most poorly paid. Yet given the strictures established by the very productivity problems such improvements sought to address, as well as the runaway growth of the work force, even minimal changes could be made only at the expense of those who were in the best position to organize and fight.

To be sure, the dynamism of Russian railroad development still created opportunities for advancement. The rapid growth of the work force in the decade before 1905 thrust many older workers into new positions of authority: senior telegraph operators became stationmasters, workshop machinists and greasemen became enginedrivers. Yet these men rose at a time when conditions were stagnating, even deteriorating, most in the higher ranks they were

65. Ibid.
66. For instance, *ZhN*, January 15, 1899, pp. 22–24; January 22, 1899, pp. 37–40; April 30, 1899, pp. 260–63; May 6, 1899, pp. 282–84.
67. Tregubov, p. 117.

entering. Calls for reform came, then, not only as appeals to rationalize and systematize, but also as a manifestation of the railroads' inability to continue providing what had been offered at an earlier, less strained point.

In the workshops the deteriorating economic position was a product of, and interpenetrated with, the breakdown of older production relations. In a certain sense a similar pattern was repeated throughout railroading as pressure grew for a shift—already begun—from capital-intensive to labor-intensive development. The rapid growth of the railroads, as of all industry in late imperial Russia, strained the production relations through which that development had previously proceeded. In the context of the overall economic and political crisis preceding 1905, economic grievances could be raised and supported across the board by all segments of railroad labor, but the crisis hit hardest those most capable of fighting back—the administrative and communications workers, railroad industrial labor, and the engine-drivers. An expanding work force thus allowed special dissatisfactions to emerge simultaneously both among veteran workers who had risen through the ranks and among younger newcomers impatient with stagnation. This hardly boded well for the success of reformist solutions.

Four

The Railwayman's Life

The social position of the Russian worker is usually defined in terms of factory and village. Yet large segments of the working class were also part of a broader urban community, and their problems were also defined by life in the city. On the railroads, most administrative, communications, industrial, and skilled operations workers were urban dwellers. To some extent, however, railroad workers lived in a special "railroad world," or, more precisely, in several overlapping railroad communities. In small towns and medium-sized junctions, the railroad station might stand at the heart of town life. In major industrial centers railroad workers could merge into a broader fraternity of skilled or white-collar labor, but they were still drawn together by the specificity of railroad operations and by distinct institutional structures established by railroad management.

How did railwaymen live? What can be said of their health, housing, diet, family situations, and cultural experiences? Among contemporaries awareness of the conditions of railroad life was limited; in 1904 the Bolshevik and middle-level railroad bureaucrat A. G. Shlikhter wrote that despite all the talk of the need to improve the everyday lives of railwaymen, the authorities knew almost nothing about what those lives were actually like.[1] Yet the historical record affords a surprisingly full picture. In addition to memoir sources, the railroad press published considerable material, some of it systematic and statistical, on housing, living condi-

1. *Zhel.*, 72, October 12, 1904, p. 3.

tions, education, and cultural life. The annual reports of the pension fund also yield statistical data. Of particular value, however, are the reports and other published and unpublished records of the railroad public health section, an institution that merits separate attention.

The railroad medical service can be traced to the start of railroad construction. In 1842 the first medical section was established under the Department of Communications as a special branch of the military health service, and in 1870 this still rudimentary system was transferred to civilian management and decentralized. On most roads, however, available care was extremely limited, though probably better than what could be found in most factories. In 1879 a St. Petersburg meeting of railroad medical personnel recommended establishing a central organization directly under the ministry. A similar 1881 meeting in Moscow called for periodic congresses of railroad doctors. These proposals were considered by the Baranov Commission, which, in the 1885 general charter, mandated the construction of hospitals at major terminals and of first aid facilities at each station. In March 1886 the first congress of railroad doctors discussed a charter for a new, centralized public health section, which was approved June 12. It was not until June 20, 1893, however, that operative regulations and funding were confirmed and work began in the wake of the disastrous cholera epidemic that followed the 1891–92 famine.[2]

The tasks of the public health section were to provide medical care to railroad employees and their families and to victims of railroad accidents and those taking ill while traveling by train; to ensure that railroad workers were in sufficiently good physical and mental health to guarantee safe train operation; and to supervise the overall sanitary condition of the roads and of the communities attached to them, with the particular intent of checking the spread of epidemic infections. According to the new rules, each road was divided into medical sections of no more than 120 versts in length, each served by a doctor and clinic. Large stations and workshops employing more than 1,500 workers were to be separate sections.

2. TsGAOR, f. 6865, d. 49, ll. 49–54; S. L. Tregubov, *Opyt izucheniia v sanitarnom otnoshenii byta zheleznodorozhnykh sluzhashchikh v predelakh Kursko-Kharkovo-Sevastopol'skogo zh. d.* (Kharkov, 1904), pp. 165–68.

Treatment was offered free of charge to all railwaymen with an annual salary below 1,200 rubles.[3]

These requirements, however, were initially closer to targets than norms. During its first half decade, the public health section was absorbed in organizational work and in combating epidemics of diphtheria and smallpox in the southeast. An 1898 congress of railroad doctors noted that medical care continued to be marked by "extreme diversity" in both availability and quality. As a result, the rules were strengthened in 1899, with the maximum length of each medical division lowered to 100 versts. In general, care was better on state lines than on private ones, although by 1904 the average expenditure per worker was actually slightly higher for private than for state roads. In 1900, according to one report, the number of people eligible to use a single hospital or infirmary bed ranged from a low of 225 on the state Transcaucasian Railroad to a high, among state lines, of 2,512 on the Riga-Orel Railroad and, among private roads, of 4,813 on the Moscow-Kazan line.[4]

In 1903 the public health section began issuing standardized annual reports. These included general comments by the chief railroad doctor and detailed, systematic, and uniform statistics on both the service and facilities of the section and the incidence of some 125 different categories of health problems in some thirteen different groupings of railroad workers, family members, and others.[5] The reports indicate a gradual, but significant, expansion of medical care. On the eve of 1905 the railroad network was divided into 544 medical divisions, served by small, often rudimentary, clinics situated an average of 60 miles apart and serving an average population of 4,369. These divisions were staffed by 697 doctors, 1,557 nurses, and 330 midwives, a notable gain over the 304 doctors, 706 nurses, and just 84 midwives employed in 1894. In 1904 there were eighty-three railroad hospitals with 2,626 beds as compared to thirty-seven hospitals with only 884 beds ten years earlier. Railroad health facilities were available in 1904 to some 2,361,923 people—railroad employees, their immediate families, students at railroad

3. TsGAOR, f. 6865, d. 49, ll. 56–57; TsGIA, f. 273, op. 8, d. 180, ll. 206–9; op. 12, d. 407, ll. 25–27; Tregubov, pp. 168–69; *VMPS*, June 8, 1896, pp. 581–82.
4. TsGAOR, f. 6865, d. 49, l. 59.
5. These reports were compiled from annual reports of different lines, many of which are in TsGIA, f. 273, op. 8.

schools, and gendarmes. The budget of the public health section for all lines was over five million rubles.[6]

Despite these not unimpressive figures, the work of the public health section was seen as "less than shining" and "poorly organized" by most railwaymen.[7] Common targets of criticism were the railroad hospitals and infirmaries, which were still limited in number and size, often poorly located, and almost always overcrowded. Both the Saratov *zemstvo* and the Moscow *duma* complained that railroad doctors routinely placed patients in province and city hospitals owing to lack of beds in their own facilities (although in some towns the opposite was true, with *zemstvo* doctors relying on railroad hospitals). The situation in Moscow was especially scandalous; in 1903 the country's largest junction could claim just 20 railroad infirmary beds.[8]

First aid stations and clinics were sometimes accessible only with difficulty. It was not simply that managers and foremen tended to discourage visits (although this was a frequent problem). On most lines clinics were located at irregular intervals and generally open just two hours each morning, which often compelled workers who had traveled considerable distances to wait overnight in station sitting rooms for treatment.[9] Medicines were in short supply and, when available, of poor quality; on the Siberian Railroad, workers complained that castor oil was prescribed for nearly every malady.[10] Complaints against medical staff were also common. To obtain treatment a bribe was often necessary, the railroad press charged. Although some new doctors were thought to approach their work with concern, they were said soon to be overwhelmed by a pervasive atmosphere of bureaucratism and indifference. *Zheleznodorozhnik* charged that the role of the railroad doctor was "to a significant degree that of a policeman."[11]

6. *Vrach-san otchet*, 1905, pp. 6–7, 20–21; VMPS, March 29, 1897, p. 360.
7. M. K. Dymkov and D. Ia. Lipovetskii, *1905 god na Kazanke. Sbornik* (Moscow, 1925), p. 30; ZhD, 1904, 9, p. 81. In 1905 the director of the Riazan-Ural Railroad reported that the care guaranteed by ministry rules did not exist "in practice" (TsGIA, f. 273, op. 12, d. 325, l. 77).
8. ZhN, January 26, 1903, p. 47.
9. ZhN, March 2, 1902, p. 113, April 28, 1901, p. 261; ZhD, 1904, 9, p. 81; Vech. poch., 207, August 21, 1905.
10. *Bir. ved.*, 8554, February 6, 1905, p. 6; Zhel., 71, October 5, 1904, p. 17; 64, August 17, 1904, pp. 15–16.
11. ZhN, April 28, 1901, pp. 261–62; Zhel., 142, March 13, 1906, p. 4.

Such complaints were not fully merited, however. The common notions that railroad doctors were novices, for instance, and that many viewed railroad service as a stepping stone to more lucrative private practice do not seem justified. A 1906 report of the Saratov section of the Imperial Russian Technical Society indicated that the age distribution of railroad doctors did not differ noticeably from that of doctors generally. If railroad employees complained of the indifference and insensitivity of medical personnel, the latter could with some justice respond that patients were not always courteous.[12] Like their counterparts in private practice, railroad doctors were generally underpaid by comparison to other professions and felt overburdened and inadequately equipped. Many brought to their work the genuine concern with social problems that was a notable characteristic of their profession at this time. In 1905 railroad doctors themselves emerged as the most articulate critics of the public health section, forcefully demanding increased funding and various improvements from management.[13]

The real problem with the public health section was not personnel, but that, owing to inadequate funding, improvements could not keep pace with the rapidly increasing demand for health care, which outpaced even the breakneck expansion of the work force. On the Nicholas Railroad, for example, between 1899 and 1908 the population served by the public health section grew by 33.8 percent, the number of doctors by 37.5 percent, and the number of hospital beds by 52.6 percent, but the number of patient visits increased by nearly 200 percent.[14] Yet the ministry was committed to only a "gradual improvement" of the system. Between 1903 and 1907 annual expenditures on railroad health care per employee rose from 7.36 rubles to 9.44 rubles, but expenditures per patient visit remained stable, rising insignificantly from 1.53 to 1.57 rubles. To be sure, the rate of expenditure per worker compared rather favorably to the 1907 average of just 6.19 rubles in private

12. TsGIA, f. 273, op. 8, d. 180, ll. 304–5; *Zhel.*, 64, August 17, 1904, pp. 15–16.
13. TsGIA, f. 273, op. 8, d. 180, l. 209, 320; op. 12, d. 350, ll. 52–54; d. 407, l. 27. On the status of doctors, see Nancy Frieden, *Russian Physicians in an Era of Reform and Revolution, 1856–1905* (Princeton, N.J., 1981), especially pp. 200–221. Nowhere in this otherwise admirable study is the railroad public health section mentioned.
14. TsGIA, f. 273, op. 8, d. 133, l. 385.

industry (up from 3.91 rubles a decade earlier), but, still, the tsarist government spent more on the upkeep of police horses than on railroad medicine.[15]

The reports and records of the medical service confirm accounts in the railroad press and elsewhere that despite their relatively privileged position in the working class, the majority of both blue- and white-collar railwaymen lived in a pitifully poor state. "I have seen the ranks of the railwaymen, emaciated by the yoke of their economic plight," wrote a correspondent to *Zheleznodorozhnik* in 1905. "They fall before my eyes, worn out to the point of destruction, victimized by rheumatism and tuberculosis. I have seen them blinded by thousands of sleepless nights, jaded, crippled, and thrown away to die on the roadway."[16] According to the annual reports of the public health section, railroad workers suffered most from infectious diseases, digestive disorders, traumas, and lung diseases, including tuberculosis. Among the nine departments into which the section divided the work force, the rate of illness was invariably highest among telegraph operators, followed by locomotive and train crews, then shop craftsmen. Station and administrative employees were next on the list, with workers in track repair and maintenance enjoying the lowest rate.[17]

Many illnesses plaguing railroad workers were undoubtedly connected to job conditions. The widespread incidence of physical trauma, especially among shop craftsmen and train crews, has already been discussed as a product of safety conditions. Problems with tuberculosis and other lung disorders, prevalent among telegraph operators and administrative employees, may be attributable in part to work in stuffy, overcrowded offices. The spread of a wide variety of infectious illnesses, including regular epidemics of typhus, cholera, scarlatina, and diphtheria, was facilitated by regu-

---

15. *VMPS*, March 17, 1901, p. 153; *Vrach-san otchet*, 1903, p. 5; 1907, p. 5; TsGAOR, f. 6865, d. 49, l. 81; Rostov, *Zheleznodorozhniki v revoliutsionnom dvizhenii 1905 g.* (Moscow and Leningrad, 1926), p. 14. An article in *ZhN*, January 26, 1903, p. 46, complained that railroad health care was "much worse" than that available to factory workers.

16. *Zhel.*, 106, June 13, 1905.

17. *Vrach-san otchet*, 1907, p. 37. The surprisingly low rate of disease among the line repair crews probably reflects a reluctance by these rural and often seasonal hands to use the railroad medical facilities and/or their limited access to them.

lar travel through both urban and rural breeding grounds of infection. But the maladies to which railroad workers were subject were also products of their overall quality of life. Most railroad workers, especially in large industrial centers, lived a squalid existence, even if they stood a cut above millhands and fully outside such notorious urban slums as Moscow's Khitrovka and St. Peterburg's Haymarket.

The prevalence of digestive disorders, the single most frequently treated category of illness, surely reflected the abominable sanitary conditions and inadequate diet of the urban working class. In Ekaterinoslav the chief doctor of the Catherine Railroad reported that at only a handful of points on the road did drinking water approach satisfactory quality.[18] It has been estimated that the average urban factory worker spent as much as half his income on food, and the available budgets of railwaymen indicate a similar proportion. Although on the lines railroad workers could sometimes supplement their diets with garden vegetables, at large junctions high prices compelled consumption of more limited fare. A survey of lower administrative employees on the Nicholas Railroad revealed that most ate but one full meal a day, and many existed almost solely on tea and dark bread. A clerk on the Riga-Orel Railroad earning 30 rubles per month found this "not enough for milk and food for the children, nor for vegetables . . . or even tobacco." A telegraph operator on the Moscow-Brest Railroad receiving 25 rubles spent some 17.19 each month on food for his family, almost three-fourths of which went for staples such as flour, butter, salt, and tea. Even among a group of semi-rural Ukrainian track repair workers and switchmen, 80 percent of whom tilled railroad land and even owned farm animals, a family of four spent 10.80 rubles of an average monthly income of just 13.70 rubles on food, mainly sugar, tea, and flour.[19]

Especially at provincial junctions, high food prices and the frequently unscrupulous practices of local merchants drew many railwaymen into consumer cooperative societies. By 1904 there were forty-six officially approved cooperatives on the railroads, a fifth of all such groups in the country.[20] Ostensibly, these were indepen-

18. TsGIA, f. 273, op. 8, d. 126, ll. 18–19.
19. Rostov, *Zheleznodorozhniki*, pp. 11–12; *Zhel.*, 90, February 15, 1905, pp. 13–14; *ZhD*, 1902, 34–35, p. 331; *Zhel.*, 39, February 22, 1904, pp. 3–5.
20. L. V. Olkhovaia, "Rabochaia kooperatsiia kak forma organizatsii proletari-

dent organizations run by the workers themselves. In practice, however, real worker participation was minimal: the governing bodies were completely subordinate to railroad management, which not only dominated most cooperative activities, but usually held a veto over all significant society decisions. The consumer group of the Samara-Zlatoust Railroad had 1,500 official members, but the "huge majority" were "indifferent" to its affairs. On the eve of 1905 an election to the society's board attracted only 190 voters.[21] Still, in some places the consumer groups did offer a limited arena for worker organization and oppositional agitation. In 1902 the railroad cooperatives played an important part in the first Moscow congress of consumer societies, which managed to address several pressing social and political themes. "At that time, the majority of the congress was already on the side of the liberals," a delegate from the Kovrov workshops of the Moscow-Kursk Railroad recalled, "and several were even partisans of the revolutionary tendency."[22]

It is likely that the majority of railroad workers, especially those with families, ate at home. But for single workers, those whose residence was more than a short commute from the job, as well as for train and locomotive crews in transit, some large stations, depots, and workshops provided special cafeterias.[23] The food offered at such places was usually of poor quality, however, and where it was not was often priced well beyond the means of the average worker. At the Aleksandrovsk workshops of the Kursk-Kharkov-Sevastopol Railroad, for instance, for fourteen kopeks a worker could obtain a bowl of *borshch* with some meat, kasha or potatoes, and bread. "I dropped in on the cafeteria [at Aleksandrovsk] without notice," reported Pavlovskii in 1904,

and found the kitchen and dining room in good order, with no trace of cooking odors. The *borshch* had the aroma of fresh beets and cabbage that one might find in the best railroad buffets for twenty-five kopeks a plate.

ata," in *Rossiisskii proletariat: oblik, bor'ba, gegemoniia*, ed. L. M. Ivanov (Moscow, 1970), p. 262. See also *VMPS*, July 6, 1896, pp. 699–700; TsGAOR, f. 6865, d. 111, ll. 240–77.

21. TsGIA, f. 1287, op. 9, d. 2643, 2671. On participation in the Samara-Zlatoust society, see *Soiuz potrebitelei*, 7, May 2, 1905, pp. 198–99, in TsGAOR, f. 6865, d. 111, l. 240.

22. TsGAOR, f. 6865, d. 122, ll. 8–9.

23. TsGIA, f. 273, op. 8, d. 126, l. 18; *ZhD*, 1903, 46–47, p. 496.

As for the meat in the soup, while a bit lean [Russians traditionally prefer fatty meats in soup], it was of fine quality, which was also the case with the second course of roast potatoes. I would prefer this lunch to many I have had in the finest homes. . . . Yet, it seems there is not much demand for such meals. The cafeteria is used daily by no more than fifty people, sometimes even fewer. Evidently the price is more than a working-class family can budget for just one of its members. . . . [As for single workers] often at lunch break one notices young unskilled hands and apprentices buying some dried fish, cucumber, and bread at a nearby stand for seven or eight kopeks. For such a worker, too, fourteen kopeks is too high.

According to Pavlovskii, workers who could afford to eat at the cafeteria often passed up the opportunity so that they might have some money for vodka. Others, he claimed, avoided the place because they found the presence of the women who staffed it intimidating to conversation. "Many workers simply prefer to lunch at their work stations, where they read aloud and discuss the morning newspaper among themselves."[24]

Railroad doctors frequently attributed medical problems to overcrowded and unsanitary housing, which offered "favorable soil for infectious diseases."[25] Indeed, the housing problem was "one of the most pressing questions" facing railroad workers and managers alike, and it garnered considerable attention in the railroad press. A central concern was the chronic shortage of residence space. On the Samara-Zlatoust Railroad, for example, several stations were understaffed simply because there was no place to house the full complement of employees. On the Catherine Railroad a similar problem was solved by housing workers in refurbished freight cars.[26]

The housing shortage was at first most pressing in semi-rural areas and small towns opened to commerce by rail transport, but by the twentieth century the crunch was gravest in the cities, swollen to the bursting point with new migrants following more than a decade of rapid industrial growth. About 20 to 25 percent of all railwaymen lived in housing provided by the roads under the support program discussed in the preceding chapter. Such hous-

24. *ZhD*, 1904, 9, p. 80.
25. Tregubov, p. 141.
26. *ZhN*, January 7, 1900, p. 8; *Zhel.*, 57, June 29, 1904, p. 19; TsGIA, f. 273, op. 8, d. 126, l. 15.

ing, however, was mainly available at smaller junctions, rural stations, and repair facilities and switching posts on more isolated sections. In the cities the railroads seem not to have followed the pattern established by the many factories that built dormitories for their workers. Instead, at the largest junctions the great majority of administrative and communications employees, shop craftsmen, and operations personnel were compelled to find quarters on the private market. On the South West Railroad, for instance, of some 150,000 workers and family members counted by the public health section in 1903, about a fifth lived in railroad apartments at 310 different stations and turnabouts, another 4 percent in 744 barracks, and some 9 percent in 2,272 cabins for switchmen and track watchmen. The remainder, almost two-thirds, lived in privately rented space, including in 1901 all but 204 of 2,150 workers and employees at the line's main Kiev terminal.[27]

Housing patterns could foster social isolation. Compelled by line rules or circumstance to live near stations, shops, and yards, many railwaymen, especially in small to medium-sized junctions, lived in segregated communities. In larger urban centers, however, where most factory workers lived near their plants, the majority of railwaymen were somewhat dispersed, with many commuting by train from scattered suburbs.[28] To be sure, the housing pattern varied among different cities, but in almost every instance a major section of the work force was spread throughout the broader working class community. This was of considerable significance, although in two contradictory ways. On the one hand, the dispersal of railwaymen facilitated their integration into the working class as a whole. On the other hand, the lengthy and often tiring commute could combine with the long and irregular work schedules of such railroad occupations as telegraph operator, engine-driver, or conductor to keep workers away from home for considerable stretches, reinforcing the "separateness" of railroad life and encouraging the development of narrowly professional consciousness.

27. TsGIA, f. 273, op. 8, d. 148, l. 94.
28. ZhN, January 8, 1899, pp. 8–11; ZhD, 1902, 30–31, p. 298; 1904, 9, p. 79. On housing in private industry, see Victoria E. Bonnell, *The Russian Worker: Life and Labor Under the Tsarist Regime* (Berkeley and Los Angeles, 1983), pp. 20–21. These housing patterns were similar to those on mid-nineteenth-century American railroads (see Walter Licht, *Working For the Railroad: The Organization of Work in the Nineteenth Century* [Princeton, N.J., 1983], pp. 228–29).

Whether provided by the railroads or privately rented, most housing available to railroad workers, especially in large cities, was overpriced, overcrowded, and frequently just barely habitable. Most apartments were too small to accommodate the number of people living in them, and were poorly lit, inadequately heated, and lacked proper ventilation. In Moscow and St. Petersburg, where railwaymen lived almost exclusively in private apartments, the housing situation was especially atrocious; like other proletarians, railroad workers were frequently forced to crowd several families in a flat, or, worse yet, they might rent just a corner of a room, or a section of one of St. Petersburg's notorious dank and fetid basements, periodically flooded by overflowing sewage. Those somewhat better off might be lucky enough to rent a small cottage near one of the suburban stations. The situation was not much better elsewhere. The public health section of the Riga-Orel Railroad noted that in Riga and Dvinsk private accommodations did not even fulfill "the most modest sanitary requirements." One worker described the space occupied by many employees as "no larger than a coffin" and the conveniences available as those of "the very worst pigsty." On the Samara-Zlatoust Railroad, nearly half of all housing provided by the road was said to be "overcrowded, dirty, and lacking adequate cesspools and toilet facilities." Private apartments were "even worse, though, in most cases at least, they have baths."[29]

White-collar railwaymen lived no better than their blue-collar counterparts. In 1900, concerned about the increasingly high cost of living in Kiev, Nemeshaev appointed a commission to study the housing situation. The commission distributed questionnaires to nearly 2,000 employees and workers attached to the Kiev terminal who lived in private housing, of whom nearly 75 percent responded, including 900 employees of the central administration. Of this latter, white-collar group, 670 lived with their families and 230 were single. Of those with families, for whom the housing problem was most acute, 180 resided in apartments of three rooms (plus kitchen) at rents ranging from 7 to 50 rubles per month, an average of 19.87 rubles. Each such apartment was inhabited by be-

    29. TsGIA, f. 273, op. 8, d. 138, ll. 72–73; *Zhel.*, 90, February 15, 1905, p. 13; *Privol. kr.*, 145, June 18, 1904, p. 3.

tween two and twelve individuals. Another 145 families lived in two-room flats, paying between 9 and 25 rubles to house from two to nine people. The remaining 167 families lived in four- and five-room communal apartments. The commission found Kiev rents rising at an average rate of between 2 and 6 percent annually. Of the 670 families surveyed, just 135 lived in apartments with running water, and only 113 had access to a sewer. According to the survey, apartments of three rooms or fewer housed an average of two people per room, and larger ones an average of 1.21 per room.[30]

These Kiev statistics are enlightening from another standpoint too, for they suggest that a good portion, if not a majority, of white-collar railwaymen lived with their families. In fact, evidence seems to indicate that this was also true of blue-collar craftsmen and many operations personnel. The "bifurcated household," in which male peasant workers left wives and young children in the villages, which Robert E. Johnson found to be a characteristic feature in the lives of late-nineteenth-century Moscow millhands, seems to have been exceptional—or certainly a rapidly disappearing custom—among urban railwaymen in most parts of European Russia. To be sure, both the housing shortage and the peculiar demands of rail-roading as a transport industry often necessitated extensive family separations, but this was generally not a matter of choice, and the compulsion to maintain "two homes" was universally condemned as an evil, from which newly hired workers suffered especially.[31] Urban railwaymen of all categories sought to establish a home and family where they worked, and by the early twentieth century it appears that many, if not most, succeeded. "We are all family men," began the petition of striking workers at the Moscow depot of the Moscow-Kazan Railroad in February 1905.[32]

According to pension fund figures, about 75 percent of male permanent staff were married. About half of all pension fund participants had children, with an average of 2.6 per family and an

30. *ZhN*, February 24, 1901, pp. 120–21.

31. See, for instance, the following comment in *ZhN*, January 27, 1901, p. 54: "A good number of employees are compelled to leave their families somewhere in a distant home town [*na rodine*] and to live in two homes, which causes them to miss their families terribly." On the "bifurcated household," see Robert E. Johnson, *Peasant and Proletarian: The Working Class of Moscow in the Late Nineteenth Century* (New Brunswick, N.J., 1979).

32. TsGIA, f. 273, op. 12, d. 328, l. 131.

average age per child of 7 years, 4 months.[33] It is impossible, of course, to judge from such numbers how many families actually lived together, but on the basis of numerous references in the railroad press and, later, in the demands raised by railwaymen in 1905 for schools, child care, and maternity facilities, it seems certain there were many. The annual reports of the public health section include statistics from which it can be inferred that a large number of railroad wives and children lived with their working husbands and fathers in single, largely urban, households. In 1905 railroad health care was available to a population of 2,470,807, of whom 709,531 were workers; 57,710 students at railroad schools, and the rest the wives and children of railwaymen.[34] Although family members tended to utilize railroad health care facilities much less frequently than the workers themselves, the statistics still suggest that a very high proportion had access to the system, which surely meant that they lived near their husband's place of employment rather than in a distant village.

Especially revealing were figures on maternity care. In 1905 some 29,966 children were born to the wives of railroad workers under the care of the public health section. Assuming the accuracy of pension fund statistics on the percentage of married workers, this converts to about 6 percent of all railroad wives. Since it is doubtful that many women would—or could—travel from their home village to a distant railroad hospital or midwife to give birth, it can probably be assumed that a majority, if not all, of these new mothers lived with their husbands near the line. The rapid increase in the number of midwives employed by the public health section between 1894 and 1904—almost twice the rate of increase in the number of doctors—testifies as well to an increasing demand for such care, and, by inference, to the growing urbanization of railroading families. If anything, birth statistics published by the public health section may tend to underestimate the extent of family life. It may be reasonably assumed that the lion's share of births represented families who lived together near the railroad and its supporting institutions, but it should not be assumed that all such families could or did use railroad facilities. In Moscow, for

33. *Statistika*, 1902, pp. 62, 68.
34. *Vrach-san otchet*, 1905, pp. 266–73.

instance, the notorious inadequacy of railroad health care and the increased, though, no doubt, still limited, access of workers to alternative medical and child delivery options may well have encouraged some railroad families to bypass the public health section altogether.

Another interesting statistical indicator of railroad family life is provided by public health section figures on the incidence of syphilis and other venereal diseases among railwaymen. In urban areas these afflictions were most common among males who were single or lived for long stretches separated from their wives.[35] On the eve of the 1905 revolution the public health section was treating some 5 percent of all railwaymen for venereal diseases, a rate several times greater than the national average. Such comparison is essentially meaningless, however, because in Russia as elsewhere, venereal diseases were far more prevalent in urban than rural environments, and the overwhelming majority of the population were peasants. More suggestive is a comparison between the Nicholas Railroad and the city of St. Petersburg, where the rates were nearly identical, which meant that the rate among railwaymen was actually a good deal lower than that among the city's male workers, who comprised about a third of the capital's venereal disease patients. According to one study, in 1904 "employees in communications and transport" accounted for only 2.3 percent of St. Petersburg's syphilitics.[36]

35. According to one 1910 study of venereal disease in St. Petersburg, over two-thirds of all patients were male, and 71.9 percent of all male sufferers were single. Of the remainder, just half lived permanently with their wives (K. V. Goncharov, *O venercheskikh bolezniakh v S. Peterburge* [St. Petersburg, 1910], p. 80). That married railwaymen living with their wives were less likely to contract venereal diseases is also suggested by both common sense and the much lower incidence of such illnesses among railroad wives. In 1905, 6.89 percent of all railroad workers, but only 1.23 percent of their spouses, were treated by the public health section for venereal disease (*Vrach-san otchet*, 1905, pp. 266–73). Assuming that an infected male would pass the condition to a spouse with whom he lived, the inference is clearly that a much greater proportion of those contracting such infections were single, or married but living alone. It may be reasonably concluded, then, that sections of the work force with a lower than average incidence of venereal disease had a higher proportion of relatively stable married workers living in a single household.

36. For the Nicholas Railroad, see TsGIA, f. 273, op. 8, d. 133, l. 83. For the city, see Goncharov, p. 12. According to Goncharov, there were in 1904 some 32,749 recorded cases at city hospitals and about a third were male factory work-

The incidence of venereal disease varied considerably between different railroad lines. Among nine major roads whose annual health reports were found in the Leningrad archive, the rate of treatment tended to be noticeably higher on lines situated in less developed and more recently urbanizing regions to the south—with a rate of nearly 20 percent on the Transcaucasian Railroad—and lowest in the industrial center and north. This suggests, perhaps, a greater degree of family stability on roads in older industrial areas. Newly developing regions in any case surely had higher rates of venereal disease overall owing, on the one hand, to a relatively unstable population of recent, largely male, and single immigrants, and, on the other, to less developed health care. The difference in reporting may also stem from factors other than the actual incidence of venereal illness, since the moral shame and intimacy attached to these afflictions might have compelled some to seek private treatment, which was more readily available in older industrial centers.

A more interesting and revealing variation was that among different railroad departments. Not surprisingly, the incidence of venereal disease was lowest among semi-rural and more socially isolated workers in track maintenance; station workers also had a below-average rate. The incidence of venereal disease among the skilled craftsmen of the repair shops, however, was only slightly above the average for all railroad workers, which is especially significant given that in society as a whole blue-collar industrial workers like these were among the most likely to contract venereal illnesses. At the St. Petersburg workshops of the Nicholas Railroad the rate was well below that of the line as a whole and just three-fourths the city rate. The rate in the Administrative Department was somewhat higher, which takes on added significance when it is recalled that this department had a relatively greater number of women. Clearly the life-style associated with higher rates of venereal disease was by no means simply a blue-collar characteristic. In fact, although the next highest rates were among train and locomotive crews—reflecting, most likely, their extensive time on the

---

ers. Given that the male proletariat of the city numbered about 250,000, the venereal disease rate for this group can be estimated at over 4 percent, significantly higher than the 2.47 percent for railwaymen.

road—the very highest rate was that for telegraph operators, an important segment of the administrative work force, among whom the incidence of venereal disease was four times that among all railwaymen, reaching the astronomical level on the Vladikavkaz Railroad of nearly 60 percent in one year.[37]

The situation of telegraph operators merits special comment. Not only was the incidence of venereal disease among them considerably greater than in other departments, but they had the highest rate of illness in general, which attracted the attention of railroad doctors, who usually attributed their health problems to "youth and unsatisfactory material conditions."[38] But official data may actually underestimate the extent to which telegraphists suffered. In 1902 the chief doctor of the Moscow-Brest Railroad delivered a sobering report to the Pirogov Society on a two-year study of 420 telegraph operators, 360 men and 60 women, on his road. The group, from which administrators and apprentices were excluded, was typical of the composition of the telegraph staff; the majority were under 25 and earned 300 rubles or less per year. Over the course of the study only 90 members of the sample avoided serious health problems. Of the others, more than a third suffered from various lung disorders, including 23 cases of tuberculosis, and another 19 percent developed vision problems. The most shocking statistic, however, was that during this period 18 operators died, including 12 of tuberculosis, an extraordinary annual mortality rate of 2.25 percent, closer to the national rate for 50- to 60-year-olds than to that for young adults. It was also well above the officially reported rate of 0.42 percent for Moscow-Brest operators, a discrepancy which the doctor attributed to the official practice of not reporting deaths of those who left railroad work shortly before passing on.[39]

On the Moscow-Brest Railroad, as on most state lines, only senior operators were entitled to railroad housing; junior telegraphists lived mainly in "low-ceilinged, dark, and crowded" private rooms. It

37. *Vrach-san otchet*, 1905, pp. 266–73.

38. TsGIA, f. 273, op. 8, d. 160. *Vrach-san otchet*, 1907, p. 37, traces the overall illness and mortality rates for the years 1903 to 1907. In each year the rate of illness for telegraph operators was about one-and-a-half times the overall rate, and significantly above the next highest group, locomotive crews.

39. *ZhD*, 1902, 34–35, pp. 329–32.

was mainly this latter group whose medical problems were worst. Of the 90 operators in the sample without problems, just 35 percent lived in private housing. Of the majority who took ill, however, 82 percent were quartered in private rooms.[40] The living conditions of these young telegraph operators reflected a different sort of urban experience. According to Dr. S. L. Tregubov of the Kursk-Kharkov-Sevastopol Railroad, teenage telegraph operators, "lacking any supervision and leadership, frequently spent their meager salary in an extraordinarily irrational way, leaving nothing for tolerable housing." Most young telegraphists lived several to a room, where, according to Tregubov, they frequently went months without a change of bedding or linen, and for weeks without sweeping the floor and tidying up. "Often the young operator sleeps on bare boards, with no bedding of his own, using the linen of his room-mate at work."[41]

One telegraph operator on the Riazan-Ural Railroad recalled how young railroad employees spent their leisure:

At holidays we generally drank, sang popular songs, and partied. The junior employees would gather in groups at the stations and go off to wish a happy holiday to our superiors, who in turn would give us money for tea, which, of course, we used to treat ourselves to more vodka. . . . Most of all the young employees chased after the daughters of merchants and others of the lower middle class (*meshchanskoe obshchestvo*). On the other hand, many railwaymen found satisfaction exclusively in drink.[42]

Heavy drinking was also common among shop craftsmen, "not a few of whom drank up a good half their salary," and engine-drivers, who often "stopped off for a few shots" after a long shift. "Alcoholism is one of the biggest evils of railroad service," lamented one observer. "Completely sober employees are a minority."[43]

If younger, often single, railroad workers shared a common escape with their more family-oriented elders, they were still easily distinguished from preceding generations by higher levels of education and greater sophistication. This is, perhaps, suggested

40. Ibid., p. 331.
41. Tregubov, p. 50.
42. TsGAOR, f. 6865, d. 39a, l. 2.
43. *ZhN*, June 16, 1901, p. 377; November 24, 1902, p. 720; *ZhD*, 1895, 35–36, p. 318. Drinking was also important on American railroads (see Licht, pp. 236–38).

by the attraction to the daughters of merchants reported above. Summarizing his observations of fifteen major railroad workshops, Pavlovskii concluded that younger railwaymen were quite well-informed:

For the past quarter century education and the means of communication have become so accessible that our worker knows very well how workers live, not only in other European states, but across the ocean too. A great many of our machinists, turners, braziers, and forge workers, whom we know as unintelligent men resigned to the same monotonous work in our shops until the end of their days, have sons with even a university or higher technical education. These youths, the children of railroad workers, do not attend seminaries or enter military service; they strive with special energy toward higher education because they are surrounded by countless examples of the good life enjoyed by the engineering corps. Such educated youths are quite sensitive to the conditions of life of their foreign counterparts, and they eagerly seek out news of factory conditions abroad, and especially in America. These workers know quite well where and by whom things are done in their behalf on our own roads.[44]

During the last years of the nineteenth century the level of literacy of the Russian working class rose dramatically. By 1900 it was estimated that six of every ten male factory workers could read. In Moscow the proportion was about 10 percent higher, and in St. Petersburg the level of working-class literacy was triple the national figure.[45] Although comparable data could not be found for railwaymen specifically, indications are that, especially in larger cities, they were more literate than most. To be sure, among track watchmen and repair crews, switchmen, and signalmen, and at small and medium-sized stations, education and even literacy could be exceptional. In the workshops, however, the situation was different: in 1896 the ministry reported that of 5,108 apprentices in railroad workshops between the ages of fourteen and twenty-five, 2,286, or 44.8 percent, had completed "a full course of primary school," and just 214 were judged illiterate.[46]

Increasing numbers of second- and third-generation railroad workers obtained much of their education at establishments maintained by the Ministry of Communications. Of these the most de-

44. TsGIA, f. 273, op. 8, d. 46, l. 591.
45. W. Bruce Lincoln, *In War's Dark Shadow* (New York, 1983), p. 131.
46. *Zhel.*, 39, February 22, 1904, pp. 3–5; TsGAOR, f. 6865, d. 45, l. 35.

veloped were the technical academies established to train skilled personnel in railroad operation. The first such academy opened in 1869, but it was not until 1886 that the ministry centralized the administration of twenty-eight private institutions. By 1903 the number of technical academies had grown to forty-six, and more than 60 percent of graduates were employed on the Russian railroads, over half as engine-drivers, about a fourth as road foremen, and the remainder split between the telegraph service and the chancelleries. Between 1890 and 1902 the percentage of academy graduates who were children of railroading families rose dramatically, even as the total number of graduates also increased. Where in 1890 just 36.4 percent of academy graduates were children of railroad workers, in 1902 the figure stood at 56.7 percent.[47]

More unevenly developed, but rapidly expanding, were primary schools for younger students, established on many roads during the 1890s in response to a growing need for basic education. Unlike the technical academies, railroad primary schools were not centrally administered, nor was their establishment mandated by the ministry. Individual roads set up educational programs to attract and maintain a skilled work force composed increasingly of family men. On most roads, even the very best, classroom space was sorely limited. The Moscow-Kursk Railroad was considered an especially "shining" example: In 1892 there were 358 students in three schools; a decade later this had risen to 1,561 students in fourteen schools, which still amounted to only 37 percent of all eligible children. The South West Railroad also claimed a respectable program. In 1894, when the road was still under private management, there were eight primary schools with 42 teachers, 1,453 students, and an annual budget of 25,000 rubles. By 1900 the system had grown to include twenty-nine primary schools with 165 teachers, 4,571 students, and a budget of over 75,000 rubles. Yet here, too, less than half those eligible were able to attend. More typical was the Moscow-Kiev-Voronezh Railroad, where by 1907 nine schools taught 1,980 pupils, just 19 percent of workers' children between the ages of seven and fourteen.[48]

47. *ZhN*, May 25, 1902, pp. 302–5; *Zhel.*, 23, November 2, 1903, p. 3.
48. *ZhN*, March 9, 1902, p. 125; July 7, 1901, pp. 423–24; *ZhD*, 1902, 13–14, p. 139; Maruta, p. 26. See also on the Catherine Railroad, TsGIA, f. 273, op. 8, d. 126, ll. 16–17, and the Riazan-Ural Railroad, *ZhD*, 1903, 46–47, p. 495.

Such educational facilities were just part of a broader network of cultural institutions—including libraries and tea rooms, lectures and theater programs—that some railroads began to offer workers in the 1890s. *Popechitelstvo* (literally "guardianship," a term used to designate largely paternalistic programs aimed at promoting "enlightenment" and "sobriety" among the workers) was in general most extensively practiced in provincial centers, where often the railroad terminal, its depot, shops, and offices, stood somewhat apart from city life. Railroad cultural institutions were less extensive at smaller stations, where railwaymen were fewer and more scattered, and in Moscow and St. Petersburg, where they could more readily mingle with other workers and urban facilities were somewhat more accessible and developed.

Two lines that paid considerable attention to cultural programs were the South West Railroad and the Kursk-Kharkov-Sevastopol Railroad. In 1897 the former began an extensive program of Sunday lectures and readings. In 1900–1901, 143 lectures with a total attendance of nearly 100,000 were held at nine different stations. At the road's Kiev workshops lectures were accompanied by performances of a small workers' orchestra and chorus. Although the first library only opened on the South West Railroad in 1896, shortly after Nemeshaev took over, within two years there were ten branches with 23,000 volumes, serving 1,500 dues-paying readers. In addition, two railroad library cars, each with a collection of about 1,500 volumes, toured the line regularly, like bookmobiles on rails, to provide service to more isolated stations. At the Aleksandrovsk shops of the Kursk-Kharkov-Sevastopol Railroad, the *Popechitelstvo o narodnoi trezvosti* (Guardianship for Popular Sobriety), chaired by the workshops' manager, ran a small cultural center that included a theater with seating for 340, a tea and reading room, and a recreation hall for dances and games. In 1902, 34 theatrical performances, 30 lectures, and 18 dances were held for the workers.[49]

On these and other lines both the content and patronage of cultural programs were limited. A great proportion of both guest speakers and library materials were religious, and many workers no doubt resented the programs' very obvious propagandistic and

49. *ZhN*, April 6, 1902, pp. 192–94; March 17, 1900, pp. 167–69; *ZhD*, 1903, 13–14, p. 154; 1904, 9, pp. 79–81; 10, pp. 89–91.

paternalist character. At the Aleksandrovsk shops more than half the titles in the reading room were devoted to religious themes, and almost 90 percent of patrons were under seventeen, mainly sons and daughters of railroad workers.[50] Reports published in the railroad press on patronage and reading patterns in libraries on the South West, Perm, Samara-Zlatoust, and Siberian Railroads, however, indicate that library patrons could be found among adults too and at all levels of the work force, both white- and blue-collar. A library serving the Kursk terminal of the Moscow-Kiev-Voronezh line boasted nearly 9,000 volumes in 1909, with more than 100 checked out each day. In 1901 a branch opened at the road's Konotop workshops, but it closed two years later. A 1903 strike demanded its reopening, which came in February 1904. Within a year the library had 2,184 books and 921 regular subscribers.[51]

Readers evidenced a strong interest in popular literature, the Russian classics, travel books, and works of popular history. On the Riazan-Ural Railroad it was reported in 1905 that railwaymen spent 48,378 rubles per month on newspaper and journal subscriptions, or 1.5 percent of the line's wage bill, although the most popular publications were mass journals such as *Niva* and *Rodina*, with 1,697 and 949 subscriptions respectively. In some cases the libraries and *popechitelstvo* programs could even in a very limited way offer access to oppositional thought, despite the clear intent of management to use such programs to divert workers from revolutionary temptations. At the Kovrov shops of the Moscow-Kursk Railroad, the library and "sobriety" group were staffed by local *zemstvo* activists, mainly future Kadets, who, according to the memoir of one craftsman, surreptitiously introduced library patrons to literature critical of the established order and assisted in forming the first socialist circles at the workshops.[52]

At the start of 1905 the Russian railroads were ripe for revolutionary unrest. Leaving aside for a moment the general and deeply

50. TsGIA, f. 273, op. 12, d. 46, l. 600.

51. *ZhN*, February 11, 1900, pp. 91–92; March 17, 1900, pp. 167–69; August 4, 1900, pp. 488–89; *Zhel.*, 61, July 27, 1904, pp. 21–22; Ivan Maruta, *Ocherki po istorii revoliutsionnogo professional'nogo dvizheniia na Moskovsko-Kievo-Voronezhskoi zh. d.* (Kursk, 1925), pp. 24–25.

52. *Privol. kr.*, 9, January 13, 1905, p. 3; TsGAOR, f. 6865, d. 29a, l. 43. See also d. 122, l. 8.

rooted economic and political crisis gripping the entire empire, the railroads themselves had by 1905 reached a critical point. With productivity stagnant at best, and growth of the work force uncontrolled, railroad managers found it impossible to continue the largely ad hoc labor policies of autocratic paternalism that had predominated in the nineteenth century. Simultaneously, railroad workers saw their economic position declining relative to that of other sections of the working class, even as educated and urbanized youth with higher expectations were beginning to play a more important part in the railroad economy and as the general educational and cultural level of railroad labor continued to rise.

Given the crisis of the railroad economy, in which managers were already crying for a restructuring of labor relations, workers sought to redefine their roles. Shop craftsmen were motivated by more than a concern with wages and hours. Forced to respond to changes in the organization of work, their principal demand would be greater *participation* in production decisions. Demands for participation could also appeal to administrative staff and engine-drivers who sought to actualize the promises of paternalism. Insofar as this concern motivated rebellious workers, the transition from economic grievances to political activism would not be very hard. Demands for participation and respect on the job led inexorably to similar demands of society.

When the railroads were young, many railwaymen could and did understand their situation as unique. They were Russia's industrial pioneers, white- and blue-collar together, technical engineers and engine-drivers alike, extending modernity to the furthest corners of the empire. Hence, a special and separate professional aura grew up around railroad work. By 1905, however, the changing position of railroad workers was tending to draw many of them into the larger world of the urban working class. If the special mystique of the "railroad family" could help keep the bulk of railwaymen relatively passive in the nineteenth century, by 1900 professional ties could offer an effective vehicle for mobilization as part of a broader opposition.

Participation within a broader opposition would, however, force railroad workers to examine the divisions within their own ranks. Were railwaymen a unified professional group, or were some railwaymen part of a larger class, the proletariat, whose interests differed from those of other railwaymen who were not members of this class? That question, moreover, was inextricably joined with the problem of which brand of politics offered railroad workers a motivating vision and explanation of their situation and a practical road out of it.

Part Two

Railroad Workers in Revolution

The goals of the railroad employees are, in
essence, those of all Russian society.
Birzhevye vedomosti,
February 24, 1905

Five

First Assaults and the Time of Petitioning

Labor disturbances on Russian railroads began among the private and state serfs recruited to build new lines during the 1840s and 1850s. These peaked in 1860, after which unrest among construction laborers was drastically reduced by passage of more favorable regulations governing peasant labor.[1] The first strikes in railroad operations and repair came in the early 1870s. According to incomplete figures compiled by I. M. Pushkareva, from the first known strike—at the Aleksandrovsk workshops of the Catherine Railroad in 1872—to 1905, there were at least 237 recorded disturbances, confrontations with management, and strikes on Russian railroads. Twenty-nine incidents took place between 1875 and 1884, 33 between 1885 and 1894, and 171 between 1895 and 1904.[2] Before 1905 unrest developed almost exclusively among shop craftsmen. Although wage cuts and deteriorating working conditions were protested, these issues were closely linked to another precipitant of unrest, the evolution of work organization.

1. G. I. Ionova, "Rabochee dvizhenie v Rossii v period revoliutsionnoi situatsii, 1859–1861 gg.," in *Iz istorii rabochego klassa i revoliutsionnogo dvizheniia*, ed. M. V. Nechkina et al. (Moscow, 1958), and S. Tokarev, "Volneniia rabochikh na postroikakh zheleznykh dorog v 1859–1860 godakh," *Voprosy istorii*, 1949, no. 1: 88–92.
2. I. M. Pushkareva, *Zheleznodorozhniki Rossii v burzhuazno-demokraticheskikh revoliutsiiakh* (Moscow, 1975), pp. 75–76. TsGAOR, f. 6865, d. 29a, ll. 161–78, contains a useful chronology of important strikes on Russian railroads before 1905.

During the late 1870s and 1880s, between the two railroad construction booms, efforts to systematize labor relations in the workshops more effectively created unrest. With demand for skilled labor slackening, standardized work procedures were increasingly introduced and a more formalized wage structure instituted, often resulting in attacks on the advantages enjoyed by craftsmen. Strikes also arose in response to wage cuts and especially to the often confusing and irregular system of pay, including the failure of management to release wages on schedule, an all-too-common occurrence, especially on private railroads.[3] The increasing involvement of the state in railroading could also cause problems.[4]

Workers objected to the introduction of more restrictive procedures, to the absence of a clearly defined shop order, and to the foreman's emergence as an agent of management. Hostility was often focused on especially unpopular managers or foremen, and specific outrages would often provoke resentment. An official investigating one disturbance noted that much dissatisfaction stemmed from "confusion among the workers concerning rules and fines." He charged that no pay-books and no copies of the labor contract had been distributed, although in practice the shops were burdened with an overabundance of superfluous regulations.[5]

Although striking railroad metalworkers could still command substantial bargaining power, most railroad strikes in this period remained defensive and were easily defeated. According to Pushkareva's survey, before the 1890s only two railroad strikes—in the workshops of the South West Railroad in Kiev and the South East Railroad in Voronezh, both in 1879—achieved even partial victories. Typical of this period was the battle waged by workers at the St. Petersburg shops of the Nicholas Railroad between 1877 and 1880. On October 25, 1877, workers in the carriage shop pelted the director with mud to protest new regulations that only thinly

3. *Rabochee dvizhenie v Rossii v XIX veke: Sbornik dokumentov i materialov* (Moscow and Leningrad, 1950–63), vol. 2, pt. 2, pp. 235–36, 300, 458–60; TsGAOR, f. 6865, d. 29a, l. 6; d. 39b, l. 1; A. Elnitskii, *Istoriia rabochego dvizheniia v Rossii* (Moscow, 1924), vol. 1, p. 27.

4. Ivan Maruta, *Ocherki po istorii revoliutsionnogo professional'nogo dvizheniia na Moskovsko-Kievo-Voronezhskoi zh. d.* (Kursk, 1925), p. 21.

5. TsGAOR, f. 6865, d. 45, l. 29; *Rabochee dvizhenie*, vol. 2, pt. 2, p. 548; vol. 3, pt. 1, pp. 396–98, 411–13, 529–31, 533–35.

disguised a cut in the piece rate. The next May another set of rules was distributed, first in the boiler shop and then in the forges, where 400 workers protested a provision that workers could be employed on Sundays and holidays. Finally, on May 10, 1880, a crowd of a thousand workers demonstrated at the gates demanding a just wage, and 1,500 struck. According to an official report, these incidents stemmed from two causes. One was the economic slowdown of these years, but another was the poorly defined character of labor relations, stemming in this instance from the incompetence and lack of interest of a foreign management team. There was no written contract, so the British manager was free to operate "secretly." His staff were also of little assistance, as all the foremen were foreigners and most could speak hardly a word of Russian.[6]

The breakneck expansion of the railroad system during the 1890s was accompanied by an acceleration of the strike movement, which was still, however, restricted to shop and depot craftsmen. The pace of unrest began to pick up during the first half of the decade, but between 1895 and 1904 the number of railroad strikes was three times that of the previous two decades combined. Of 171 strikes during these years, 154 involved shop craftsmen, and only 17 operations, administrative, or track maintenance personnel.[7] The issues that had sparked resistance in previous decades, centering about the transformation of the factory order, remained paramount in the 1890s, as the pace at which work organization was changing quickened. The strikes of the late 1890s grew more assertive and less defensive, however.[8] After 1900 workers responded to the onset of economic crisis with increasingly militant resistance, in which railroad metalworkers often acted in concert with craftsmen in private industry, and political agitators, mostly Social Democrats, made significant headway.

6. *Rabochee dvizhenie*, vol. 2, pt. 2, pp. 203–4, 292–93, 423. See also TsGAOR, f. 6865, d. 29a, l. 40; d. 39b, l. 1.
7. Pushkareva, *Zheleznodorozhniki*, p. 79.
8. A prolonged and successful strike at the Rostov-on-Don shops of the Vladikavkaz Railroad in 1894 marked a key turning point. See TsGAOR, f. 6865, d. 29a, ll. 25–37; "Stachka zheleznodorozhnykh rabochikh v Rostove-na-D. v 1894 g. (rasskaz rabochego-ochevidtsa)," *Byloe* 18 (1921): 124–27; Henry Reichman, "Russian Railwaymen and the Revolution of 1905," Ph.D. diss., University of California, Berkeley, 1977, pp. 95–98.

Acquisition of formerly private railroads by the state treasury during the Witte years contributed to labor unrest, since the reorganization of recently purchased lines offered managers a convenient opportunity to attack worker privileges and workers transferred during the transition sometimes spread the lessons of previous disturbances.[9] Transfer of control from one private entrepreneur to another could also provoke resistance. On June 23, 1893, 1,200 workers in the Moscow shops of the Moscow-Kazan Railroad, which had recently passed into the hands of new owners, struck to protest establishment of the new ministry pension fund, which the strikers feared could mean the loss of deposits in a company savings plan.

Although the shop craftsmen walked out, a group of office employees also filed a petition of protest, which placed the strike in a broader context of changing labor relations:

In the past, when the road's administration was in the hands of intelligent, decent, and honorable men . . . the very idea of protest would not even have occurred to us, because in those good times management was attentive to its employees and dealt with them in a Christian and human way. Wages were paid according to assigned rates for each position and not at half those rates as now. In those days appropriate housing subsidies were paid to all, where now only a few receive them. In a word, the employee had no cause to complain of a poor life—he was valued by management, not driven from service, repeatedly fined without cause, and burdened by overwork, in short, treated not as a dog, but as a man.

But times have changed. . . . Employee salaries are cut in hâlf, as are the wages of craftsmen. At the same time working hours are increased while the number of engine-drivers, switchmen, conductors, and employees is reduced to the very minimum. . . . Under the old administration there were no deductions for the pension fund. Usually management and shareholders assigned a designated percentage of income to pension payments and did not reach into workers' pockets. . . . Now the employees themselves, the majority of whom will never receive a pension, are taxed. . . . Moreover, not a single employee has been given an account book in which deductions can be recorded and their accuracy checked. . . . From all sides they take our money, but say nothing of how it will be used.

9. For examples, an 1892 strike on the Kursk-Kharkov-Sevastopol Railroad, an 1895 walkout on the Moscow-Kursk line, and an 1898 strike in the Tiflis shops of the Transcaucasian Railroad (TsGAOR, f. 6865, d. 45, ll. 27, 30–32; d. 39b, l. 2; d. 127, l. 20; d. 29a, l. 9).

The petitioners complained that the company store sold expensive, but shoddy, goods and that the railroad and the Ministry of Internal Affairs frustrated efforts to organize a consumer cooperative. They pointed out that the line was one of the wealthiest in Russia and had recently received a hefty allocation from the state to finance expansion from its former terminus at Riazan. "The current manager," the petition concluded, "is a German Jew who can't stand Russians and replaces them at each opportunity with German Jews. Can one really expect any good from this non-Russian? He is one of the main causes of dissatisfaction among the craftsmen and is responsible for many oppressive measures."[10]

If a transfer of ownership could concentrate and crystallize grievances, the developments feared by workers in such circumstances were to some extent universal. Although articulated appeals to an idealized past like this Moscow-Kazan petition were exceptional, by the mid 1890s many railroad workers, especially in the workshops, were growing conscious of their ebbing power over the pace and organization of work. Some of this was surely imagined, but in the context of the rapid and chaotic expansion of railroading, such changes no doubt seemed especially threatening.[11]

By 1900 a typical program of demands was emerging as the frequency of strikes rapidly increased and their impact broadened. Everywhere workers fought over the setting of hourly wage and piece rates and protested the depredations of their foremen, demands that reflected an attempt to maintain control over the work process. Strikers were also concerned about the length of the work day. Demands for early Saturday closings and holiday pay were subsumed into calls for the establishment of nine- or even eight-hour days. According to a report by the Administration of Railroads, of thirty-three strikes in railroad workshops between 1899 and 1903, thirteen called for establishment of the eight- or nine-hour day.[12]

10. TsGAOR, f. 6865, d. 23, ll. 13–18. The craftsmen of the Moscow-Kazan shops struck again in 1895 to protest pension fund deductions, inaccurate wage payments, and "discourteous treatment" by foremen (TsGAOR, f. 6865, d. 29a, l. 8; d. 30, ll. 7–9).

11. *Rabochee dvizhenie*, vol. 4, pt. 1, pp. 247–49, 355–56, 367, 737; pt. 2, p. 359; TsGAOR, f. 6865, d. 29a, l. 9; d. 39b, l. 3; d. 24; *Rabochee dvizhenie v Ekaterinoslave* (Geneva, 1900), pp. 3, 8–9.

12. TsGIA, f. 273, op. 12, d. 354, l. 30.

Most important, however, was the increasing politicization of the strike movement and its growing connection to unrest among other industrial workers. Revolutionary agitation in the railroad shops can be traced as early as the late 1870s. In the 1890s young Marxists spread their influence among railroad craftsmen in Moscow, St. Petersburg, and various cities in the south. The Moscow shops of the Moscow-Kazan Railroad—where a revolutionary circle was organized by the daughter of the priest at the nearby Pokrovsky Church, the future wife of the noted Bolshevik M. V. Bonch-Bruevich—and the Moscow-Kursk Railroad, as well as those of the Vladikavkaz Railroad in Rostov-on-Don, where revolutionary work had continued sporadically since the early 1880s, were key centers of agitation. In 1898 Social Democratic literature was even found in the shops of the Perm-Tiumen Railroad in distant Ekaterinburg.[13]

Gradually such agitation produced a small core of radical worker-intellectuals. Although many such men were at most cautious organizers and somewhat elitist in their attitudes toward fellow workers, it was they who often conveyed radical ideas to more restive younger craftsmen. For instance, A. Liakhin, a metalworker at the Kovrov shops of the Moscow-Kursk line, recalled how upon becoming an apprentice in 1895 he almost immediately fell under the wing of Fedor Matveevich Ivanov, "who treated me as a son." Before working on the railroad Ivanov had served in the navy and worked in Petersburg, Helsinki, and "even, he claimed, in France." Liakhin remembered him as the "first worker in all the shops who, if not an organizer, was at any event a participant in the workers' movement. By comparison with run-of-the-mill workers, he was more developed, but not so much as to organize a group or circle. His convictions were by no means clear—he still considered himself a peasant, but adopted the title 'socialist.'"

It was Ivanov who introduced young Liakhin to dissident literature, beginning with the oppositional newspaper *Syn otechestva*. More important, the aging craftsman communicated an important sense of self-respect and resistance to authority. He preached that workers "should read and not drink vodka." Ivanov ordered his young disciple never to remove his cap for the director, threatening to cut off all contact if he dared do so. "It's funny now to recall such

13. Reichman, "Russian Railwaymen," pp. 88–89, 92, 94–95.

a trifle," Liakhin later wrote, "but then this was a sharp challenge, whose consequences could not be foreseen, as generally only the highest administrators conversed with the director wearing a hat. Even the old men would stand a half hour in the cold capless, but we dared and the result was unexpected—the foreman warned us we could be fired for such impudence; nonetheless our wages increased ten kopeks a day."[14]

When the rapid development of the 1890s stalled abruptly in response to a tightening of the international money market in 1898 and other factors, the ensuing five-year downturn, which saw more than 3,000 enterprises close their doors and over 100,000 workers turned out of work, brought to a head the festering contradictions of the tsarist system. The crisis was particularly acute in the new industrial regions of the south, where it was compounded by poor harvests. The railroads were also affected by the depression, but railwaymen did not face the employment pressures of private industry, as the number of workers continued to grow and labor fluidity stayed high. Consequently, the railroad strike movement remained vigorous. Especially in provincial centers, railroad workshops and depots were often prime targets of revolutionary agitation and played a disproportionate part in the small, but ominous, May Day and other demonstrations of these years. Railroad craftsmen often galvanized broader sections of the working class into motion, most notably in the series of general strikes that swept south Russia and the Caucasus in 1902–3.[15]

Two events in 1900, the May Day street demonstrations in Kharkov and the major summer strike in the Tiflis workshops of the Transcaucasian Railroad, together marked a turning point in the emergence of the railroad labor movement. In Kharkov workers at the repair shops and depot of the Kursk-Kharkov-Sevastopol Rail-

14. TsGAOR, f. 6865, d. 29a, ll. 40–42.
15. Petr Liashchenko, *History of the National Economy of Russia* (New York, 1949), p. 656, was the first to stress the role of the railroad workshops in the strike movement of the early twentieth century, although he tended to exaggerate the extent of unrest. In a 1903 secret report, the Black Sea *guberniia* governor noted that "the highest degree of agitation in Chernomorskaia *guberniia*, as in the entire southern Rostov and Caucasian region, is observed precisely among the railroad workers. This is not without cause: there is no control, no supervision over the actions of the railroad administration, no regularized work rules" (TsGIA, f. 273, op. 12, d. 46, l. 512).

road composed the overwhelming majority of the nearly 2,000 workers who marched behind red flags on May 1 and clashed with police in what Lenin later greeted as a major moment in the political emergence of the Russian working class.[16] The Tiflis strike was the largest railroad walkout yet, and the first to affect freight movement seriously. It began in late July after a group of machinists refused overtime, but the struggle soon expanded, and the entire depot closed for nearly two weeks. The strikers demanded shorter hours, improved wages and piece rates, and "courteous treatment" by foremen and managers.[17]

Similar demands were raised in strikes on the Riazan-Ural Railroad in Saratov and Tambov, the Nicholas Railroad in St. Petersburg, the Briansk shops of the Moscow-Kiev-Voronezh line, and again in the Tiflis shops in 1901; at the Krasnoiarsk shops of the new Siberian Railroad in 1902; and in the St. Petersburg shops of the St. Petersburg-Warsaw road and the Borisoglebsk shops of the South East Railroad in the first months of 1903.[18] The most important walkout, however, was the great Rostov general strike of November 1902, in which a disturbance at the workshops of the Vladikavkaz Railroad quickly expanded into a paralyzing citywide strike. The Rostov events were especially significant because the movement quickly took on a political character. Foreshadowing 1905, strikers and middle-class supporters gathered in illegal mass meetings of up to 30,000 to hear Social Democratic and other dissident orators call for political freedom and socialism, but "for the whole time the strike of workers at the Rostov railroad shops remained at the core of the movement."[19]

16. "Zabastovka v Kharkove na Mae 1, 1900 g." *Krasnyi arkhiv*, 93 (1939): 189–207; *Pervoe maia v tsarskoi Rossii, 1890–1916 gg. Sbornik dokumentov* (Moscow, 1939), pp. 37–38; *Maiskie dni v Kharkove* (Geneva, 1901); TsGAOR, f. 6865, d. 35, ll. 223–27; d. 45, ll. 43–44.

17. TsGIA, f. 273, op. 12, d. 45, ll. 200–221; "Stachka rabochikh zheleznodorozhnykh masterskikh v Tiflise (1900 g.)," *Krasnyi arkhiv*, 94 (1939): 32–63; S. T. Arkomed, *Rabochee dvizhenie i Sotsial-Demokratiia na Kavkaze* (Moscow, 1923); and Reichman, "Russian Railwaymen," pp. 102–10.

18. On Saratov and Tambov: TsGIA, f. 273, op. 12, d. 45, ll. 328–38, 475–80, and *Iskra*, 7, p. 5; 9, p. 6. On the Nicholas road: TsGIA, f. 273, op. 12, d. 45, ll. 325–27. On Briansk: Maruta, pp. 28–29, and *Iskra*, 15, p. 4. On Tiflis: *Iskra*, 12, p. 3. On Krasnoiarsk: TsGIA, f. 273, op. 12, d. 45, ll. 340–56. On Borisoglebsk: TsGIA, f. 273, op. 12, d. 46, ll. 323–82; d. 226, ll. 563–83; *Iskra*, 44, p. 5.

19. V. A. Posse, *Vseobshchye stachki* (Geneva, 1903), p. 91. On the Rostov events and their significance for both railwaymen and the revolutionary move-

Government officials were growing increasingly concerned about the spreading unrest. On November 4, 1902, just as the Rostov disturbances were beginning, a special meeting "to discuss measures for terminating criminal assaults on the security of railroad movement" convened in St. Petersburg with Minister of Internal Affairs V. K. von Plehve in the chair and Khilkov, Witte, Minister of War A. I. Kuropatkin, and other leading bureaucrats attending. Several railroad directors, including Nemeshaev of the South West Railroad, recommended concessions to some of the most pressing worker demands, including the eight-hour day and increased benefits for shop craftsmen. But a preparatory commission agreed with Khilkov to offer only periodic bonuses to permanent staff employees. The meeting itself decisively rejected economic concessions, particularly the eight-hour day, which as "a slogan of the socialist parties in the West and one of the central elements of foreign revolutionary propaganda among our workers" could have an "undesirable and wrong effect." The meeting accepted Plehve's proposal to increase the size and funding of the railroad police. More important, in order "to create among the workers a more settled cadre hostile to alien influences," it was agreed to extend permanent staff status to an additional 40,000 craftsmen. These proposals were approved by the tsar on August 20, 1903, but never fully implemented. The modest steps taken were not popular among railroad administrators, who complained of the cost and also recognized the futility of seeking to assuage unrest by expanding the ranks of the privileged when this group itself, although not yet striking, was also growing restive.[20]

Signs of such restiveness could be seen in the unprecedented general strikes that rocked Tiflis, Baku, Odessa, Kiev, Ekaterino-

ment, see Henry Reichman, "The Rostov General Strike of 1902," *Russian History* 9, pt. 1 (1982): 67–85. Also: A. Stanchinskii, "Rostovskaia stachka v 1902 godu," *Proletarskaia Revoliutsiia*, 1927, no. 12(71): 141–70; and Amvrosii (pseud.), *Pravda o Rostovskikh sobytiiakh* (Stuttgart, 1903).

20. Minutes of the meeting were leaked to the underground press and appeared in *Osvobozhdenie*, no. 38 (14), December 25, 1903, pp. 255–57. See also TsGAOR, f. 6865, d. 29a, ll. 14–15; N. Rostov, *Prolog pervoi revoliutsii. Zheleznodorozhniki i pervaia vseobshchaia zabastovka v 1903 godu* (Moscow, 1928), pp. 13–16; and Rostov, "Zheleznodorozhniki v pervoi revoliutsii," *Proletariat v revoliutsii 1905–1907 gg.* (Moscow, 1930), p. 130.

slav, and other southern cities in the summer of 1903.[21] In Tiflis the movement was by 1900 dominated by Georgians, for whom the assertion of class demands and the following of Marxist leadership were closely linked to the emergence of nationalism; in 1903 and again in early 1905 a small minority of "exclusively Russian" shop workers opposed strike actions and declared their loyalty to the regime. In Baku, by contrast, railroad workers were predominantly Russian, and as such were largely isolated from the city's mainly Muslim and Armenian labor movement. Where in Tiflis the railroad shops emerged as a center of activity for all the city's workers, in Baku the strike of railwaymen, though significant, was in the end subsumed into the larger movement of oil workers. Most important, however, "the disorders in Tiflis and Baku were echoed along all lines of the Transcaucasian Railroad." Strike activity occurred among engine-drivers and station operations personnel in Batum, Chiatur', Toroplin, Sharopan', Kvirily, and Borzhoma, linked in part with growing peasant disorders and strikes among manganese miners.[22]

In Odessa, where the city was engulfed by a movement of elemental force, a strike in the shops of the South West Railroad, perhaps inspired by activists in the Zubatovist Independent Labor Group, began the rebellion, although the railwaymen returned to work after Nemeshaev arrived from Kiev with concessions and the citywide strike that followed was dominated by longshoremen, artisans, and urban transport workers. In Kiev the strike was planned by local Social Democrats, whose leadership was concentrated in the administration and workshops of the South West Railroad, where the strike began and remained centered. The Kiev walkout not only disrupted the city and the movement of trains, but revealed divisions within the government, as the Ministry of Internal

---

21. On the role of railroad workers in the 1903 strikes, see Rostov, *Prolog pervoi revoliutsii*, pp. 20–120, and Reichman, "Russian Railwaymen," pp. 152–98. Also: TsGAOR, f. 6865, d. 35, ll. 86–114; TsGIA, f. 273, op. 12, d. 46, ll. 6–7, 139–46, 419–32; "Svedeniia o volneniiakh rabochikh proiskhodivshikh v iule i avguste 1903 goda," *Krasnyi arkhiv* 88 (1938): 76–122; A. Lopukhin, "Zapiska direktora departmenta politsii Lopukhina stachkakh v iule 1903 g. v Odesse, Kieve i Nikolaeve," *Krasnaia letopis'* 4 (1922): 382–95; the documents in *Vseobshchaia stachka na iuge Rossii v. 1903 godu. Sbornik dokumentov* (Moscow, 1938); and F. E. Los', ed., *Revoliutsiia 1905–1907 gg. na Ukraine* (Kiev, 1955), vol. 1.

22. TsGIA, f. 273, op. 12, d. 322, ll. 53–55, 263; "Svedeniia," p. 82.

Affairs lodged vigorous protests against the actions of Nemeshaev, who in several speeches to striking railwaymen promised concessions, a conflict that would resume in 1905. Railroad workers were also central to the general strikes in Ekaterinoslav, headquarters of the Catherine Railroad, and Konotop, site of the main shops of the Moscow-Kiev-Voronezh line.[23]

Although confined to the south, these strikes reflected the development of unrest in the working class—and among railroad craftsmen in particular—that was national in scope. In Moscow, the largest railroad center, similar tensions were percolating below the surface. The Moscow Zubatovists found a following in the workshops of the Moscow-Kursk line, but contrary to the plans of these "police socialists," the contacts developed in Zubatovist tea rooms and libraries also spurred the organization of Social Democratic groups; in early 1904 the first Social Democratic circle was formed in the shops of the Moscow-Kazan Railroad.[24] A few Moscow employees and engine-drivers were beginning to consider organizing, turning to the liberal activists of the Museum for Assistance to Labor for aid.

Before 1905 the movement of railroad workers was not a professional one. The craftsmen of the railroad repair facilities were distinct from other metalworkers, but their strikes tended to expand outward into other branches of the metalworking industry and then further on a citywide basis to other sectors of the working class rather than along the railroad lines. This reflected, too, their alienation from other segments of the railroad work force. Still, a significant development of the 1903 strikes was the extent to which they began to attract support from railroad workers outside the shops, on the Transcaucasian Railroad especially. In the Ukraine the strike wave "was localized in separate workshops only because the older engine-drivers refused to support the *manevrushki* and rank-and-file workers."[25]

The war with Japan put a temporary halt to the developing unrest; railroad reformers like the editors of *Zheleznodorozhnik* ini-

23. TsGAOR, f. 6865, d. 35, ll. 103–4; TsGIA, f. 273, op. 12, d. 46, ll. 419–20, 32–33.
24. TsGAOR, f. 6865, d. 127, l. 36; A. I. Gorchilin, *1905 god na Kazanke* (Moscow, 1934), p. 6.
25. TsGAOR, f. 6865, d. 45, l. 66.

tially greeted the declaration of war with patriotic enthusiasm, and so did many workers. But, as previously noted, wartime disruptions ultimately exacerbated problems, and the transfer of workers to war-burdened lines tended to spread unrest and feelings of solidarity. Moreover, once the initial wave of patriotism subsided, the war, coupled with the somewhat more liberal policies of the government in the wake of Plehve's assassination, acted to broaden the horizons of some workers. In the Kovrov shops, one activist later recalled, the war "provoked heated debate . . . which created an opportunity for open propaganda." Among employees on the Vladikavkaz Railroad in Rostov-on-Don the war occasioned a "desire to read newspapers" among hitherto narrow-minded clerks. "Gradually a group emerged from the more developed and energetic who, at first cautiously, only among themselves, but then ever louder began to say that our failures at the front were a direct consequence of the existing regime."[26]

With the war going poorly, by late 1904 Russia stood on the eve of a major crisis. During Prince Sviatopolk-Mirsky's liberal "spring" the intelligentsia opposition, reformist and revolutionary, gained strength and boldness—the revolutionaries despite the internecine fighting between Bolshevik and Menshevik Social Democrats. But it was workers, acting by and large independently of the organizational influence of the liberation movement, who finally sparked the conflagration. The first flash came in December 1904 in Baku, where a 22-day general strike paralyzed the city. The walkout mainly affected the oil fields and refineries, but its force was also felt in the railroad shops and depot, where a foreman was murdered on December 21. Several days later railroad workers joined the strike.[27]

The decisive match was struck, however, in St. Petersburg.

26. TsGAOR, f. 6865, d. 29a, l. 45; *1905 vo vospominaniiakh ego uchastnikov* (Rostov-on-Don, 1925), pp. 6–7.
27. TsGIA, f. 273, op. 12, d. 322, l. 6. On the Baku strike, see E. L. Keenan, "Remarques sur l'histoire du mouvement révolutionnaire à Bakou (1904–1905)," *Cahiers du monde russe et sovietique* 3, no. 2 (1962): 225–60, and Solomon M. Schwarz, *The Russian Revolution of 1905* (Chicago, 1967), pp. 301–14. For Soviet views, see V. Nevskii, "Dekabr'skaia zabastovka 1904 g. v Baku," *Proletarskaia revoliutsiia*, 1924, no. 2 (25): 46–84, and A. N. Guliev, "Stachka Bakinskikh rabochikh v dekabre 1904 goda," *Voprosy istorii*, 1954, no. 12: 26–38.

Here the Assembly of Russian Factory Workers, a unique and fascinating movement led by Father Georgii Gapon, had quietly built a major following in working-class districts. A December dispute over the firing of four Assembly members at the giant Putilov plant soon snowballed into a major strike movement, and by the close of work on January 7 all but 25,000 of the capital's 175,000 factory workers were out. The purpose of the strike was not always entirely clear to those who joined, but as the movement grew, political questions began to be raised. The Gapon organization hit upon the idea of sponsoring a peaceful march to the Winter Palace demanding a redress of grievances. Their petition, couched in terms of humble loyalty to the monarchy, was a crude amalgam of the liberal political program with measures designed to alleviate the workers' economic misery. The march was scheduled for Sunday, January 9, and its result is well known. The brutal slaughter of innocent workmen marching peacefully with their families, many carrying icons and portraits of the tsar, singing religious hymns, galvanized oppositional sentiment and, more than the march's program of political demands itself, began the transformation of a basically economic strike movement into a political revolution.[28]

Although Gapon and his Assembly of Russian Factory Workers seemed to disappear virtually overnight, the St. Petersburg strikers continued their walkout and were joined by other workers, students, and professionals. In Moscow strikes began January 10; by January 12 other Russian cities were engulfed, and within a week there was unrest in virtually every industrial area. Nearly 500,000 workers struck in January 1905—more than the combined total for the entire previous decade. By the month's end the movement had ebbed somewhat, but in early February new strikes began, centered now on the Moscow railroad junction. By the middle of the month there was a near-general railroad strike in several regions and industrial walkouts continued in most major cities.

28. The quantity of literature on Bloody Sunday is staggering: the 1930 Soviet bibliography *Pervaia Russkaia revoliutsiia: ukazatel' literatury* (Moscow, 1930), pp. 92–96, alone lists seventy-six Russian-language entries. For collected documents, see N. S. Trusova, ed., *Nachalo pervoi revoliutsii, ianvar'–mart, 1905 god* (Moscow, 1955), pp. 3–126. In the Western literature, see Walter Sablinsky, *The Road to Bloody Sunday* (Princeton, N.J., 1976), and Gerald Surh, "Petersburg's First Mass Labor Organization: The Assembly of Russian Workers and Father Gapon," *Russian Review*, pt. 1, 40, no. 3 (1981): 241–62; pt. 2, 40, no. 4 (1981): 412–41.

In his account of 1905 Trotsky wrote of the January events that "the railway personnel act as detonators of the strike. The railway lines are the channels along which the strike epidemic spreads."[29] But a more sober Menshevik rendering pointed out that though "in February, railroad strikes seized nearly all the networks of roads, in January only the first signs of this movement could be noted."[30] In January strikes seized workshops in St. Petersburg, Moscow, and several other cities, but service was affected only in Poland, the Baltic provinces, the Caucasus, and, in Russia proper, on the Riazan-Ural Railroad.

Response to the Gapon movement among St. Petersburg railroad workers was weak, with only a few branches of the Assembly of Russian Factory Workers functioning in the railroad workshops. The first railroad shops to join the strike movement were those of the Nicholas Railroad, where on January 7 strikers issued a list of demands "in full solidarity with the demands of a general character raised by workers of other plants." They were joined the same day by craftsmen at the depots of the Baltic and Moscow-Vindau-Rybinsk Railroads. On January 8 workers at the depot of the St. Petersburg–Warsaw Railroad also walked out. All other railroad workers and employees in St. Petersburg, however, remained at their posts until January 9.[31]

After Bloody Sunday St. Petersburg railwaymen continued to offer the movement lukewarm support. Strikes continued at the workshops that went out on the eve of the big demonstration, but only the shops of the St. Petersburg–Warsaw line struck afterward, and then only on January 17. On the Baltic Railroad the walkout ended on January 12, well before the national reaction peaked.[32] The largest strike was on the Nicholas road, where on January 12 workers in the locomotive department released a new list of thirty-five demands, mainly economic, but including a call for a constituent assembly based on universal suffrage and freedom of speech, the press, assembly, to form unions, and to strike. A crowd of over

29. Leon Trotsky, *1905*, trans. Anya Bostock (New York, 1972), p. 81.

30. E. Maevskii, "Obshchaia kartina dvizheniia," in *Obshchestvennoe dvizhenie v Rossii v nachale XX veka*, ed. Iu. Martov (St. Petersburg, 1909–14), vol. 3, pt. 1, p. 54.

31. B. Krugliakov, "Zabastovki sredi zheleznodorozhnikov v nachale 1905 godu v Peterburge," *Krasnaia letopis'* 12 (1925): 59–60.

32. Ibid., p. 65.

1,000 strikers assembled to present this petition to management, but "in view of the absence of solidarity" among them, the director decided to read the list aloud. When the first paragraph of the declaration, concerning the constituent assembly and democratic rights, was read, he reported, the crowd cried out "as one man" that "they didn't read this to us and we don't want it." Similarly, in the carriage department a fifteen-point declaration with five political demands was prefaced by a statement that these latter were "not obligatory." By January 13, 350 of 1,610 strikers had returned to work in the locomotive shops, and 560 of 1,705 in the carriage shops. On January 14 the strike ended.[33]

Workers in Moscow, the central railroad junction, were among the first to respond to the St. Petersburg shootings, and by January 14, the peak of the strike movement there, some 30,000 workers from various industries were out. But the response of Moscow railwaymen was limited, poorly organized, and short-lived; "in general the demands of the railwaymen were not met."[34] The workshops of the Moscow-Kursk Railroad were the first to go out on January 12, in support of a list of shop demands concerning wages, hours, and conditions. They were joined on January 13 by the Perovo workshops and on January 14 by the Moscow shops of the Moscow-Kazan Railroad; on January 15 the Moscow-Brest shops walked out. On all three roads the strike was confined to craftsmen; engine-drivers, who on the Moscow-Kazan line in particular would become exceptionally militant later in the year, continued to work. On the remaining Moscow lines repressive measures kept things relatively quiet.[35]

Elsewhere in Russia the movement spread sporadically among railwaymen. At the workshops of the Catherine Railroad in Ekaterinoslav craftsmen were locked out January 18 when they sought to join a "peaceful" general strike begun by the printers three days before.[36] Craftsmen also struck the Kovrov shops of the Moscow-

33. TsGIA, f. 273, op. 12, d. 316, ll. 4–6. Ibid., p. 61.

34. V. I. Nevskii, *Rabochee dvizhenie v ianvarskie dni 1905 goda* (Moscow, 1930), pp. 431, 447; Nevskii, "Ianvarskie dni 1905 g. v Moskve," *Krasnaia letopis'* 2–3 (1922): 12.

35. Nevskii, *Rabochee dvizhenie*, p. 445; Trusova, ed., *Nachalo*, pp. 252–53, 264–67; M. K. Dymkov and D. Ia. Lipovetskii, *1905 god na Kazanke* (Moscow, 1925), p. 33; TsGIA, f. 273, op. 12, d. 343, ll. 6–7.

36. *Vpered*, 9, February 23, 1905; Nevskii, *Rabochee dvizhenie*, pp. 350, 358–59.

Kursk road, the Strogan' shops near Smolensk, the depot and work-shops of the Kazan line in Alatyr, the Samara shops and depot of the Samara-Zlatoust Railroad, and the Kozlov workshops in Tam-bov.[37] In Rostov-on-Don the Menshevik *Iskra* reported that "a strike of the railroad workers is anticipated," but planning meet-ings—already divided by disputes between activists and workers over the utility of posing political demands—were broken up by arrests and the strike was stillborn.[38] In Gomel, where the re-sponse to Bloody Sunday was led by the Jewish Bund, "only the Jewish workers struck. It seems that the Russians, and in particular the workers from the railroad depot, remained oblivious." In Kiev attempts to foment a railroad strike failed owing to similar divisions and repression. A Menshevik attempt to organize a strike at the Odessa shops was also unsuccessful.[39]

In Poland the strikes began at the Warsaw workshops of the Warsaw-Vienna Railroad on January 11 under the leadership of the Polish Socialist Party. By January 14 the movement had seized over half the city's industrial enterprises. By January 17 freight traffic in and out of Warsaw had ceased. The strike began among craftsmen, but spread rapidly to other railwaymen. On January 16 a crowd of strikers attacked switchmen who were not yet out, driving them from work. The next day line repairmen joined the fight, and on January 18 some engine-drivers went out.[40] From Warsaw the strike fever spread to provincial workshops and stations. In Radom the railroad shops joined four other plants in a January 18 walkout. At Skarzhisko on the Vistula Railroad strikers clashed with troops, leaving 25 dead. A tremendous struggle took place at the Sosno-wice railroad junction, where a persistent strike was finally sup-pressed by a great show of military force, which left 44 dead. According to the London *Times*, "strikers in the Dombrova dis-trict . . . went to the railway station at Strshemeschiz and seized

37. Nevskii, *Rabochee dvizhenie*, pp. 453, 460, 474, 495, 497; *Iskra*, 86, Feb-ruary 3, 1905; 91, March 6, 1905; TsGIA, f. 273, op. 12, d. 364, l. 6.

38. *Iskra*, 85, January 27, 1905; 86, February 3, 1905; *1905–1907 gg. na Donu: sbornik dokumentov* (Rostov-on-Don, 1955), pp. 24–27.

39. *Iskra*, 91, March 6, 1905; Nevskii, *Rabochee dvizhenie*, pp. 274–75; V. I. Nevskii, "Ianvarskie dni 1905 g. v provintsii," *Krasnaia letopis'* 4 (1922): 97–100.

40. Nevskii, *Rabochee dvizhenie*, pp. 166–68; "Provintsii," pp. 54–56; Richard Donald Lewis, "The Labor Movement in Russian Poland in the Revolution of 1905–1907," Ph.D. diss., University of California, Berkeley, 1971, p. 104.

and bound with ropes the men employed there. They then totally wrecked the station buildings and forcibly prevented trains from leaving in either direction."[41]

Economic demands dominated the petitions issued by Polish railroad strikers, but even where political demands were not clearly articulated, the strikes were everywhere accompanied by such virulent displays of nationalism—as evidenced by attacks on state vodka stores, widespread destruction of Russian property and symbols, and unprovoked attacks on soldiers and police—as to make their threatening political character unquestionable. In most areas workers endorsed proclamations issued by revolutionary groups supporting the St. Petersburg workers and demanding restoration of Polish national rights. The peak was reached during the Warsaw street demonstrations of January 15–17, which left 90 dead, 176 injured, and 733 under arrest. On the railroads the Polish strike continued sporadically into February, when it merged with the empirewide railroad strike.[42]

National antagonisms also intensified grievances against tsarism in the Baltic area. In Riga railroad workers joined the strike movement on January 12, when a crowd of factory workers appeared outside the terminal of the Riga-Orel Railroad. By the next morning all the city's railroad shops were empty. That afternoon a crowd of 25,000 under the leadership of the Latvian Social Democratic Labor Party marched on the Tukum railroad bridge, where they were met by troops. Shots were fired and the crowd broke ranks, many running onto the ice of the Dvina, which gave way. Riga railroad craftsmen returned to work on January 18, but strikes spread to other Baltic workshops in Revel, Kovno, Mitau, and Libau. Train assemblers, couplers, and track repairmen on the Riga-Orel line also struck briefly, but their action was "poorly organized and went almost unnoticed."[43]

In the Caucasus unrest began in the Tiflis shops as early as December 20, when workers demonstrated in support of the Baku strikers. After January 9 agitation intensified, and on January 18

---

41. Nevskii, "Provintsii," pp. 90–93; *The Times* (London), February 4, 1905.
42. Lewis, pp. 110–31; Nevskii, "Provintsii," p. 66.
43. TsGIA, f. 273, op. 12, d. 335, ll. 1–7; Nevskii, *Rabochee dvizhenie,* pp. 232–37; "Provintsii," pp. 103–4, 115; A. Paulish, "Zabastovochnoe dvizhenie na Rigo-Orlovskoi zh. d.," *Proletarskaia revoliutsiia,* 1925, no. 11 (46): 153.

the Tiflis shops went out. Several factories joined the movement, and a mass demonstration of 3,000 marked the peak of the walkout, which came to an end on February 1. More impressive, however, was the response of railwaymen at smaller stations in the Caucasian hinterland. The strike on the Transcaucasian Railroad actually began on January 11, when workers at Novo-Sekaki station walked out. They were joined by the Kvaloni station on January 14, the Rion station on January 16, and the large Batum station on January 17. By January 20 line maintenance and repair personnel had shut down the entire Batum to Samtredi stretch, and the next day three versts of track were torn up outside Batum. Between January 22 and 25 the strike spread to Abaria, Chalodidi, Nigoriti, Sadzhevako, Kopitari, Natanebi, Mukhiani, Kutais, Kvirili, Sharopani, and Chiatur'. In the northern Caucasus workers at the Groznyi depot of the Vladikavkaz Railroad struck from January 31 to February 4, and at the Tikhoretskaia station there was a confrontation with Cossacks.[44]

The outstanding exception to the generally weak response of railwaymen in Russia to the Bloody Sunday events was the general strike of workers on the Riazan-Ural Railroad in Saratov.[45] An agrarian center in the heart of the Black Earth region, Saratov was an important transit point for moving grain from the Volga to central Russia. The city thus stood at the hub of vital railroad connections, and by 1905 it had emerged as a significant regional junction. Owing to its nonindustrial character, however, Saratov was not a center of the nascent labor movement. The Socialist Revolutionaries and not the Social Democrats—who in Saratov sympathized

44. S. Maglakelidze and A. Iovidze, eds., *Revoliutsiia 1905–1907 gg. v Gruzii. Sbornik dokumentov* (Tbilisi, 1956), pp. 65–87; V. I. Nevskii, "Ianvarskie dni 1905 g. na Kavkaze," *Proletarskaia revoliutsiia*, 1925, no. 4 (28): 40–53; M. Sh. Shigabudinov, *Bor'ba rabochikh severnogo kavkaza nakanune i v period revoliutsii 1905–1907 gg.* (Makhachkala, 1964), pp. 81–82.

45. On the Saratov strike, see TsGIA, f. 273, op. 12, d. 325, ll. 17–38, and Trusova, ed., *Nachalo*, pp. 379–400. Important secondary accounts are M. I. Semenov, "1905 god v Saratovskoi gubernii," *Proletarskaia revoliutsiia*, 1926, no. 3 (50): 197–217; G. M. Denkovskii, I. M. Raschetnova, and M. S. Semenova, "1905 god v Saratove," *Istoricheskie zapiski,* 54 (1955): 74–104; I. S. Sokolov, *1905 god na Riazansko-Uralskoi zh. d.* (Saratov, 1925), pp. 19–22; G. A. Malinin, "Saratovskie zheleznodorozhniki v revoliutsii 1905–1907 gg.," *Uchenye zapiski Saratovskogo gos. universiteta* 55 (1956): 124–54. Also see Nevskii, *Rabochee dvizhenie*, pp. 476–92, and Rostov, "Zheleznodorozhniki," pp. 131–34.

mainly with the Bolsheviks—were dominant in the revolutionary movement. Though few in number, the Social Democrats concentrated their work in the railroad shops, where by January 1905 a core of activists had been established. Oppositional activity in Saratov was also strengthened by the many exiled dissidents sent to the city as a way-station to Siberia. These highly politicized individuals were encouraged to seek employment, and a number found work in the offices of the Riazan-Ural Railroad.[46]

The engineers and administrative personnel of this road were known for their liberalism. Indeed, Saratov province was noteworthy for dissent: its *zemstvo* was one of the most radical provincial *zemstvos* and one of only five to endorse the full program of the liberal November 1904 *zemstvo* congress.[47] Dissent also received a boost in Saratov from the governor, Petr Stolypin, who was eager to utilize the liberal movement against his political rivals, Prince Sviatopolk-Mirsky and Police Director A. Lopukhin. On January 8, on the eve of a zemstvo congress, mass meetings of nearly 2,000 people heard speeches of a liberal and even revolutionary bent; the congress itself, chaired by Stolypin, considered demands for a constitution and civil liberties. The city was thus already politicized when word of the St. Petersburg events arrived on January 10.[48]

The news spread rapidly through the city. The next morning at the railroad workshops a Social Democratic worker distributed statements of solidarity and called for a strike; other workers demanded an armed demonstration. At the administrative offices a clerk called for a political strike of white-collar employees. That evening 40 craftsmen met under Social Democratic auspices to plan a strike, which began on January 12 at the Bering machine-tool plant when a hundred workers walked out and proceeded to the railroad shops, where they were joined by a crowd of over 1,000 craftsmen. The strikers then proceeded to the railroad depot, where they encouraged 300 switchmen and repair workers to go out. According to police this was achieved by force, but the *Saratovskii dnevnik* said the men joined voluntarily. At any rate, the depot

46. Semenov, pp. 197–99; Sokolov, pp. 14–15.
47. Roberta Thompson Manning, *The Crisis of the Old Order in Russia: Gentry and Government* (Princeton, N.J., 1982), pp. 86, 91.
48. Nevskii, "Provintsii," p. 121; Nevskii, *Rabochee dvizhenie*, p. 478.

emptied, and by day's end the number of strikers stood at 4,000. By late afternoon all freight traffic in and out of Saratov had stopped, although passenger trains continued to run.[49]

That evening the Riazan-Ural line was occupied by troops and 94 activists, including 86 workers, were arrested, but this failed to halt the movement's progress. Representatives from various departments of the administration gathered with city and *zemstvo* employees to discuss demands proposed by revolutionary groups. They elected Petr Nikolaevich Kazantsev, a retired teacher of liberal sympathies who would later play a major part in the organization of the All-Russian Railroad Union in Saratov, to head a strike committee. The next day some 1,700 white-collar employees were out, as well as a group of engine-drivers and the telegraph personnel. From Saratov the strike spread to neighboring stations and to the shops of the Tambov-Ural Railroad. By January 15 the total number of strikers in all industries was 7,500, but, according to police, the railroad workers were "the most stubborn." The walkout reached its zenith on January 16, when from 3,000 to 5,000 workers and supporters held a political demonstration organized by the Social Democrats, the SRs, and some *zemstvo* and railroad liberals— the largest of several strike meetings reminiscent of the great Rostov assemblies of 1902. On January 19 railroad management agreed to several major concessions, and the strike came to a victorious conclusion. Of seventeen demands raised by craftsmen, nine were fully and four partially met. Although the eight-hour day was not won, the railroad consented to nine-hour shifts. Of fourteen economic demands put forward by the administrative employees, eleven were satisfied.[50]

In the eyes of Saratov authorities the strike was directed "against the political and economic structure of Russia."[51] Demands extended beyond job issues to calls for a constitution and civil liberties; revolutionary and liberal oppositional propaganda circulated broadly among the strikers and a volatile anti-authoritarian mood gripped much of the city's population. However, the main thrust of

49. TsGIA, f. 273, op. 12, d. 325, l. 17; Denkovskii et al., p. 74; Trusova, ed., *Nachalo*, pp. 386, 686, 383.

50. Trusova, ed., *Nachalo*, pp. 384–89; Nevskii, *Rabochee dvizhenie*, p. 480; Nevskii, "Provintsii," p. 123. On Kazantsev, see Sokolov, p. 26.

51. Trusova, ed., *Nachalo*, p. 385.

the strike remained economic. The list of demands issued in the workshops, although prefaced by an amorphous political statement, stressed economic issues, including the eight-hour day, modifications in piece rates, higher wages, and improved conditions. The demands of the engine-drivers contained no political references.[52] The only list of demands that raised political issues was the declaration supported by the employees of the Riazan-Ural administration. The first political statement by railroad labor in 1905, this document called for

1. Immediate rescinding of all laws and administrative dictates that infringe upon the inviolability of person and home, restrain freedom of travel, freedom of speech and of the press, freedom of assembly, freedom to strike and form unions, and freedom of religion.
2. No punishment for political crimes; freedom and restoration of rights to all those charged with such.
3. To fulfill all the above we deem essential the immediate convocation of an all-popular constituent assembly, elected on the basis of general, equal, direct, and secret suffrage (a) to abolish the economic and legal survivals of serfdom; (b) to work out a constitution for the Russian empire securing for the people of the country free participation in legislation and administration of the country; (c) to bring to an end the war and conclude peace with Japan.

In these political demands we see the sole guarantee of the improvement of our economic position. . . .[53]

A list of fourteen economic demands followed, and the petition concluded with a call for the release of arrested strikers.

That such a boldly political—even radical—document came from the white-collar administrative employees and not the workshops is certainly significant. It contrasts with the still very limited development of political awareness among railroad craftsmen and operations workers. But this political appeal perhaps less reflected the political consciousness of striking employees than the unusually high degree of reformist sentiment among the city's railroad bureaucrats and engineers, who strongly influenced their strike. According to Stolypin, the demands issued by both employees and

52. TsGIA, f. 273, op. 12, d. 325, ll. 18–19; Trusova, ed., *Nachalo*, pp. 381–83; Nevskii, "Provintsii," pp. 126–27; *Rabochee dvizhenie*, pp. 484–86.
53. Trusova, ed., *Nachalo*, pp. 379–80.

workers were formulated by outsiders. In discussions with management "the employees often interrupted and, turning to the director, declared, 'Read directly from the fourth point,'" indicating that the group of three political demands could be passed over.[54] To those operating within the highly charged political atmosphere permeating professional and white-collar circles in Saratov, the strike movement was a welcome source of pressure for acceptance of the reform program. In an appeal addressed to Prince Khilkov, a group of sixty-seven railroad engineers, department heads, and chief accountants declared that "currently threatening social phenomena have their basis in the Russian people's lack of rights, and only a full reconstruction of the entire civic legal order" on the basis of the proposals of the *zemstvo* congress in November 1904 "will let the country develop peacefully and spare it serious upheavals in the future."[55]

In Saratov, as elsewhere in January, strikes predominantly of blue-collar railroad workers were spontaneous and only implicitly political, with an as yet rather isolated handful of revolutionaries, principally Social Democrats, straining to elicit class solidarity and consciousness. What was distinctive about the Volga city was that here reformist railroad officials appealed to white-collar employees and in so doing succeeded in explicitly politicizing strike activity. This politicization, however, was still separate from the more spontaneous activity of railroad labor.

Word of the victory won by the Riazan-Ural railwaymen and of the virtually unprecedented solidarity between blue- and white-collar workers that had facilitated it spread rapidly among railroad personnel in central Russia and the border regions, infusing the strike movement with new energy and illustrating how in 1905 revolutionary initiative could come almost as readily from the provinces as from St. Petersburg and Moscow.[56] No sooner had the first wave

54. Ibid., p. 390.
55. TsGIA, f. 273, op. 12, d. 325, l. 38. The appeal is not dated, but judging from its placement in the archival file and its wording, it was undoubtedly written in January or early February.
56. On the impact of the Saratov strike, see Rostov, *Zheleznodorozhniki v revoliutsionnom dvizhenii 1905 g.* (Moscow and Leningrad, 1926), p. 39; V. Romanov, "Dvizhenie sredi sluzhashchikh i rabochikh Russkikh zh. d. v 1905 g.," *Obrazovanie*, 1906, no. 10: 35.

of industrial unrest begun to ebb in Poland, St. Petersburg, and elsewhere, than a second, larger wave of railroad strikes began. The first rumblings were felt in Belorussia, where on January 29 a strike occurred at the Pinsk shops of the Polessky Railroad; on February 1 the Minsk shops of the Moscow-Brest road went out. On February 3 the railroad strike reached the Ukraine, as workers in the Kharkov shops of the Kursk-Kharkov-Sevastopol Railroad ceased work.[57]

Among Moscow administrative employees unrest began on January 31, when the employees of the Moscow-Vindau-Rybinsk Railroad met to work out a list of economic demands, copied almost word for word from the Saratov petition. These were presented to management the next day, but on February 4, the strikers' deadline for response, local officials declared they were powerless to act without consulting the ministry. Even before this became known, spontaneous walkouts began at several stations outside the city. In Moscow a delegate assembly, informed of management's response, voted to endorse the actions taken by the rank and file, and called on the entire road to strike. By the next morning all freight and passenger traffic had ceased, and only military trains could get through. The walkout continued until February 7, when the ministry conceded to several key demands.[58]

Workers on the South East Railroad in Voronezh were also among the first to copy the Saratov experience. Here, as in Saratov, the initiative came from a group of liberal professionals in the administration, headed in this case by the accountant Ivan Leonidovich Shingarev, also a future leader of the local branch of the All-Russian Union of Railroad Employees and Workers. This group convened a "representative" assembly of employee delegates on February 1 to formulate a program of twenty economic demands. On February 4 the employees walked out and were joined by shop craftsmen, who released their demands the next day. The strike quickly spread in a wide arc extending out of Voronezh. On Febru-

57. Trusova, ed., pp. 518, 521–22; Nevskii, *Rabochee dvizhenie*, pp. 269–70; *The Times* (London), February 17, 1905; TsGIA, f. 273, op. 12, d. 375, ll. 6–15; Los', ed., vol. 2, pt. 1, pp. 88–89.
58. Romanov, 1906, no. 10, pp. 43–44; *Vpered*, 12, March 16, 1905; Trusova, ed., *Nachalo*, p. 300.

ary 8 the workshops and depot of the line's Novocherkassk station walked out. The entire line remained inoperative on February 10.[59]

Largely because proposals for improving conditions had been circulating before 1905 and consciousness of the urgency of reform was already developed, the Ministry of Communications responded quickly to the initial unrest with concessions, though these were minimal. But it should not be assumed that this response was either informed or consistent. The ministry remained largely ignorant of the sources of labor unrest and railroad bureaucrats alternately put the blame on outside agitators, youthful hotheads, and insensitive or overly compliant managers. The ranks of the railroad administration continued to be divided between advocates of relatively extensive reform and those who called for repression, and throughout 1905 policy shifted clumsily between these alternatives.

As early as January 13 Dumitrashko, the director of the Administration of Railroads, met with the directors of the St. Petersburg junction. Among other concessions, the meeting voted to recommend extending to railroad workshops the law of June 10, 1903, permitting elected factory elders (*vybornye starosty,* or simply *vybornye*) to act as spokesmen for their fellow workers in dealings with management. The law had not been well received either by private capitalists or their workers, who frequently boycotted the elections. Since compliance was voluntary, only a few dozen factories in all of Russia participated. But in January 1905 the St. Petersburg railroad directors hoped such a system might undercut the organizational basis of unrest; only the hard-line head of the Nicholas road, Lt. General Nikolai K. Schaffgauzen-Schenberg-Eck-Schaufus, spoke against it as a practice that might further encourage worker initiative. On January 21 Khilkov urged the tsar to adopt the elder system in the shops and proposed review and standardization of pay-books. He would also implement and extend the 1902 decision to grant "staff" status to senior workers.[60]

As the movement began to snowball in early February, Khilkov dispatched the chief inspector of the Administration of Railroads to survey the situation. His reports indicated that even on lines as yet

59. *1905 god na Iugo-Vostochnykh zh. d.* (Moscow, 1925), pp. 16–22; Romanov, 1906, no. 10, pp. 38, 44; Nevskii, *Rabochee dvizhenie,* p. 409, 462.
60. TsGIA, f. 273, op. 12, d. 354, ll. 19, 27, 44–51.

untouched by unrest, or where brief strikes had been suppressed, agitation was widespread and finding fertile soil. Meetings with local officials confirmed these conclusions. In Kharkov the directors of the Catherine, Kharkov-Nikolaev, and Kursk-Kharkov-Sevastopol lines met with Khilkov on February 1 to urge ministry approval of the nine-hour day, a general wage increase in the workshops, and elected elders. The day before directors in Moscow had reached similar conclusions. Thus on February 8, as a strictly temporary measure, the ministry granted local managers the right to introduce the nine-hour day, to establish additional holidays, to adjust piece rates in consultation with "older, more experienced" workers, and to introduce elected elders.[61]

Such meager offerings failed to take the steam out of the movement, however, as the possibility of attaining tangible and immediate gains only aroused workers further. On the very day the new regulations were announced strikes began on the Moscow-Briansk section of the Moscow-Kiev-Voronezh line, at the Rostov shops of the Vladikavkaz Railroad, and the Novocherkassk station of the South East Railroad. On February 9 the St. Petersburg workshops of the Nicholas Railroad went out. They were joined by the Moscow shops of the Moscow-Kursk Railroad and by the Kaluga shops of the Syzran'-Viazma line. On February 10 the struggle reopened on the Tambov-Ural and Riazan-Ural roads in Saratov, now extending outward along the lines to include lesser stations, and unrest began at the Catherine Railroad shops in Aleksandrovsk. On that day the Moscow junction of the Moscow-Kazan Railroad, where unrest had been smoldering for weeks, also went out. On February 11 the strike moved outward from the nodes where it had begun to the Samara-Ufa section of the Samara-Zlatoust Railroad and the Moscow-Riazan section of the Moscow-Kazan line and again to the Riga-Orel Railroad in Latvia. On February 17 the Lugansk workshops of the Catherine Railroad struck.

61. Romanov, 1906, no. 10, p. 30; TsGIA, f. 273, op. 12, d. 354, ll. 70–72, 116, 256–58. The February 8 telegram is in N. S. Trusova, ed., *Revoliutsionnoe dvizhenie v Rossii vesnoi i letom 1905 goda, aprel'–sentiabr'* (Moscow, 1955–57), vol. 1, pp. 866–69. It was followed by more extensive "temporary rules" on February 17. See B. A. von Raaben, *Sbornik pravitel'stvennykh rasporiazhenii otnosiashchikhsia do sluzhby podvizhnogo sostava i tiagi zh. d. so vremeni obrazovaniia Ministerstva putei soobshcheniia po 1-omu ianvaria 1914 goda* (Petrograd, 1915), pp. 215–29.

At the headquarters of the South West Railroad in Kiev, the largest administrative offices in the railroad system, white-collar employees struck with the cooperation of blue-collar craftsmen and won significant victories. On February 7 groups of employees ceased work and gathered to discuss demands. The next day a thousand staffers from the statistics office marched down a nearby street calling for a strike; several thousand employees were soon crowding the halls and stairwells of the line headquarters. This often chaotic meeting—in effect an occupation of the railroad offices—elected a strike committee of eighty headed by the accountant Aleksandr Grigor'evich Shlikhter, a prominent Bolshevik, who addressed the strikers for nearly two hours. Shlikhter would later emerge as the chief Social Democratic leader in the All-Russian Railroad Union. Late in the afternoon the road director, Nemeshaev, arrived from St. Petersburg and tried to speak with the strikers. His words were greeted with derision, and only after Shlikhter implored the meeting to listen could he finish his speech. A telegram from Witte appealing to "former colleagues" to maintain his old line's "traditional discipline" was similarly ineffective.[62]

On February 9 Nemeshaev offered to negotiate concessions if the employees returned to work. They refused and once again occupied the halls. A marathon meeting heard political speeches—in addition to Shlikhter the strike leadership included at least one other Social Democrat and several Socialist Revolutionaries—and extended the list of demands to forty-one. In a move later criticized severely by the Kiev governor, Nemeshaev decided to open negotiations with the strikers. For the next two days a formal administrative hearing considered the demands formulated by the strike committee meeting next door; in a victory for the strikers, twenty-seven demands were met and fourteen others referred to the ministry for consideration. On February 12 Nemeshaev informed employees that continued voluntary absence from work could result in dismissal and imprisonment. Declaring that the strikers had been given the opportunity "to voice their views, formulate demands and elect delegates," he called on them to end the strike. Two days later, bolstered by promises of amnesty and a

62. TsGIA, f. 273, op. 12, d. 345, ll. 16–18; TsGAOR, f. 6865, d. 29a, l. 97; d. 31, l. 5; Los', ed., vol. 2, pt. 1, p. 109.

pledge to implement the concessions of February 9 and 10, the employees of the South West Railroad returned to work.[63]

Concessions also rekindled the Polish powderkeg. On February 9 the Warsaw-Vienna line went out again, and within days unrest had spread to the Vistula Railroad and the St. Petersburg–Warsaw road. Within a day the Russian empire's rail connections with western Europe were completely cut. There was no link possible between the two largest Polish cities, Warsaw and Lodz. Given the growing threat of famine in this situation, St. Petersburg could do little but concede to the demands of the Polish strikers.[64]

Within days of promulgating the temporary rules the autocracy itself undercut their effectiveness by placing the rail system under martial law. On February 7, as the ministry was preparing to release its program of concessions, the chairman of the Moscow-Kazan Railroad requested troops to break the strike being threatened on his road, declaring that he would "sooner lay gold rails to Kazan than concede to the demands of the workers." Ignoring Khilkov's pleas to give the temporary measures a chance, the tsar granted the request. On February 11 he released a declaration on "The Position of Railroad Workers in Wartime," which not only dispatched military trains to strike-torn junctions, but granted local officials the right to place any worker or employee under arrest for up to seven days without showing cause. Jail sentences of four to eight months could be imposed for quitting or failing to show up for work without a proper excuse.[65]

In reality, however, according to one strike activist, martial law had only a "near mythical" significance, as enforcement proved difficult. It may well have placed more pressure on harried officials, who were helpless to take control of the situation, than on the workers. The new ruling did not force workers back on any road, and though the peak soon passed, new strikes continued sporadically through February and March. Agitators even found in the

63. TsGIA, f. 273, op. 12, d. 345, ll. 24–35, 52–65, 96–104, 116; TsGAOR, f. 6865, d. 31, l. 8; Los', ed., vol. 2, pt. 1, p. 111.

64. Reichman, "Russian Railwaymen," pp. 245–46.

65. *Zheleznodorozhniki v 1905 g.* (Moscow, 1922), p. 8; TsGAOR, f. 6865, d. 30, ll. 8–9; Pushkareva, *Zheleznodorozhniki,* pp. 99–100. For the text of the martial law decree, see Trusova, ed., *Vesnoi i letom,* p. 874, and Romanov, 1906, no. 10, pp. 39–40.

decree a convenient vehicle for politicizing what was still mainly an economic struggle; a February 12 leaflet of the Moscow Social Democrats, for instance, announced in the wake of the martial law proclamation that "the autocracy has declared war on the railroad workers."[66]

A total of twenty-seven railroad lines were touched by strikes during the first two months of 1905. Fourteen experienced major walkouts involving several grades of workers that stopped freight and/or passenger traffic on major sections. All fourteen were struck during February, and four, the Warsaw-Vienna and Vistula roads in Poland, the Transcaucasian Railroad, and the Riazan-Ural Railroad, experienced such strikes in January too. Twelve other roads suffered strikes by individual workshops, depots, or stations without interruption of traffic.

The strikes varied greatly in length and intensity. At some depots and workshops walkouts lasted for only a day or two, or even a few hours, as at the Rostov shops of the Vladikavkaz Railroad February 8. Elsewhere, however, whole lines were shut down for several days, with sections remaining out for as long as two weeks. The "most stubborn" strike paralyzed the Moscow-Kazan Railroad for sixteen days, but this was exceptional. In February the average strike lasted 6.9 days, in January the walkouts averaged just 3.5 days.[67]

Both geographically and with respect to the category of railroad worker involved, the February strikes were centered among workers who had not previously been known for rebellion. The railroad strikes of 1900–1904 had been most prevalent in the newer industrial regions of the Ukraine and south Russia, but now, though major strikes certainly took place in the south, the movement's center of gravity seemed to shift toward the more crucial Moscow junction. Moreover, for the first time several major railroads were struck in separate parts of the country simultaneously by different segments of the work force, sometimes acting in concert. Given pre-

66. M. B. [M. Bogdanov], *Ocherki po istorii zheleznodorozhnykh zabastovok v Rossii* (Moscow, 1906), p. 21; Trusova, ed., *Nachalo*, p. 304.

67. Romanov, 1906, no. 10, p. 45; Trusova, ed., *Nachalo*, pp. 291–306; Pushkareva, *Zheleznodorozhniki*, p. 105.

1905 patterns, unrest could be expected among shop craftsmen, but the emergence of white-collar protest was almost unprecedented. The broad sweep of the February strikes made it seem to some that the strikers commanded a level of organization that in fact did not exist. At the peak of the movement the London *Times* informed its readers that "the labor organization" was "prepared to simultaneously interrupt southern grain traffic, military transport for Siberia and communications with Poland," and planned "to proclaim a general strike over the whole region on March 4 [February 19 Old Style], the anniversary of the abolition of serfdom." Such wild stories would be merely entertaining if a similar paranoia had not also been evident in government circles; the regime gave serious consideration to an equally spurious report from its Paris ambassador of an alleged "plot" to foment a general railroad strike.[68]

In fact the February movement was almost entirely spontaneous, and the rudimentary organizations that emerged were largely ephemeral. The level of discipline and coordination that did characterize the strikes were as much products of the tight organization and command apparatus of the railroad industry as of conscious activism. The very structure of railroading facilitated the formation of local commissions, assemblies, and strike committees. These organs, formally prohibited under the martial law decree but generally tolerated by local managers, met to work out demands and strike tactics. In some places a primitive strike apparatus first emerged in January but gained strength and legitimacy in February. In Moscow tentative efforts at cooperation between roads began, as the Museum for Assistance to Labor opened its doors to organizing meetings attended mainly by employees of Moscow administrative offices. Several hundred were present at the largest of these gatherings, and from these sessions grew the first shoots of the All-Russian Railroad Union to be founded in April.[69]

Employees stood at a distinct advantage over craftsmen in such organizing efforts since their position in the railroad structure placed them in closer contact with other stations and lines. Within the industrial section of the work force, though there was more ex-

68. *The Times* (London), February 24, 1905; TsGIA, f. 273, op. 12, d. 354, l. 299.
69. Romanov, 1906, no. 10, p. 55.

perience in labor activism, organizing was still carried out mainly
by revolutionary socialists who operated under the burdensome
conditions of illegality and factional strife. But whether in the
workshops or offices, those who stepped to the forefront of strikes
at the start of 1905 were all to some degree outsiders. The presence
of an especially dynamic individual—Kazantsev in Saratov, Shlikhter in Kiev, Shingarev in Voronezh—could prove more important
than political ideology or organizational development. Both liberals in the lower and middle levels of the railroad bureaucracy and
revolutionary Social Democrats with links to the workshops were
concerned at this stage first and foremost with politics, and each
group sought to utilize the spontaneous outpouring of railwaymen
for political ends. Neither approached the strike movement with
trade union organization as a primary goal, but the largely economic spontaneous movement of the workers, who sought both improvements in their material situation and greater control over production relations, ultimately forced the activists to elaborate a
professional program.

To be sure, in the post–Bloody Sunday political conjuncture,
railroad strikes could not but have a tremendous political impact,
no matter what demands were raised and who the leaders were,
and surely many, if not most, railroad workers were aware of this.
The extraordinary zeal with which railwaymen formulated demands during these weeks alone gave them a significance beyond
their specific content. This was the "time of petitioning," as hundreds of lists of demands were presented to railroad authorities
from large and small groups of craftsmen, employees, telegraph
operators, and engine-drivers, including many who did not resort
to strikes. On the Moscow-Kazan Railroad alone between January 13 and March 9, forty-one separate petitions were filed by various groups of workers.[70] Economic demands were regularly accompanied by calls for worker participation in the organization and
regulation of work, which in the context of the paternalistic tsarist
system held implicit political significance. As the newspaper *Birzhevye vedomosti* commented, such demands touched more than

70. TsGIA, f. 273, op. 12, d. 328, ll. 73–169. Similar *dela* in the archive of the
Administration of Railroads include more petitions from these weeks. TsGAOR,
f. 6865, d. 99, collects well over a hundred lists from this period culled from
newspapers.

the narrow economic and legal interests of the strikers, but were implicitly consistent with sentiments "expressed by workers of various cities, the zemstvos, city dumas, engineers, doctors, teachers, professors, Moscow factory owners [!], and actors."[71]

Nevertheless, the demands of January and February were with few exceptions still explicitly economic and professional. The economic demands raised were almost as many and varied as there were individual shops, stations, and offices. A survey of issues raised by shop and depot craftsmen on eighteen state roads compiled by the ministry listed ninety-seven different requests. These, as well as demands raised by other railwaymen, can be grouped in five categories: (1) demands for higher wages; (2) demands for shorter hours; (3) demands concerned with working conditions; (4) demands concerned with fringe benefits and pension funds; and (5) demands for worker participation and/or control over the pace and organization of work.[72]

Demands in the first category, including increased daily minimums, piece-rate formulas, and holiday and sick pay, appeared on all eighteen workshop lists surveyed by the ministry and on each of eight lists in a representative sample of petitions submitted by employees.[73] Demands for shorter hours were also put forward by all the shops, with half calling for an eight-hour work day and half for a nine-hour shift; demands in this category were found on all but two of the selected office petitions. Two-thirds of the state workshops demanded "improvements in the technical and sanitary conditions" of the work place. In the fourth category, ten workshop lists requested changes in the public health section and "courteous treatment of workers by doctors"; lesser numbers called for the institution or improvement of various benefit programs, including

71. *Bir. ved.*, 8687, February 24, 1905.
72. TsGIA, f. 273, op. 12, d. 354, ll. 139–54. A list of fifteen basic demands raised by railroad workers in January and February compiled in 1906 by M. B., pp. 19–20, and repeated in B. Fain, "Zheleznodorozhniki v revoliutsii 1905 goda," *Zheleznodorozhnik*, 1930, no. 6: 17, is somewhat misleading, since it combines demands raised separately by different categories of workers and fails to distinguish adequately between demands raised almost universally and lesser, though still important, issues. This list does, however, include all key issues and can be broken down according to the schema presented here.
73. For data on the employee list and another analysis of sample workshop demands yielding similar results to that of the ministry compilation, see Reichman, "Russian Railwaymen," pp. 263–65, 282.

calls by five shops for the construction of bathhouses, two for the establishment of a library and cafeteria, and two simply for "an attentive attitude to the needs of the workers." Among the employees a major issue was reform of the pension fund. Seventy-five percent of the employee lists sampled—including all those from the largest walkouts in Moscow, Kiev, and Saratov—demanded a thorough review of pension operations, and some called for employee participation in fund management.

Of special interest are the demands included in the final category. Here one finds a dizzying array of highly specific requests touching on start-up and finishing routines, break times, production norms, and the authority of foremen in the workshops. Most common, however, were demands for the participation of elected worker representatives in dismissal and grievance procedures (raised in eleven workshops) and in establishing piece rates (raised in eight workshops). Eight workshops articulated a call for "courteous treatment" of workers by foremen and managers, but in only three instances did craftsmen request the dismissal of a specific foreman, a significant change from nineteenth-century patterns suggesting, perhaps, that workers were developing a more systematic response to changing work relations. Employees were also concerned with participation and control, though in a slightly different way. Much of the unrest over pension adminstration can be viewed as evidence of this concern, as can the demand for an elected grievance bureau found on five of eight employee lists. Significantly, though, only one of eight offices surveyed called for "courteous treatment" by superiors, even though arbitrary tyranny was often a part of the white-collar world too.

In the course of the February upsurge many of these demands were met by harried local officials or by the ministry in its February 8 concessions. Wage increases were granted, and the nine-hour day became standard in the workshops. The institution of elected elders in the shops also sought to respond to worker concerns with participation, while at the same time widening divisions between older, allegedly more stable, men and young activists. These "authorized representatives" of the workers were to be chosen by each trade for the express purpose of articulating worker petitions and appeals to management. According to "temporary rules" released by the ministry on February 8, only appeals communicated through such representatives were legitimate. Elected elders could also participate "with a consultative voice" in commissions on the dismissal of veteran workers and in the mediation of other questions deemed appropriate by road directors. Voting in the election of representatives was restricted to workers above the age of twenty-one employed for at least one continuous year. Candidates were to be at least twenty-five years old, literate, and with a minimum of three years' continuous service. Electoral meetings were to be held by department. If a quorum of two-thirds of those in a given shop was present, the meeting would choose four candidates. From this group the director of the Department of Engines and Rolling Stock was empowered to select one elder and an alternate. The selected elder was entitled, with the permission of management, to call future shop assemblies.[74]

Given the many restrictions placed on the electoral process and the fact that the final choice remained with management, it was not surprising that the reform was greeted with indifference or even "hostility" by the workers in affected shops and depots, although in many places craftsmen decided "to utilize the elections to illustrate their bankruptcy."[75] On many roads the delegate elections and assemblies never really got off the ground; in September *Zheleznodorozhnik* published an "obituary" for these institutions on the Nicholas Railroad that dated their passing to March 23, just a month and four days after their establishment on that line.[76] On the Riazan-Ural Railroad, however, the new institution was welcomed by liberal activists in the lower and middle levels of the bureaucracy, who sponsored a campaign for introduction of elected delegates "in a revolutionary way," and succeeded in calling together an electoral meeting even before the new rules were formally promulgated.[77]

Where elected elders were successfully introduced there was either minimal activism or the "official" representatives were soon subordinated to more genuine expressions of grass-roots organiza-

74. TsGIA, f. 273, op. 12, d. 361, ll. 66–69.
75. As in the Kovrov shops of the Moscow-Kursk Railroad (TsGAOR, f. 6865, d. 29a, l. 49). There was a similar response in the Moscow shops of the Moscow-Kazan Railroad (Dymkov and Lipovetskii, pp. 43–49).
76. *Zhel.*, 119, September 13, 1905, pp. 9–10.
77. Sokolov, p. 25; *Privol. kr.*, 23, February 4, 1905.

tion. Although, as will be seen, the real spurt of rank-and-file
organizing did not come until the fall, in February unofficial delegate assemblies on many roads elected representatives and even
"strike committees" to negotiate with foremen and managers well
before the new rules could be implemented. Where such meetings
and elections were approved by managers on the basis of the new
rules, workers often ignored the procedural niceties mandated by
the ministry.[78] In a survey of road directors taken by the ministry in
1906 to assess the functioning of the elected elders, road managers
were virtually unanimous in their dissatisfaction with the new institution. The worker representatives, they complained, interfered
with production and work routines by seeking to exercise worker
control. Appointment of officially recognized spokesmen did not
prevent workers from continuing to present demands en masse,
and shop meetings only facilitated discussion of political issues and
increased the influence of "extremists."[79] Moreover, because the
elected elders were to some degree a creation of management,
where elections were held according to the rules worker suspicions
could defeat their very purpose. The manager of the Alatyr workshops of the Moscow-Kazan Railroad complained that it was as difficult to negotiate with elected delegates as with a mass meeting
since the representatives were powerless to act without approval
from the rank and file.[80]

Insofar as the election of elders, along with the extension of
"permanent staff" status to additional craftsmen in the shops and
depots, aimed at heightening the influence of older, more stable
workers, they were also largely unsuccessful. As the manager of
the Moscow-Kazan Railroad pointed out, such measures could
have quite the opposite effect. "In the disturbances," he argued,
"it was noted that the youngest employees were the leaders of the
movement. The old employees, the most prudent and stable, exercised no influence whatsoever." Expanding the rights of the stable
men "would also create a huge gulf between the two groups. The
influence of the older group would be lessened still more, and

78. Pushkareva, *Zheleznodorozhniki*, pp. 97–98.
79. TsGIA, f. 273, op. 12, d. 361, ll. 97–119. Responses were received
from the directors of the Kharkov-Nikolaev, Moscow-Kursk, Kursk-Kharkov-
Sevastopol, Catherine, Samara-Zlatoust, and Riga-Orel Railroads. Only the director of the last road offered even a tepidly positive assessment of the elder system.
80. TsGIA, f. 273, op. 12, d. 328, l. 211.

there would be no hope of their gaining influence in the ranks of the workers; their opinion would always be considered that of a privileged .group."[81] Actually, the situation was quite complex, since young militants often needed the experience of older workers. On the South East Railroad in Voronezh, striking telegraph operators faced this contradiction in choosing representatives: "Were the delegates to be chosen from among the most militant and staunch of the younger operators, then the 'old men' and senior operators wouldn't strike. But if the delegates were acceptable to the older workers, then they would not stand firm in defending the interests of all employees." In the end these operators elected three middle-level officials, including the leader of the whole telegraph department, and a lone junior operator to represent them. The situation was similar in other departments, and as a group the elders were said to present a "sorry picture." Continual tensions emerged between the rank and file and their "representatives." One memoirist even charged that the delegates evolved into "a Black Hundred group."[82]

By late February the strikes on the railroads had subsided, although the Odessa workshops of the South West Railroad were struck for the first time on March 4, and on March 16 the Ekaterinoslav shops and depot went out again.[83] The ministry, meanwhile, continued to straddle the fence between reform and repression. Between March 11 and 16, Khilkov convened a special conference of all state and private railroad directors. The meeting aimed to work out a new "legal order" on the railroads, but yielded only a general statement promising a "fair approach" and emphasizing the need for discipline and order. Still, as originally released and distributed, the report of the meeting listed a large number of measures to be studied that promised hope for improvements. But later a paragraph was added stressing that no "final decisions" had been reached and that all proposals were subject to the legislative process and approval by other departments of government. This failure to act decisively was probably fatal to any hope of railroad reform. "Perhaps the participants in the meeting did not understand how easy it would have been *at that moment* [emphasis in

81. TsGIA, f. 273, op. 12, d. 430, ll. 55–56.
82. *1905 god na Iugo-Vostochnykh zh. d.*, p. 17.
83. Trusova, ed., *Nachalo*, pp. 470, 753.

original] to bribe the railroad masses with a mess of pottage, that the professional demands raised by the masses were quite limited in scope and extremely modest," wrote V. Romanov, a leader of the All-Russian Railroad Union.[84]

As the immediate pressures of February faded the attitudes of railroad officials gradually changed; concessions were abandoned and the new watchword became "patience." On March 28 the decree on martial law was strengthened, although it remained relatively ineffective. Then on March 29 a circular was released over Khilkov's signature that gave "a clear and determined response to all the demands" of the railroad workers. Stressing the necessity of maintaining regular service, it forbade all violations of discipline. The right to meet to express grievances was again denied. Demands calling for additional funding were termed fiscally unfeasible and rejected. Although it retained the elders, the circular prohibited any permanent worker organizations. "It would have been suitable for a journal of satire had it not been so cynical," wrote Romanov. "The time of hopes and expectations has ended," moaned the editors of *Zheleznodorozhnik.*[85]

84. TsGIA, f. 273, op. 12, d. 354, ll. 275–80; *Zhel.*, 98, April 12, 1905, pp. 2–7; M. B., p. 23; Romanov, 1906, no. 11a, pp. 18–19.

85. TsGIA, f. 273, op. 12, d. 354, ll. 294–95; Romanov, 1906, no. 11a, p. 23; *Zhel.*, 97, April 5, 1905, pp. 3–4; 98, April 12, 1905, pp. 1, 2–7; 105, June 5, 1905, p. 2.

Six

The All-Russian Union of Railroad Employees and Workers

The March 29 circular took from railroad workers much that had been won through strikes, but enforcement of its provisions was necessarily uneven. Fearing renewed trouble, cautious administrators could be slow to retract concessions. Still, by April initiative had passed from workers to management, and for the next several months railwaymen found themselves increasingly on the defensive. Strike activists thus sought ways to institutionalize the new power relations temporarily established at the beginning of the year. On one level this meant increasing interest in political affairs, but also important were efforts to build more permanent organizations.

The most important organization proved to be the Moscow-based All-Russian Union of Railroad Employees and Workers (henceforth referred to as the Railroad Union). Founded in April 1905, this group played a key part in sparking the October general strike, but for all intents and purposes it perished in the severe repression that followed the abortive December uprisings. During its brief history the Railroad Union was not the only organization to mobilize railroad workers, but it alone had national pretensions. Although the union tried to remain neutral in dealing with conflicting opposition groups, it was itself never a strictly economic organization. The Railroad Union program contained an amalgam of political demands acceptable to proletarian socialists and middle-class liberals alike. Formally the union embraced all railroad workers and employees from engineers and stationmasters to switchmen and depot craftsmen, but in reality the organization was based almost exclusively—at least until October—among white-collar administrative employees.

Soviet historians have minimized the role of the Railroad Union. Even in the 1920s, when its contributions were more likely to be acknowledged, it was regarded as representing "objectively . . . the left tendency among railroad officialdom"[1] (that is, as not being fully proletarian). More recent Soviet literature has distinguished the leadership from the organization itself, which is rightly seen as more amorphous, but the essential attitude has not changed. Although Western scholars have also paid little attention to this organization, one American historian has sought to reaffirm its role as a "popular organization" and a "genuine expression of mass discontent and popular democracy." Although the Railroad Union was surely more significant than the Soviet literature would suggest, this latter conclusion is also misleading.[2]

It is difficult to pinpoint exactly what kind of organization the Railroad Union was. Its records—to the extent they ever existed—were destroyed in 1905, and, though important documents have survived along with scattered police reports in the archives, the principal source of information on union activities and composition remains memoir literature. Such sources must always be handled with caution, but in the case of the Railroad Union problems arise

1. B. Krugliakov, "Professional'noe dvizhenie zheleznodorozhnikov v 1905–1907 gg.," *Krasnaia letopis'*, 18 (1926): 81. To another writer the union was a "prototype of Vikzhel" (TsGAOR, f. 6865, d. 29a, l. 114).

2. Walter Sablinsky, "The All-Russian Railroad Union and the Beginning of the General Strike in October, 1905," in *Revolution and Politics in Russia*, edited by Alexander and Janet Rabinowitch with Ladis K. D. Kristof, (Bloomington, Ind., 1972), pp. 114–15. Laura Engelstein, *Moscow, 1905: Working-Class Organization and Political Conflict* (Stanford, Calif., 1982), p. 98, more accurately notes, "The railroad union represented in microcosm the dynamic political formula of the 1905 revolution: white-collar leadership of a united front of working class and professional groups, using the strike and the trade union—characteristically "proletarian" instruments—to achieve democratic or basically liberal aims, such as greater economic equality and the right to self-representation." This formulation tends to overestimate the unity of the working class, however, as well as the solidity of the "united front" of resistance to tsarism in 1905. The appeal of the Railroad Union to blue-collar elements was limited and depended on the cooperation of Social Democracy.

from more than the weakness of human memory: the conflicting recollections of union activists and of radical organizers who dealt with the union also reflect the organization's very slippery and internally disputatious character. In 1925 railroad activists from 1905 assembled in Moscow in honor of the twentieth anniversary of the revolution, for several public evenings of reminiscence, of which a stenographic record has been preserved.[3] What is perhaps most striking about the debates was how the memories of activists were so thoroughly colored by old political affiliations. Indeed, the 1925 sessions saw the rekindling of ancient disputes among Social Democrats, Socialist Revolutionaries, and more moderate professional activists, with even the recollection of very basic facts shaped by old loyalties.

The Railroad Union was never principally an expression of the spontaneous activism of rank-and-file workers and employees; it was mainly a battleground upon which rival groups of political activists fought for influence in the professional context. Although it is arguable that institutions such as the St. Petersburg and Moscow soviets provided structure for a de facto united front of skilled and unskilled, blue- and white-collar, artisan and industrial labor, the Railroad Union should not be viewed principally as a body that united a disparate profession. Given the divisions and rivalries that existed among all parties, the Railroad Union was organizationally unstable, even ephemeral, from the start. Its program and two national congresses provided opportunities for various local activists—Social Democrats, Socialist Revolutionaries, and liberals—to channel their efforts within a broader national context.

Nationally, the union was defined by its Central Bureau, which in both composition and orientation reflected the influence of politically unaffiliated, but mainly left-liberal, administrative employees of the Moscow junction. This body, all of whose members were regularly employed in the railroad bureaucracy, commanded meager resources and could boast few direct ties with the rank and file, even in Moscow, where it was based. Organization was very loose, with most authority and the administration of strike and operating funds vested locally. Individual branches were frequently dominated by one or other political grouping, or by loose associa-

3. TsGAOR, f. 6865, d. 120.

tions of liberal or vaguely radical nonparty railroad officials. When they existed at all, the links between such units were weak; in most areas (especially outside Moscow) the Central Bureau established ties with previously existing groups that were not always representative of those for whom they spoke.[4]

Until October the union was not involved in a single strike. Even in October, however, when the Central Bureau emerged as the apparent initiator of the national railroad strike, its influence was in great measure symbolic, its role principally that of a galvanizing, rather than mobilizing, agent. After October blue-collar and other rank-and-file railwaymen poured into the union's ranks from below, which not only transformed the union's role, but most frequently posed a challenge to its largely white-collar and liberal-oriented leadership. In the tumultuous final weeks of 1905, the Central Bureau uncomfortably rode the crest of a leftward tide, and a confrontation between the group's liberal-democratic and revolutionary-socialist wings, one professional-political in orientation, the other more class-oriented, was avoided only by the violent eclipse of both in the aftermath of the unsuccessful December actions.

Although perhaps exaggerated, the assessment of the Railroad Union's position offered in an unpublished essay by a Soviet historian in the 1920s remains essentially correct:

The union was organically incapable of uniting the variegated and ill-assorted railroad masses, who composed, by their ideology, two diametrically opposed parts. On one side stood the administrative and managerial employees situated under the influence of the liberal intelligentsia, while on the other were the craftsmen and workers, coming to class consciousness under the leadership of the Social Democratic party. The entire railroad army was divided, as it were, into two camps, but the commonality of goals and tasks . . . ameliorated all internal contradictions, demanding a unity of forces.[5]

o   o   o

4. Ibid., d. 29a, l. 114.
5. TsGAOR, f. 6865, d. 29a, l. 103. More recent Soviet historiography downplays the divisions and rivalries within the labor movement, paying homage to the success of the Bolsheviks' alleged united front tactics. See I. M. Pushkareva, *Zheleznodorozhniki Rossii v burzhuazno-demokraticheskikh revoliutsiiakh* (Moscow, 1975), passim.

Among railroad workers the idea of trade union organization began to gain support on the eve of the 1905 revolution. Although white-collar employees and some skilled operations personnel were involved in pension fund and consumer cooperative administration, in tsarist Russia the formation of protective, mutual aid, and benefit societies was strictly limited by a political environment hostile to nearly all forms of voluntary association, and such organizations remained under strict bureaucratic control. The first organizing efforts thus took place through other channels.[6]

Before 1905 rank-and-file groupings among shop craftsmen were largely ephemeral, especially since underground socialist circles largely eschewed union organizing. Still, in 1904 craftsmen in the Vladikavkaz Railroad shops organized an illegal union under the leadership of I. I. Stavskii, a Social Democratic worker prominent in the 1902 general strike. By early October this group boasted 572 members in Rostov-on-Don and another 117 in nearby Tikhoretskaia.[7] The first effort to create a true union of railwaymen was initiated, however, by white-collar personnel in Voronezh in August 1903. In an appeal "to the railroad employees of south Russia," an Organizing Committee of Employees on the Railroads of Southern Russia lamented the failure of operations and administrative railwaymen to support their blue-collar colleagues. This apparently short-lived group called on railroad workers to unite in the struggle for "political and social freedom," but pledged only to coordinate communication and distribute propaganda.[8]

Of more long-term importance were a series of meetings held under the sponsorship of the Museum for Assistance to Labor under the Moscow section of the Imperial Russian Technical Society beginning in late 1904 after the publication of several reports on railroad life by engineers associated with the society attracted the attention of some opposition-minded lower- and middle-level railroad officials. Founded in 1901, the Museum briefly partici-

6. On the origins of trade union organization generally see Victoria E. Bonnell, *Roots of Rebellion: Workers' Politics and Organizations in St. Petersburg and Moscow, 1900–1914* (Berkeley and Los Angeles, 1983), pp. 74–103.

7. TsGAOR, f. 6865, d. 37, l. 4.

8. Ibid., d. 29a, ll. 95, 128–33. See also N. Rostov, "Zheleznodorozhniki v pervoi revoliutsii," *Proletariat v revoliutsii 1905–1907 gg.* (Moscow, 1930), pp. 134–35.

pated in the Zubatov experiment, but withdrew after police involvement was revealed. The Museum provided educational and cultural services for workers and, after appointment of a left-liberal board of directors in March 1905, functioned as a center of labor organizing. As previously noted, in January and February the Museum invited striking railwaymen to use its facilities.

Among the activities organized under Museum auspices was a commission formed to assess proposals for creating representative institutions on the railroads in line with strike demands and the regulations governing elected elders released by the ministry. Assembling a wide range of proposals and temporary regulations, the commission tried to formulate a "Model Constitution of Elected Representatives on the Railroads." But as the ministry stiffened its response to railroad unrest in March, this effort became increasingly academic and was finally rendered irrelevant with release of the March 29 circular. Yet the body did not disband. Instead, four of its members hit upon the idea of organizing a national railroad union, utilizing the contacts they had made and the program and structure they had already begun to develop. The idea was presented to a broader meeting at the Museum, where it was agreed that the four should begin work on a draft program to be submitted to representatives of the Social Democratic and Socialist Revolutionary parties for approval.[9]

The program was written by V. N. Pereverzev, a railroad engineer destined to play a major, if controversial, role in the stormy history of railroad labor. A man of amorphous democratic convictions seasoned with a healthy measure of personal ambition and conceit, Pereverzev had been active in populist circles since 1894 and considered himself a Socialist Revolutionary—he was a contributor to the SR newspaper *Revoliutsionnaia Rossiia*—though he was most often viewed by others as a "nonparty democrat," or even a "semi-Kadet, semi-SR."[10] Pereverzev believed the program

9. TsGAOR, f. 6865, d. 29a, ll. 107–11; V. Romanov, "Dvizhenie sredi sluzhashchikh i rabochikh Russkikh zh. d. v 1905 g.," *Obrazovanie*, 1906, no. 10: 57–64; V. N. Pereverzev, "Pervyi vserossiiskii zheleznodorozhnyi soiuz 1905 goda," *Byloe*, 1925, no. 4 (32): 40–41; Rostov, "Zheleznodorozhniki," p. 136; S. I. Mitskevich, *Revoliutsionnaia Moskva* (Moscow, 1940), pp. 357–63. On the Museum for Assistance to Labor, see P. Kolokolnikov and S. Rapoport, eds., *1905–1907 gg. v professional'nom dvizhenii* (Moscow, 1925), p. 156; *Obshcheprofessional'nye organy 1905–1907 gg. Vypusk 1* (Moscow, 1926), pp. 93–94.

should reflect prevailing currents of opinion as revealed in the programs of other groups, but was convinced the new union should be open to railwaymen of all tendencies and not be linked to any single party; in Social Democratic jargon, it should be a corporative and not a class organization. After March 29, however, most of those active in the incipient Moscow railroad movement were convinced, as one later put it, that "the main enemy was lack of political rights."[11] Pereverzev's program thus espoused certain popular political goals endorsed by both liberals and socialists, such as convocation of a constituent assembly and the granting of political and civil rights.

Pereverzev's draft was approved by both factions of Social Democrats and the Socialist Revolutionaries and submitted to the first congress of the Railroad Union, held secretly in Moscow on April 20 and 21. The meeting was attended by some fifty to sixty delegates representing employees from ten state and private lines, of which seven were headquartered in Moscow and three, including the Orenburg-Tashkent Railroad still under construction, in other provinces. Representatives of the revolutionary parties were present with an advisory vote. Also invited were two members of the Museum for Assistance to Labor and an individual claiming to be in touch with a new Social Democratic union in Kharkov.[12]

The first item on the agenda was a discussion of the goals and programs of the new union. Pereverzev's draft proclamation was accepted with minor alterations. Treading a fine line between political advocacy and professional interest, the proclamation articulated a political program essentially subordinate to professional concerns. Indeed, despite endorsement of revolutionary demands, the politics formally espoused by the new organization were fundamentally trade unionist and liberal, since political change was advocated mainly as a prerequisite for progress in the economic struggle.

"Any petitions and appeals of the employees and workers concerning the betterment of their position will remain futile and use-

10. Sablinsky, "All-Russian Railroad Union," pp. 120, 364 n. 34; Pereverzev, p. 41; Pushkareva, *Zheleznodorozhniki*, p. 111; M. I. Vasiliev-Iuzhin, *Moskovskii Sovet rabochikh deputatov v 1905 g.* (Moscow, 1925), p. 96.

11. M. B. [M. Bogdanov], *Ocherki po istorii zheleznodorozhnykh zabastovok v Rossii* (Moscow, 1906), p. 25.

12. Romanov, 1906, no. 11a, p. 28.

less while [this] position . . . depends exclusively on the arbitrary rule of the all-powerful bureaucracy," the program proclaimed. Calling on railwaymen to "direct all their efforts to the creation of a trade union," the program cautioned that

the vitality and fruitfulness of this effort will be unthinkable without the availability of those state-legal norms that alone can guarantee the successful development of any such independent social activity. . . . Hence, *as a secondary consequence*, following from the general conditions of any professional struggle, it is necessary to place the activity of the union of railroad employees on a political footing [emphasis added]. . . . The goal of the union is the defense of the material, legal, cultural, and service interests of the employees and workers of all railroads, which can be achieved only under a democratic state structure. Thus, as its central task the union raises the demand for a transformation of the existing state structure, and, as a logical consequence of this, the demand for the convocation of an assembly of popular representatives with legal powers, elected by all the people of the country through general, equal, direct, and secret ballot without distinction by sex, nationality, or religious denomination.[13]

The delegates to the congress clearly intended to formulate a program attractive to a wide variety of dissenting opinion and capable of mobilizing the railwaymen who in January and February had revealed their economic militancy. But intentions aside, the program also reflected the outlook of a stratum of railroad officialdom and white-collar labor concerned with liberal reform and, inseparable from this, the enhancement of professional status. Although the document was approved by the revolutionary parties, its approach differed fundamentally from that of the socialists. The choice of professional and "corporate" organization over class mobilization, whatever the political veneer adopted, contained seeds of conflict. It also represented a radically different assessment of the potential organization and consciousness of the working class, as well as of its role in social change. As Pereverzev later recalled, the socialist parties

did not yet have the forces to tie all the many hundreds of thousands of the railroad army to a single, unified goal; in the first place, because the great majority of the railroad workers were far from any kind of socialism and would be completely alienated by any party affiliation, [and] in the

13. M. B. [M. Bogdanov], pp. 25–28; Romanov, 1906, no. 11a, pp. 32–34; Pereverzev, p. 42; Krugliakov, p. 78.

second place, because a large section of the railwaymen . . . consisted of intellectuals and *raznochintsy*—that is, of elements belonging to the petty bourgeoisie, far removed from the class consciousness of the laboring masses and consequently also little susceptible to party propaganda.[14]

With the program approved, the congress turned to organizational matters. The delegates discussed methods of struggle and agreed that the union should participate in strikes where possible, but for the present the main effort would be directed toward expanding and consolidating its influence in preparation for a later nationwide outpouring aimed at winning fundamental change in the political order as the key to achieving professional goals. For reasons of security, however, it was nonetheless decided to accumulate strike funds locally to guard against the possibility of the organization's total assets being seized at one stroke. Such funds were to be raised through a dues assessment of one-half of 1 percent of the regular wage of each union member.[15]

Selection of the Central Bureau sparked controversy. Many delegates wanted all members of the leading body elected openly, but others argued that to do so under prevailing conditions would be suicidal. It was finally resolved to hold an election but to make the results known only to the elected. Perhaps because of this, accounts of the body's composition differ.[16] It seems certain, however, that Pereverzev became chairman and V. Romanov, also an engineer, vice-chairman. Other members were I. I. Bednov, a senior telegraph operator from the Moscow-Kazan line; K. D. Nametnichenko, a legal advisor in the administration of the Moscow-Kursk road, an accountant, and two others, one said to be sympathetic to the Bolsheviks and the other an anarchist who soon dropped from sight. The Central Bureau was given the right to coopt additional members, and it soon did, recruiting M. I. Bogdanov, a pension fund manager, G. B. Krasin, head of the technical department of the Moscow-Iaroslavl-Archangel Railroad, two accountants, a bookkeeper, and another engineer. After the October general strike, two militant engine-drivers from the Moscow-Kazan Railroad, both

14. Pereverzev, pp. 44–45.
15. Romanov, 1906, no. 11a, p. 31; M. B. [M. Bogdanov], p. 28.
16. Pereverzev was not even consistent in his own recollections of the Central Bureau's makeup. See TsGAOR, f. 6865, d. 120, l. 82, and *Zheleznodorozhniki v 1905 g.* (Moscow, 1922), p. 9, but mainly Pereverzev, p. 43. See also Romanov, 1906, no. 11a, p. 31.

formally SRs, were added. The Central Bureau reflected the white-collar and administrative character of the new group. Its political sympathies were divided, but mainly reflected a liberal–SR trend. Of the original five *intelligenty* members, three were said to favor the SRs and one was sympathetic to the Mensheviks. According to one Bolshevik, Romanov and later Krasin did not "formally belong to the party, but were considered 'our men,'" although Romanov's own account, which points to Nametnichenko as the Bolshevik voice on the Central Bureau, is so critical of Bolshevik policy as to render this doubtful.[17]

Combined the two factions of the Social Democratic delegation constituted the largest force at the congress. They were led by the Kiev Bolshevik Shlikhter, leader of the February strike in the administration of the South West Railroad. But the Social Democrats were in the minority when jointly opposed by independent liberals and SRs. The different perspectives of the two forces came out at the congress in a debate over the union's attitude toward political parties. The Social Democrats argued that since the program approved by the congress directed the union to pursue political goals, it should be designated a political and not a professional-economic or corporate group. In that case, they said, the union would increasingly have to link up with the Russian Social Democratic Labor Party (RSDLP), the party of the working class. The liberal–SR bloc responded, however, that the union's political aims were designed to achieve conditions under which it could function as a professional body pursuing the economic welfare of its members. In other words, the group was not advocating any special political program other than the minimum needed to develop the trade union movement. The question came to a vote and the Railroad Union was declared an exclusively economic organization independent of all political affiliation.[18]

o o o

17. Pereverzev, p. 43; Mitskevich, p. 391; Romanov, 1906, no. 11a, pp. 42–48. According to Rostov, "Zheleznodorozhniki," p. 137, Nametnichenko was sympathetic to the Mensheviks. During 1905 organizations that were primitive and minuscule by foreign standards gained unexpected prominence, and for many railwaymen who joined a political party, such affiliations were essentially fortuitous or merely formal. Often political labels were determined casually, depending less on conviction than chance acquaintanceship and the influence of personal ties.

18. Romanov, 1906, no. 11a, p. 29.

The dispute was more profound than a simple tactical difference over the applicability of *partiinost'* to trade union organization. It reflected a fundamental political disagreement between mainly Bolshevik Social Democracy and the Railroad Union organizers, a disagreement rooted, moreover, not only in differing conceptions of the railroad proletariat, but also in that each group found support among, and sought to express the interests of, a different segment of that work force. Although formal unity was maintained throughout 1905, the conflict would in many respects determine the history of the new organization. The Central Bureau sought to preserve its political independence, but the approach of the Social Democrats was ambivalent. On the one hand, they sought to penetrate and eventually control the Railroad Union as an organization with influence among white-collar and operations employees. On the other hand, both factions of Social Democracy continued to work independently among railroad workers, especially in the depots and workshops, and to build party organizations, strike committees, and even rival Social Democratic unions, at times in direct opposition to the efforts of the Railroad Union's Central Bureau.

Considerable confusion prevailed among Social Democrats on how to approach the new union. As Romanov recalled, "This was a period when directives of the party center on the question of trade unions were still weak, and . . . party thinking itself was still searching for more productive paths for its work, testing various methods."[19] The confusion was not a product of factional strife, however, as the two factions tended to cooperate in railroad work. Although the attitudes of Bolshevism and Menshevism toward the trade union movement were headed in fundamentally opposed directions, the differences were still ill-defined, and many party activists remained independent. Menshevik railroad organizing was limited to the Moscow workshops and depot of the Moscow-Brest Railroad, described by one partisan memoirist as "our Menshevik citadel," and some employees in Kharkov. The Bolsheviks, on the other hand, were considerably more active among railwaymen. Consequently, they tended to determine Social Democratic policy toward the Railroad Union, with the Menshevik *Iskra* generally defending the Bolshevik approach.[20] As the year progressed, how-

19. Ibid., p. 42.
20. P. Garvi, *Vospominaniia sotsial demokrata* (New York, 1946), p. 547; *Iskra*, 98, April 23, 1905; 109, August 29, 1905.

ever, the Leninists developed ideas about the role of trade unionism in the revolution that would bring the party into growing conflict with the aims and sympathies of the Railroad Union and its
leadership.

The Bolshevik approach to trade unionism was based on Lenin's
well-known thesis (first elaborated in *What Is to be Done?*) "that
the working class by its own effort is able to develop only trade
union consciousness."[21] For Lenin the urge to organize in unions,
although not necessarily harmful to the workers' cause, was not itself revolutionary. As an approach to the problems faced by the
workers, trade unionism was wholly acceptable to the bourgeoisie
and at times even encouraged by it as an alternative to political
class consciousness. Lenin saw the spontaneous gravitation of workers to trade unionism as a reflection of the dominant *external* influence on workers of bourgeois society and bourgeois political consciousness, and hence he did not oppose socialist organizing to
genuine grass-roots labor activism. Indeed, Lenin had previously
written that "the party's task is not to concoct some fashionable
means of helping the workers, but to join up with the workers' movement, to bring light into it, to assist the workers in the struggle they
themselves have already begun to wage."[22] For Lenin this struggle
was a prerequisite for the acceptance of advanced ideas, but it
could not alone guarantee such acceptance. Nor could it help but
reflect mixed political influences.

Because the bourgeoisie is dominant in capitalist society, its ideology is also dominant, Lenin reasoned. Hence, "the task of Social
Democracy is to *combat spontaneity, to divert* [emphasis in original]
the working-class movement from this spontaneous, trade unionist
striving to come under the wing of the bourgeoisie, and to bring it
under the wing of revolutionary Social Democracy."[23] Lenin emphasized the role of an outside agency because he believed that a
class conscious worker had to be aware of the proletariat's role

21. V. I. Lenin, "What Is to Be Done?," in *Collected Works* (Moscow, 1961),
vol. 5, p. 375. "What Is to Be Done?" is a much misunderstood work, but a full
discussion is beyond the scope of this book. The starting point for any real understanding of Lenin, however, is a close reading of his actual text. A useful corrective
to distortions of Lenin's thought as "Jacobin" and elitist is to be found in Neil Harding, *Lenin's Political Thought* (London, 1977), vol. 1, pp. 161–76.
22. V. I. Lenin, "Draft and Explanation of a Programme for the Social Democratic Party," in *Collected Works*, vol. 2, p. 112.
23. Lenin, "What Is to Be Done?," pp. 384–85.

within the entire spectrum of political and social relations. As a Marxist, Lenin agreed that the industrial environment, and the factory in particular, provided a powerful socializing force. However, he recognized that the factory is not a microcosm of society, and, moreover, that the division of society into separate production units reflects at a most fundamental level the commodity relations and division of labor associated with capitalism. In short, Lenin recognized the centrality of the total social experience in the formation of class consciousness, from which followed his emphasis on the central role of political exposure, and of agitation and propaganda.

Given the rush to organize unions that began in several industries as early as spring 1905, and the lingering hesitation of many workers to endorse political demands, the Bolsheviks feared the 1905 upsurge might easily be sidetracked from revolutionary goals and succeed only in paving the way for the victory of trade unionism. To the Bolsheviks—indeed, at this stage, to nearly all Social Democrats—the triumph of trade unionism could mean only the predominance in the working class of trade unionist and not socialist politics; that is, of a working-class political program subservient to the terms of the economic class struggle under capitalism. Yet although the Bolsheviks were suspicious of the developing union movement, like others they were incapable of standing outside it. The thorny problem faced by the Bolsheviks and Social Democracy generally was *how* to enter the emerging union movement so as to *turn* it onto a Social Democratic path and to facilitate the development of class-conscious politics within it.

The first Bolshevik effort to grapple with this problem theoretically was an article on "The Trade Union Movement and Social Democracy," probably written by V. V. Vorovskii, which appeared in *Proletarii* in early July. Approaching the new unions with extreme caution, the author complained that "enthusiasm for the economic struggle is dividing the proletariat into trade groups, alienating it from its class interests—that is, its political interests; not only that, but it frequently turns [the proletariat] against the political struggle and Social Democracy." Hence, the article concluded, the party must make an effort to build unions that recognized the primacy of political organization and must firmly "unite these unions under the leadership of the party."[24]

24. *Proletarii*, 8, July 4, 1905.

Although not opposing the formation of unions, this somewhat hazy formulation stressed the party ties unions should establish. In "The First Steps of the Trade Union Movement," published some weeks later, Vorovskii returned to the question, quoting at length from a proposed constitution for party unions worked out by the Saratov Bolsheviks, who had established a Social Democratic union at the shops and depot of the Riazan-Ural Railroad. This document declared "the basic goal of the union" to be "the full solidarity of its members with the views of the RSDLP on the tasks of the working-class movement." After briefly explaining what these views were, the proposed constitution noted two additional, but subordinate, aims: "raising the level of class consciousness of its members" and "leadership of the struggle for economic improvements." This statement of purpose was followed by twenty-two articles of organization, including the statement that "a union is a party organization whose activity is under the control of the local party committee; it is guided in its activity by the decisions of the committee." Although "welcoming the initiative of the Saratov comrades," Vorovskii criticized the constitution on the grounds that it would both limit trade union membership and dilute party purity. "The tasks of the trade union movement are not the same as those of the party," he declared. "In our opinion it would be better to consider unions not party organizations but organizations connected with the party. . . . Our task is to make the unions Social Democratic in the sense of their recognizing the party's guidance and the tenets of its program." [25]

The Saratov constitution was the high-water mark of the trend toward "party unions." In October *Proletarii* published an article by one M. Borisov, "The Trade Union Movement and the Tasks of Social Democracy," with favorable comments by Lenin. Borisov demanded that the party acknowledge the mass character of the new unions. Unions are "an inevitable fact of life," he wrote, and the socialist attitude toward them must "not be friendly neutrality but active assistance." Borisov did not abandon the principle of party leadership, but advocated a retreat from the "party union" concept to facilitate this. "While encouraging the creation of trade unions, we must restrict their activity to purely economic limits,"

25. *Proletarii*, 11, July 27, 1905; V. V. Vorovskii, *Izbrannye proizvedeniia o pervoi Russkoi revoliutsii* (Moscow, 1955), pp. 357–62.

he argued. The unions should not be allowed to compete with the party in the political arena. If the unions espoused no political programs of their own, Social Democratic unionists could agitate freely for their own program within them.[26]

The Borisov article marked a break with the sectarian approach to many of the mass organizations of 1905, but there was no retreat from the struggle for party leadership. Even during the heyday of the "party union," the Bolsheviks continued to "bore from within" in independent union groups. As early as June Lenin noted that owing to the democratic character of the revolution, various nonparty elements were drawn into the struggle and played a significant role in organizing unions. Although stressing that "actually nonpartyism, with its appearance of independence, implies utter lack of independence and utter dependence on the ruling party," he nonetheless warned that "it would be unpardonable doctrinairism for the Social Democrats to adopt a snobbish or contemptuous attitude towards the 'nonparty' workers belonging to such groups." Lenin compared the problem faced by Russian Bolsheviks to that presented to European socialists by the development of Catholic unions. He noted that even in the democratic countries the notion that all workers can become conscious Social Democrats under capitalism is considered utopian. He therefore urged "no concealment of Social Democratic views, but no slighting of the revolutionary workers' groups that do not share these views. So long as these groups have not officially joined any non–Social Democratic party, we are entitled, nay, obligated to regard them as *associated with the RSDLP.*"[27]

In the context of this unfolding discussion, Bolshevik railroad organizers sought to work with the Railroad Union. From the union's April founding congress until the October general strike, the Social Democrats followed an ambiguous course, determined not only by their own political confusion but by practical realities as well. Even before the Railroad Union congress, on April 8, a leaflet announced the formation of a railroad "Party Union of the Moscow Committee of the RSDLP," and after the congress, on

26. *Proletarii*, 21, October 4, 1905. The true identity of M. Borisov, described as "a comrade active in Russia" has been lost.

27. *Proletarii*, 4, June 4, 1905; V. I. Lenin, "A New Revolutionary Workers Association," in *Collected Works*, vol. 8, pp. 499–510.

May 5, *Vpered* greeted this group's founding. The union promised to struggle for the economic interests of railwaymen, but beyond this declared that "railroad employees, by their socioeconomic position, belong to the great family of the proletariat . . . as this is so, then the Russian Social Democratic Labor Party, the party of the proletariat, is our party, and we must unite with its program and its organizations."[28] Similar party railroad unions were formed in Riga, on the Siberian, Trans-Baikal, and Transcaucasian Railroads, in Saratov, and in several locations in south Russia.[29]

But the Social Democrats could not ignore the Railroad Union. For one thing, with its connections among radical railroad administrators and employees, the Central Bureau offered one avenue through which they might approach white-collar and operations personnel. "The union very quickly began to develop its activity mainly among railroad employees and unorganized workers; the skilled organized workers being attracted primarily by party organizations," Pereverzev recalled. "The forces of the Railroad Union consisted primarily of employees based in the actual structure of the railroad apparatus." As Bednov later explained, such workers were difficult for Social Democrats to reach because "the party men were unprepared for mass professional work and their ranks were very thin. Before 1905 party organizations were virtually nonexistent. . . . [Moreover,] party activists did not know the psychology of the railwaymen and thus found it difficult to approach them. . . . It was easier to work in the depots and workshops where there was a concentrated proletarian group. Other railwaymen were dispersed throughout the system."[30]

Independent railroad unions were often created by the Social Democrats as vehicles for penetrating the Railroad Union and strengthening the influence of the "proletarian element" within it. According to N. N. Mandelshtam, a leader of the Bolshevik-led Moscow Social Democratic Committee who was in charge of railroad organizing in 1905, the party union in that city was established "to wrest the leadership of the union from the hands of the

28. *Vpered*, 18, May 5, 1905; *Listovki Moskovskikh bol'shevikov v period pervoi Russkoi revoliutsii* (Moscow, 1955), p. 128. Three additional leaflets produced by the Moscow Social Democratic Union are in TsGAOR, f. 6865, d. 79.

29. *Vpered*, 18, May 5, 1905; Krugliakov, "Professional'noe dvizhenie," p. 81; *Proletarii*, 22, October 11, 1905.

30. TsGAOR, f. 6865, d. 120, ll. 203–4; l. 105.

liberals." From the beginning it was "organized . . . along the lines of the Railroad Union, so that we would have corresponding organs and thus be able to gain control." Moreover, members of the Social Democratic group "entered the central establishment of the Railroad Union and selflessly worked in it."[31] Penetration was not always readily achieved, however. Mandelshtam recalled that among railroad craftsmen there was "stubborn resistance to the idea of entering this union. 'This is not our union, it is the management union [*soiuz nachal'stva*] and there is no place for us there,' the workers told us. It was only with considerable effort that we finally convinced them it was essential to work in this organization and utilize it to expand our influence."[32]

To be sure, before October only relatively small groups were mobilized by either the Central Bureau or the Social Democrats, and for many workers the distinctions between different organizations were difficult to perceive. Still, by summer predominantly Bolshevik Social Democracy had greatly expanded its influence on the railroads and in the Railroad Union, with relatively strong organizations among depot and workshop craftsmen. And although the amorphous organizational structure of the Railroad Union still kept developing factional differences localized and largely divorced from the experience of rank-and-file railwaymen, it could not prevent a confrontation provoked by the demands of a third force, Polish nationalism, from breaking out at the union's second congress, which was held July 22–24 in Moscow.

In the three-month period between the two congresses of the Railroad Union the organization gradually extended its influence, organizing mainly "from the top down."[33] Union leadership was most active in Moscow, where two representatives of each of between six and nine roads—including several members of the Central Bureau—formed a junction committee. Although the precise composition of this body cannot be determined and the extent of its activity chronicled, it is clear that Social Democrats, SRs, and independent liberals both cooperated and vied for influence within

31. N. N. Mandelshtam, "Iz proshlogo," in *Piatyi god*, edited by S. Chernomordik (Moscow, 1925), vol. 1, pp. 78, 83–84; Romanov, 1906, no. 11a, p. 42.
32. TsGAOR, f. 6865, d. 120, l. 39.
33. Krugliakov, "Professional'noe dvizhenie," p. 80.

it. Since the Social Democrats enjoyed their greatest support in the workshops, union organizers associated with the Central Bureau mainly directed its efforts toward operations personnel, especially telegraph operators and engine-drivers, the "nerves and arteries" of the railroad economy. Only on the Moscow-Kazan Railroad, however, did they enjoy measurable success with these groups; on other Moscow lines the union following remained a mixed assortment of lower-level officials, employees, and mainly Social Democratic shopmen.[34]

Outside Moscow organizing proceeded largely independent of the central leadership.[35] In Kovrov on the Moscow-Kursk Railroad, according to the recollections of one worker, railwaymen seeking to establish a union organization sent a delegate to Moscow to seek affiliation with the Railroad Union and learn its programmatic and organizational principles, but he received minimal concrete advice and the organization was built "by our own efforts."[36] On June 19 thirty-five employees of the Samara-Zlatoust Railroad met in Samara and announced formation of a Samara section of the Railroad Union. Reminding railwaymen they were "not only railroad agents but citizens of the fatherland," the group declared its support for the principle of "popular representation." On the South West Railroad in Kiev the Bolshevik Shlikhter returned from the April Moscow congress to organize a "western section" of the Railroad Union before he was dismissed from railroad service in late May.[37]

Outside Moscow the two most important centers of independent Railroad Union organizing were the Riazan-Ural Railroad in Saratov and the South East Railroad in Voronezh, where liberal activists embraced the union cause with enthusiasm, though not without opposition from the left. In Saratov, where the movement of railwaymen had won its first victory in January, the decision of the local Bolshevik organization to establish a separate party union in the workshops enabled the liberal group of engineers and officials associated with Kazantsev to establish effective control over the Saratov Railroad Union, which quickly branded the Social Demo-

34. TsGAOR, f. 6865, d. 29a, l. 150; d. 120, l. 107; d. 128a, l. 4.
35. Ibid., d. 29a, ll. 113–14.
36. Ibid., d. 120, l. 61.
37. Ibid., d. 29a, l. 144; d. 63, ll. 33–36; ll. 100–115.

cràtic group dual unionists and "disorganizers." On May 14 an assembly of white-collar railwaymen organized by the self-proclaimed Saratov bureau of the All-Russian Railroad Union voted 130 to 60 to affiliate with the Moscow-based Railroad Union rather than forming a "separate class union" as proposed by some left-wing employees.[38] In Voronezh union organizing began in May under the leadership of administrative personnel in the central accounting office, among whom I. L. Shingarev was the most active. A June 12 meeting of some 50 white-collar employees voted to affiliate with the Railroad Union and released a proclamation declaring that petitions and appeals had proved fruitless and railroad workers should prepare for a "general railroad strike." The group called for a broader mass assembly, which was held openly in the workshops on July 3 with attendance estimated by the police at about 500 railwaymen. That meeting elected a larger, but still overwhelmingly white-collar, steering committee of three administrators, a leading engineer, six senior clerks, a telegraph operator, an engine-driver, a workshop technician, and two shop craftsmen.[39]

In late June, when the Central Bureau distributed a formal "call" to the union's second congress, it could claim some sort of affiliate on each of seventeen different lines. Moreover, the leadership counted four functioning regional committees: Moscow, involving the Moscow-Brest, Moscow-Vindau-Rybinsk, Moscow-Kazan, Moscow-Kiev-Voronezh, Moscow-Kursk, and Moscow-Iaroslavl-Archangel Railroads; Saratov, including the Riazan-Ural and South East Railroads; Warsaw, where the Warsaw-Vienna, Lodz, and Vistula Railroads were active; and Vilna, where the committee claimed representation from the Libau-Romny, Polessky, and Riga-Orel Railroads. The most significant expansion of the infant organization's influence had come in May, when representatives of seven Polish and Baltic lines organized by the Polish Socialist Party met in Vilna and voted to join. In its call to the second congress the Central Bureau reported, however, that the Vilna meeting voted to supplement the program adopted in April with a statement favoring "political and cultural-national autonomy" for minority nation-

38. I. S. Sokolov, *1905-i god na Riazansko-Ural'skoi zh. d.* (Saratov, 1925), pp. 29–32.

39. *1905 god na Iugo-Vostochnykh zh. d.* (Moscow, 1925), pp. 24–43; TsGAOR, f. 6865, d. 63, ll. 27–33; TsGIA, f. 273, op. 12, d. 377, ll. 63–71.

alities and the "complete legislative-administrative autonomy of the Kingdom of Poland."[40]

The second congress of the All-Russian Railroad Union convened secretly in Moscow on July 22, 1905, just as a lengthy walkout on the Vladikavkaz Railroad, the largest railroad strike since February, was coming to an end. Twenty separate roads were represented with votes and another three, whose organizations were controlled by Social Democrats, had a consultative voice, as did representatives of the Socialist Revolutionary party, both factions of Social Democrats, and the Jewish Bund, for a total of 120 delegates.[41] By recommendation of the Central Bureau, a maximum of 5 delegates per road were to have been nominated secretly by union organizers rather than elected by the membership. Although this was to insure the meeting's security, and the congress call stressed the desirability of naming at least one delegate from the engine-drivers, one from the shop craftsmen, and a third from line personnel, the nomination process surely strengthened the hand of the administrative element. Representative assemblies or similar mass organizations from large stations or workshops were invited to petition the Central Bureau for independent representation, but apparently no such bodies did so.[42]

On the first day the congress, assembled in suburban Mikhailovka with Shlikhter in the chair, heard reports from the various lines. The next day the body moved into Moscow proper, and a representative of the Polish roads, a Polish Socialist party (PPS) member, announced that the lines represented at the Vilna meeting had decided to join the Railroad Union provided the group pledged to continue any general strike until Poland gained national autonomy.[43] Members of both factions of Social Democracy, whose program opposed the autonomy principle, favoring instead guarantees to the right of self-determination, rose immediately to object. The SRs supported the Polish demand, but were unable to persuade many of their liberal allies, who objected to the introduction of a bluntly political issue not directly related to the union's own avow-

40. TsGAOR, f. 6865, d. 63, ll. 51–52.
41. Pereverzev, p. 48.
42. TsGAOR, f. 6865, d. 63, ll. 55–56.
43. Pereverzev, p. 48; M. B. [M. Bogdanov], pp. 29–30; Krugliakov, "Profesional'noe dvizhenie," p. 83; Rostov, "Zheleznodorozhniki," p. 142.

edly economist politics.[44] The Poles held firm, however, and to avoid a split the congress, now chaired by the independent M. D. Orekhov of the Riazan-Ural Railroad, agreed to postpone debate.

Other items on the agenda evoked little controversy; although Social Democratic delegates criticized the Central Bureau for affiliating the union with the liberal professional Union of Unions, the criticism was muted since the bureau itself had already retreated from serious involvement with that group.[45] Discussion of the proposed general strike evoked surprisingly little debate. It was agreed to begin strike preparations immediately, but a decision on precisely when to start the walkout was left to the Central Bureau, which was urged and empowered to coordinate efforts with other groups and the revolutionary parties. It was resolved that any strike should continue until demands for political and civil rights and for a constituent assembly were met. The congress voted unanimously that the strike be peaceful and that damage to property should be avoided.[46] These plans met no organized opposition, but members of the Social Democratic group must have been a bit uneasy. For the Bolsheviks, a general strike was irrelevant at best, destructive at worst, if not planned in strict coordination with a well-prepared strategy for launching a classwide armed uprising. The Mensheviks were less skeptical, however, and *Iskra* later claimed that the decisions on the general strike were "thrust upon" the congress by the Social Democratic delegates.[47]

After disposing of some organizational matters and empowering the Central Bureau to draft a constitution for the union, on its third and final day the congress returned to the thorny question of Polish autonomy. A vote was taken and the Poles won the support of twelve delegations, including all those that had attended the Vilna meeting. Three delegations voted against the Polish proposal, one abstained, three "refused to participate," and one was hopelessly divided. At this point the Social Democrats declared the decision unacceptable and withdrew from the organization. Among those de-

44. For the Social Democratic position, see *Iskra*, 109, August 29, 1905. The SR position was argued in *Revoliutsionnaia Rossiia*, 73, August 15, 1905.

45. TsGAOR, f. 6865, d. 63, ll. 53–54; Romanov, 1907, no. 6a, p. 29; 7, 1907, p. 71.

46. M. B. [M. Bogdanov], p. 29; Romanov, 1907, no. 7, pp. 65–66; Krugliakov, "Professional'noe dvizhenie," p. 82.

47. *Iskra*, 109, August 29, 1905.

parting the congress were delegates from the Moscow-Brest, South West, Orenburg-Tashkent, Syzran-Viazma, Riga-Orel, Moscow-Kursk, Moscow-Iaroslavl-Archangel and Moscow-Vindau-Rybinsk Railroads.[48]

The Central Bureau now faced a serious dilemma. Although the Social Democrats had been a minority at the congress, their influence was far greater among railwaymen than was reflected at that meeting.[49] Without Social Democratic participation the Railroad Union's independence and its ability to unite varied trends would be seriously compromised and its inherent inability to stand on its own eventually revealed. Hence, as soon as the congress closed, the Central Bureau organized a referendum of local groups on the Polish question, explaining that "the majority of voting delegates had not received definite instructions with respect to this question from their local committees and had thus expressed personal views and not those of their organizations."[50] Forced to choose between Russian socialism and Polish nationalism, the local groups rejected the Polish demand, allowing the Central Bureau to rescind the resolution. The Poles responded by leaving the Railroad Union to form, under PPS sponsorship, the National Circle of Railwaymen (Narodowe Koło Kolejanzy [NKK]), which was destined to become "the most important influence among Polish railroad workers."[51] Most of the dissenters were pacified and withdrew their resignations, although the Moscow Social Democrats did not. The Moscow city prefect gleefully informed the police that "although the workers of the Moscow railroad center decided on a political strike, the withdrawal of the extreme revolutionary group from the All-Russian Railroad Union will postpone a strike on the railroads to the distant future."[52]

Such optimism in the ranks of the authorities was unwarranted,

48. Romanov, 1907, no. 7, p. 72; Rostov, "Zheleznodorozhniki," p. 142.

49. This point is stressed by Romanov, 1907, no. 7, p. 73.

50. TsGAOR, f. 6865, d. 59, l. 1.

51. Richard Donald Lewis, "The Labor Movement in Russian Poland in the Revolution of 1905–1907," Ph.D. diss., University of California, Berkeley, 1971, p. 273.

52. Pereverzev, pp. 48–49; *Iskra*, 109, August 29, 1905; Mitskevich, p. 391; A. Kats and Iu. Milonov, eds., *1905: professional'noe dvizhenie* (Moscow and Leningrad, 1926), p. 254.

however. The Railroad Union had been saved. Even in Moscow individual Social Democrats continued to work within its ranks, while continuing to build party organizations in depots and workshops where the largely white-collar Railroad Union had little influence. Neither Social Democratic faction assumed a publicly hostile posture toward the Central Bureau, and they largely ignored its work in their newspapers. Nonetheless, the union's ties among the rank and file remained tenuous, and the divisions in its ranks could no longer be ignored. If the growing unrest of late summer and early fall and the rising sentiment for a general strike among widely varied segments of the working class tended to overwhelm the differences that divided the second congress, it was still the case, as Pereverzev later acknowledged, that after that meeting "the atmosphere of internal ideological struggle thickened even more, and after just three months in existence the organization was in fact already split."[53]

While a segment of the administrative apparatus turned toward trade unionism in the wake of the February upsurge, the railroad strike movement ebbed, though there was still considerable unrest by pre-January standards. By midsummer, however, a new strike upsurge again put railroad authorities on the defensive. I. M. Pushkareva has recorded 235 separate instances of railroad strike activity during the first nine months of 1905, almost equal to the total number of railroad strikes during the previous thirty years.[54] March and April marked the nadir of the strike movement, as railroad administrators, bolstered by the March 29 circular, stood firm against demands for new concessions and on many roads whittled away at those already won. Even the reform-minded administration of the South West Railroad got tough; in mid April, seventy-seven employees active in the February walkout, including the Bolshevik leader Shlikhter, were dismissed, apparently after pressure was exerted on Nemeshaev by local police. For the rest of the spring railwaymen struck mainly to defend gains won in winter;

53. TsGAOR, f. 6865, d. 29a, l. 122.
54. There were 49 strikes in January, 62 in February, 11 in March, 13 in April, 20 in May, 22 in June, 31 in July, 12 in August, and 15 in September and the first days of October (Pushkareva, *Zheleznodorozhniki*, pp. 104–5).

strikes were again centered overwhelmingly in workshops and large depots.[55]

In private industry the period immediately after May 1 was marked by a new round of strikes. Among railwaymen, however, the response to May Day was mixed; in some cities railroad shop-men joined industrial workers in demonstrations and walkouts, but elsewhere railwaymen stood apart from struggle.[56] Soon, however, the bitter eight-week strike of Ivanovo-Voznesensk textile workers, the June strike and street fighting in Polish Lodz, and the mutiny on the battleship *Potemkin* and subsequent rioting in Odessa quick-ened the revolutionary pulse. Although railroad workers did not participate in these events, the changing mood in the country be-gan to shift initiative from the railroad authorities. Beginning in late June, a new series of strikes swept railroad lines, mainly in the south, forcing both the ministry and private railroad managers back on the defensive. Significantly, the most impressive of these strikes came where the Railroad Union enjoyed little or no influence.

On June 20 a strike began in the Tiflis workshops of the Trans-caucasian Railroad, and within two days the entire road shut down, reopening under military control a week later. The precipitant was the administration's failure to satisfy demands supposedly granted

55. Henry Reichman, "Russian Railwaymen and the Revolution of 1905," Ph.D. diss., University of California, Berkeley, 1977, pp. 285–86; *Zhel.*, 102–3, May 23, 1905, p. 23; An April 1 walkout on the Transcaucasian Railroad was broken after ten days (N. S. Trusova, ed., *Revoliutsionnoe dvizhenie v Rossii ves-noi i letom 1905 goda, aprel'–sentiabr'* [Moscow, 1955–57], vol. 1, p. 122; *Pro-letarii*, 4, June 3, 1905).

56. On May Day generally, see I. Volkovicher, "Pervomaiskii prazdnik v 1905 g.," *Proletarskaia revoliutsiia*, 1925, no. 3 (38): 82–117. In Belorussia the Minsk shops of the Moscow-Brest Railroad greeted May Day with a strike, as did the shops in Dvinsk, though in Gomel the railwaymen "cover[ed] themselves with shame" as the only workplace remaining open during a May 12 walkout called by the Bund to protest a pogrom in nearby Zhitomir (TsGIA, f. 273, op. 12, d. 343, ll. 52–59; Trusova, ed., *Vesnoi i letom*, vol. 1, pp. 217–25; *Proletarii*, 5, June 13, 1905). Railroad shopmen struck unsuccessfully on May 1 and 2 in Samara, Novoros-siisk, and Rostov (TsGIA, f. 273, op. 12, d. 364, ll. 79–80; *1905–1907 gody na Donu* [Rostov-on-Don, 1955], pp. 60, 62, 64–65; Reichman, "Russian Railway-men," pp. 295–97). In Kharkov the railroad shops stood aside from a "colossal" May Day celebration, and agitators complained they were met with hostility and treated as "outsiders" (*chuzhaki*) at the shops of the Kursk-Kharkov-Sevastopol Railroad (Volkovicher, pp. 108–10; S. Kramer, ed., *1905 god v Kharkove* [Khar-kov, 1925], pp. 33, 36, 38; TsGIA, f. 273, op. 12, d. 375, ll. 65–72; F. E. Los', ed., *Revoliutsiia 1905–1907 gg. na Ukraine* [Kiev, 1955], vol. 3, pt. 1, pp. 272–74).

in January.[57] In Kharkov the Bolsheviks and Mensheviks agreed to organize a citywide strike jointly in sympathy with the Odessa rebels, which closed down most of the city's industry, including the workshops of the Kursk-Kharkov-Sevastopol Railroad, from June 27 to 29.[58] June and July saw a series of strikes on the Catherine Railroad, and the Ufa depot and workshops of the Samara-Zlatoust Railroad struck on July 5, demanding freedom of assembly and the liberation of arrested activists, as well as economic improvements.[59] On the Moscow-Kazan Railroad, the Alatyr workshops struck on July 6 and remained out most of the month, until a partial victory was secured. No sooner had they returned, than the line's Moscow depot and large Perovo workshops walked out, although this strike was broken two days later when the Perovo manager threatened to have all strikers drafted and shipped east.[60]

The largest—and bloodiest—railroad strike in Russia between March and October 1905 paralyzed the Vladikavkaz Railroad during the second half of July.[61] Although this private line was not linked to the Railroad Union, it was an activist hotbed, with Socialist Revolutionary, Menshevik, and, mainly, Bolshevik organizers extremely active. The road's main workshops and depot in Rostov-on-Don had a long tradition of worker unrest, but by mid 1905 there was active organizing as well at depots and stations in Novorossiisk, Tikhoretskaia, Groznyi, Derbent, Baladzhari, and Mineral Waters. In late March road management granted several relatively minor concessions, but in June a strict new disciplinary order "poured oil on the fire" of unrest.[62] Throughout June and early July

57. Trusova, ed., *Vesnoi i letom*, vol. 1, pp. 120–21.
58. Kramer, pp. 38–39.
59. TsGIA, f. 273, op. 12, d. 350, ll. 180–230; d. 364, ll. 98–120; Reichman, "Russian Railwaymen," pp. 301–5. There was also a July 26 walkout of telegraph operators in Samara (Trusova, ed., *Vesnoi i letom*, vol. 1, pp. 245–52).
60. Trusova, ed., *Vesnoi i letom*, vol. 1, pp. 227–34. There were railroad strikes as well in St. Petersburg on July 9 and on the Riga-Orel Railroad in late July (*Proletarii*, 14, August 16, 1905; Trusova, ed., *Vesnoi i letom*, vol. 1, pp. 238–39).
61. On the Vladikavkaz Railroad strike, see TsGAOR, f. 6865, d. 70; Trusova, ed., *Vesnoi i letom*, vol. 1, pp. 83–102; *ZhD*, 1905, 46–47, pp. 527–29; M. Sh. Shigabudinov, *Bor'ba rabochikh severnogo Kavkaza nakanune i v period revoliutsii 1905–1907 gg.* [Makhachkala, 1964], pp. 106–9; Reichman, "Russian Railwaymen," pp. 307–12.
62. The order was actually issued March 30, but only implemented in June. TsGAOR, f. 6865, d. 70, l. 207; d. 74, ll. 1–6.

all three revolutionary factions agitated for a strike. Though there was some factional maneuvering, cooperation was maintained and effective joint strike committees organized. Lists of political as well as economic demands were discussed and presented to the administration.

The walkout began at Mineral Waters on July 11, and within five days the entire line was shut down. On July 17 six hundred Rostov strikers clashed with Cossacks, but the most violent confrontation came in Novorossiisk on July 19, "Bloody Thursday," when a riotous crowd of several thousand strikers attempting to halt a mail train was attacked by Cossacks, leaving fifteen dead and twenty seriously injured.[63] Although some minor concessions were won, the strike met with firm resistance from line management and, at least initially, from the ministry, which on July 16 ordered the road to make no concessions and to take all measures necessary to restore service. Striking stations, depots, and shops were occupied by troops, and military train crews from the Transcaucasian Railroad (already under martial management after the June strike there) were mobilized as strikebreakers.

The harsh response was perhaps prompted by the strikers' extraordinary political militancy. At Groznyi the railroad police reported that "the attitude of the crowd, in comparison with the two previous strikes in February and June, is significantly more aggressive, bold, and defiant."[64] According to the principal police summation of the walkout, "the economic demands play a very insignificant role and serve the leaders as a starting point for agitation among the semideveloped and even the completely undeveloped shopmen and drivers." Demands raised included the eight-hour day; an end to martial law on the railroads; freedom of assembly, unions, speech, the press, and to strike; a constituent assembly; prohibition of police participation in hiring and firing; and rescinding of the March 29 circular.[65] The most active strikers were in the workshops, but an important part was played by engine-drivers, especially at the Mineral Waters depot. Here the railroad police chief reported that "as men of greater development" the drivers

63. TsGAOR, f. 6865, d. 70, ll. 208, 215; Reichman, "Russian Railwaymen," pp. 310–11.
64. TsGAOR, f. 6865, d. 71, l. 2.
65. Trusova, ed., *Vesnoi i letom*, vol. 1, pp. 99, 86–88; Shigabudinov, p. 109.

were less swayed by agitation than shop craftsmen. "Their political thinking," however, "was noticeably affected [by the strike], even more in this respect than other workers." Although the breakdown of passenger service to and from the Mineral Waters spas disturbed prosperous travellers "seeking not so much treatment as flirtations and diversion," the strike won broad support from the local press, students, and the general public; according to the police, collections were taken up for the strikers "in private homes, parks, and at sessions of the Balneological Society."[66]

Once more a provincial road ran ahead of the movement in Moscow. But a more significant fact about the strike on the Vladikavkaz Railroad was the strikers' attitude toward politics. Concern with immediate material issues seemed now to be expressed directly through political demands. This was also happening, of course, in the Railroad Union, but in a very different way. The Railroad Union was essentially an organization of the administrative centers; the strike on the Vladikavkaz Railroad saw the mobilization of line workers not through established administrative channels but independently by shop craftsmen and engine-drivers. As administrators, the Railroad Union leaders did not, perhaps, wish to directly challenge the structures of authority in railroading, but instead to rationalize them, albeit quite radically. On the Vladikavkaz Railroad, however, political initiative came from a very different source. It was probably not yet clear to anyone at the time, but even as the Railroad Union was dividing into hostile political factions, at the grass-roots level two quite different—if still intermingled—movements of railwaymen were emerging simultaneously.

66. TsGAOR, f. 6865, d. 70, ll. 46, 54, 52.

Seven

The Pension Congress and the October Strike

The regime responded to the rising tide of protest with a clumsy combination of repression and concessions. Strikes met increased resistance; where police had been lax, troops were used. Yet at the same time concessions to the student movement opened newly autonomous university campuses to antiwar agitation and labor organizing. On August 6 the tsar released the long-awaited legislation establishing the so-called Bulygin Duma, to most oppositionists a woefully inadequate measure, but an effort nonetheless to coopt the rapid growth of dissent. Still, the apparent vacillations in policy were evidence more of weakness and confusion than of a sophisticated strategy aiming to divide moderates from radicals, or workers from the middle classes.

On the railroads a subtle shift toward conciliation followed the Vladikavkaz Railroad strike and the second congress of the Railroad Union.[1] Although the ministry had encouraged the Vladikavkaz management's resistance to the strikers, in early August the road was ordered to rehire all dismissed workers, which provoked a bitter response from its manager. Voicing sentiments typical of the private roads, he blamed unrest on outside political agitators and the government's timid response to their assaults. Bemoaning the absence in Russia of professional strikebreakers like the American Pinkertons, he called for "special laws with strict punishments for

1. N. Rostov, "Zheleznodorozhniki v pervoi revoliutsii," *Proletariat v revoliutsii 1905–1907 gg.* (Moscow, 1930), p. 139.

participation in strikes." However, the director of the Siberian Railroad, vacationing at Mineral Waters during the July strike, reported that worker demands had been "in the main completely just" and that similar concessions had already been granted elsewhere by the ministry and introduced on the Siberian line. Dumitrashko's report charged that the road had ignored concessions granted in February. He blamed the strike on management's "failure to take preventive measures and respond to the repeated appeals" of the workers.[2]

On September 20 the ministry convened a crucial congress of participants in the railroad pension fund in St. Petersburg to consider modifications in the fund's structure and management. A representative meeting to work out recommendations for pension reform was first proposed by Khilkov on May 24, but delegate elections were not held until midsummer. Each road with more than 12,000 fund members was given two delegates, smaller roads got a single representative, and leading fund administrators designated by the ministry and private railroad managers were also granted voice and vote. Elections were held in two stages: eligible participants voted for representatives to a roadwide electoral meeting, which, after discussion and debate, chose the final congress delegates.[3] The very notion of an elected body recommending policy, even on a relatively minor matter such as pension affairs, still ran counter to the bureaucracy's paternalistic creed. But the pension system had been a source of unrest in February, and the ministry hoped to use the issue to pacify white-collar strata.

The first railroad pension fund was established on the Warsaw-Vienna Railroad in 1857, and by the mid 1880s various pension and/or insured savings plans functioned on perhaps a third or more of Russia's railroads. Attempts by the ministry to regulate highly diverse private pension programs in the 1870s met stiff resistance, however. Only in 1888 did the State Council adopt legislation compelling railroads to establish either pension or savings plans. On June 3, 1894, the separate private and state pension programs were merged into a single state-managed fund enrolling all permanent staff on state and private roads. Such a massive retirement

2. TsGIA, f. 273, op. 12, d. 373, ll. 263–64, 324–26; TsGAOR, f. 6865, d. 70, l. 56.
3. Rostov, "Zheleznodorozhniki," p. 149.

plan, which within two years controlled a capital fund of over five million rubles, was unprecedented in Russia and, according to the ministry, virtually unique in Europe.[4] As previously noted, the plan was in theory jointly financed by workers and management, but according to one study the latter's contribution was less than the amount received by the ministry to cover administrative expenses. Administration was in principle elective, but as one critic put it, the electoral process was "grossly deformed." On each line the fund was overseen by a committee of fifteen, elected by all fund participants earning more than 240 rubles annually and with at least one year's service. Candidates for election were limited to participants residing at the road's administrative headquarters, with at least three years' service and a minimum salary of 600 rubles. Even this group had limited powers, since according to the 1894 rules the railroad director, who served as fund chairman, was "personally responsible" for the administration of pension affairs. The majority of elected representatives remained "passive, fearing to contradict management." On the national level, control over the central investment lay with a group of five designated ministry officials.[5]

The pension fund was never popular with railroad employees. Its establishment was greeted with protests on several lines and many railwaymen suspected its real purpose was related only incidentally to their future welfare. By 1905 it was reported that only a third of all money going into the fund came back to workers in benefits, with the remainder financing various often questionable projects favored by railroad bureaucrats. Older workers who only began to contribute in mid career suffered especially, but the rules governing dispersals were restrictive for all. Those leaving railroad service before the ten-year minimum tenure required to receive a pension regained just two-thirds of their original contribution, without interest. Fund participants who died before retirement could pass only a small portion of their investment on to family members. The widow of one worker with twenty-two years' seniority, who had put in over 6,000 rubles, received just 472 back;

4. TsGAOR, f. 6865, d. 49, ll. 66–72; *VMPS*, June 22, 1896, 25, pp. 644–45. For a comparison with other countries, see Walter Licht, *Working For the Railroad: The Organization of Work in the Nineteenth Century* (Princeton, N.J., 1983), pp. 212–13.

5. TsGAOR, f. 6865, d. 29a, ll. 21–23; d. 34, l. 13; Rostov, "Zheleznodorozhniki," pp. 127–28.

an unmarried man served sixteen years and accumulated nearly 850 rubles, but could pass on nothing to his mother, whom he had supported. On the Moscow-Kazan line an old railroad inspector died with more than 11,000 rubles in the fund, but his two orphaned daughters got nothing.[6]

In 1901 the ministry appointed a commission to review proposals to improve the positions of older workers and orphans and to enhance the fund's profitability. In 1903 "a series of fundamental reforms . . . designed to make railroad service more attractive" were announced, but these brought few real changes and criticism continued to mount.[7] In February 1905 striking fund participants called almost unanimously for a "fundamental review" of pension affairs. "The basic principle of a new constitution for the pension fund must be the supposition that all pension capital consists of the inviolable property of the employees and can be used only for their needs," declared striking employees on the Moscow-Kazan Railroad.[8]

When the ministry announced plans for the pension congress the Central Bureau of the Railroad Union advised railwaymen to boycott the electoral process and maintained this stance until well after the St. Petersburg meeting began. The union leaders objected that a large proportion of the delegates would be appointed by fund directors and that the indirect character of the elections guaranteed a compliant group.[9] There was also considerable sympathy for a boycott among the Social Democrats, and on a few lines railwaymen refused to send delegates. On the Moscow-Vindau-Rybinsk Railroad, the August 12 electoral meeting voted eighteen to two for a boycott on the grounds that "the commission [the meeting was sometimes called the Pokotilov Commission, after the chief administrator of the pension fund] will consist of administrators and fund managers and cannot express the desires of the employees." The representatives called for liquidation of the old fund and establishment of a new system of life insurance for which

6. TsGAOR, f. 6865, d. 29a, l. 22; *Russkie vedomosti*, February 4, 1905, 33; *ZhD*, 1905, 21–22, pp. 250–51; 37, p. 460; Rostov, "Zheleznodorozhniki," p. 128.

7. Ministerstvo putei soobshcheniia, upravlenie zheleznykh dorog, #9302, "Ob izmenenii i dopolnenii Polozheniia o pensionnoi kasse sluzhashchikh na kazennykh zh. d.," February 24, 1903; *Zhel.*, 53, June 1, 1904, pp. 5–8.

8. TsGIA, f. 273, op. 12, d. 328, l. 78.

9. The text of the union boycott call is in TsGAOR, f. 6865, d. 63, ll. 79–80. See also Rostov, "Zheleznodorozhniki," p. 149.

"a new state order based on freedom of conscience, of speech and of the press, inviolability of home and person, freedom of assembly and unions, and participation of the people in legislation" was essential.[10] On the Transcaucasian Railroad, sixty-five representatives decided it was "not worth" sending a delegate to the capital. They "came to the conclusion that paternalistic management does not want to understand that the employees of the Transcaucasian Railroad have already succeeded in transforming themselves from ordinary philistines into citizens and thus demand something more than just daily bread."[11]

Where electoral meetings refused to cooperate, as well as on several smaller roads, delegates were simply appointed by the director, as on the Kharkov-Nikolaev road, where the election results were falsified. Elsewhere, according to *Zheleznodorozhnik*, the proceedings were generally "insipid and boring," indicating widespread lack of trust in the procedure and the abiding influence of conservative administrators on participants.[12] On more than a few lines, however, radical-minded employees ignored the boycott, packed the electoral meetings, and managed to initiate discussion of political issues. The electoral meeting on the South West Railroad, held at the Zhmerinka station, proceeded "in a very lively atmosphere, full of hope and expectation." On the Kursk-Kharkov-Sevastopol Railroad, the meeting expelled the road director from the chair and selected as delegates two independent leftists, who later recalled that "a huge majority of the railroad proletariat were hostile to the declared boycott and wanted to participate in the congress." A similar incident took place on the Riga-Orel Railroad. According to the police, all eighty-five delegates to the electoral meeting on the Vistula Railroad were "of known socialist views."[13]

10. TsGAOR, f. 6865, d. 118, ll. 362–64; *Golos zhizni*, 8, September 17, 1905; *Zhel.*, 122, October 4, 1905, p. 18.

11. The quote is from an illegal newspaper, *Soiuz*, published by Tiflis railwaymen in September 1905, found in TsGAOR, f. 6865, d. 93, l. 8.

12. *Privol. kr.*, 185, September 13, 1905; *Zhel.*, 116, August 23, 1905, pp. 1–2.

13. TsGAOR, f. 6865, d. 35, l. 153; S. Kramer, ed., *1905 god v Kharkove* (Kharkov, 1925), pp. 175–76; A. Paulish, "Zabastavochnoe dvizhenie na Rizhsko-Orlovskoi Zh. D.," *Proletarskaia revoliutsiia*, 1925, no. 11 (46): 154–55; I. M. Pushkareva, *Zheleznodorozhniki Rossii v burzhuazno-demokraticheskikh revoliutsiiakh* (Moscow, 1975), p. 145; L. M. Ivanov, ed., *Vserossiiskaia politicheskaia stachka v oktiabre 1905 goda* (Moscow-Leningrad, 1955), vol. 1, p. 296.

Congress preparations were especially lively on the Riazan-Ural Railroad. In fact, it is possible that the idea for a representative meeting originated there, since at least a week before the ministry proposed the Petersburg assembly, plans had already been announced for a Riazan-Ural pension conference, to be held in Tambov. The elections were marked by political controversy. At Ranenburg station a Social Democratic employee managed to turn the electoral assembly into a political meeting.[14] In Saratov the administrative employees elected delegates affiliated with the Railroad Union (who apparently ignored the boycott), but the engine-drivers chose the Social Democrat Molchanov, who immediately demanded that shop craftsmen be allocated ten delegate positions despite their lack of pension coverage. This was refused, but when those elected gathered on July 7 conditions in the workshops were the subject of extensive discussion. In fact, the Tambov conference expanded its agenda to address not only pension matters but other burning economic and political issues, and the delegates quickly divided into "right" and "left" wings, with an "extreme left" composed of three Saratov Social Democrats.[15] At the final session on July 20 the delegates approved a program of demands for all railroad workers, including craftsmen, and a bureau of twelve was chosen to continue organizing. On September 18 this body convened a second congress, which elected as St. Petersburg delegates Mikhail Dmitrievich Orekhov, who had been a delegate to the Railroad Union congress in July, and Aleksandr Mikhailovich Arkhangelskii; both were railroad engineers and middle-level officials. The two were instructed to participate in the St. Petersburg congress only if its sessions were public, with personal inviolability and free speech guaranteed to all delegates; if votes were limited to elected representatives; if the chair were elected from the ranks of the delegates and not officially designated; and if the proposals produced were ultimately subject to a vote of all railwaymen.[16]

Thus, when the pension congress opened on September 20 in the quarters of the St. Petersburg Railroad Club on the Neva embankment near Senate Square, there were already signs that gov-

14. *Privol. kr.*, 95, May 18, 1905; TsGAOR, f. 6865, d. 39a, l. 14.
15. I. S. Sokolov, *1905 god na Riazansko-Uralskoi zh. d.* (Saratov, 1925), pp. 34–36; *Privol. kr.*, 140, July 14, 1905.
16. *Privol. kr.*, 166, August 18, 1905; 192, September 22, 1905.

ernment hopes of pacifying a segment of the railroad work force were unfounded.[17] The assembly's composition was decidedly non-proletarian: of fifty-seven elected delegates (thirteen with voice but no vote) all but two engine-drivers and one railroad doctor were upper- or middle-level managers. With attending pension administrators, ministry officials, and managers of private roads, there were approximately seventy-five participants, of whom sixteen considered themselves loosely "on the left." This group, which began to meet as an informal caucus almost immediately, was quite influential, however, since even the most conservative among the elected delegates opposed a meeting stage-managed by the ministry.[18]

The congress opened with a speech by Dumitrashko surveying various pension fund problems and proposed solutions, after which the fund director, A. D. Pokotilov, assumed the chair. Immediately Arkhangelskii rose to demand a temporary adjournment so that the elected delegates might meet separately. This was granted, and the elected group reconvened in private session, with Mark Elizarov, senior accountant general of the Nicholas Railroad, Lenin's brother-in-law and a Bolshevik, temporarily in the chair. (Elizarov's extreme politics probably played little role in his selection; on the eve of the congress he had published a lengthy and thoughtful critique of the pension system in *Zheleznodorozhnik*, and this, no doubt, gained him respect and name recognition.) Arkhangelskii then outlined the conditions for participation mandated by the Riazan-Ural electors. "We wish to work," Orekhov added to this report, "but not as a bureaucratic commission and not so that Pokotilov can simply shelve the results of our efforts." The group voted unanimously to demand an elected chair for all sessions, but when the proposal was put to Pokotilov, he countered with a weak compromise. The next morning, however, the ministry withdrew its objections to an elected chair and the delegates proceeded to put Orekhov in the post by a margin of thirteen votes, with Elizarov and Bronislaw Skupevsky, one of Nemeshaev's deputies on the South West Rail-

17. The Railroad Club, which catered to the engineer corps, was at 6 English Embankment (now Red Army Embankment), two doors from the present reading room of the Central State Historical Archive. It is today marked by a memorial plaque commemorating the "First All-Russian Congress of Railroad Workers."

18. *Zhel.*, 121, September 27, 1905, pp. 4–6; Rostov, "Zheleznodorozhniki," p. 150; Kramer, p. 177.

road, vice-chairs. With this victory under their belts the delegates were in a truculent mood. By a vote of twenty-six to eight they expelled the appointed delegate of the Kharkov-Nikolaev Railroad, replacing him with one claiming an electoral mandate. "As an organized force we must demand, not beseech and propose," Orekhov declared. "We must put forward demands that cannot be fulfilled."[19]

The congress was rechristened the "First All-Russian Delegate Congress of Railroad Employees," a sort of railroad constituent assembly seeking to bring democracy and a kind of professional control to railroad management, an idea that recalled an appeal for a similar body issued by strikers on the Nicholas road in February.[20] Congress minutes were carried in *Zheleznodorozhnik*, which became the unofficial voice of the meeting, and detailed reports also appeared in the socialist daily *Nasha zhizn'*. Support from offices, stations, depots, and workshops was little short of overwhelming, as meetings passed resolutions of support and instructions demanding "fundamental changes in legal and political conditions." At small rural stations news of the congress rebellion sparked agitated debates among railwaymen, even where the workers could barely articulate "what precisely we were agitated about." Messages of solidarity were telegraphed to St. Petersburg at a rate of nearly thirty each day.[21] From the Riazan-Ural road came praise for the "staunch fighters for the interests of the railroad proletariat." Employees on the Vladikavkaz road expressed the conviction that "the day is not far when each railwayman can participate in solving the problems posed by his own professional interests and needs." Engine-driver G. O. Tsimoshenko, a delegate from the Polessky road, told the congress the roads were "capitalist enterprises" and railwaymen of all stripes "hired proletarians." "Proletarians indeed we are," responded Dr. Ia. Liakhovskii of the Trans-Baikal road,

19. *Zhel.*, 121, September 27, 1905, pp. 1–3; *Nasha zhizn'*, 276–77, September 21–22, 1905.

20. *Zhel.*, 98, April 12, 1905, pp. 7–10.

21. *Nasha zhizn'*, 294, October 1, 1905; *1905 vo vospominaniiakh ego uchastnikov* (Rostov-on-Don, 1925), p. 64. M. N. Pokrovskii wrote that "the importance of the commission [pension congress] lay not in the activities of the delegates meeting in St. Petersburg but in how it was conceived all over the country. For the railroad workers this was a kind of constituent assembly. To them it seemed that the commission was about to proclaim a democratic republic" (*Russkaia istoriia v samom szhatom ocherke* in *Izbrannye proizvedeniia* [Moscow, 1962], vol. 3, p. 409).

"but in most cases our employer is the state. To nationalize such an enterprise we need only free democratic control by all the people, and first of all by railroad employees."[22]

But behind such militant rhetoric the congress was notably less radical, reflecting the limitations of its essentially elite composition. A. A. Tsvetkov, a left delegate from the Vladikavkaz road, recalled how the congress responded to a speech he delivered calling for the overthrow of the regime: "These engineers . . . looked at each other with fear, pinched themselves and asked whether I was really such a revolutionary."[23] Significantly, for the next seventeen days, with attendance declining, debate focused almost solely on professional questions, with highly technical exchanges on the relative merits of various forms of pension finance. Here the "radical" position was for a comprehensive system of state-financed disability insurance, which the congress accepted in principle on October 4, much to the ministry's displeasure. But the elected delegate of the Kharkov-Nikolaev road was by no means far from the mark when he announced that "neither pension and savings fund nor state insurance can in the present state of affairs satisfy railwaymen." Hence the congress endorsed, though by only a narrow margin and with more than a few delegates absent, a resolution offered by Arkhangelskii declaring that state insurance would only be subverted "under the existing police-bureaucratic regime. . . . A just security for the ill and the aged will be possible only after the existing system is replaced by a democracy."[24]

The opening of the pension congress coincided with a revival of industrial strikes. In St. Petersburg, 260 strikes involved 40,000 workers in September, but the center of unrest was Moscow, where a walkout of printers at the Sytin Co. quickly spread to include many of the city's printers, tobacco workers, bakers, carpenters, and metalworkers. Although the movement lacked coordination, at its peak, September 23–25, crowds of strikers roamed the streets, stirred by revolutionary agitators and sometimes clashing violently with Cossacks. By the end of the month, the street disturbances had died down and the number of strikers was declining, but un-

22. TsGAOR, f. 6865, d. 70, ll. 1–2.
23. TsGAOR, f. 6865, d. 120, l. 21.
24. TsGAOR, f. 6865, d. 70, ll. 4–6.

rest did not abate completely and the atmosphere remained tense. The spontaneous demonstration of students and middle-class oppositionists occasioned by the October 3 funeral of the liberal rector of Moscow University, Prince Trubetskoi, who died while on business in St. Petersburg, and the indignation in liberal circles following the Cossack attack on that demonstration, revealed that impatience for change was mounting in educated society.[25]

Moscow's railwaymen were not unaffected by these developments. On September 27 a meeting of nearly 500 workers at the shops of the Moscow-Kursk Railroad condemned the Bulygin Duma and expressed solidarity with the printers. The same day 1,000 workers at the workshops of the Moscow-Brest Railroad, the Menshevik-led "brain of the [Presnia] district," walked out, presenting a list of twenty-nine economic demands. Administrative employees and operations workers remained on the job, however, and the ministry refused to negotiate. On October 3 there was sporadic strike activity in the Kazan and Iaroslavl shops and among Kursk conductors. It was only with considerable effort that the Central Bureau of the Railroad Union managed to persuade its Moscow units not to join the Brest walkout individually, but to prepare instead for a general strike.[26] Rumors that began circulating during the first week in October to the effect that the pension congress had been dispersed and the delegates arrested, though unfounded, added further to the building tension.[27]

At its July congress the Railroad Union, with little debate and almost as an afterthought, had declared itself in favor of a general strike at an appropriate moment in the near future. By late Sep-

25. On the September events in Moscow, see Laura Engelstein, *Moscow, 1905: Working Class Organization and Political Conflict* (Stanford, Calif., 1982), pp. 73–96.

26. Ivanov, ed., vol. 1, pp. 85–87; P. A. Garvi, *Vospominaniia sotsialdemokrata* (New York, 1946), pp. 546–53; Engelstein, p. 105; Leon Trotsky, *1905*, trans. Anya Bostock (New York, 1972), p. 86; Walter Sablinsky, "The All-Russian Railroad Union and the Beginning of the General Strike in October, 1905," in *Revolution and Politics in Russia*, edited by Alexander and Janet Rabinowitch with Ladis K. D. Kristof (Bloomington, Ind., 1972), p. 126.

27. The rumors added to the agitated mood, to be sure, but they were not, as some contemporaries believed, the precipitant of the October general strike. The authorities did place the lodgings of some delegates under surveillance on October 8, but this was surely a *response* to the Moscow strike, which had already begun, and the rumors began somewhat earlier. See Kramer, ed., p. 236.

tember this relatively cautious pronouncement acquired considerable urgency, since the idea had begun to seize broad sectors of both the railroad work force and the Moscow populace. Along with most of the socialist groups, the Central Bureau hoped to coordinate strike plans with the scheduled opening of the Bulygin Duma and the first anniversary of Bloody Sunday in January. It seemed, however, that events demanded swifter action. Moreover, the St. Petersburg pension congress had emerged as a potential rival to the Moscow-based Railroad Union for leadership of the professional movement. When the congress declared its independence of the government, the Central Bureau retracted its ineffective boycott and Romanov went to the capital to act as a liaison. Still, union activists could not help but retain a suspicious attitude toward the leadership pretensions of the legally constituted and still formally government-sponsored St. Petersburg body. Challenged from one side by the growth of Social Democratic influence, especially among shop craftsmen, and from the other by the pension congress's appeal to the administrative hierarchy, the Railroad Union was in something of a bind.

By October, then, the Central Bureau was convinced that a general railroad strike was both necessary and possible. Pereverzev later compared the mood among Moscow's railwaymen to "a saturated salt solution into which but a single crystal need be tossed for crystallization to ensue." But the union leaders were reluctant to take on sole organizational responsibility for a walkout; in their view the "party organization," not the Central Bureau, could "best play the role of the crystal."[28] Meetings were arranged with revolutionary groups and unions, but the most important negotiations took place with members of the Bolshevik-led Moscow Social Democratic Committee. In view of the ebb of the September strike movement, the Social Democrats, and a minority of the Central Bureau itself, were skeptical of the strike proposal, but agreed that "in the workshops of several roads where they had organizations they would begin a strike," though only on a local basis.[29]

Although not quite what the union leaders wanted to hear, this

28. TsGAOR, f. 6865, d. 120, l. 87.
    29. V. N. Pereverzev, "Pervyi vserossiiskii zheleznodorozhnyi soiuz 1905 goda," *Byloe*, 1925, no. 4 (32): 50; M. B. [M. Bogdanov], *Ocherki po istorii zheleznodorozhnykh zabastovok v Rossii* (Moscow, 1906), p. 31; Rostov, "Zheleznodorozhniki," p. 151.

was enough. Telegrams went out to provincial branches informing them that a national railroad strike would begin on October 4. On that day, at the second meeting of the newly formed Council of Representatives of the Five Professions, a delegate of the Central Bureau announced that the strike would actually begin the following afternoon on the Moscow-Kazan line and that plans were afoot to have other roads join.[30] At some time during this confused period (probably on October 3) the Bolshevik railroad organization circulated a leaflet calling on railroad shopmen to strike, ending with the words "we await your answer." There was, however, no response, either to this Social Democratic appeal or to the efforts of the Central Bureau. The first attempt by the Railroad Union to organize a general strike together with the Bolshevik-led Moscow Committee had failed.[31]

It seemed that the concern of the Moscow Bolsheviks that the strike call was premature had been well-founded after all. On October 1 the police reported that "the spirit of the striking workers has noticeably declined, and there is reason to believe that the majority of strikers will return to work." Where on September 29, 15,000 Moscow workers were still on strike, by October 4 the number had fallen to 12,789, and on that day most newspapers, suspended owing to the printers' walkout, resumed publication.[32] The

30. Rostov, "Zheleznodorozhniki," p. 151; *Materialy po professional'nomu dvizheniiu rabochikh*, vol. 1 (St. Petersburg, 1906), p. 15; Sablinsky, p. 127. Pushkareva, *Zheleznodorozhniki*, p. 149, says the October 2 meeting of the Council of the Five Professions endorsed the general strike call, but, according to Engelstein, p. 265, there is no mention of this in the meeting protocol.

31. We know of these words from the Bolshevik leaflet only because they are quoted in a subsequent one (Ivanov, ed., vol. 1, pp. 415, 678 n. 193). Pereverzev, p. 50, makes it apparent, however, that the leaflet was a product of the Bolshevik negotiations with the Central Bureau. He also told a 1925 audience that after several days of negotiations the Moscow Social Democrats agreed to issue a strike call on October 4, which was distributed, but, according to the "extremely embarrassed" SDs themselves, "made absolutely no impression." See TsGAOR, f. 6865, d. 120, l. 87. The position of M. B. [M. Bogdanov], p. 31, that "the call of the Social Democratic railroad organization to strike had no success whatsoever," echoed by Sablinsky, p. 127, is misleading. It is clear from all accounts that this unsuccessful effort was initiated by the Railroad Union with only reluctant and limited cooperation from the Bolshevik group, no matter which organization ultimately distributed the unsuccessful appeal. It was *not* an attempt by Social Democratic railroaders to foment a strike independently.

32. Ivanov, ed., vol. 1, p. 98; A. V. Shestakov, "Zheleznodorozhniki Moskovskogo uzla v revoliutsii 1905 g.," *Partiinyi rabotnik zheleznodorozhnogo transporta*, 1940, no. 3: 277.

Central Bureau nonetheless remained committed to its strike plan. On October 5 it convened a meeting of the Moscow junction. The majority of those attending supported a renewed strike call, but according to a police agent they encountered forceful opposition based on three main arguments: insufficient preparation; the ebb of the strike movement; and fear that the union would be crippled by arrests. The majority held firm, however, with the strongest strike advocates being the Moscow-Kazan telegraph operator Bednov and his comrades the engine-drivers A. V. Ukhtomskii and N. K. Pechkovskii, both formally affiliated with the Socialist Revolutionary Party. These *Kazantsy* put forth a bold plan, which the meeting ultimately adopted: the strike was set to begin on October 7, when the Moscow-Kazan drivers would stop departure of freight and call out shop craftsmen and employees. Striking telegraphists would spread the word by wire.[33]

The walkout actually began around 2 P.M. on October 6, when engine-drivers on the Kazan road refused freight runs. Late that evening two groups of engine-drivers set out along the line. Commandeering a shunt engine, one group, led by Bednov and Ukhtomskii, proceeded to the Nikolaevka station, where there was a brief skirmish with railroad police and drivers reluctant to strike. The other detachment, under Pechkovskii, proceeded to Perovo, where the stationmaster was a union member. Here the prearranged telegram was dispatched signaling a national railroad strike. During the night the agitators moved through the junction linking the Kazan road to the Nicholas and Iaroslavl lines. Windows were smashed at station offices and depots, and after strike messages had gone out telegraph equipment was destroyed.[34]

By morning police had rounded up many of the instigators, including Bednov and Pechkovskii, but the arrests only further inflamed the situation. Early on the morning of October 7 a small, but angry, crowd assembled in front of the police station where the arrested leaders were being held, and the authorities prudently yielded the men. The jubilant strikers then organized a meeting of

33. Pereverzev, p. 51; M. B. [M. Bogdanov], pp. 31–32; TsGAOR, f. 6865, d. 63, l. 120; Ivanov, ed., vol. 1, p. 488; Rostov, "Zheleznodorozhniki," p. 152.

34. Ivanov, ed., vol. 1, pp. 210, 266–67, 488; M. K. Dymkov and D. Ia. Lipovetskii, eds., *1905 god na Kazanke* (Moscow, 1925), pp. 59–60; TsGAOR, f. 6865, d. 120, ll. 108–9; Pereverzev, p. 51; M. B. [M. Bogdanov], p. 32; Rostov, "Zheleznodorozhniki," p. 152.

about sixty to seventy employees in the hall of the main administration building. Chosen as chair, Bednov presented a report on the progress of the walkout, and a list of demands was read. The meeting voted to support the strike, and its participants dispersed to spread the word through the Moscow junction.[35]

The situation on the Moscow-Kazan Railroad on October 7 was confused, as varied segments of the work force and diverse political factions responded to the initiative taken by a relative handful of militant Railroad Union members. The authorities later charged that most workers were coerced into striking, but more likely the walkout was greeted with enthusiasm, since oppositional sentiment was well prepared. More problematic were difficulties arising from political rivalries within the work force. Crowds of railwaymen had been meeting in the woods around Perovo all summer to listen to revolutionary speeches, including debates between rival organizations. The Kazan shops were filled with lively political debate, mainly between SRs, who tended to sympathize with the Railroad Union, and Social Democrats affiliated with the Moscow Committee. In September the Bolsheviks felt strong enough to hold a political rally at the gates of the shops. One who spoke at that meeting was a nineteen-year-old metalworker named Aleksandr Gorchilin, known to comrades by the party name "Grenadier." Gorchilin was named by party leaders to a newly formed party railroad district and was coopted to the city leadership body.[36]

It was Gorchilin who led the walkout at the Moscow-Kazan workshops and depot on October 7. Speaking at a 1925 anniversary meeting in Moscow, he said that the walkout had begun "almost spontaneously" on October 6 after each shop had prepared its own list of demands "known to all the workers." In a published, and certainly more reliable, account, however, he recalled that owing to lack of time the strike and its demands had been prepared at the last minute by a "tight group of Bolshevik *Kazantsy*," with repre-

35. Ivanov, ed., vol. 1, pp. 267–68; Dymkov and Lipovetskii, p. 60.
36. N. S. Trusova, ed., *Revoliutsionnoe dvizhenie v Rossii vesnoi i letom 1905 goda, aprel'–sentiabr'* (Moscow, 1955–57), vol. 1, pp. 226–27; Dymkov and Lipovetskii, p. 56; A. Gorchilin, *1905 god na Kazanke* (Moscow, 1930), pp. 9–14. N. N. Mandelshtam recalled that Bolshevik railroad organizing in Moscow—principally in the workshops—expanded from a circle of just seven at the beginning of the year, to a network of about six hundred at the start of the October strike (TsGAOR, f. 6865, d. 120, l. 39).

sentatives from the Moscow Committee and the Iaroslavl and Kursk Bolshevik organizations, and that the actual walkout began at noon on October 7. Although Gorchilin remained silent about the actions of the union engine-drivers the previous day, it is clear his group was responding to that fait accompli. When the shopmen walked out they gathered in a large crowd to hear Gorchilin greet the strike and a prominent SR call for cooperation with the Railroad Union. After electing a committee consisting of four Social Democrats and the SR, the strikers proceeded to join willing engine-drivers and depot workers in crippling locomotive engines. From here the crowd moved to the terminal to rouse the office employees and telegraph operators.[37]

When the striking craftsmen arrived, the group around Bednov had, of course, already called white-collar railwaymen out. But there were divisions among the administrative staff too. Bednov represented the Railroad Union, but a Bolshevik clerk named D. M. Kotliarenko could also claim a following. He had assembled another meeting, which was in session—and wavering in its support for the strike—when the shopmen arrived. "Comrades, you're here discussing this question, but we've already decided it!" the employees were told. At this point the offices began to empty spontaneously and the various factions merged in a common crowd of strikers, which moved across Kalanchevskaia Square to the terminal of the Moscow-Iaroslavl-Archangel Railroad, where the Railroad Union had one of its strongest units. By the middle of the afternoon the terminal was entirely shut down.[38]

On October 8 striking railwaymen made the rounds of the city's terminals. "The administrative personnel, mainly young men and women, went in crowds to all the stations in the Moscow junction to persuade the workers and employees to leave their posts," Pereverzev recalled. They "were responsible for spreading the strike among the very workers in the workshops who, according to the original plan, should have begun the strike themselves."[39] Other

37. TsGAOR, f. 6865, d. 120, l. 11; Gorchilin, pp. 15–20.
38. See Kotliarenko's 1925 account in TsGAOR, f. 6865, d. 120, l. 109, 112–14, and Gorchilin, p. 20. Kotliarenko's unspoken implication that there was but one meeting in the administration, which he and not Bednov chaired, is clearly false. On the Iaroslavl walkout, see Ivanov, ed., vol. 1, pp. 268, 282.
39. Pereverzev, p. 51.

reports confirm that the initiative mostly came from a section of the administrative personnel and then spread to the depots and shops. On the Moscow-Kursk Railroad a mass meeting addressed by Railroad Union and Social Democratic representatives voted to strike, but the walkout began when a crowd arrived from the Kazan and Iaroslavl terminals. By October 9 the Moscow railroad junction was under armed guard. By October 10 traffic had ceased on all lines, with incoming trains forced to stop at suburban stations. Passenger terminals were crowded with stranded travellers, who were housed in spare railroad cars and given a small stipend. On October 7 the Central Bureau approved a list of eleven political and economic demands and circulated a leaflet calling on workers to strike "for freedom and a better life." A similar call came October 8 from the Bolshevik-led Moscow Committee. In a second leaflet, released on October 9, the Central Bureau advised "no negotiations whatsoever with the government" until the tsar conceded political rights.[40]

On the night of October 8 ten leading members of the Railroad Union were arrested, including Pereverzev, Bednov, and Ukhtomskii. Within days eight more leaders were seized, including Bogdanov of the Central Bureau and Pechkovskii.[41] But arrests had little effect on the strike, which was spreading with increasing rapidity to other sections of labor and society. On October 10 Prince Khilkov met with a delegation of some forty railroad workers. "The deputies insisted on demands that are beyond my power to grant: that is, political rights and the liberation of individuals arrested by the police," he reported. "Material questions are of secondary importance." The minister enraged his audience with patronizing tales of his years as a cabman; forced to confess his ignorance even of the fact that railroads had been under martial law since February, he was openly mocked. As if to add insult to injury, the highest transportation official in Russia was compelled to return to St. Petersburg by private carriage, the Nicholas Railroad being halted by the strike.[42]

40. TsGAOR, f. 6865, d. 127, l. 39; Ivanov, ed., vol. 1, pp. 201–2, 210–13, 217–20, 264–65, 269, 278–79, 415; *Proletarii*, 24, October 25, 1905.

41. TsGAOR, f. 6865, d. 63, ll. 115–19, 134–36.

42. *Pravo*, 45–46, November 20, 1905, supplement, p. 12; *Zhel.*, 125, November 1, 1905, p. 6; *Nasha zhizn'*, 309, October 13, 1905, p. 2; S. I. Witte, *Vospominaniia* (Moscow, 1960), vol. 2, p. 553; *Proletarii*, 24, October 25, 1905.

Who began the October general strike? During the 1920s most Soviet historians accepted the contention of Railroad Union leaders that the strike was initiated by the Central Bureau. Writing in the 1925 collection edited by M. N. Pokrovskii, A. Shestakov charged that "the Petersburg and Moscow Bolshevik committee took a waiting attitude; it is apparent that they overdid their cautiousness." This view gained support in the 1940 memoirs of S. I. Mitskevich.[43] By the mid 1950s, however, Soviet historians were forthrightly declaring that "the October strike was prepared and executed by the Russian proletariat under the leadership of the Bolsheviks."[44]

Key to all recent Soviet accounts is the contention that on October 6 Bolshevik workers from the Kazan, Iaroslavl, and Kursk lines met and decided to strike, and that this decision was endorsed by a meeting of the Moscow Committee that evening. According to one 1975 history, "The Central Bureau of the All-Russian Railroad Union also declared a general railroad strike."[45] Although these Bolshevik meetings were mentioned in most every secondary work published for the fiftieth anniversary of the revolution, I was unable to locate a single reference to them in the mammoth collection of primary documents and materials produced for that occasion.[46]

43. Pokrovskii, *1905*, vol. 1, p. 90; S. I. Mitskevich, *Revoliutsionnaia Moskva* (Moscow, 1940), pp. 289–90. Neither of these men, however, was involved in railroad organizing. Even in the 1920s, former Bolshevik railroad organizers would not grant a leading role to the Railroad Union.

44. L. K. Erman, "Uchastie intelligentsii v oktiabr'skoi politicheskoi stachke," *Istoricheskie zapiski*, 49 (1954): 367. Western observers have attributed this change in emphasis to "the advent of Stalinism," as in Sablinsky, p. 129. It was not until after Stalin's death, however, that obviously distorted efforts to downplay the Railroad Union's role appeared. With the exception of Mitskevich's memoir, little of relevance was published during the 1930s and 1940s, although in 1940 A. V. Shestakov credited neither the union nor the Social Democrats with starting the strike. Pushkareva, *Zheleznodorozhniki*, p. 149 n. 21, states that an overemphasis on the role of the Railroad Union was characteristic of Soviet historiography from the 1920s through the 1940s.

45. Iu. O. Korablev et al., *Revoliutsiia 1905–1907 gg. v Rossii* (Moscow, 1975), pp. 142–43. Pushkareva, *Zheleznodorozhniki*, pp. 148–49, offers a similar account.

46. See, for examples, G. D. Kostomarov, ed., *1905 god v Moskve* (Moscow, 1955), p. 84; A. V. Piaskovskii, *Revoliutsiia 1905–1907 gg. v Rossii* (Moscow, 1966), p. 121; Korablev, pp. 142–43. Apparently Soviet historians also find it difficult to document these meetings. Wherever the story is repeated, it is rarely accompanied by a note indicating its source. Pushkareva, *Zheleznodorozhniki*,

Perhaps one source is Gorchilin, who recalled an October 6 meeting of Bolshevik *Kazantsy* with party railroad leaders. Walter Sablinsky points out that it would hardly be surprising if these Bolshevik meetings did take place, "since the strike was already in progress, and the Bolshevik organization had to clarify its policy towards it." But Sablinsky's response to Soviet historiography tends too far in the other direction in concluding that "the evidence, then, clearly indicates that the initiative and execution of the massive railroad strike of early October, 1905 was the result of a planned effort on the part of the Central Bureau" and by implying that the Bolsheviks opposed the strike until October 10.[47]

Actually, the failure of the first strike call issued by the Moscow Social Democrats with the cooperation of the Railroad Union indicates that *no one was in effective control of the situation*. What is most startling is that despite the initial failure and the apparent retreat of the September movement, the Central Bureau remained committed to a strike. Union leaders must have realized that were they to back down they stood a real chance of losing all hope of leadership of the railroad movement. In this situation the persistence and enthusiasm of the *Kazantsy* must have seemed persuasive indeed. As Bednov later recalled, "Our attempt to begin [the strike] from above had not succeeded." Hence the Kazan union group "decided to offer the Central Bureau a new initiative" and the strike was actually started by "only about six or seven individuals."[48] Explaining the origin of the strike to the pension congress delegates on October 10, Romanov allowed that "the employees struck spontaneously; recognizing the inevitability of a strike on the Moscow-Kazan Railroad, the union found it necessary to support a strike on the remaining roads of the Moscow junction."[49] Far from being well planned by the Central Bureau, the October railroad strike began as something of a last gasp effort to salvage a situation that for several days had been confused and even deteriorating.

---

p. 149, for example, credits only an unfootnoted passage in the 1956 *Istoriia Kommunisticheskoi partii Sovetskogo Soiuza*.

47. Gorchilin, pp. 15–20; Sablinsky, p. 129.
48. TsGAOR, f. 6865, d. 120, ll. 107–8.
49. *Zhel.*, 127, November 17, 1905, Bulletin 10, p. 16.

As for the Bolsheviks, they were even more the temporary prisoners of events than the Railroad Union. Even assuming the meetings of October 6 did take place, clearly the Social Democratic organization was powerless to do much more than support the decisions taken by the Central Bureau at the initiative of the *Kazantsy*. Certainly the strike was not the result of Social Democratic initiative or leadership, but once it was under way the Bolsheviks did work actively to develop it and cooperated with other forces in providing direction. By all indications the Bolsheviks lived up to the agreement they had reached with the Railroad Union leaders the previous week. According to Mitskevich, "Our railroad district energetically supported the strike, having linked the railroad workshops to it."[50]

In the crush of events, however, it was probably not apparent who could claim the initiative, and to most workers this hardly mattered. When Moscow activists assembled twenty years later to reminisce about those event-filled days, the question of, as Kotliarenko put it, "who said A"—that is, who began the strike—was a hot one. Pereverzev and Bednov argued that the strike had been started by the Railroad Union, while Gorchilin, Mandelshtam, and Kotliarenko attributed the initiative to their party. It soon became evident, however, that the varied political forces among railwaymen had in fact all been acting separately and often unknown to one another, and much confusion probably stemmed from this.[51] At the same time, organizational labels could be less important than personal ties and work affiliations. There was a rough coordination of action among rank-and-file Social Democrats, Socialist Revolutionaries, and trade unionists even though these groups formally functioned apart from one another and their leaders engaged in vigorous political sparring.

50. Mitskevich, p. 389. A Social Democratic worker in the shops of the Moscow-Kursk road recalled: "As a party organization we stood completely apart from the work and movement of the railroad union. But we actively participated in all events, leading the working masses of our shops" (TsGAOR, f. 6865, d. 127, l. 40).

51. TsGAOR, f. 6865, d. 120, passim. It seems likely that people such as Gorchilin were essentially honest in their claims to have begun the walkout; this is simply how it appeared to them when viewed from the fragmented perspective of underground labor politics at this confusing moment. Since prominent party historians would continue for some time to credit the Central Bureau with the October initiative, it seems unlikely that those who recalled otherwise in 1925 were simply responding to latter-day partisanship.

Although the Bolsheviks supported the railroad walkout, they were skeptical about extending the movement into a national or even citywide general strike.[52] For one thing, the Leninists distrusted amorphous strike movements, preferring to focus attention on the question of state power, and consequently on armed insurrection. But their skepticism was founded on more pragmatic grounds too. In the spring a call for a general strike by the Moscow Committee had "failed to get the support of a single enterprise."[53] Even after the start of the Moscow-Kazan strike the number of strikers in Moscow remained stable for several days. On October 8 the authorities counted 10,213 workers out; by October 12 the total had reached just 10,865. Yet the spirit of the railroad workers was contagious, and there was strike talk everywhere among workers and middle-class professionals alike, although there was little organized connection between the railroad walkout and renewed unrest in industrial districts. On October 10 a conference of the Moscow Bolshevik organization voted to endorse a nationwide general strike.[54]

The railroad strike that began in Moscow rapidly spread to the farthest corners of the empire. The strike formally began with the Railroad Union's telegraphed call on October 7, and on October 9 provincial newspapers published the rumors that had been circulating in Moscow that the pension congress delegates were under arrest. It was only after October 10, however, when Moscow was completely shut off, that most other cities were affected. Fully to trace the paths along which the movement spread chronologically and geographically is close to impossible, since it was like a wildfire, spontaneous and beyond control. The largest railroad centers were ripe for unrest, but in some places the strike call was initially "not so successful," or even "came like a bolt from the blue," although in the end all but two minor roads joined the movement.[55]

52. Sablinsky, p. 129, tends to confuse the question of Bolshevik support for a railroad strike with support for a general strike of the entire working class. Reluctance to endorse the latter did not necessarily indicate opposition to the former.

53. Account of Mandelshtam in S. Chernomordik, ed., *Piatyi god* (Moscow, 1925), vol. 1, p. 85. Also quoted in Sablinsky, p. 129.

54. Ivanov, ed., vol. 1, pp. 535–37; Mitskevich, p. 392.

55. Kramer, p. 177; Ivan Maruta, *Ocherki po istorii revoliutsionnogo professional'nogo dvizheniia na Moskovsko-Kievo-Voronezhskoi zh. d. Vypusk pervyi.*

On the railroads the October general strike was like a collection of local strikes, with the extent and nature of participation, leadership, and militancy varying significantly.

Although this volume is concerned specifically with railroads, the October railroad strike was soon subsumed within a much broader strike movement. Affecting all sorts of enterprises, both industrial and commercial, as well as students, professionals, and other members of the educated classes, it was perhaps the most extensive general strike in history. It is hardly surprising that the railroad walkout should have sparked a broader uprising, since the political heterogeneity and apparent coalescence of professional, class, and general civic interests that seemed to characterize the railroad movement appealed to varied strata. The October general strike united skilled and unskilled, blue- and white-collar workers, even employers and employees—for instance, pharmacists and their clerks—in common struggle. It was a repetition of the pattern, first seen in Rostov-on-Don in 1902, in which labor conflict—now, as then, a railroad strike—aroused middle-class political opposition. There was no common program of demands, but the goals were generally recognized to be "freedom" and a "constitution," although these terms were understood differently by different groups.

The alliance between classes was often more symbolic than real, however, as workers were frequently hostile to their intellectual and professional allies and many in the middle class were equally suspicious of labor. In Moscow, according to Laura Engelstein, the October factory strikes were not as well organized as they had been the previous month, spreading along neighborhood rather than industrial lines. As the printers had in September, striking railroad workers "provided a free-floating mass to which other strikers could then attach themselves." After October 13 it seems that most factories shut down owing to outside intimidation or as a result of employer lockouts. Although most striking industrial workers sought improvements in their economic situation, political agitation was widespread. Still, "the example of the strike itself was

---

1905 g. (Kursk, 1925), p. 37; TsGAOR, f. 6865, d. 120, ll. 60, 45. For a chronology of all railroad strike activity between October 6 and 16 compiled by the Ministry of Communications, see Ivanov, ed., vol. 1, pp. 217–20.

more effective than political propaganda in winning recruits in the factory districts."[56]

Workers in Moscow played a much smaller role than did the middle class in directing the movement. Although railroad and factory workers were out for almost a week before significant numbers of white-collar employees and professionals joined the strike, the strike committee that formed on October 12 included only a handful of factory delegates. The Railroad Union Central Bureau was represented, as were strike committees of individual lines. They were joined by member organizations of the Union of Unions; associations of technicians, engineers and municipal employees; telephone workers; bank and retail clerks; and just three blue-collar groups. The three socialist parties participated independently, and the Social Democrats tried in vain to increase worker participation, with the Mensheviks also going outside the committee to organize a Soviet modeled on the one in St. Petersburg. Such a representative body of workers would not take shape in Moscow until late November, however.[57]

Where in Moscow the initiative taken by railwaymen aroused other segments of the population, in St. Petersburg railroad workers struck together with other groups. As in Moscow, the death of Prince Trubetskoi became a lightning rod for political opposition. On October 2 the Social Democrats organized a demonstration of about six hundred workers and students to follow his cortege to the railroad station. On that day the city's printers declared a strike in solidarity with their Moscow comrades. Within a few days the printers were joined by workers at the Neva Shipbuilding Works, the Obukhov steel mill and other plants. On October 4 a one-hour walkout and mass meeting closed the workshops of the Nicholas Railroad.[58]

As in Moscow, for several days the strike seemed unable to make up its mind, but as news of the Moscow railroad walkout arrived the movement was rejuvenated. At first St. Petersburg railwaymen looked to the pension congress for leadership, but that body lacked roots among local railroad employees and workers, especially shop craftsmen. When word arrived of the events on the Kazan line, the

56. Engelstein, pp. 112–13.
57. Ibid., pp. 114–16.
58. Ivanov, ed., vol. 1, pp. 342–49.

congress voted to telephone Moscow to dissuade the strikers from action, since their rumored arrests were believed to have started the trouble.[59] When the congress did address the questions posed by the general strike in a special Sunday session on October 9, local elements had already seized the initiative in the city and the attention of the delegates was focused on the national scene.

On October 8 representatives of the St. Petersburg lines met at the Military-Medical Academy to discuss a strike. They decided to focus on the workers of the Nicholas Railroad, where a walkout of switchmen began that evening. This line was already crippled by the strike at its Moscow terminus, but since the main offices, workshops, and depot were in the capital, traffic was still moving north of Tver. After a day of agitation the Nicholas Railroad ceased operation on October 10. On October 11 some ten thousand factory workers, students, and others assembled in various professional and local groupings on the campus of St. Petersburg University. A meeting of railroad employees voted unanimously to strike.[60] On October 12 every railroad line serving the city was shut down, including the St. Petersburg–Warsaw, Vindau-Rybinsk, Baltic, and Nicholas roads. On October 13 employees of the Administration of Railroads and the Ministry of Communications joined the strike, by which time the Petersburg walkout had become general, vastly exceeding the January movement in scope.[61]

If accusations that the Bolshevik-led Moscow Committee was overly cautious in endorsing the general strike are exaggerated, similar charges against the St. Petersburg Bolsheviks are largely valid. Only after the movement had spread throughout the working class and was rapidly gaining white-collar and middle-class support did they come out in favor of the strike.[62] It fell instead to the Mensheviks, who controlled the St. Petersburg Social Democratic organization, to seize the initiative. On October 10 they proposed a citywide body of worker delegates, an idea that won the support of leading left-liberals. This body, which met for the first time on October 13, and adopted the title Soviet of Workers' Deputies four days later, invited the participation of white-collar and artisan

59. TsGAOR, f. 6865, d. 120, l. 20.
60. Ivanov, ed., vol. 1, pp. 291–92, 355.
61. Pushkareva, *Zheleznodorozhniki,* p. 153.
62. Gerald Surh, "Petersburg Workers in 1905: Strikes, Workplace Democracy and the Revolution," Ph.D. diss., University of California, Berkeley, 1979, pp. 402–15.

groups, but it was dominated by factory workers. At its peak in late November the soviet could count 562 deputies representing 147 factories and 34 shops. Two-thirds of the factory delegates were metalworkers, who constituted only about a third of the city's industrial work force.[63]

The new "workers' parliament" exercised leadership over the revolutionary movement in the capital for the next fifty days, until its leading members were placed under arrest in early December. Besides acting as a strike committee, the soviet organized a militia, served as a coordinating center for workers' organizations, and negotiated with government officials and railroad administrators. Like the Railroad Union, it was officially nonpartisan; although the Social Democrats were the largest organized political group within it, they could not impose their views on others. The soviet was headed by the liberal attorney G. S. Nosar' but its most dynamic figure was the young Leon Trotsky, the vice-chair, who, although nominally a Menshevik, voiced the emerging nonfactional spirit of the Social Democratic rank and file.[64]

According to Nosar', sixteen unions were officially represented in the soviet, including the Railroad Union, which had only a consultative voice. But the soviet was not a professional or trade union council. Although Victoria Bonnell has shown convincingly that unionists had a more significant voice in the soviet than their formal representation would indicate, the dominant organizational principle was not representation by industry, trade, or profession, but by enterprise.[65] Nationwide, the St. Petersburg soviet came to symbolize the leading role within the revolution of the class-conscious workers. With its formation, initiative in the struggle seemed to shift away from the Moscow railroad employees and back to the industrial workers of the northern capital, who had first begun the revolution in January.

In St. Petersburg railwaymen did not play the pivotal role they had in Moscow and would in many provincial centers. The reasons for this are many, among which must surely be included the differ-

63. Georgii S. Nosar', "Istoriia soveta rabochikh deputatov," *Istoriia soveta rabochikh deputatov g. S. Peterburga* (St. Petersburg, 1906), p. 147.

64. On the soviet, see Oskar Anweiler, *The Soviets* (New York, 1973), and Surh, pp. 425–45.

65. Victoria E. Bonnell, *Roots of Rebellion: Workers' Politics and Organizations in St. Petersburg and Moscow, 1900–1914* (Berkeley and Los Angeles, 1983), pp. 171–80.

ences between the Social Democratic movements in the two cities. But the principal factor was that the northern capital was more a center of car repair and freight shipment than an administrative hub and transport junction. Central ministry authority was much stronger here, and shop craftsmen seemed to be more part of the city's increasingly militant and politically aware metalworking industry and less distinctively railroad craftsmen than in Moscow. Moreover, where in Moscow the presence of a large group of engine-drivers could act to bring together the administrative and workshop groups, drivers on the St. Petersburg roads were generally stationed at depots outside the city, if only because (as noted in Part One) housing was hard to come by in the capital. The liberal professional movement among railwaymen was decidedly weaker in Petersburg than in Moscow, while the *class* movement represented by the soviet was stronger. The dominance of the metal trades in the soviet in particular meant that rebellious railroad craftsmen could find an alternative mode of expression for their militancy to more narrowly professional forms of mobilization such as the Railroad Union.

Outside the capitals the spread of the strike followed no single discernible pattern, but almost everywhere "the atmosphere was so electrified that only a single small spark was enough" to set off the conflagration.[66] Indeed, in several places railroad strikes began even before word of the Moscow events arrived. As in St. Petersburg and Moscow, however, the relationship of railroad workers to the broader strike movement depended as much upon the relationship of different sorts of railwaymen—and of different political tendencies in railroading—to one another as on external factors.

In Kharkov agitators from neighboring industrial plants disrupted work at the depot and shops of the Kursk-Kharkov-Sevastopol Railroad as early as October 4. Four days later two clerks from the Aleksandrovsk station addressed a meeting at the Kharkov workshops, where a resolution of employees and telegraph operators calling on all railwaymen to join striking shop craftsmen was read. That evening telegraph operators walked off at several stations on the Kursk-Kharkov-Sevastopol and Kharkov-Nikolaev roads.[67] Thus

66. *1905 vo vospominaniiakh ego uchastnikov*, p. 64.

67. Ivanov, ed., vol. 2, p. 144; F. E. Los', ed., *Revoliutsiia 1905–1907 gg. na Ukraine* (Kiev, 1955), vol. 2, pt. 1, p. 426.

when trains from Moscow stopped arriving on October 9, the Kharkov railroad strike had already been under way for several days.

On October 10 railroad employees and local intellectuals gathered at the main Kharkov terminal to discuss how to respond to the rumored arrests of the pension congress delegates; a simultaneous meeting in the workshops voted to join the employees. The strikers moved to a lecture hall at Kharkov University where they voted unanimously to endorse demands for political freedoms and a constituent assembly. The next day a group of strikers heading toward the university clashed violently with a patriotic counterdemonstration and soon barricades had risen in the streets surrounding the university. The city was placed under martial law and for two days the university district lay under military siege, defended by students and striking workers, including large contingents from the railroads. Further bloodshed was avoided, however, when military authorities agreed to permit a peaceful demonstration in memory of those killed in the revolution in exchange for a dismantling of the barricades.[68]

In Ekaterinoslav disturbances began as early as October 6, when shop craftsmen on the Catherine Railroad chased a German-born foreman from the shops. On October 10 the employees walked out and proceeded to the main terminal, where they were joined by the craftsmen. Confronted by troops, most of the crowd dispersed, but a sizable contingent seized a train, which they directed to nearby Nizhnedneprovsk, where the shops and depot emptied and 3,000 strikers marched along the tracks. The next morning about 1,500 strikers assembled at the Ekaterinoslav terminal. They refused an order to disperse, and Cossacks fired into the crowd. Soon barricades appeared in the streets and on Briansk Square in the city center. Troops launched several assaults on the makeshift fortifications, and by nightfall six workers were confirmed dead and over a score lay injured. Meanwhile at Nizhnedneprovsk a crowd commandeered a train, in which agitators proceeded to smaller stations on the Catherine road.[69]

All major stations on the Moscow-Kiev-Voronezh Railroad, which

68. Kramer, ed., pp. 236–38; Ivanov, ed., vol. 2, p. 148; TsGIA, f. 273, op. 12, d. 375, l. 122.

69. Ivanov, ed., vol. 1, p. 239; 2, pp. 98, 102–9; Los', ed., vol. 2, pt. 1, pp. 393–402.

linked the central industrial and agricultural regions with the Ukraine, struck in solidarity with the Moscow walkout. The strike began October 10 in the line's main workshops in Konotop and at the depot of the Briansk station, the Kiev station, and the Kursk depot and shops. At Konotop the movement began in the workshops, but the strike leaders were employees. In Kiev, too, the depot craftsmen walked out first, but most strikers were employees. They were joined two days later by the employees of the South West Railroad administration, who once again chose the Bolshevik Shlikhter, dismissed from railroad service five months earlier, as their leader.[70] In Kaluga trains dispatched from Moscow on the Moscow-Kiev-Voronezh line stopped arriving on October 9. This did not at first affect workers on the Syzran'-Viazma Railroad, but that evening, upon receipt of a telegram reporting the rumored arrests in the capital, telegraph operators on that line walked off after dispatching strike messages to surrounding junctions. The next day the strike spread to the Kaluga depot and shops and to Penza, Tula, and other stations. With the Syzran'-Viazma line shut down, mail service to the Samara terminus of the Samara-Zlatoust Railroad ceased, and by October 12 that road was also closed to traffic.[71]

On these lines there was close cooperation between the different segments of the work force, largely because shop craftsmen took the lead. In southern industrial cities such as Kharkov and Ekaterinoslav the railroad workshops became focal points for working-class organizing, and the workers' movement in turn galvanized other strata. But where more strictly professional organization was more developed, the situation could differ. During the summer the Railroad Union continued to gain influence on the South East Railroad. With a strong base among telegraph operators and administrative personnel in Voronezh, union activists began to organize lesser stations. By September ties had been established with all stations on the road, and in early October a train loaded with agitators was dispatched to expand union activity. When word arrived from Moscow of the Central Bureau's strike call, the Voronezh union leaders hesitated, waiting several days to see what neighboring roads would do.

70. Maruta, pp. 37–45; Ivanov, ed., vol. 1, p. 274.
71. Ivanov, ed., vol. 1, pp. 320, 325; TsGIA, f. 273, op. 12, d. 364, l. 480; f. 1405, op. 530, d. 219, ll. 51–57.

Finally, with the walkout spreading rapidly, they decided to act: on October 12 the South East Railroad joined the strike.[72]

The Saratov headquarters of the Riazan-Ural Railroad was the other key provincial center of Railroad Union organizing. Here activists responded to the strike call with more alacrity, but it is unclear whether the initiative was not ultimately taken by the Social Democrats. Already on October 8 there were disturbances in the depot and workshops. The next day word arrived of the Moscow walkout. A meeting of administrative employees organized by the Railroad Union took place with Social Democratic representation and cooperation. The session agreed to strike and elected a committee of representatives from each branch of the administration. The strike began the next morning, and a second meeting, organized now by the Social Democrats, convened outside the workshops with extensive participation by employees. This lengthy session, attended by as many as three thousand striking railwaymen, broke up amidst considerable confusion as, to the dismay of sympathetic railroad officials hoping to limit the walkout to railroad professionals, agitated strikers took to the streets to rouse workers in the city's industrial enterprises. Although memoirs differ, one of these meetings apparently saw a conflict over strike demands between the Social Democrats and white-collar railwaymen associated with the Railroad Union. In the end, it seems, the Social Democratic program was accepted, although organizational leadership remained in the hands of the employee-dominated strike committee. Even before the strike began in Saratov, shop and depot craftsmen and station employees at Balashov and Atkarsk went out, and by October 12 representatives of striking railwaymen from virtually every station on the Riazan-Ural line were arriving in Saratov to join the strike committee.[73]

In January and February the most militant and extensive strikes had been launched by railwaymen in Poland, the Baltic provinces, and the Caucasus. On the railroads, however, the October strike

72. *1905 god na Iugo-Vostochnykh zh. d.* (Moscow, 1925), pp. 38–45.
73. Sokolov, pp. 40–42; G. G. Sushkin, "Oktiabr', noiabr', i dekabr' 1905 g. na Riazansko-Uralskoi zh. d. (vospominaniia)," *Katorga i ssylka*, 1930, no. 12: 146–48; I. Kh. Danilov and P. G. Sdobnev, eds., *Zheleznodorozhniki v 1905 godu* (Moscow, 1940), pp. 104–6; G. A. Malinin, "Saratovskie zheleznodorozhniki v revoliutsii 1905–1907 gg.," *Uchenye zapiski Saratovskogo universiteta* 55 (1956): 136–38.

was most powerful in Russia proper, centered in Moscow but encompassing every major railroad from Belorussia to the Urals,
Archangel to Odessa. The minority regions were nonetheless still
affected. In the Baltic provinces the strike began on lines directly
linked with St. Petersburg, but its center was Riga. Here telegraph
operators, clerks, switchmen, and shop craftsmen struck jointly
October 13.[74] In Poland the strike began October 12 at the Warsaw
terminals of the St. Petersburg–Warsaw and Warsaw-Vienna roads,
and by October 13 it had spread to Lodz, where striking clerks demanded use of the Polish language in railroad bookkeeping and correspondence. Although the strike ultimately shut down most Polish
rail traffic, its spread was hindered by the attitude of the Narodowe
Koło Kolejanzy. Still smarting from its rejection after the Railroad
Union congress, the Polish union refused to support the October
strike, arguing that Russian strikers did not support Polish autonomy and that the walkout was unexpected and unprepared.[75]

In the Caucasus the strike began late but continued longer than
in other regions. The Vladikavkaz Railroad, a center of militancy
during the summer, did not strike until October 13.[76] On the Transcaucasian Railroad the strike did not begin until October 15, when
the Tiflis terminal walked out. One likely reason for the delayed
response of the Caucasian railwaymen was the emergence of national disunity in the Tiflis shops, where a sizable minority of Russian workers organized in a Society of Patriots opposed the increasingly Georgian labor movement.[77] In both the Caucasus and Poland
national diversity, which had made these regions special hotbeds
earlier in the year, now tended to hold some workers back from full
participation in the strike.

The general strike triggered an explosion of rank-and-file organization, but the walkout itself spread chaotically and, especially on
the national level, remained largely leaderless. To be sure, the Railroad Union initiated the strike, and many railwaymen responded to
its call, pledging allegiance to its commands. A Rostov strike meeting on the Vladikavkaz Railroad, hitherto hostile to the Moscow-

74. Ivanov, ed., vol. 1, pp. 237, 297; Paulish, p. 156.
75. Ivanov, ed., vol. 2, p. 327; Richard Donald Lewis, "The Labor Movement
in Russian Poland in the Revolution of 1905–1907," Ph.D. diss., University of
California, Berkeley, 1971, p. 228.
76. *1905 v vospominaniiakh ego uchastnikov*, pp. 11–12.
77. Ivanov, ed., vol. 1, pp. 248–56; vol. 2, pp. 262–90.

based group, declared the road "in full solidarity with the principles of the union," and pledged to work "under the flag of the union" and support its demands. Telegrams of solidarity were sent to the Central Bureau from as far away as Askhabad, where the employees and workers of the Central Asian Railroad pledged their loyalty.[78] But the leadership provided by the Railroad Union remained more inspirational than concrete.

The general strike did little to develop sorely needed links between the largely autonomous local sections and the Central Bureau; most locals functioned in reality as independent strike committees or quasi-soviet organs. After the first days of the strike in Moscow the Central Bureau's activity was at best limited; arrests of the most active members dealt a crippling blow to its leadership pretensions. Between October 9 and 18 there is no record of the Central Bureau issuing even a single instruction to union locals, and the memoirs of its leaders are noticeably silent concerning events of these days. In fact, the upsurge of rank-and-file organizing sparked by the strike tended to strengthen the influence both of local leadership factions and revolutionary parties at the expense of the nominally independent Central Bureau, especially as the strike came to involve new occupational categories.

In addition to arrests of its members, the principal cause of the Central Bureau's failure to capitalize on the opportunities presented by the general strike was the Railroad Union's organizational disparateness and political ambiguity. Railroad activists had been talking about a general strike for some time, but had never reached unity on the purpose this would serve. The Central Bureau apparently had some vague notion that the government could be pressured into negotiations by the strike, and that once such talks began victory was inevitable.[79] They could see little use either for the Bolshevik call to transform the strike movement into an armed uprising or for ideas of popular "self-government" as expressed in the emergence of organizations such as the St. Petersburg soviet. The Central Bureau could only advise strikers to sit tight and wait it out, a strategy that failed to capture the imagination and channel the energies of the broad strata of the railroad work force the unprecedented scope of the movement had brought into motion.

78. Ibid., vol. 1, pp. 238–39, 313–14.
79. Ibid., vol. 1, p. 202.

The Central Bureau was also concerned that the pension congress might seize strike leadership and come to represent the rebellious railwaymen in talks with the government. However unfounded, rumors of the delegates' arrest played an important part in the strike's initial spread, and in the early days of the walkout the number of solidarity messages received by the congress multiplied. Although the St. Petersburg body approached the strike with considerable caution, by October 9 the delegates acknowledged that they had heretofore been concerned with the needs of "no more than 10 percent of the railroad army" and that "life is more than the fulfillment of professional obligations." Meeting in extraordinary session, the congress endorsed a lengthy document on key political and economic issues, but the next day several proposals calling on the delegates to play a more active role and even seize control of the strike were defeated.

Like the Railroad Union, the congress responded to the initiative from below, but the St. Petersburg body sought to play more of a mediating, rather than leadership, role.[80] On October 11 delegates were chosen to meet with Khilkov and Witte to urge concessions "in order to avoid a bloodbath." The first delegation, headed by Arkhangelskii, was unable to see the minister, but the second group, under Orekhov, gained an audience with Witte. The chairman of the Council of Ministers was polite—the delegates themselves, in visible awe, were, it seems, almost obsequious— but he rejected any immediate concessions, saying, "First things will have to settle down, and then [we can have] reforms."[81] The delegates reported back to a mammoth meeting of railwaymen at St. Petersburg University, but the congress returned to its agenda.

When it came to formulating a program of demands for the railroad strike, however, both the union and the pension congress

80. *Zhel.*, 127, November 17, 1905, Bulletins 9 and 10. Sablinsky's notion (p. 131) that by formulating a program of demands the congress was "joining forces with the union leadership" misses the still quite detached relationship between the two groups. While endorsing the principle of "corporate organization," the congress was silent about the Moscow group. Similarly, in St. Petersburg the Central Bureau member Romanov opposed an active strike role for the congress. See Kramer, ed., p. 179.

81. *Zheleznodorozhniki v 1905 g. [ocherki iz istorii soiuza]* (Moscow, 1922), pp. 10–15; Danilov and Sdobnev, pp. 100–102; *Pravo*, 45–46, November 20, 1905, supplement.

played significant parts. In February the separate lines had formulated their own lists, with some repetition, but frequently with little awareness of what others were demanding. In October many lines still drew up local lists, but most often this came together with endorsement of the much broader strike programs offered by the union or the congress. The demands formulated by these groups were telegraphed throughout the railroad system and generally embraced by railwaymen, and often by striking factory workers and their supporters as well.

In calling the strike on October 7, the Central Bureau defined its basic goals: "Freedom of speech and of the press, freedom of assembly, to form unions and to strike, the convocation of an assembly of popular representatives, freely elected on the basis of general, equal, direct, and secret suffrage." The union also called on railwaymen to strike for the economic demands they had been raising all year, but cautioned that "without political freedoms they are meaningless."[82]

On October 9 the Central Bureau published a program of eleven demands, which enjoyed wide circulation and support:

1. Higher pay for all railroad workers
2. An eight-hour workday
3. Establishment of elected bureaus of worker deputies to meet with management to resolve disputes concerning hiring and firing
4. Abolition of the existing pension fund and institution of a state insurance system
5. Reform of the public health section
6. Construction of schools, libraries, and reading rooms for railwaymen and their families
7. Freedom of speech, press, and assembly; right to union organization and to strike; personal inviolability and the sanctity of the home
8. Convocation of a congress of employee and worker delegates to discuss a new railroad labor charter
9. A constituent assembly based on "four-tail" suffrage, "since under the existing police-bureaucratic structure the above demands cannot be met"

82. Ivanov, ed., vol. 1, pp. 201–2.

10. Legal immunity for strike participants and freedom for those arrested
11. Amnesty for all political and religious prisoners[83]

This program was already in circulation when the pension congress met to formulate its strike concerns on October 9. The delegates enumerated fifteen economic demands, which, although formulated in much greater detail, were substantially similar to those articulated by the Railroad Union. More important, however, the congress worked out a relatively detailed program of democratic worker-employee participation. The delegates recognized the railwayman's "right to corporative organization" and called for a second delegate congress to work out rules and procedures. As a temporary measure, they called for establishment on each railroad line of a "permanent bureau of elected representatives" with nine basic functions, including "regulations of relations and resolution of conflicts between employees and management and among the employees themselves; establishment of rules of internal order and work assignment"; control over transfers, firings, vacations, and housing assignments; investigation of grievances; convocation of general meetings; and, finally, working out of a new charter for railroad labor. In addition, each road was called on to establish a disciplinary council, with equal representation from labor and management, and, recalling one of Nemeshaev's more successful reforms, a system of "comradely courts" to adjudicate complaints. Periodic road congresses were also mandated.

But "establishing the beginnings of a professional-legal life for railroad employees and workers does not exhaust their demands," the delegates insisted, and the congress added seven political demands:

1. An immediate and unconditional end to martial law and all similar laws and decrees limiting the rights of Russian citizens; control of the police by organs of popular self-government; abolition of the railroad gendarmery
2. Abolition of the death penalty
3. Amnesty for political and religious prisoners
4. Freedom of communication, speech, and press; inviolability of home and person; freedom to strike, form unions, assemble, and demonstrate

83. Pereverzev, p. 52; M. B. [M. Bogdanov], pp. 33–34.

5. Release of all those arrested in railroad strikes
6. Elimination of all national restrictions and recognition of the right of each nationality to self-government [this was supplemented by a specific call to support the demands of Polish railwaymen for the introduction of the Polish language and other reforms requested by delegates from the Polish roads sympathetic to the NKK]
7. Convocation of a constituent assembly

These political demands were followed by a proposal that the congress delegates prepare a second national meeting. An organizing bureau of five was named, and all delegates were instructed to build local committees by November 15.[84]

To be sure, a certain resistance to political agitation continued among some workers. One Bolshevik organizer recalled that when "the genuine gray masses from the workers' districts" joined the movement

agitators could no longer introduce political slogans without difficulty. "We thought that real business would be discussed here, and once again they're trying to stuff us with politics!" Such outbursts were heard frequently from those workers who were completely new to the mass movement. This suspiciousness was especially strong among unqualified railroad workers—signalmen, line workmen, and the like.[85]

In some places freight handlers and porters idled by the walkout attacked picket lines. At the Moscow terminal of the Moscow-Iaroslavl-Archangel Railroad, where the Railroad Union had considerable support, the political demands posed by the Central Bureau won approval only after extensive debate. Elsewhere strikers did not fully understand the politics they endorsed: at the Ekaterinodar depot of the Vladikavkaz Railroad workers enthusiastically cheered every political speech, be it Social Democrat, Socialist Revolutionary, or even monarchist. Cynical railroad officials charged that backward workers were won to political demands only through "unbelievable promises" of an immediate improvement in their material position.[86] Still, in marked contrast to the strikes of

84. *Zhel.*, 127, November 17, 1905, Bulletin 9, pp. 25–28. Ivanov, ed., vol. 1, p. 203.
85. Quoted in Engelstein, p. 109.
86. *Nasha zhizn'*, 209, October 27, 1905; Ivanov, ed., vol. 1, pp. 282–83; I. Masliev, "Krasnodarskie zheleznodorozhniki v 1905 godu," *Proletarskaia revoliutsiia*, 1926, no. 6 (53): 161; Dymkov and Lipovetskii, p. 83.

January and February, the October movement was explicitly and self-consciously political; endorsement of demands for civil rights and a constitution was nearly universal.

In the end, though, it was the strike itself, its spirit of rebellion, of standing up for the dignity and well-being of the working class and the whole Russian people, that can be said to have most deeply motivated the strikers. There was for many strikers a close, if not clearly articulated, relationship between economic demands for participation and control on the railroads and calls for the democratization of society and the state. Like a contagious disease, the strike seemed to affect even those only briefly exposed to the virus. No matter how many declarations and demands were issued, many workers knew that the near-total shutdown of economic life spoke for itself most eloquently. In Odessa three hundred switchmen and line watchmen joined the walkout October 13. They demanded a two-ruble increase in monthly pay, which in desperation local officials granted. The workers decided to continue the walkout anyway, without demands.[87]

As the general strike initiated by the railroad workers gradually engulfed the country, the forces of "order" demanded stern measures, but the government was immobilized. Officials could not even travel between St. Petersburg and Moscow. An October 12 conference of ministers called by the tsar to restore railroad operations all but threw up its hands in despair. As opposition snowballed, the tsar turned to a man whose "constitutional career was built wholly on combatting revolution," Count Sergei Witte.[88] Witte's energy and intelligence were all but intolerable to the dull-witted Nicholas, and he had languished in the largely ceremonial position of chairman of the Council of Ministers for three years. But since January 9 Witte's star had been rising. Despite his words to the pension congress delegation, the former railroad administrator argued that the situation could be brought under control only if the tsar took the initiative by granting a constitution and civil liberties. The plan was anathema to Nicholas, but when on October 15 even the notoriously repressive Trepov was forced to agree, the die was cast. Early on the evening of October 17, Nicholas signed an imperial

87. Los', ed., vol. 2, pt. 1, pp. 408–9.
88. Trotsky, p. 119.

manifesto that, if implemented, would transform the nation's political life: the tsar promised civic freedom, an expanded franchise, and a guarantee that no law would take effect without approval by the elected Duma.

The response was electrifying. All urban Russia went wild with celebration. Yet the strikers were keenly aware that thousands remained in prison. Quickly the cry rose to continue the struggle and, in particular, to fight for a general amnesty. In St. Petersburg a massive demonstration demanded the liberation of political prisoners. In Moscow a similar crowd forced the governor-general to release arrestees. In Simferopol a mob broke through the prison gates to free those inside. In Odessa and Revel angry crowds forced local officials to yield to the demand for amnesty.[89] In Minsk, however, jubilant strikers on the Libau-Romny Railroad were attacked by troops, leaving fifty dead.[90]

As the cry for amnesty grew, representatives of the Union of Unions and the Peasants Union arranged for release of the Railroad Union leaders. Immediately the Central Bureau caucused and decided that the strike had achieved its goals. On October 18 they dispatched a telegram announcing that the manifesto made the Railroad Union a legal organization and thus fulfilled the demands for which railwaymen had been fighting. The Central Bureau called on all railroad strikers to return to work.[91]

The Railroad Union leaders based their decision almost exclusively on the situation in Moscow, where the strike fever had already begun to cool before the manifesto was issued. The days immediately preceding the tsar's announcement had been ones of growing desperation among Moscow railwaymen, whose meager resources were quickly running low. By October 15, one activist recalled, "the situation was so unclear that the railroad union, formerly nerve center of the entire strike movement, had already begun to contemplate liquidating the strike."[92] Gorchilin recalled how the daily strike meetings had lost their previously festive air:

89. Ivanov, ed., vol. 1, pp. 376–78, 451; *Proletarii*, 24, October 25, 1905.

90. TsGIA, f. 273, op. 12, d. 330, ll. 153, 171–72; Ivanov, ed., vol. 1, p. 263. Similar incidents were reported from Poltava, Kishinev, and Odessa (*Zhel.*, 126, November 11, 1905).

91. Pereverzev, p. 53; M. B. [M. Bogdanov], p. 36.

92. Quoted in Engelstein, p. 133.

We saw the workers gather silently and clearly sensed a shift in their mood, observed a fear for the immediate future, for the final outcome of the strike. . . . On October 17 I was proceeding to the meeting with Belorussov when we ran into Korotkov who warned us not to go, since today, as never before, the old men had turned the workers against continuing the strike.[93]

Thousands of employees and workers quickly endorsed the union call, and by October 19 work had resumed in all the city's railroad offices and many shops, including those of the Kazan line.[94] In the workshops of the Moscow-Kursk Railroad, where a revolutionary minority debated for two hours with a priest summoned by icon-bearing workers to offer prayers of gratitude, there was "great faith in the manifesto."[95]

Outside Moscow, however, there was considerable suspicion, and the call to end the strike won little support. To be sure, in places where the movement was not very developed, railwaymen returned to work as soon as they heard the news. But all over the country railroad strikers branded the Central Bureau's telegram a government provocation and demanded that delegates from Moscow personally ask them to return. On the Riga-Orel line the manifesto spurred striking workers to elaborate new political demands and to organize fighting detachments and a branch of the Railroad Union. In Saratov the strike committee of the Riazan-Ural Railroad meeting at the railroad terminal on October 19 was dispersed by pogromists, but not before voting 164 to 11 to continue the strike, with only the local Railroad Union leaders advocating a return to work. Nevertheless, two days later a telegram went out to stations on the line calling an end to the walkout. It was later discovered that this message had been sent by a minority of five local Railroad Union leaders without strike committee approval.[96]

In St. Petersburg strikers on the Nicholas Railroad returned on October 19, but walked out again the next morning. On October 19 workers on the Baltic Railroad assembled for a mass meeting marked

93. Gorchilin, pp. 25–26. See also TsGAOR, f. 6865, d. 120, l. 12, and Dymkov and Lipovetskii, p. 77.
94. M. B. [M. Bogdanov], p. 37; Gorchilin, p. 27; Dymkov and Lipovetskii, p. 81.
95. TsGAOR, f. 6865, d. 127, l. 40; *1905 god na Moskovsko-Kurskoi-Nizhegorodskoi i Muromskoi zh. d.* (Moscow, 1931), p. 81.
96. Paulish, p. 158; Sushkin, pp. 150–51; Sokolov, p. 44.

by bitter debate. Several engineers proposed a return to work, but were rebuked by two shop craftsmen and a delegate from the pension congress, who argued that the regime had not changed. A conductor rose to declare that since the manifesto satisfied 95 percent of their political demands, only economic questions should be discussed. He was ejected from the meeting, prompting protests from several workers. By this point tempers had begun to boil and the strike committee proposed a vote to resume work on October 21. The motion was defeated in an apparently close and confusing count.[97]

Such indecision was shared by the pension congress delegates. On October 18 the congress met to discuss the manifesto and agreed it did not satisfy the strikers' demands. They pointed out that the manifesto did nothing to repeal the declarations of martial law issued in several regions and on the railroads, and that it left the death penalty intact. "The life and rights of the citizens remain dependent on the police and gendarmes," they concluded. Encouraged by this, left-wing delegates attempted one final time to get the body to seize leadership of the strike, at least in the capital. But this was defeated and the pension congress returned to technical matters. By October 23 its participants began to head home.[98]

If the manifesto did not bring the strike to an immediate end, it did manage to open a crack in the hitherto united wall of resistance the strikers had presented. With the passage of several days that crack widened. The Moscow strike committee, dominated by railroad employees, "temporarily" called off the strike on October 19. The St. Petersburg Soviet voted to call workers back on October 21. On October 22 traffic started to move on the Moscow-Kiev-Voronezh railroad. On October 23 the St. Petersburg junction went back. The Riazan-Ural line started up on October 24. That day the Administration of Railroads issued a 24-hour ultimatum to the remaining strikers. Ten days after publication of the manifesto, service had been restored on all lines except the Transcaucasian Railroad and several Polish roads, where martial law was again proclaimed.[99]

97. Ivanov, ed., vol. 1, pp. 294–95, 385–86.
98. *Zhel.*, 128, November 24, 1905, Bulletin 11; Ivanov, ed., vol. 1, p. 207; Kramer, ed., p. 180.
99. Ivanov, ed., vol. 1, pp. 222–37, 261, 304.

Eight

The Rush to Organize

Though a victory for liberal aspirations, the manifesto still had to be implemented, and most opposition leaders were skeptical of the government's intentions. It soon became clear that far from a genuine opening to compromise, the manifesto marked the limit beyond which the regime would not retreat. The Witte government was convinced that a successful transition to limited constitutionalism presupposed the restoration of order; the new prime minister had communicated just that conviction to the pension congress delegates. It has been argued that although the manifesto encouraged the widening of political divisions within the opposition, the government's obstinacy in the months that followed kept the revolutionary alliance together. That may be true, but refusal of further compromise was hardly short-sighted from the regime's point of view. For although government cooperation with the moderate opposition might have weakened the radicals, it would not necessarily have strengthened the government. Witte sought cooperation with the moderate middle class, but on his own terms, and this presupposed a decisive victory over working-class radicalism. It was not simply that Nicholas's personal intransigence provoked confrontation, but rather that the kind of constitutional reform from above envisioned by Witte was predicated upon prior liquidation of independent mass politics.

If the strike undammed new reservoirs of popular opposition, it likewise revealed that the regime could also command reserves of support. Businessmen and other conservatives intimidated by the elemental power of the mass movement welcomed the prospect of a more orderly path to change. Frightened by spread of the conflict to the countryside—during the last third of 1905 peasant disturbances were reported in 291 of 501 *uezds* in European Russia—gentry landowners shifted their sympathies away from the forces of reform to those of order. Black Hundred mobs had already begun to mobilize and assault opposition meetings in several cities before October 17. With release of the manifesto the enemies of reform vented their anger with new virulence at any group they thought responsible for the strike and its unwanted outcome. The final weeks of October saw a veritable orgy of pogromist bloodletting, and street fighting between defenders and opponents of the old order far surpassed the turbulence of the strike itself, which had been relatively peaceful. Jews were a favored target of pogromists, especially in the Ukraine, but mobs could lash out blindly at demonstrators, strikers, and students of all nationalities.

Though it has never been conclusively determined whether the regime directly instigated anti-Semitic and right-wing assaults, local police rarely bothered to conceal their sympathies. The manifesto ushered in an unprecedented period of political and civil liberty, but official recognition of the newly declared freedoms did not last long. These were fully acknowledged only insofar as they were exercised through acceptance of the newly emerging "constitutional" system. Buoyed by the support the Black Hundred movement revealed, and taking full advantage of the breathing space the manifesto had won, the government stiffened its spine and prepared for—even sought—a new and more decisive confrontation.

In railroading reformism was subsumed by calls for a firm hand. In October many railroad managers cooperated with the strikers, partly out of sympathy with strike goals, but mainly because of impotence and fear. The police had "virtually disappeared and gave the impression of being terrorized." By the strike's end road managers often enjoyed only "the superficial appearance" of authority, in reality commanding "neither the power nor force to act." In mid November one railroad inspector described the administration of the Kursk-Kharkov-Sevastopol Railroad as "a boat without oars and rudder, sailing helplessly on a general course, striving only to maintain momentary equilibrium." Arriving at the Ekaterinoslav terminal of the Catherine Railroad on November 27, another inspector found "total disorder and anarchy. . . . The situation on the road is such that the director and higher officials are isolated from power and besieged by all kinds of delegations, which demand everything and request nothing."[1]

The manager of the Moscow-Kazan Railroad complained that the chaos was an inevitable product of the ministry's failure to take a clear and unyielding position. Criticizing such decisions as the convening of the pension congress and the establishment of elected shop elders, he traced the problem back to

the start of the year, when, eager to restore the appearance of tranquility, management, right up to the Minister of Communications, revealed an unexpected tractability, and, worst of all, by its actions granted amnesty to strikers, agreeing to pay wages for time lost striking. This inspired in the workers and employees the belief that it was their right to strike, and that to pay wages for strike time was the obligation of the state and employers. . . . The workers and employees could recognize that the highest administration had no clear notion of permitted limits.[2]

Such sentiments had been heard from the private lines all year. To a great extent the complaints were unfounded, since the ministry had engaged in its share of repressive actions as well, but vacillation had rendered the techniques of both compromise and resistance ineffective, and now calls for order came from new quarters. The railroad police, virtually impotent during October, drafted a new five-point plan to suppress strikes.[3] In early November the newspaper *Nachalo* created a minor scandal by publishing the text of a secret report by a high-ranking military transport official. "We must exterminate forever in the consciousness of railroad employees the very thought that strikes are possible," the report declared. To achieve this all roads must be taken over by the government and all staff must formally enter state service with no right to strike. "Pretexts must be found," the report continued, to fire agitators. Delegate assemblies of workers were permissible, but no standing bodies or permanent representation should be allowed. Finally, the officer proposed amending the martial law declaration (still formally in effect) so that "every railroad employee, without

1. TsGIA, f. 273, op. 12, d. 364, l. 479; d. 375, l. 122; d. 350, ll. 340–42.
2. TsGIA, f. 273, op. 12, d. 328, ll. 359–61. See also M. K. Dymkov and D. Ia. Lipovetskii, eds., *1905 god na Kazanke* (Moscow, 1925), pp. 83–87.
3. TsGIA, f. 273, op. 12, d. 354a, ll. 153–54.

regard to position, age, or sex, will be drafted into actual military service."[4]

On October 25, discredited, seriously ill, and lacking Witte's confidence, Prince Khilkov submitted his resignation to the tsar. To replace him Witte turned to the reform-minded director of his old line, Nemeshaev. The choice was, perhaps, conditioned by the views of striking railwaymen. During his audience with the pension congress delegates on October 10, Witte had asked his visitors who among present railroad administrators enjoyed the kind of popularity that he and Bunge could claim in former years. The answer had been Nemeshaev. And, indeed, when the choice was announced, railroad circles were hopeful. *Zheleznodorozhnik* called the new minister a "bright exception" in a "regime of not a few dark personalities."[5]

Yet the appointment of Nemeshaev hardly signaled a decisive victory for reform. Shortly before Khilkov's exit, his subordinate Dumitrashko was replaced by the vigorous hard-line director of the Nicholas Railroad, Schaufus, a career military man disposed to use of force in labor relations. More important, when Nemeshaev unveiled his reform program, it hardly proved very novel, despite his claim "to be inspired by the new beginning heralded on October 17." Not surprisingly, its centerpiece was the renewed promise of a new charter, disciplinary code, and revised norms on wages and hours mainly applicable to staff employees. The minister also proposed new regulations governing assignment of state housing and the establishment of a network of railroad educational institutions. He pledged to seek increases in the ministry's budget to finance improvements, and on November 11 the Council of Ministers assigned sixteen million extra rubles to improve the conditions of railroad employees.[6]

Nemeshaev's approach to reform, like Witte's, was consistent with the maintenance of autocratic control and stood in conflict with the democratic and participatory goals of the revolution. In

4. *Nachalo*, 8, November 6, 1905, pp. 5–6.
5. *Zheleznodorozhniki v 1905 g.* [*ocherki iz istorii soiuza*] (Moscow, 1922), p. 14; *Zhel.*, 126, November 11, 1905, p. 2.
6. TsGIA, f. 273, op. 12, d. 345, ll. 237–38; f. 229, op. 2, d. 1645, ll. 14–18; TsGAOR, f. 6865, d. 118, l. 414. N. Rostov, "Zheleznodorozhniki v pervoi revoliutsii," *Proletariat v revoliutsii 1905–1907gg.* (Moscow, 1930), p. 157.

April the Administration of Railroads had revived the commission charged with formulating a railroad labor charter and disciplinary code, and draft documents were circulated to all road directors in late July. The drafts were formulated as "temporary rules," however, and in August Nemeshaev, supported by several other directors, submitted a blistering criticism of their failure to offer a "*legislative* solution." The main emphasis, he avowed, should be on defining the rights and responsibilities of personnel in order to improve their quality. The spirit in which the new minister understood such rights and responsibilities was suggested by his later comment, following suppression of the December risings, that "where officials were themselves permeated with consciousness of service duty, stood close to subordinates, took an interest in their needs, knew their wants, and, together with this, demanded strict fulfillment of service obligations," grounds for unrest were minimal.[7] Nemeshaev may well have been personally sympathetic to the plight of the ordinary railwayman, but his principal concern remained rationalization of the command structure and consolidation of a kind of labor aristocracy in support of the existing order. Although he recognized the dangers of arbitrary and unsystematic management, his response did not stray outside the confines of autocratic paternalism.

Since January, however, the strike movement had moved beyond complaints against arbitrary management, increasingly demanding participation and control, and it was precisely popular participation that the "constitutional" order was expected to deliver. Hence, even Nemeshaev's admirers quickly voiced dissatisfaction with his approach. *Zheleznodorozhnik* was skeptical of the new minister's promise that "all will be completely subordinate to the living participation of employee representatives." The editors headlined their commentary on his program "All According to the Old Road," noting pointedly that the chief failure of the proposals was that they did not involve participation by railwaymen themselves. "The times have changed too much," concluded *Zheleznodorozhnik*, "the demands themselves are now already not those of the liberalism of the old school. . . . Now it will no longer be enough to

7. Henry Reichman, "Tsarist Labor Policy and the Railroads, 1885–1914," *Russian Review* 42, no. 1 (1983): 68–69.

work out a rational charter or to sweep away sinecures and costly idling."[8]

If the October events pushed the government toward a more uncompromising and repressive stance, they also decisively transformed the mass movement. Despite the continuing struggle and the emergence of Black Hundred reaction, there was good reason for the Russian people to brand the weeks following the strike the "days of freedom." Everywhere the tsar's pronouncement was interpreted as if it were already a guarantee of general political liberty, even where rights were exercised to denounce the new constitution as a sham. Newspapers and magazines ignored the censorship. Political parties, hitherto banned, emerged into the open, although their legal status had yet to be formally amended. People were spurred by both the satisfaction of a partial victory and the challenge of the unresolved fight.

Before October the movement of railwaymen had been relatively narrow and controlled. Although the Railroad Union took rapid root among a segment of the white-collar work force, it still mainly reflected the interests and influence of a relatively limited group of liberal and left-wing railroad administrators, and its organized power was at best shaky. There was considerable unrest in the workshops, but, with notable exceptions, economic issues remained primary there, and only some craftsmen were dedicated to political change. The energy surrounding the pension congress had hinted at the depth of ferment, but until October most roads were functioning with only periodic disruptions.

During the final quarter of the year, however, "discipline among employees and workers declined swiftly," and virtually the entire railroad network was thrown into what seemed to many like total anarchy, what one tsarist official described as a "chronic passive strike."[9] To say that after October the mood shifted drastically to the left would be accurate, but inadequate. As heretofore inactive strata joined the movement, the situation altered in various complex and often ambiguous ways. Ultimately, the final months of the

8. *Zhel.*, 130/131, December 17, 1905, pp. 6–7; 126, November 11, 1905, p. 2.
9. A. L. Sidorov, ed., *Vysshii pod'em revoliutsii 1905–1907 gg.: vooruzhennye vosstaniia, noiabr'–dekabr' 1905 god* (Moscow and Leningrad, 1955), vol. 3, pt. 2, p. 800; I. M. Pushkareva, *Zheleznodorozhniki Rossii v burzhuazno-demokraticheskikh revoliutsiiakh* (Moscow, 1975), p. 185.

year saw the emergence of a nascent political class consciousness among railroad workers, expressed not only in a new sense of radicalism but also in a powerful spurt of organizational activity. Yet this new consciousness also stood partially in contradiction to the professional form of worker mobilization inherited from the pre-October months.

The October strike and the "days of freedom" that followed aroused railwaymen previously untouched by the revolutionary fever. Some of these workers seemed less committed to the political demands of the liberation movement than they were aroused by the prospect of concrete economic benefits, a phenomenon many railroad administrators were eager to emphasize. On the Catherine Railroad it was reported that after the manifesto "the strike was declared over, since the leaders were satisfied, but, the masses, uninterested in politics and seeking only to improve their material welfare, were secretly disappointed." The manager of the Moscow-Kazan Railroad claimed that the success of the October strike was attributable to "the skill with which agitators managed to use the uneducated mass in the struggle for political goals, seducing them with simultaneous promises of immediate and decisive improvements in the material position of the majority. In conversations with employees, political demands were expressed in dark, undefined form, and usually remained in the background."[10]

In reality, however, these officials failed to comprehend the real transformation of labor politics at this time. That the formal victory of the October strike was not accompanied by significant changes in the material position of most railwaymen surely left a deep reservoir of resentment, but it did not in the main lead to political cynicism. Instead, it prompted a search for a redefinition of politics that could more forcefully express worker aspirations. Although the extraordinary broadening of the social base of the working-class movement after October certainly aroused apolitical elements, far more significant was the rejection by many worker activists of a certain *kind* of politics—the politics of the middle-class "liberation movement"—and the gradual emergence of an inchoate, but nonetheless very real, alternative class politics that sought to combine liberal demands with proletarian material concerns in a striking

10. TsGAOR, f. 6865, d. 78a, ll. 13–14; Dymkov and Lipovetskii, p. 83.

new way. The main questions animating the rank and file were not, as the authorities naively believed, narrowly conceived economic concerns, but the actualization of the political ideals of participation and democracy in economic and social relations on the immediate local level.

In the wake of the strike, political discussion and debate took on an unprecedented mass character. By late November, the ministry learned, "the platforms and halls [of the Ekaterinoslav railroad terminal] were crowded with railroad employees, postal-telegraph workers, and various outsiders of unidentified callings. The mood was extremely agitated; everywhere there were loud discussions, debates among junior railroad employees, the open distribution of all sorts of printed sheets."[11] For many railwaymen the real victory won in October lay, not in the specific terms of the manifesto or any other desired reform, but in the somewhat intangible, though no less important, sense of confidence and pride they had won: "Yesterday we were slaves, but today masters."

Perhaps ironically, this sense may well have been strongest in former political backwaters, at smaller stations and medium-sized junctions. An employee from a station on the Kharkov-Nikolaev line recalled:

Only yesterday a drunken Makar Mikhailovich was chasing the plump buffet girl around the station demanding "more vodka on credit"; today he is a delegate to the Liubotin railroad congress, a top-notch speaker, and the first to sing the "Marseillaise." . . . It is difficult to convey the joyous agitation with which we greeted our entry into social affairs. . . . In the first days of the strike everyone felt not quite himself; the institutional structure of everyday life that had existed for years was broken at the root.[12]

In Samara railroad officials reported that "the magic word 'freedom,' understood by them [the workers] to mean that one can do what one wants, attracts the youth and creates scandalous behavior in the supposition that such behavior is necessary and demanded by the goal of achieving freedom."[13]

11. TsGIA, f. 273, op. 12, d. 350, l. 341.
12. *1905 vo vospominaniiakh ego uchastnikov* (Rostov-on-Don, 1925), pp. 62, 69, 70.
13. TsGIA, f. 273, op. 12, d. 364, l. 479.

Following the manifesto radical activists reached greater numbers of workers than ever before, and socialist ideas gained many converts. To be sure, the political programs of all three socialist groups, Bolsheviks, Mensheviks, and SRs, did not diverge significantly from the demands of liberals for genuine civil liberties and a constituent assembly. But the socialists, especially the Social Democrats, could better articulate within this program the special goals of the workers, in part through emphasis on Marxist ideas of class conflict. As Victoria Bonnell has pointed out, "the idea of class struggle was especially important in shaping workers' attitudes during 1905 because it went to the very core of official ideology, which stressed the mutual compatibility of workers' and employers' interests and the possibility of their reconciliation within the framework of the tsarist state."[14] But perhaps equally significant for railroad workers was the fact that this concept also called into question the kind of professional mobilization that had up to this point shaped railroad activism and the reconciliation on a professional basis of divergent class interests within the "liberation movement" itself. The Social Democrats placed special stress on the fight against craft particularism. In railroading this meant, first, "the merger of the railwaymen with the rest of the country's workers," which began in November, but also an intensified struggle against the influence within the professional movement of dissident officialdom.[15]

The concept of class struggle enabled many railwaymen to express the differences they had with middle-class liberals, including many railroad officials, in terms other than the often mechanical distinction between politics and economics. The eventual goal of socialism itself, though rarely understood as an immediate alternative to tsarism, likewise gave coherent political form to a still vaguely felt consciousness, simultaneously exposing a streak of often naive utopianism that colored the workers' mood. Political language in 1905 could be wildly imprecise; as has been seen, managerial delegates to the pension congress freely declared their membership in the exploited "proletariat." Definitions of socialism also varied considerably. Still, endorsement of a socialist future was

14. Victoria E. Bonnell, *Roots of Rebellion: Workers' Politics and Organizations in St. Petersburg and Moscow, 1900–1914* (Berkeley and Los Angeles, 1983), p. 168.

15. Rostov, "Zheleznodorozhniki," p. 179.

another way rank-and-file railwaymen could distinguish their concerns from those of middle-class and managerial allies. Noteworthy in this light was a resolution of the Delegate Assembly of Workers of the Catherine Railroad, which met in Ekaterinoslav in late October, calling for establishment in Russia of the "kingdom of socialism" (*tsarstvo sotsializma*). According to this document the new socialist order would be one "under which all—land, factories, and establishments of art and science—will belong to the people. In the kingdom of socialism there will be neither rich nor poor, oppressed nor oppressors; all will labor equally and everyone will have everything necessary for the satisfaction of their physical and spiritual needs."[16]

The changing consciousness of railroad labor found expression in the "feverish organizational work" that began during the October strike and intensified exponentially after its victorious conclusion. On the Moscow-Kazan Railroad, "the long-pent-up striving toward organization emerged so forcefully that until the beginning of December there remained almost no nook or cranny on the Kazan line where the workers and employees were not organizing in one way or another."[17] The organizations that emerged were difficult to characterize; loose in form, they frequently seemed to have no clearly defined purpose. Trade union groups often assumed a political character, and ostensibly political organizations took up economic concerns. Moreover, it was within these new organizations that the rapidly emerging contradictions within the oppositional movement were played out.

The new sense of freedom emerging in the wake of the manifesto offered opportunities for relatively open association, but the rush to organize had already begun during the October strike. As has been seen, that movement was spontaneous and uncoordinated, with no true national direction. As a result, the police later noted, "during the strike committees were formed by the strikers on each of the railroads to provide organization and leadership."[18] These local strike committees grew out of the specificity of the

16. Sidorov, ed., vol. 3, pt. 1, p. 33.

17. *1905 god na Moskovsko-Kurskoi-Nizhegorodskoi i Muromskoi zh. d.* (Moscow, 1931), p. 64; Dymkov and Lipovetskii, p. 93.

18. A. Kats and Iu. Milonov, eds., *1905: professional'noe dvizhenie* (Moscow-Leningrad, 1926), p. 255.

October struggle, and their functioning reflected that movement's varied experience. Sometimes—this was especially true in large industrial centers—railwaymen participated in citywide organizations involving workers of different industries and railroad strike committees interpenetrated with such forms in amorphous ways. In a few places delegate assemblies representing several sections of a line, or the railwaymen of a given area served by several roads, were elected. But in October most strike committees were based at a single station, terminal, depot, or office.

Committees were formed to endorse demands, organize picketing and demonstrations, represent the strikers to the authorities, and communicate with other stations and roads. In carrying out these assignments strike committees often had to provide monitors to ensure the peaceful character of the strike. In Ekaterinoslav and Kharkov, however, the committees were formed in the heat of violent confrontation with police and troops, and one of their goals was the formation of fighting squads. Termination of rail transport created monumental problems in feeding the population, providing medical supplies, and maintaining communication. In some locales railroad strike committees took charge of food distribution and often found themselves dispatching and regulating special supply trains. On the Riazan-Ural Railroad the committee seized the Saratov grain elevators and equipped a special train to deliver bread to striking stations. On the Samara-Zlatoust Railroad the central strike committee used a train to distribute strike funds and wage payments.

The October strike was initiated by office employees and engine-drivers and, though all sectors of the work force were involved, white-collar employees tended to play a disproportionately large role in strike leadership. Active shop and depot craftsmen were often "represented" by delegates from the Social Democratic committees who, alongside largely independent professionals, dominated virtually every delegate body above the station level.[19] At the

19. On the Riga-Orel Railroad, for example, a "Central Bureau of Employees and Workers" was formed in Riga by about fifty delegates, each representing a hundred men. A Bundist, Aleksandr Paulish, served as chair, and, though the group had local branches at most stations, its central leadership was dominated by technical staff and representatives of the revolutionary parties (A. Paulish, "Zabastavochnoe dvizhenie na Rigo-Orlovskoi zh. d.," *Proletarskaia revoliutsiia*, 1925, no. 11 (46): 159; L. M. Ivanov, ed., *Vserossiiskaia politicheskaia stachka v oktiabre 1905 goda* [Moscow and Leningrad, 1955], vol. 1, pp. 299–301).

grass roots, however, the strike committees varied widely in composition. At Kinel', on the South East Railroad, there were two station employees, two telegraph operators, and a coupler; at Zilan, on the South West Railroad, three depot craftsmen, two engine-drivers, a foreman, a medical assistant, a telegraph operator, and a station clerk; at Briansk, on the Catherine line, it was two railroad doctors and three engine-drivers. At the Konotop workshops of the Moscow-Kiev-Voronezh Railroad the strike committee was led by an engineer, and initially there was little participation by organized political groups. Within days, however, the committee was dominated by an assortment of Social Democrats, Socialist Revolutionaries, and even anarchists.[20]

Organizing was facilitated by the activities of so-called "delegate trains," which traveled the rail lines spreading the strike. Assembled by striking railwaymen and dispatched under the control of striking crews, the trains were generally connected to strike committees at major junctions, although harried railroad directors were frequently compelled to approve their formation. The functions of these trains varied from a purely agitational role to serving as vehicles of communication and organization, bringing delegates together from stations hundreds of miles apart. The arrival or departure of a delegate train could occasion a major display of revolutionary fervor. At Belgorod on the Kursk-Kharkov-Sevastopol line a train was greeted by a demonstration of more than a thousand strikers and citizens, who sang revolutionary songs as the agitators set out for the road's Kursk terminus. Often the arrival of a delegate train served to free workers at smaller stations from the influence of conservative stationmasters and other line officials. Pushkareva has found evidence that delegate trains were active on at least twenty different railroad lines.[21]

One example of how the delegate trains spread not only the strike but also political and organizational activity is the Samara-Zlatoust Railroad, where, according to one official lament, such a train "played a tremendous negative role." On October 16 the road

20. Pushkareva, *Zheleznodorozhniki*, p. 166; Ivan Maruta, *Ocherki po istorii revoliutsionnogo professional'nogo dvizheniia na Moskovsko-Kievo-Voronezhskoi zh. d. Vypusk pervyi. 1905 g.* (Kursk, 1925), p. 40.
21. Ivanov, ed., vol. 1, pp. 258–59; I. M. Pushkareva, "Zheleznodorozhniki Rossii—uchastniki oktiabr'skoi politicheskoi stachki," *Voprosy istorii*, 1958, no. 12: 165.

director agreed to give striking workers a train in order to arrange a meeting of delegates in Ufa. In exchange the strikers pledged not to hold demonstrations at stations through which the train passed. However, at Raevka, where there had as yet been no organized strike activity, the train was met on the evening of October 17 by nearly all station employees and officials, who gathered in the first-class dining hall. Here a speaker from the train noted the presence of managers in front of whom workers would be "hesitant to speak." At his suggestion, the workers moved to the conductors' room and within hours the strike had seized this formerly isolated station. Delegates were chosen to join the train and a strike committee was elected.[22]

On the Moscow-Kiev-Voronezh Railroad a delegate train played a key role in politicizing the movement. Here the strike center was in Kursk, where a committee led by a Socialist Revolutionary was very active and cooperated closely with a committee on the Moscow-Kursk line controlled by Social Democrats. The Kursk committee telegraphed all stations on the Moscow-Kiev-Voronezh road to send delegates. At Voronezh the workers met and approved a very moderate petition of demands, with no political content, which they dispatched to Kursk in a train with several elected representatives. The train made stops along the way and by the time it arrived carried nineteen different delegations, each with its own set of demands. Assisted by a member of the Kursk strike committee, the delegates worked out a joint petition, which in the end endorsed calls for civil liberties and a constitution. Another delegate train originated at the line's Kiev station, where the strike was led by the stationmaster. On October 14 violence broke out when the authorities tried to dispatch troops to Kharkov. After the strikers set fire to the coal bins and fuel storage tanks, the stationmaster and other strike leaders fled to Konotop, where they joined the strike committee at that workshop junction.[23]

The trains also spread the strike and antigovernment feeling to other sections of the population, especially the peasantry. Striking

22. TsGIA, f. 273, op. 12, d. 364, ll. 482–83. For another example of how a delegate train helped spread both the strike and the urge to organize to a relatively isolated station, Dolinsk on the Kharkov-Nikolaev Railroad, see *1905 vo vospominaniiakh ego uchastnikov*, pp. 66–68, 76.

23. Maruta, pp. 40–43; Ivanov, ed., vol. 1, pp. 274–76.

railwaymen brought with them news of events in the cities. As one newspaper correspondent described the situation in the volatile Volga countryside, people would "gather in crowds at the railroad stations to meet the delegate trains . . . they would interrogate the delegates about what was happening in the towns and disperse for home agitated by what they had heard. The idea of a general strike would thus be spread through all the villages." In the Ukraine a train with as many as a thousand strikers from Nizhnedneprovsk arrived at one rural station and severed phone and telegraph lines. Then the workers spread through the district, where local peasants gathered to hear revolutionary speeches. When the train moved on, the peasants rose up, seizing forest land and attacking the manor house of a local gentry estate.[24]

During the October strike divisions among organized railroad workers were temporarily shelved as all factions cooperated in furthering the commonly accepted goals of the walkout. This was true not only of political factions, but also of divergent occupational groups. Indeed, the objective, if temporary, unity between upper and lower strata of the railroad hierarchy achieved in October probably encouraged the mobilization of broader numbers. Strike committees were often effective precisely because they could sometimes virtually duplicate the ordinary command structure of the railroad economy. At Dolinsk, on the Kharkov-Nikolaev line, for example, though the stationmaster opposed the strike, his assistant was "the most politically conscious of us all." During the first strike meeting held at this station, a German engineer, struggling to express himself in Russian, enthusiastically endorsed the movement. "The fact that the ranks of the highest station administration were taking part was an inspiration, allaying our fears of the possibly gloomy consequences [of our actions]," one young activist recalled.[25]

"After the victory of the October strike," however, "the mirage of general national unity quickly began to dissipate" and this transformed the character of grass-roots organizations.[26] To be sure, the

24. *Syn otechestva*, November 18, 1905, quoted in Pushkareva, *Zheleznodorozhniki*, p. 165; F. E. Los', ed., *Revoliutsiia 1905–1907 gg. na Ukraine* (Kiev, 1955), vol. 2, pt. 1, pp. 399–400.

25. *1905 vo vospominaniiakh ego uchastnikov*, pp. 69–70.

26. Dymkov and Lipovetskii, p. 94.

extraordinary organizing activity that took place between the October and December confrontations followed no common pattern.
Everywhere general trends were mediated by local particularities.
In the main, however, this period saw a widening rift between radical Social Democrats, whose organizational as well as political influence was growing rapidly, mainly among shop craftsmen, and the
kinds of forces that had heretofore dominated the Railroad Union.
This division took on quite varied organizational forms and was not
often clearly focused, but in general the emergence of increasingly
militant class consciousness conflicted with, and often burst, the
bounds of professional forms of mobilization.

The soviets were one important form through which railroad
workers were able to unite with other sections of the working class.
In a number of medium-sized and smaller cities railroad strike
committees and branches of the Railroad Union provided nuclei for
the new class bodies, especially where railroad workshops were the
largest industrial establishment. In the northern Caucasus and the
Don basin the workers of the Vladikavkaz Railroad were central to
creating soviet bodies, especially in Rostov and Novorossiisk. Even
where soviets were not formed, local groups of railwaymen made
concerted efforts to establish links with the soviet movement. The
railwaymen of Dvinsk, for example, decided to sever ties with the
Central Bureau of the Railroad Union and take leadership instead
from the St. Petersburg soviet, which had emerged as Russia's most
prestigious working-class organization.[27]

Participation in the soviets was linked to the growing influence
of shop craftsmen and consequently of Social Democracy among
railroad workers, although this was certainly highly uneven. In the
soviets the shopmen were able to associate with other industrial
and skilled craft workers, and this resulted in an observable tendency to pull other railwaymen away from the more liberal professional trend, which was stronger among white-collar employees.
Hence there could be sharp debate over the advisability of affiliating with other workers. On the South East Railroad in Voronezh
some office employees balked at proposals to invite factory delegates to join an assembly organized by railwaymen. They wanted to

27. Pushkareva, *Zheleznodorozhniki*, p. 188.

retain a strictly railroad organization, but were defeated by shop and depot delegates who called for a soviet.[28]

The emerging class militancy was not in principle hostile to professional forms; the conflict was rather between competing conceptions of proletarian politics. Even as new class organizations such as the soviets were developing, professional organizations also mushroomed. However, the professional movement was itself increasingly divided. Many diverse factors, including especially local particularities, played roles in this, but in general there were two intimately connected conflicts. Increasingly radical and class-conscious workers, mainly young shop and depot craftsmen (but also many telegraph operators, engine-drivers, and even some lower white-collar employees), sought to break the dominance of the professional movement by members of the administrative hierarchy. At the same time the Social Democrats were engaged in a political battle against liberal influence.

The Bolsheviks wanted professional forms to restrict their concerns to economics, leaving the party free rein in the political sphere, but this was impossible since many workers sought to express essentially socialist politics in the professional milieu. Professional forms of organization were often the most immediately accessible to newly awakened workers, even if the concerns of these workers and their mode of expressing them often stood in contradiction to a narrowly interpreted professional philosophy. There often was almost a spontaneous syndicalism in this: to reach the "kingdom of socialism," declared the assembled delegates of the Catherine Railroad, the working class must organize in unions.[29] Bonnell has argued that a peculiar characteristic of the Russian labor movement was a "telescoping of phases," evidenced by the simultaneous emergence of class consciousness and professional organization.[30] But, at least in railroading, class politics was not necessarily hostile to professional organization, seeking instead to fundamentally reshape the outlook and leadership of the professional movement. Hence, Social Democratic practice was perforce

28. N. N. Demochkin, *Sovety 1905 goda—organy revoliutsionnoi vlasti* (Moscow, 1963), pp. 66–67.
29. Sidorov, ed., vol. 3, pt. 1, p. 33.
30. Bonnell, *Roots of Rebellion*, p. 446.

flexible, even inconsistent: in some places socialists fought for a "purely professional" approach to union organizing, while elsewhere they could advocate quite the opposite.

In all sections of the working class, especially in St. Petersburg and Moscow, the weeks after the October strike were marked by a furious upsurge in the organization of unions. In November forty-two unions were established in St. Petersburg and forty-one in Moscow. Many of these organizations were almost ephemeral, however, "hardly more permanent than the meetings that ratified their existence."[31] Moreover, many unions were as much political as professional associations. According to a government report, "unions were formed initially to regulate the economic relations of the employees, but soon, under the influence of propaganda hostile to the state, they took on a political aspect and began to strive for the overthrow of the existing state and social order."[32]

The Railroad Union was already a relatively established organization in October, but it, too, grew rapidly during the "days of freedom," especially in the Moscow area, where it remained based. "The railroad union came out from the underground," recalled the Bolshevik clerk Kotliarenko, "holding open meetings of both road committees, which were generally open to all who wished to be union members, and representative assemblies from the various lines in the Moscow area." According to Pereverzev, the Railroad Union began to advertise its meetings in the press and there was a "colossal increase in membership." The Central Bureau opened a public office in Moscow and accumulated a treasury of more than ten thousand rubles.[33] On the Moscow-Kursk Railroad, where Social Democratic influence was relatively weak and the Railroad Union fairly powerful among the employees, a new line bureau was formed of representatives from all branches of railroad service. There were fourteen delegates from the Moscow administration, nineteen from operations personnel in the Department of Traffic Management, sixteen from the workshops and depots, five from the Track Maintenance Department, two telegraph operators, two

31. Ibid., pp. 122–23; Laura Engelstein, *Moscow, 1905: Working Class Organization and Political Conflict* (Stanford, Calif., 1982), p. 155.

32. Sidorov, ed., vol. 3, pt. 2, p. 800.

33. I. Kh. Danilov and P. G. Sdobnev, eds., *Zheleznodorozhniki v 1905 godu* (Moscow, 1940), p. 138; TsGAOR, f. 6865, d. 120, l. 88.

workers from the railroad print shop, and someone from the Public Health Section. The group met regularly throughout November under the chairmanship of K. D. Nametnichenko, a member of the Railroad Union Central Bureau.[34]

Greater participation by the masses, however, tended to increase the influence of political parties and to diffuse the leadership of both the Central Bureau and those largely independent liberal members of the administrative hierarchy who supported it and were so important to the initial organizing. A Riazan-Ural engine-driver recalled that the October manifesto "split the Railroad Union into two camps," although, as has been seen, the beginnings of that split could be traced to the union's summer congress.[35] On one side stood the liberals and some SRs, supported by a section of mainly white-collar railwaymen still tied to the administrative hierarchy, who essentially welcomed the terms of the manifesto and now hoped to fight for its implementation and to establish the union as a professional support for an evolving constitutional regime. They were not so naive as to be deluded that the regime had fundamentally changed its character, but they were fearful that a new confrontation would destroy gains already won, including the union's de facto legalization. They faced, on the other side, a growing revolutionary tendency, mainly led by the Social Democrats, but supported increasingly by more radical SRs, which demanded that the Railroad Union unite with the rest of the working class to continue the revolutionary struggle. The Central Bureau itself was divided and tried to stand aloof from the controversy. Pressure from below combined with government intransigence pushed the union leaders leftward, however, although they moved in that direction with increasing unease. Lower union bodies in Moscow were likewise torn and could be virtually paralyzed. Even on the relatively unified Moscow-Kursk road the line bureau could not resolve whether to send representatives to the blue-collar, socialist-led Moscow soviet or to the increasingly white-collar and ineffective strike committee.[36]

In Moscow the formal break between Social Democracy and

34. *1905 god na Moskovsko-Kurskoi-Nizhegorodskoi i Muromskoi zh. d.*, pp. 26–29.
35. *Zheleznodorozhniki v 1905 g.*, p. 21.
36. *1905 god na Moskovsko-kurskoi-nizhegorodskoi i muromskoi zh. d.*, p. 37.

the Railroad Union came before October, but the Central Bureau and the Bolshevik-led Moscow Committee continued to cooperate during the general strike. Afterward, however, the Moscow Social Democrats launched a full-scale political assault on the railroad liberals. Pereverzev recalled how "party workers arrived at every union meeting and called on all comrades to leave this petty-bourgeois union and join the party."[37] Once again the Moscow Committee attempted to build a separate union affiliated with the party, which attracted support in several railroad workshops. On October 18 the city's Bolshevik and Menshevik groups formally reunited, and the new union was begun in the Menshevik-dominated shops of the Moscow-Brest Railroad. Meeting on November 8 to endorse a charter for a "purely worker union," the Brest railwaymen declared they could not enter the Railroad Union "in view of its hybrid composition." The new union formally eschewed politics in order to unite with nonparty workers; its purpose was defined as "the struggle to better the material position [of railroad workers], but also to assist in their intellectual and political development."[38]

Shop craftsmen on the Moscow-Kazan Railroad also affiliated with the Social Democrats on an independent basis in November.[39] Dissatisfaction with the Railroad Union even seized white-collar *Kazantsy:* "after the October strike our administration began to break away from the union," the Central Bureau member Bednov recalled. "At that time neither the union nor the Social Democrats, nor any other party engaged the workers and employees; there were only conversations like this: 'To whose meeting are you going? I'm going to Kotliarenko. I'm going to Bednov.'"[40] Nonetheless on November 17 a meeting of employees of the Moscow-Kazan administration debated the relative merits of the Railroad Union and the Social Democratic railroad group. A representative of the Rail-

37. TsGAOR, f. 6865, d. 120, ll. 88–89.

38. TsGAOR, f. 6865, d. 119, ll. 164–69; Dymkov and Lipovetskii, p. 96. The Mensheviks began organizing on the Brest road in September, but the first meeting of the new union came on October 23 and involved over a thousand workers, including some office employees with Social Democratic sympathies. See Engelstein, p. 238.

39. Dymkov and Lipovetskii, p. 94; Engelstein, p. 238, is mistaken in designating the Union of Moscow-Kazan Railroad Shop Workers as a "member-union of the All-Russian Union of Railroad Workers and Employees."

40. TsGAOR, f. 6865, d. 120, l. 109.

road Union opened the discussion; he was followed by two Social Democrats, who denounced the Central Bureau as "bourgeois" and invited employees to join the union begun by the Brest craftsmen.[41]

A leaflet distributed by the Social Democrats explained the difference between the two unions:

The professional railroad union is striving to improve the material and legal position of the railwaymen. The Social Democrats are striving to educate and organize all workers, including railwaymen, for the struggle to improve their everyday lives, not in separate industries, but in all industries, in all professions. The Social Democratic railroad union poses for itself the goal of developing the consciousness of the workers so that they may feel and recognize themselves as members of the great united family of the working class. . . .

. . . the Social Democratic railroad union is not hostile to the professional railroad union. On the contrary, it welcomes it as it does any stirring of opposition political thought and action in Russian society, no matter how immaturely and naively expressed. Besides, as does any trade union, the professional railroad union facilitates Social Democratic organizing. It offers the possibility of recruiting new proletarian forces. But all the same the Social Democrats will always enter trade unions with a critical attitude, always speak out on the irreconcilable contradiction between the proletarian elements and the top employees.[42]

On almost every major railroad line during October and November workers created new forms of professional organization. In some places this occurred nominally under the auspices of the Railroad Union, but nearly everywhere the organizations were effectively independent of the Moscow group. The principal form was the delegate assembly, or congress. These brought together representatives of all railroad departments, railroad workshops, offices, and smaller stations. Held openly under the new freedoms granted by the manifesto, the meetings were more than incipient trade union conventions; they could become political forums.[43]

Several delegate assemblies declared support for the Social Democrats, but, mostly, political sentiments did not coincide pre-

---

41. *Moskovskaia gazeta*, 10, November 20, 1905, as cited in Dymkov and Lipovetskii, pp. 89–90.

42. Dymkov and Lipovetskii, pp. 99–102.

43. Sidorov, ed., vol. 4, pp. 11, 14; vol. 2, p. 13; vol. 3, pt. 1, pp. 497–98.

cisely with those of any special organized tendency. Sometimes the meetings were convened by Railroad Union chapters, sometimes by local revolutionaries. On several roads delegate assemblies were organized by returning pension congress delegates, or even the road administration, to discuss the results of the St. Petersburg sessions. Usually the meetings elected some form of permanent bureau or other leadership group to function on a regular basis, sometimes as a chapter of the Railroad Union, sometimes as an independent local body. On virtually every road there was tension and conflict between liberals associated with the administration and predominantly blue-collar forces often mobilized under socialist leadership. This could, however, take different forms in different places.

In St. Petersburg, where the proportion of shop craftsmen within the railroad work force was significantly higher than in Moscow, the bulk of blue-collar energy seems to have been directed toward the work of the soviet. Although the Railroad Union only had a consultative voice in that body, it was represented on the second executive committee, elected on November 19.[44] Railroad craftsmen also elected delegates to the soviet, including several Social Democrats.

Strictly professional organizing continued, however. On the Nicholas Railroad elected delegates assembled on November 14 to hear Elizarov report on the work of the pension congress. The meeting voted to demand that road managers permit local meetings at all significant stations and terminals, with higher officials and police barred, so that workers could discuss the congress.[45] On the Baltic and St. Petersburg–Warsaw lines, and on the St. Petersburg network of the Moscow-Vindau-Rybinsk Railroad, delegate assemblies approved local union charters and confirmed their affiliation with the Railroad Union. In fact, by late November the Railroad Union claimed to have signed up as many as 80 percent of the capital's railwaymen. However, on November 28 a citywide meeting of railroad employees and workers called by the union turned into a "very stormy" debate between Social Democrats and Socialist Revo-

44. Georgii S. Nosar', "Istoriia soveta rabochikh deputatov," *Istoriia soveta rabochikh deputatov g. S.-Peterburga* (St. Petersburg, 1906), pp. 71, 153–54.

45. *Nachalo*, 3, November 16, 1905; *Novaia zhizn'*, 14, November 16, 1905.

lutionaries when the subject of the union's relations with political parties arose.[46]

On some roads delegate meetings were first convened during the October strike. On October 13 workers and employees at the Kharkov terminals of the Kursk-Kharkov-Sevastopol and Kharkov-Nikolaev Railroads met in congress to affirm that "the pacification of railroad employees is possible only with the pacification of all citizens" by granting constitutional rights. Two days later delegates from most stations on these lines gathered in Liubotin to endorse a similar call. The October strike and the weeks that followed in Kharkov saw the eclipse of the initial strike committee dominated by administrative employees and the emergence of a new group centered in the workshops. Efforts to organize a union of railroad workers were frustrated, however, when police broke up an organizing meeting on November 10 and a subsequent session was torn by a factional dispute between Bolshevik Social Democrats and a group of anarchists.[47]

On the Riazan-Ural Railroad delegates from various parts of the line assembled in Saratov on October 12 to form a central strike committee initiated by the liberal Railroad Union group, which had led the professional movement since January. Five days later the meeting was surrounded by troops and dispersed, with several arrests. The next day, however, word arrived of the tsar's proclamation, and the arrested delegates were released. The group reassembled on October 19 and, despite the urgings of the local Railroad Union leaders, voted overwhelmingly to continue the strike. Before the issue could be decisively resolved, however, the assembly was surrounded by an angry Black Hundred mob, which had begun an anti-Jewish pogrom in the city. Committee leaders appealed to Governor Stolypin to act against the pogromists and protect the railroad workers, but he responded by banning all railroad assemblies in the province. It was in this situation that the local Railroad Union leaders dispatched the much-disputed telegram ter-

46. TsGAOR, f. 6865, d. 63, ll. 138–39; d. 56, ll. 6–12; d. 163, l. 29; *Novaia zhizn'*, 13, November 15, 1905, p. 3; 14, November 16, 1905, p. 3; *Nasha zhizn'*, 347, November 30, 1905, p. 4.
47. TsGIA, f. 273, op. 12, d. 375, l. 122; L. M. Finkelshtein, "Liubotinskaia respublika," *Proletarskaia revoliutsiia*, 1925, no. 12 (47): 182; S. Kramer, ed., *1905 god v Kharkove* (Kharkov, 1925), pp. 241–42.

minating the strike in the name of the central strike committee.[48]
A rump body of union leaders, Social Democrats and Socialist
Revolutionaries, soon began to organize a new congress in cooperation with the returning pension congress delegates. On November 15 approximately 150 delegates, including "depot and shop
workers, switchmen, greasemen, conductors, engine-drivers, track
repair workers, stationmasters and their assistants, and even department heads," assembled in Moscow beyond Stolypin's reach.
Pension congress leader Orekhov, also affiliated with the Railroad
Union group, was selected to chair the meeting at the head of a
presidium divided in roughly equal proportions among Railroad
Union members, Social Democrats, and SRs. The meeting broke
into sections by department and occupation to work out economic
demands. An initially vocal minority of railroad engineers objected
to the organized presence of political parties at the meeting and
warned of the dangers and "treachery" of a new strike, but in the
increasingly radical atmosphere of Moscow the entire congress
moved steadily leftward. Still, in the words of the leading Bolshevik
delegate, G. G. Sushkin, "newly conscious and uneducated workers
often feared debate with articulate engineers and administrators."[49]

The November delegate congress on the Riazan-Ural Railroad
saw the final eclipse of the liberal leadership group that had introduced the political struggle on the railroads at the beginning of the
year. The struggle came to a head when the congress addressed the
question of permanent professional organization. Sushkin and a
Socialist Revolutionary, Lutskii, presented reports on the principles of union organization and called on the congress to begin
organizing. Members of the Railroad Union protested that a union
of railwaymen already existed, and a fierce debate began, which
lasted two sessions. The speakers and their supporters countered
that the Railroad Union was really a political group, not a professional one, and that, moreover, its politics were hostile to those of
the revolutionary proletariat. Ultimately the congress approved a
resolution submitted by the Social Democrats:

48. N. Sushkin, "Oktiabr', noiabr', i dekabr' 1905 g. na Riazansko-Ural'skoi zh.
d. (vospominaniia)," *Katorga i ssylka*, 1930, no. 12: 146–52; I. S. Sokolov, *1905
god na Riazansko-Ural'skoi zheleznoi doroge* (Saratov, 1925), pp. 43–44; *Zheleznodorozhniki v 1905 g.*, p. 20. TsGAOR, f. 6865, d. 38a.
49. Sushkin, pp. 152–56; Sokolov, p. 48; *Privol. kr.*, 234, November 27, 1905.

Recognizing the expediency of trade unions for the successful struggle for economic and legal demands and as a means of organizing all railwaymen, [it is resolved] to take up their organization as soon as possible. The organization of the union executive group must be based on broad democratic foundations and on the principle of general electoral rights.[50]

Upon its conclusion at the start of the December general strike, the congress chose a 21-member temporary executive committee dominated by the socialist parties and chaired by Sushkin, from which the liberal Railroad Union leaders were excluded.

The Railroad Union also received a rebuke from blue-collar workers on the Catherine Railroad, where the delegate assembly rejected an invitation by a group of office employees to organize a union local. "We workers . . . have nothing in common with the engineers and higher employees," who were friends only in words, the assembly bureau declared. Only the lower employees, telegraph operators and clerks, were deemed worthy allies. The others "don't have to listen to the cries of hungry children. . . . They are not our comrades. They are prepared to struggle with us only to better their own position."[51] Although local judicial authorities later declared that Catherine Railroad delegates were "not representatives of the masses, but revolutionary loudmouths," it was, as these same authorities recognized, precisely because the blue-collar ranks were dissatisfied with the October outcome that the delegate assembly took on such an ominous character.[52]

On the Vladikavkaz Railroad, where the Railroad Union had had no influence before October, the "days of freedom" brought the group initial success, but soon a process of radicalization and decline in union influence occurred here too. At the start of the general strike a mass meeting of employees and shop craftsmen at the Rostov railroad administration agreed to "work under the flag" of the Railroad Union. A 56-member organizing bureau headed by Ivan Shvedov, a senior clerk, and B. F. Nazarevich, a pension congress delegate, was chosen to prepare a delegate congress. Trains were sent to outlying stations, and on October 23, one day after freight traffic resumed, 214 delegates gathered in the Rostov workshops. There was immediate agreement that the delegates should

50. *Privol. kr.*, 242, December 8, 1905; Sokolov, p. 50.
51. Sidorov, ed., vol. 3, pt. 1, p. 34.
52. TsGAOR, f. 6865, d. 78a, l. 13.

create some form of permanent professional organization, but a proposal to endorse the decision to affiliate with the Railroad Union taken ten days before at Rostov ran into obstacles, as the delegates debated whether the union was "strictly professional" or a political organization and whether it should or could cooperate with the Social Democrats.[53]

With discussion stalemated, the congress accepted a Social Democratic offer to table the question. For the next two days the body met in ten separate sections according to occupation in order to formulate a program of economic demands. On the evening of October 26 the plenary session was again called to order and debate began about a union platform, but that discussion was also curtailed when rumors of a Black Hundred assault on the railroad shops brought the meeting to a close. The next day the congress established local organizing bureaus and agreed to designate the Rostov body as the central bureau. This group was directed to establish a more permanent organization by December and to organize a second congress no later than February 1. When the congress adjourned on October 28, the issue of affiliation with the Railroad Union remained unresolved, but the great majority of those elected to leadership were senior office employees and engine-drivers, and the Railroad Union advocate Shvedov was chosen to head the Rostov bureau.[54]

In the following weeks local organizing proceeded at a "feverish" pace. As early as October 20 the railroad's private management complained that the situation in the Caucasus was "close to anarchy," with trains and stations under continued assault by both workers and criminal elements whose "goal was simply plunder." The road agreed to give the organizing bureaus access to the railroad telegraph system, partly in the hope that they might bring some order to the situation, but mainly out of weakness. Mass meetings were held in just about every significant station. In Rostov craftsmen and employees gathered on November 8, 9, 15, and 26 to debate both economic and political questions. Gradually the mood grew more radical and in mid November Shvedov was re-

53. Ibid., d. 70, ll. 14–17, 219–20.
54. Ibid., d. 75, ll. 1–4.

lieved of leadership of the Rostov bureau and replaced by a Social Democrat with Bolshevik sympathies, Solomon Reizman.[55]

In 1906 Shvedov, dismissed for strike activity after December, petitioned for reinstatement to railroad service. He claimed that he had been elected to his post at a legally constituted meeting and had always been a moderate who had tried to keep the trains running. The testimony of two employees in support of his appeal suggests much about the political and social dynamic at work on the railroads in late 1905:

. . . at one time our party of clerks had a restraining influence on the workers, but after the exit of chairman Shvedov and the election of chairman Reizman the party of workers took control.

and

. . . by its composition the bureau itself was divided into two unequal halves (workers and clerks), but the workers had a significant majority. . . . The workers always became irritated by the proper form of the chairman's messages to the administration and compelled him [Shvedov] to adopt sharper forms of expression, . . . ignoring not only the opinions but also the interests of the office delegates.[56]

Typical of the differences between the two tendencies was a dispute that emerged at a November 25 meeting where the moderates opposed use of the word "demand," which they called a "vulgar expression," in a petition to management. They argued that this limited the chances of agreement, but the resolution passed as originally proposed.[57]

The position of engine-drivers on the Vladikavkaz and other railroad lines during this period was somewhat ambiguous. By their privileged economic position the drivers stood closer to the employees, and, indeed, in Moscow at least, engine cabmen were active in Railroad Union organizing. However, engine-drivers worked

55. TsGIA, f. 273, op. 12, d. 373, l. 348; Sidorov, ed., vol. 2, p. 1127. One activist later described Reizman, who arrived in Rostov from St. Petersburg in mid November, as a "young, energetic and talented" organizer who "brought with him the mood of the Petersburg workers" (*1905 vo vospominaniiakh ego uchastnikov*, p. 18).

56. TsGIA, f. 273, op. 12, d. 374, l. 43–44, 47.

57. Sidorov, ed., vol. 2, pp. 446–47.

closely with craftsmen in the depots, and many had themselves risen out of the workshops. They could thus sympathize with blue-collar militancy and aspirations. The history of the organizing bureau at the Mineral Waters depot on the Vladikavkaz Railroad indicates how some engine-drivers were affected by the post-manifesto mood. It is worth examining in some detail also because it shows how the contradictions of these frantic weeks were mediated by local particularities.

More than 1,500 workers were attached to the Mineral Waters station and depot, which emerged as a militant hotbed in July. Both Social Democrats and Socialist Revolutionaries won considerable support among the engine-drivers, although the SRs were the larger and more active group, especially after the arrival of a talented organizer in late summer. By November they could claim that nearly a third of the station staff were attached to their organization, which on November 23 began publishing its own newspaper.[58] The two socialist groups cooperated, however, and after the Rostov congress a Social Democratic engine-driver named Ventsulevich became chairman of the Mineral Waters bureau.

According to one of his party comrades, Ventsulevich was the most "politically developed of us all," but "as a Pole he was not popular." In the view of another worker, however, Ventsulevich's problem was less his nationality than his "petty bourgeois bearing" and apparently condescending attitude toward craftsmen, which were increasingly out of place in November: "Ventsulevich spoke continually of his special technical education that distinguished him from the mass of simple machinists. He said his father had spent too much on his education for him to risk being fired."[59] No matter what the cause, on November 20 Ventsulevich was replaced by a Socialist Revolutionary engine-driver, Nikanor N. Bakliukov, who had also been a delegate to the Rostov meeting and was extremely active in the July and October strikes.

Bakliukov's biography attests that the radicalization and political splits that followed the October strike cannot be understood simply as a break between a politically liberal elite and recently mobilized young workers concerned primarily with economic issues. For not

58. TsGAOR, f. 6865, d. 71, no *list* number.
59. Ibid., d. 70, l. 175, 159.

only was Bakliukov a member of a privileged occupation, he was also an experienced political activist. Born in 1863 to a family of domestic servants, at the age of twelve he moved to Voronezh, where he completed trade school and entered a railroad technical academy. It was here that the young worker first encountered revolutionary politics, participating in an underground populist circle. Upon graduation in 1882 Bakliukov became a machinist at the Voronezh railroad shops. "Here I became part of the united worker family, became acquainted with the miserable conditions of my brothers, with their permanent need, with the ideals of the working class."

Within a year and a half Bakliukov was appointed assistant engine-driver, and two years later he became a full-fledged driver. In 1895 he came to the Mineral Waters Depot. At Mineral Waters he helped organize a mutual aid society in 1903, but it collapsed. In 1904 the society and its fund were revived, with considerable success. The group provided engine-drivers and other skilled workers with loans and established a food cooperative. More important, the society set up a small lending library of "newspapers, journals, and other literature." The underground socialist parties approached the group, but for fear of repression their leaflets were only passed hand to hand in single copies. Gradually, "on the basis of improvements in their material position, the still unconscious masses were drawn toward the revolutionary and professional movement, toward politics." In 1905 the mutual aid society was suppressed by the authorities as a "suspect and hostile revolutionary organization," and its treasury of over 800 rubles was confiscated. It was on the basis of this experience that Bakliukov came to leadership of the militant Mineral Waters railwaymen.[60]

Even on the South West Railroad, where the Railroad Union had been founded by a leading local Bolshevik, union influence declined sharply after October. Shlikhter himself, dismissed from the road in the spring, had moved to Moscow (returning very briefly in October to take on formal leadership of the strike), and it seems that without him the Kiev union group lost much of its authority with employees and workers. An assembly at the Odessa station on

---

60. Material on Bakliukov's life is from a brief autobiographical essay he wrote for Istproftran in the 1920s (TsGAOR, f. 6865, d. 70, ll. 243–44).

November 11 ignored the Railroad Union, voting instead to "unite with the tactics and program of the Russian Social Democratic Labor Party." Previously the Social Democrats had, through Shlikhter and in alliance with the Kiev SRs, established their leadership among white-collar employees of the Kiev administration. But on all lines after October it was precisely the white-collar element that was dividing into a more moderate professional component, following the leadership of liberal administrators, and a radical wing composed mainly of younger junior clerks and telegraph operators who were seeking to link up with skilled blue-collar workers increasingly led by socialists. In Kiev attention therefore shifted to the workshops, where mass meetings on November 1, 13, and 17 discussed both shop matters and national politics.[61]

Elsewhere on the line, however, leadership fell into the hands of the pension congress delegates. On November 6 the returning representatives convened a delegate assembly in Zhmerinka. Some 180 representatives of all sections of the permanent staff attended the meeting, which was in theory called to discuss only pension affairs and not the political actions taken by the St. Petersburg congress. Immediately, however, the delegates agreed to exclude the police, and the assembly "took on a lively character." The hall was physically as well as politically divided: on the right sat a group of railroad officials who voiced vigorous protests against all political manifestations. The discussion quickly moved beyond pension matters, however, as the body voted to send a telegram to the capital with demands for a constituent assembly. The meeting debated the recent pogroms in various Ukrainian towns and considered the possibility that railroad managers had helped foment them, appointing a commission to investigate this question. A second commission of eighteen delegates was elected to begin the work of organizing a trade union (no mention was made of the already-existing Railroad Union) under the chairmanship of a pension congress delegate, who also chaired the assembly itself, but this group disbanded when the ministry made it clear that such functions were outside the meeting's legal status.[62]

Polarization between liberal administrators and a section of the

61. Sidorov, ed., vol. 3, pt. 1, pp. 497–98; TsGAOR, f. 6865, d. 35, ll. 139–41.
62. TsGAOR, f. 6865, d. 35, ll. 152–56; TsGIA, f. 273, op. 12, d. 345, ll. 239–40, 288–89, 292, 299–301.

employees often associated with the Railroad Union on one side and blue-collar craftsmen and other workers and employees leaning toward Social Democracy on the other was still incipient, however, and considerable ambiguity remained. If nothing else, the increasingly provocative actions of the government, including the Ministry of Communications under Nemeshaev, tended to keep the factions together. In general, the split was more visible where a strong, usually Bolshevik, Social Democratic organization could provide leadership and where large workshops offered the most fertile soil for appeals to class over professional loyalties. Where these did not exist the situation was often less strained, although much could depend on factors peculiar to a given area. In Revel, for example, Estonian workers on the Baltic Railroad rebelled against the leadership of a small group of Russian liberal administrators who had founded a chapter of the Railroad Union in August, largely because they did not speak Estonian. Estonian Social Democracy seems to have played only a marginal role in this dispute.[63]

The varied experiences at different points on the Moscow-Kiev-Voronezh Railroad and in the central administration of the South East Railroad in Voronezh illustrate how the situation could diverge from the general pattern depending upon local political conditions. In general, organizing activity on the Moscow-Kiev-Voronezh line took place "under the slogan of the nonparty spirit [*bezpartiinost'*]."[64] In early November employees and workers at the line's Moscow station founded a committee of twenty-four delegates from the clerks, shop craftsmen, line maintenance crews, switchmen, couplers, greasemen, and station staff. Dominated by office employees, the group was not principally an organization for struggle with the administration: it selected a standing bureau to run its daily affairs, and organized a conflict commission of representatives of labor and management, a court of honor to resolve personal disagreements among employees, a mutual aid fund, and a library. A similar body at the Maloiaroslavets station formed on the eve of the December showdown was dominated by station administrators, although it was formally chaired by a railroad doctor. This group declared that its goals were to guarantee "order to the lives,

63. Sidorov, ed., vol. 4, pp. 535–37.
64. Maruta, p. 69.

health, and property of the employees and the safety and good
working conditions of the tracks and railroad property and to ensure,
where possible, the orderly movement of trains and freight."[65]

In short, these station committees reflected the views of oppositional administrators who saw political reform principally as a
means of improving and rationalizing professional life. A more
class-conscious approach was adopted in Konotop, site of the railroad's main workshops. Yet in a certain sense, probably because the
socialist parties did not have a very strong presence in this provincial town, the movement here also concerned itself principally with
trade concerns, though in a very different sort of way. Here the
issue was one of control over the work process, as expressed by the
conflict with shop foremen. On October 28 the Konotop railroad
craftsmen struck to demand the dismissal of the shop manager and
several of his foremen, who had been targets of resentment since
the 1903 walkout. Out of this action came the Konotop soviet,
which was really more like a railroad strike committee, since the
railroad shops were the principal industrial enterprise in the city.
On November 14 the railroad administration, which had threatened a lockout, agreed to negotiate with the soviet and eventually
the shop manager was dismissed.[66]

Probably the most significant center of organized activity on the
Moscow-Kiev-Voronezh line was Kursk, home of the road's central
administration, where employees organized a delegate assembly
that met from November 11 to 30. Efim Volkov, a Socialist Revolutionary accountant, was chosen as chair, although few delegates
were affiliated with any political tendency. The overwhelming concern of the meeting was the formulation of economic demands. An
illuminating insight into the spirit in which the delegates under-
took this task is afforded by a debate that took place over the formulation of minimum pay scales. A telegraph operator proposed
that these be established only on the basis of a thorough knowledge
of the income and expenditures of the railroad, so as to guarantee
to stockholders "that portion of the profits rightfully belonging to
them as capitalists." Several speakers rose to agree with this view,
but it was pointed out that the delegates did not have access to the
road's accounts. On this narrow basis the proposal was rejected.[67]

65. Ibid., pp. 61–62, 63.
66. Ibid., pp. 57–59.
67. Ibid., pp. 48–49.

The Kursk assembly was distinctly apolitical. But several delegates were also active in the Railroad Union, which had been founded in Kursk sometime in October by Efim Volkov and A. I. Masal'skii, an engine-driver. At the congress Volkov tried to win the delegates to the union banner. He met firm opposition, however, owing to the political goals in the Railroad Union platform. One clerk charged that "the program of this union is borrowed from the program of the Constitutional Democratic Party." A union, he argued, should be without party spirit and completely apolitical. Others rose to dispute these ideas, but the assembly as a whole declined to affiliate with the Railroad Union, a decision reaffirmed at the meeting's adjournment on November 30.[68] Here, then, was an instance where opposition to reformist politics did not lead workers to embrace a revolutionary alternative. Perhaps these largely white-collar employees were put off by the socialist form in which blue-collar workers converted economic concerns into political aspirations, but perhaps they were also simply less militant than others.

In Voronezh the offices and workshops of the South East Railroad presented an unusually united front throughout November. It is not entirely clear why this was so, but perhaps one explanation is that the white-collar Railroad Union leaders were unusually receptive to cooperation with local Social Democrats, who were themselves bitterly divided. Moreover, as previously mentioned, the union leaders who had emerged from the administration were even before October quite successful in winning a following among blue-collar railwaymen. In fact, according to one account, the Railroad Union was based principally in the workshops, but this seems somewhat doubtful, since the union committee formed during October consisted of eight members of the clerical staff, three telegraph operators, and just two shop craftsmen.[69]

At any rate, after the October manifesto the road administration dismissed several of the more hated managers and sought to accommodate some of the workers' demands. Two commissions were named to review complaints raised in the strike, but the delegate assembly, which met legally on October 23, refused to participate in them. Under the joint leadership of the Railroad Union chapter

68. Ibid., pp. 65–68.
69. *1905 god na Iugo-Vostochnykh zheleznykh dorogakh* (Moscow, 1925), pp. 233–38.

headed by L. I. Shingarev and the socialist parties, that assembly expanded its ranks to include industrial workers, becoming the Voronezh Soviet of Workers' Deputies. The largest group among the two hundred delegates, however, remained the railwaymen and Shingarev was chosen as chair, with a railroad craftsman and telegraph operator as his assistants.[70]

In November union organizing continued both in Voronezh and on the lines. On November 6 and 13 workshop assemblies were convened with Shingarev presiding. On November 20, 350 delegates from virtually all parts of the road gathered for a congress in Voronezh. Chaired by Shingarev, the meeting heard local reports and then broke into sections by department and occupation to discuss demands. The assembly formalized the professional organization, confirming the road's association with the Railroad Union and support for its program.[71]

The six weeks between the October and December strikes thus saw myriad complex and subtle changes in the mood of railwaymen, amidst a frantic rush to establish the most varied forms of professional and political organization. Previously quiescent groups were galvanized into action for the first time. In some places this could mean a retreat from political commitment to concern with relatively narrow economic issues. But more frequently both the newly mobilized and those who had been active for months gravitated toward a new definition of political activity. It has been seen how even before the revolution railroad workers were animated by issues of control over the work process, especially in the workshops. Now this concern began to merge with demands for political participation and democracy. The new mood among workers was generally *more* political than before, even when economic issues were in the forefront of concern.

The integration of political and economic issues came as some railwaymen began—quite fitfully and only initially—to develop consciousness of their membership in a broader class whose interests were in sharp, if not irreconcilable, conflict with those of other groups in urban society, including especially the railroad adminis-

70. Ibid., pp. 46–53.
71. Ibid., pp. 56–58, 154–58.

trative hierarchy, who had so far provided much of the direction for the railroad professional movement. This new consciousness was inseparable from the growing influence of socialist ideas among railroad workers of varying occupations, but especially shop and depot craftsmen. At the same time, it also represented a substantial change in the relationship between blue- and white-collar labor. Before the October strike the industrial workers in the railroad shops had with notable exceptions seemed more concerned about economic welfare and shop control. It had principally been the employees who entered the political arena, largely under the influence of oppositional elements in the railroad hierarchy. After October, however, the workshops were increasingly politicized, mainly on a class-conscious, often socialist, basis.

Both Social Democrats and Socialist Revolutionaries gained considerable ground among railroad workers during the October strike and in the "days of freedom" afterward, although the concept of class conflict emphasized by the former probably struck a more responsive chord than the often-ambiguous theories of the SRs. Had Social Democrats not articulated a political philosophy capable of presenting an alternative political explanation of worker grievances, labor dissatisfaction with the outcome of the October strike might well have materialized as political cynicism, leaving the liberals in command. Local factors could alter the pattern significantly, but the tendency was for the Social Democrats to gain ground among sections of the railroad work force more closely tied to industry, whereas the Socialist Revolutionaries gained among engine-drivers and some lower employees, especially telegraph operators. In general, the liberals were in retreat.

On the political level a kind of role reversal took place: previously liberal elements in the Railroad Union and among the pension congress delegates had eagerly embraced political activism, although the economist political philosophy they espoused was based mainly on the desire to achieve professional goals within a constitutional system; after the manifesto, however, the liberal professional movement tried to move away from political engagement. By contrast, the Social Democrats had previously gained their greatest success as fighters for the workers' immediate interests; now, however, their political appeals won a broad response and they were able to mobilize political consciousness precisely because they were able to link the workers' interests to politics through the concepts of class struggle and a socialist future. The liberal professional politics of the Railroad Union discredited that organization as a vehicle for professional improvement, while socialist class rhetoric was seen by newly politicized workers as the proper path for achieving workplace democracy and material gains.

The divisions that resulted remained latent, however. Although the extent of cooperation varied greatly in different cities and on different railroad lines, the liberal-revolutionary alliance that characterized the October strike held together through December, though it was increasingly strained. For one thing, liberal professionals and socialist workers still needed each other. The rush to organize in October and November was highly chaotic and no single political or social faction could dare seize undisputed leadership. Moreover, the government and railroad management increasingly took a firm stand against the turmoil that had seized the country and its railroad network. As many historians have shown, the strategy of the Witte government after October 17 seemed designed to provoke a confrontation. This alone prevented a decisive split in the movement.

Nine

The December Strike and Armed Uprisings

Government intransigence on one side and the radical politicization of the working-class masses on the other combined to make a
new crisis inevitable. The Witte government's shift from compromise and reform to repression and provocation was consistent with
earlier policy shifts in which concessions preceded new assaults on
worker rights. Forces urging the government to take a hard line
against strikes were formidable, and, more important perhaps, the
railroad reformism represented by the new minister did not stray
beyond the suffocating limits of autocratic paternalism. On the
popular side, calls to insurrection were by no means ineffective, but
it would be mistaken to attribute the December risings solely to
them. The liberal-revolutionary alliance that characterized labor
politics through the October strike crumbled in December not because of the words and deeds of the leaders, but owing to the under-
lying transformation of the alliance's social base and the awakening of
political class consciousness among new sections of the proletariat.

The grass roots organizing of late October and November took
place in an atmosphere of growing tension between the workers'
movement and the government. To be sure, in October the authorities labeled 77.6 percent of strikes in private industry political, and
only 22.4 percent economic, whereas in November just 45.1 percent were deemed political, with 54.9 percent economic. And November saw the largest monthly percentage of strikes settled by
compromise agreements between employers and strikers—nearly

60 percent.[1] But in such a politically charged atmosphere even a strike for higher wages represented a willingness to challenge government authority, which was committed to bringing the turmoil under control, especially on the railroads, where government itself was most often the employer. Many economic strikes were effectively declarations by workers that they wanted October's political victory implemented in their favor.

The movement in St. Petersburg factories to introduce the eight-hour day "in a revolutionary manner" spread to railroad lines in the capital and some provincial junctions. In many shops workers ceased work after eight hours, disrupting production and wreaking havoc with already chaotic train service. Shop craftsmen on the St. Petersburg–Warsaw Railroad did this for several days, prompting a meeting with Nemeshaev, who assured worker delegates that the eight-hour day was an impossible goal since it would unquestionably plunge the country into economic ruin. A similar incident occurred on the Orenburg-Tashkent line, where workers combined the eight-hour action with a demand that two abusive foremen be fired. In Samara a delegate from Orenburg convinced a meeting at the shops of the Samara-Zlatoust road to vote for the eight-hour day. In Ekaterinoslav shop craftsmen on the Catherine Railroad unilaterally introduced the eight-hour day toward the end of November.[2]

The St. Petersburg soviet called a strike on November 2 to protest the court-martial of several Kronstadt sailors who had mutinied in late October and the October 31 introduction of martial law in Poland. Over 100,000 of the capital's factory workers went out in response. The administrative employees on the Nicholas Railroad joined the walkout, but the engine-drivers struck only as far as the suburban Bologoe station, from whence the line ran normally to Moscow. On the Baltic and St. Petersburg–Warsaw lines, however, the strike virtually stopped traffic, spreading westward into Poland. The strike also won support on the Rybinsk-Bologoe

1. N. N. Iakovlev, *Vooruzhennye vosstaniia v dekabre 1905 g.* (Moscow, 1957), p. 44.

2. A. L. Sidorov, ed., *Vysshii pod'em revoliutsii 1905–1907 gg.: vooruzhennye vosstaniia, noiabr'–dekabr' 1905 god* (Moscow and Leningrad, 1955), vol. 1, pp. 385–86; vol. 2, pp. 689, 807–8; B. Krugliakov, "Professional'noe dvizhenie zheleznodorozhnikov v 1905–1907 gg.," *Krasnaia letopis'*, 1926, no. 3 (18): 105.

section of the Moscow-Vindau-Rybinsk line, which struck on November 5, but beyond these St. Petersburg-based railroads support did not materialize outside the city itself.[3] In Moscow all political factions agreed that the city's workers were not ready to launch a new strike, and the Central Bureau of the Railroad Union refused to respond to the call of the St. Petersburg soviet.[4]

For a month after the manifesto, then, the regime and the revolution sparred gingerly. A turning point of sorts came with the mid-November strike of employees in the government-operated postal and telegraph services. The Union of Postal and Telegraph Employees was organized after the October manifesto, although some of its founders, inspired by the success of the Railroad Union, had first conceived the idea in July. The postal union was, in fact, very similar to the railroad group: blue-collar workers played a minimal role in its leadership and those most active in its affairs generally held responsible administrative positions. The regime found the new union threatening on two counts: first, because the government did not want to grant the right to strike to public employees, and, second, because its program demanded a constituent assembly. Despite opposition from the Ministry of Post and Telegraph, which declared the new union illegal, the postal-telegraph employees pressed forward plans for a November 15 national congress in Moscow. On the eve of that meeting, however, the government responded by firing three organizers. The congress demanded their reinstatement. Receiving no reply, the delegates announced a nationwide protest strike.[5]

The postal-telegraph strike elicited broad public support, but it had a particularly profound effect on railroad workers. Many roads, including the Libau-Romny line in Minsk and the Polessky Railroad in Vilna, passed resolutions of support. In Moscow railwaymen sabotaged their own telegraph operations and refused to operate mail trains. A November 24 meeting of delegates from the Moscow terminals and the Railroad Union Central Bureau resolved to cease transmitting all telegrams "of an antisocial character" or "which

3. Sidorov, ed., vol. 1, pp. 430–31, 525–26; vol. 2, p. 218.

4. Laura Engelstein, *Moscow, 1905: Working-Class Organization and Political Conflict* (Stanford, Calif., 1982), p. 167; N. Rostov, "Zheleznodorozhniki v pervoi revoliutsii," *Proletariat v revoliutsii 1905–1907 gg.* (Moscow, 1930), p. 158.

5. Engelstein, p. 175; Sidorov, ed., vol. 1, p. 112.

have as their goal opposition to the postal-telegraph strike."[6] But the strike also marked the start of a crackdown on the revolutionary movement. The government refused to compromise with the postal workers, recruiting strikebreakers and arresting large numbers of leaders and rank-and-file strikers. By month's end the strike was lost.

Tension between the regime and its working-class opponents now escalated rapidly. In Kiev the postal-telegraph strike helped inspire a November 18 revolt among sappers of the city garrison, which was suppressed when martial law was declared. The Kiev soviet responded with a general strike that was only partially effective. On the South West Railroad, shop craftsmen walked out for nine days. In Kharkov the postal-telegraph strike merged with a citywide walkout, whose strongest base was the railwaymen. On November 10 Kharkov railroad workers organized a meeting to form a union, but this was broken up by police and rescheduled for November 12. On that date the assembled workers released a series of demands and appealed for an end to martial law, which had been operative in the city since the mid-October street fighting. Receiving no response, the railwaymen declared a strike in solidarity with the postal-telegraph walkout and the naval mutiny in Sevastopol. The strike rapidly became general, extending also to other stations on the Kharkov-Nikolaev road, and leadership passed into the hands of the city soviet.[7]

While these events rocked Kharkov, another struggle that would rally railwaymen across the empire was developing at the tiny Kushka station on the distant Central Asian Railroad. Built as the Trans-Caspian Military Railroad, the Central Asian line had been turned over to the Ministry of Communications by the army around the turn of the century, but military personnel still dominated management. On November 16 the Kushka telegraph operators walked out in solidarity with the postal-telegraph strike and an active worker was arrested. Soldiers fired on strikers demonstrating for his release. The next day the remaining railwaymen struck, and several stores closed their doors in solidarity. On November 19

---

6. Sidorov, ed., vol. 4, pp. 14, 160; TsGIA, f. 273, op. 12, d. 371, ll. 93, 95.

7. Sidorov, ed., vol. 3, pt. 1, pp. 204, 218–65, 343, 441–43; TsGIA, f. 273, op. 12, d. 375, l. 163. The strike lasted a week, but two days after it ended two battalions of the city garrison mutinied, joining railwaymen in a political demonstration. See S. Kramer, ed., *1905 god v Kharkove* (Kharkov, 1925), pp. 211–21.

troops arrested several leaders, including the popular railroad engineer L. G. Sokolov, who had represented the Central Asian road at the St. Petersburg pension congress. Three days later the commander of the Kushka fortress announced that a military tribunal had sentenced the men to execution, to be carried out within twenty-four hours.[8]

Striking telegraph operators immediately spread the grim news, and across the country railwaymen took up the cause of the Kushka defendants, demanding an end to the death penalty and to martial law. The Samara-Zlatoust Railroad struck immediately. In Odessa 4,000 shop craftsmen of the South West Railroad laid down their tools to attend a protest meeting. An assembly of employees on the Moscow-Vindau-Rybinsk Railroad threatened a general railroad strike if the death penalty was not "swiftly and categorically" abandoned. Telegrams also came from workers and employees on the St. Petersburg–Warsaw, Riazan-Ural, Nicholas, Vladikavkaz, Siberian, South East, and other railroads, as well as from dozens of local stations.[9] No one knew precisely what had transpired in Kushka, but, fearing the worst, the Central Bureau of the Railroad Union informed Nemeshaev and War Minister Rediger that a general strike would begin on November 24 if the arrested men were not released. On November 24 a meeting between delegates from the Moscow junction and the Central Bureau was torn by a stormy debate over the question of a new general strike when a telegram from Nemeshaev announced that charges against the Kushka arrestees had been dropped.[10]

The Central Bureau—along with most of the leaders of the St. Petersburg and Moscow soviets—was hesitant to embark on a new trial of strength with the government, but this seemed increasingly inevitable. For one thing, the government itself was by now committed to a policy of provocation. By November 27 the authorities had destroyed the postal-telegraph union and begun to move against other mass organizations. On November 26 Georgii Nosar', chair of the St. Petersburg soviet, was arrested. On November 28

8. TsGAOR, f. 6865, d. 125, ll. 12–23; Sidorov, ed., vol. 3, pt. 2, pp. 925–35; Rostov, "Zheleznodorozhniki," p. 160.

9. TsGAOR, f. 6865, d. 96, collects several dozen telegrams published in the newspapers *Nachalo* and *Novaia zhizn'* on November 23. See also *Zhel.*, 129, November 30, 1905, pp. 6–8.

10. Rostov, "Zheleznodorozhniki," p. 160.

labor activists on the Moscow-Brest Railroad were arrested, and two days later five active telegraph operators on the Kazan road were fired. On November 30 the police raided the Museum for Assistance to Labor.[11]

In St. Petersburg the soviet responded to Nosar's arrest with the Financial Manifesto of December 2, a declaration of economic war with the government. Endorsed by the Peasants Union and all the revolutionary parties, this document declared that henceforth its adherents would refuse to pay all taxes, redemption payments, or debts to the government, demand payment in gold for all transactions, and withdraw in gold all deposits from savings banks and the state bank.[12] Immediately the government closed eight newspapers that had printed the text and arrested their editors. On December 3 the executive committee of the St. Petersburg soviet heard Bolshevik representatives propose immediate negotiations with the railroad and postal-telegraph unions to formulate plans for a new general strike, which, it was stressed, must be "connected to street demonstrations." Even as this proposal was under discussion, the government delivered a serious blow to the revolution: soviet headquarters were surrounded by troops and 267 soviet deputies, including most of the executive committee, were arrested.[13]

On November 29 Nicholas II empowered local authorities to institute martial law to control strikes on the railroads or postal-telegraph strikes. On secret orders from Minister of Internal Affairs P. N. Durnovo, provincial governors instructed police to arrest leaders of "antigovernment" organizations. On December 2 another, more sweeping, decree was announced, banning all work stoppages and outlining penalties ranging from four to sixteen months in prison for strikers.[14] The next day, in a circular to all state and private railroads, Nemeshaev interpreted this order to mean that railroad officials were forbidden to negotiate or reach agreements with employees or workers associated with any organization that had as one of its functions the encouragement of strikes. Participation in all such groups was declared illegal, and each railroad official, employee, or worker was strictly instructed to ignore

11. *Vech. poch.*, 296, December 1, 1905.
12. Sidorov, ed., vol. 1, p. 26.
13. Ibid., pp. 146–47, 440–41.
14. Ibid., pp. 145, 147–50; Engelstein, p. 179.

all orders or decisions issued by any body not directly involved in the "financial exploitation of the railroads." Similarly, no telegrams not approved by authorized management personnel were to be transmitted via railroad telegraph. The Railroad Union, local strike committees, delegate assemblies, and soviets had, in effect, been legally banned.[15]

The government's actions forced the Railroad Union leaders to respond to the increasing militancy of the railroad rank and file. By telegram the Central Bureau informed its local committees, soviets, and other organizations that the government had "completely violated the freedoms declared on October 17." The union leaders called on railwaymen to refrain from partial or local strikes, but advised them to prepare for a nationally coordinated action to be decided by the bureau. Declaring that the union would like to spare the country the "frightful shock" of a second general strike, the Central Bureau acknowledged that there seemed little choice given the government's present course.[16] On the eve of the Kushka crisis, the Central Bureau had announced plans to convene the union's third congress in late December. On November 28, however, hesitant about committing railwaymen to a risky course of action, the union leaders dispatched a telegram inviting representatives of the lines to an extraordinary meeting in Moscow on December 5 "to decide the question of tactics."[17]

Meanwhile, especially outside the capitals, railwaymen were growing restive. The arrival of telegrams describing the situation in Kushka sparked spontaneous walkouts on several provincial roads, with much of the unrest centered in Belorussia and the Baltic provinces. In Riga word of the Kushka arrests came just as martial law was proclaimed in response to the increasingly widespread rebellion among Latvian peasants and agricultural laborers. On November 25 workers at the Riga terminal of the Riga-Orel Railroad voted to strike. The walkout quickly became general, and within days disturbances spread to parts of the Baltic and St. Petersburg–Warsaw roads. Even after the Central Bureau of the Railroad Union

15. TsGIA, f. 229, op. 2, d. 1645, l. 44.
16. Sidorov, ed., vol. 1, p. 125.
17. *Russkoe slovo*, 318, December 2, 1905, p. 3; Rostov, "Zheleznodorozhniki," pp. 160–61; M. B. [M. Bogdanov], *Ocherki po istorii zheleznodorozhnykh zabastovok v Rossii* (Moscow, 1906), pp. 42–43.

cabled the strikers to cease striking and prepare for more coordinated national action, a call soon endorsed by local strike leaders, the men refused to return to work.[18]

By late November telegrams supporting a new general strike were beginning to arrive in Moscow. From the Urals came a statement that already "all Perm is striking." From Uroch on the Moscow-Iaroslavl-Archangel Railroad came a declaration, "We are prepared to support our comrades with a general strike. We await the signal!"[19] In St. Petersburg on November 25 a general assembly of employees and workers of all lines headquartered in the capital, responding to calls for a new strike received from Samara and Riga and to government efforts "to reverse all the gains of the first all-Russian strike," declared a new general strike "inevitable." "Recognizing the necessity of unity of action," the meeting called on workers to prepare for battle, but deferred a strike call to a "general decision of all railwaymen."[20]

The desire to resist the government offensive touched all segments of the railroad work force. To be sure, there were junctions and sections where calls for a new strike fell on less than sympathetic ears. But the radicalization of the railroad proletariat after the October strike pulled some white-collar and administrative elements leftward, as the railroad movement began to merge with the overall working-class struggle and to come under increasing Social Democratic influence. If the Railroad Union leaders were cautious, *Zheleznodorozhnik*—whose editors had only recently looked to the pension congress for leadership, and just a year earlier had counseled patriotic support for the government—articulated more combative sentiments:

Let timid men whisper in fear that there has been enough struggle, that we have already achieved much, that we have reached our strongest position and that with patience the final goal will soon be ours. Let them try to scare us with the terrors of further struggle. We know that, in essence, we have yet to win a thing, that we have only ripped away a shred of wool. . . . The enemy staunchly and stubbornly defends his position. We, too, must stubbornly and staunchly attack him.[21]

18. A. Paulish, "Zabastovochnoe dvizhenie na Rigo-Orlovskoi zh. d.," *Proletarskaia revoliutsiia*, 1925, no. 11 (46): 164–67; TsGAOR, f. 6865, d. 84, l. 1.

19. Sidorov, ed., vol. 1, pp. 125–26.

20. *Nasha zhizn'*, 347, November 30, 1905, p. 2.

21. *Zhel.*, 129, November 30, 1905, p. 1.

With the St. Petersburg soviet crippled, attention again shifted to Moscow. On December 1 over a thousand railwaymen gathered in the workshops of the Moscow-Kazan line to protest the dismissal of the telegraph operators the previous day. On December 3 delegates from all lines of the Moscow junction met and decided to call a general strike.[22] In October a small group of railwaymen could initiate action on behalf of the entire working class, but by December leadership had to come from a more representative body, the Moscow Soviet of Worker's Deputies, organized in late November. The leaders of the soviet remained cautious, however, even as most recognized that there was little choice but to meet the government challenge. The coercive tactics of the regime were a sign of weakness, proclaimed the soviet's December 4 resolution. But the deputies fell short of endorsing a general strike call, instead urging workers to prepare for new battles and to hold factory meetings to discuss the question of a new strike.[23]

Even many Bolsheviks, officially committed to agitation not only for a strike but for an armed insurrection, were hesitant. A member of the Bolshevik Central Committee, I. Liubitch (Sammer), sent from St. Petersburg, addressed the Moscow soviet on December 4, but the import of his message is unclear. That evening the Bolshevik-led Moscow Committee discussed the situation, reaching agreement on the necessity for immediate action. Still, hesitancy remained, and it was felt that the final decision should be taken by a broader group. On the evening of December 5, a citywide meeting of Social Democratic organizers and workers at the Fiedler School, a popular gathering place for militant workers, debated the question of an uprising. All present affirmed the willingness of the masses to go out, but doubts were raised about the ardor of the rebellious soldiers and the preparedness of the still primitive worker fighting detachments.[24]

Even as this debate continued, delegates to the emergency meeting called by the Railroad Union—which came to be known as the Conference of Delegates from Twenty-nine Railroads—were

22. *Russkoe slovo*, 319, 320, December 3, 4, 1905; P. V. Kokhmanskii, ed., *Moskva v dekabre 1905 g.* (Moscow, 1906), pp. 5–6; M. K. Dymkov and D. Ia. Lipovetskii, *1905 god na Kazanke* (Moscow, 1925), p. 114.

23. Engelstein, p. 189.

24. Ibid., pp. 187–93.

assembling. The group had not yet begun to discuss the question of a general strike when Liubitch, accompanied by M. N. Liadov of the Moscow Committee, arrived. The two Bolsheviks urged the delegates to endorse a call for an armed uprising in connection with a general strike, but, according to Liadov, the mood of the meeting, dominated by middle-level administrators and employees, was far from militant. One delegate argued that only the unorganized were ready to go out, while union members saw a strike as a futile response to provocation. In the event that a strike did go over into an uprising, "Our only arms, comrades, are Westinghouse regulators and brakes," another noted.[25] Pereverzev, who chaired the conference, later recalled that the delegates were finally convinced by the declaration of the St. Petersburger that the capital would strike no matter what the railwaymen did. According to Liadov, however, strike endorsement came only after the two Bolsheviks threatened to go over the heads of the conference organizers and appeal directly to railroad craftsmen to initiate action. Bolstered by this victory, Liadov returned to the Bolshevik conference, which, hearing of the railroad group's support, voted to call for a strike on December 7. The railroad conference adjourned, and, departing by the final trains out of Moscow, the delegates returned home to spread the walkout.[26]

Again the Railroad Union leadership had been forced to respond to an initiative taken elsewhere—in October the rank and file of the Kazan line had set things in motion; now the Bolshevik-led Moscow Committee, responding as much to the growing pressure from below for action as to the dictates of its own militant philosophy, was the prime mover. On December 6 the Moscow soviet met to discuss the Bolshevik proposal, already endorsed by the Railroad Union. The Socialist Revolutionaries and the Moscow Mensheviks were skeptical, but, as statements of solidarity with the proposed strike and insurrection were read from plants, workshops, and workers' organizations, unity was achieved. The soviet

---

25. M. N. Liadov, *Iz zhizni partii v 1905–1907 gg.* (Moscow, 1956), p. 130; Kokhmanskii, p. 10.
26. TsGAOR, f. 6865, d. 120, l. 91–92; Liadov, p. 130. The Bolshevik clerk on the Kazan road, Kotliarenko, also recalled that it had been the militant confidence voiced not only by Liubitch but by representatives of the capital's railwaymen that turned the tide at the conference (Danilov and Sdobnev, pp. 141–46).

passed a compromise resolution calling for "a general strike, noting that this can and must pass over to an armed uprising."[27]

On the evening of December 7 the Central Bureau, in the name of the Railroad Union and the Conference of Delegates from Twenty-nine Railroads, dispatched a telegram "to all stations and offices of the Russian railroads, all employees and workers," calling on railwaymen to strike on December 7. "Those are not seditious who struggle for freedom; it is the government itself that defies its own promulgated laws," the telegram declared. "We can hold back no more. The government challenges us to a new battle; let it be so—responsibility for the consequences falls on the criminal St. Petersburg regime."[28]

The strike that began in Moscow on December 7 was more intense, more violent, and more bitterly fought than the one in October. Yet it failed to mobilize the population as extensively as the previous outbreak. In Moscow factories and among many provincial workers the second general strike met with greater enthusiasm than the first. Observers noted that in December workers often struck without any outside agitation: "Nothing comparable . . . had occurred during the October strike, when it had often been necessary to force the closing of recalcitrant enterprises."[29] However, as the proletariat defined its independence by moving politically leftward, some moderate and middle-class allies distanced themselves from the strike movement. The Constitutional Democratic party openly dissociated itself from the December actions, and much of its social base adopted a posture of, at most, studied neutrality. In October the strike won broad support among office employees and petty officials, small shopkeepers, merchants, and professionals, but such elements were not quite so willing to make a decisive commitment in December. Owing to the seeming paralysis of the government the first general strike took on an almost holidaylike atmosphere. In December, however, almost everyone was soberly

27. Iakovlev, p. 151.

28. Sidorov, ed., vol. 1, pp. 129–30; M. B. [M. Bogdanov], pp. 43–45; Dymkov and Lipovetskii, pp. 115–16.

29. P. A. Garvi, *Vospominaniia sotsial demokrata* (New York, 1946), p. 624. See also Engelstein, pp. 193–96, on the increase in the number of strikers from large plants in Moscow. A similar phenomenon was evident in many provincial cities.

aware that a showdown had come. To a great extent the regime provoked this confrontation, and once the battle was joined the government did not waver in its resolve to suppress the insurgents
forcefully and without concessions. At the same time, the virtually
unrelieved agitation and turmoil of the year, the debilitating losses
in pay during strike time, the arrests of late November, and the
onset of winter combined to drain the resources and energies of the
strikers.

Yet if the December strike failed to paralyze the country to the
degree achieved two months before, the struggle was still massive.
Although according to factory inspectors' figures the number of
strikers in December was somewhat lower than in October, the
number of strikers labeled "political" by the government reached
the highest number yet, 372,000 as compared to 330,000 in October and just 123,000 in January. Beginning in Moscow, the December strike spread to St. Petersburg, the southern industrial
centers, the Baltic provinces, and Poland. In all, thirty-three cities
and towns were affected as compared to thirty-nine in October. Although railroad transportation was not completely terminated as in
October, twenty-nine lines participated in the strike to some extent
and the involvement of secondary junctions and stations was the
most extensive and militant of the year. Nearly everywhere the
December strike led to violent confrontations of one sort or another, with widespread destruction of property, including derail-
ment of trains, uprooting of track, and organized or random looting
of freight on the railroads. Where in the main the October strike
simply shut down the railroad system, the December walkout
plunged the roads into violent chaos.

In several places, most notably, of course, Moscow, a militant
minority, supported by broader numbers, transformed the strike
into an armed uprising. Such insurrectionary activity, however,
was primitive and poorly organized. The cities in which armed revolts took place did not rise together, and it was relatively simple
for the regime to crush them one by one, especially after the
Moscow rising was suppressed. The street fighters were mostly
young and inexperienced. The Bolsheviks had agitated the most
forcefully for insurrection, but once the fighting began other revolutionary parties, soviets, trade unions, factory groups, and students willingly cooperated with them. Railwaymen probably par-

ticipated in armed actions in disproportionately large numbers, but nowhere was there a serious plan to seize the railroad system on a national or even local basis. The energies of railroad fighting detachments were divided—often unproductively—between participation in separate urban revolts and efforts to spread the rebellion along the lines.

Moscow was clearly at the center of the movement. Over 100,000 workers walked off the job on December 7; the next day industry, transportation, and communications were at a total standstill. Governor-general F. V. Dubasov withdrew police patrols and placed several labor leaders under arrest—including the Railroad Union head Pereverzev[30]—but initially made no concerted effort to oppose the movement. For all intents and purposes, the Moscow soviet was master of the city, yet as long as neither side was willing to enter into actual combat, a peaceful stalemate characterized the first two days. The authorities made their opening move on December 8 when a meeting of over 10,000 workers at the Aquarium Theater was surrounded by police and several activists were arrested, although most of those bearing arms managed to escape the dragnet. The next morning the first barricades appeared. That evening the Fiedler School was assaulted with machine guns and artillery after members of a worker fighting squad inside refused to surrender their weapons. More than 30 workers and students were killed or wounded during destruction of the building. Among the 99 arrested for participating in its defense were 6 railroad employees and 17 railroad craftsmen.[31]

The street fighting began in earnest on December 10, as barricades went up across the main boulevards to impede troop movement, and lasted for a week, involving no more than 8,000 workers, probably less than 2,000 of whom were members of partisan squads.[32] The soldiers did not go over to the insurgents, but Dubasov was unwilling to test the garrison's loyalty; after two days of battle he cabled the Interior Ministry for reinforcements. Al-

30. TsGAOR, f. 6865, d. 28a, l. 12.

31. Where not otherwise noted all information on the Moscow rising is from Engelstein's excellent and detailed account, pp. 193–225. For a railwayman's account of the Fiedler School incident, see A. Gorchilin, *1905 god na Kazanke* (Moscow, 1934), pp. 47–56.

32. E. M. Iaroslavskii, *Vooruzhennoe vosstanie: dekabr'skoe vosstanie* (Moscow and Leningrad, 1927), p. 88.

though the St. Petersburg strike, decapitated in advance by the arrest of the soviet, had not proved very threatening, troops had already been dispatched from the capital to the Baltic, so Dubasov's request was initially denied, although some troops were sent from Tver on the Nicholas Railroad, which was in government hands. On December 15 the elite Semenovskii Guards arrived. By this point the insurrection had peaked, but the new regiment insured the regime final superiority. On December 17 resistance in the Presnia district, the last stronghold of the uprising and site of the most extreme militancy, was crushed.

Moscow railroad workers participated in the strike and the street fighting in close cooperation with other sections of the city's working class. Although many employees in Moscow and elsewhere joined the strike, their role was much less central than that of shop craftsmen, especially when compared to October. The Ministry of Communications reported on December 16 that the Moscow railroad strike had begun in the workshops and that its main supporters were craftsmen and engine-drivers.[33]

The Moscow-Kazan Railroad was again the first road to go out. The late November dismissal of five telegraph operators implicated in the transmission of unauthorized cables, and the firing of the Central Bureau member and Socialist Revolutionary engine-driver A. V. Ukhtomskii shortly thereafter, had already galvanized the work force. Following an angry mass meeting the previous day, on December 2 sixty members of a fighting squad composed of craftsmen, young clerks, and telegraph operators tried to force management to rehire the men. The request was denied, and for several days protest meetings regularly disrupted work in all branches of the terminal. The demand to rehire the dismissed comrades merged with the general movement to launch a new strike. On December 6 a mass meeting of railwaymen from all departments met in the workshops and voted to begin a political strike the following day.[34] The strike began at noon on December 7, and by late afternoon the shops, depot, and station were in the insurgents' hands.

---

33. Sidorov, ed., vol. 1, p. 131. The contention of Iu. O. Korablev et al., *Revoliutsiia 1905–1907 gg. v Rossii* (Moscow, 1975), pp. 239–40, that "the higher employees of the railroad administration . . . responded . . . coldly and with hostility" is an exaggeration, however.

34. I. M. Pushkareva, *Zheleznodorozhniki Rossii v burzhuazno-demokraticheskikh revoliutsiiakh* (Moscow, 1975), p. 202.

A mass meeting, composed mainly of craftsmen and engine-drivers, elected a "Soviet of the Moscow-Kazan Railroad," which included Ukhtomskii, Pechkovskii, and Bednov from the Railroad Union, and Gorchilin and Kotliarenko from the Bolshevik group. In a telegram to all stations the soviet announced it had commandeered four locomotives for use by strikers and requested each station to assign two telegraph operators to receive information and relay strike decisions. After the meeting the Moscow-Kazan strikers poured into the streets and marched through the surrounding factory district.[35]

By December 8 the strike had spread to every major railroad in Moscow except the Nicholas line. On the Moscow-Iaroslavl-Archangel and Moscow-Kursk roads strikers barricaded the tracks with derailed passenger cars. On the Moscow-Kursk Railroad a crowd attacked two arriving trains and an engine-driver was beaten for refusing to go out. The walkout at the Moscow terminal of the Moscow-Kiev-Voronezh Railroad was successful, but railwaymen there encountered opposition from draymen who insisted on their right to pick up freight that had arrived the previous afternoon. The small Moscow shops of the Nicholas Railroad were half-empty on December 7, but the terminal continued to function normally under police and military protection.[36]

As many as 500 railwaymen were members of seven organized combat units functioning in Moscow and along suburban stretches of track. By far the largest was the detachment formed on the Moscow-Kazan road under the leadership of Ukhtomskii, Kotliarenko, and the Socialist Revolutionary V. Ia. Tatarinskii, which had 200 members, half shop craftsmen and engine cabmen and half administrative staff. There were also squads on the Moscow-Iaroslavl-Archangel Railroad, with 70 men; the Moscow-Kursk Railroad, with 40; the Riazan-Ural Railroad, with 40; the Moscow-Vindau-Rybinsk Railroad, with 37; the Moscow-Kiev-Voronezh Railroad, with 36; and the Moscow-Brest Railroad, with 25 men.[37] Funded

35. Dymkov and Lipovetskii, p. 117; Gorchilin, 44–46; Sidorov, ed., vol. 1, pp. 654, 660, 816.

36. Sidorov, ed., vol. 1, pp. 131–33, 659–60; Ivan Maruta, *Ocherki po istorii revoliutsionnogo professional'nogo dvizheniia na Moskovsko-Kievo-Voronezhskoe zh. d.* (Kursk, 1925), p. 87.

37. Kokhmanskii, pp. 121–22, 167; *Moskovskoe vooruzhennoe vosstanie po dannym obvinitel'nykh aktov i sudebnykh protokolov,* (Moscow, 1906), vyp. 1, p. 89; Leon Trotsky, *1905,* trans. Anya Bostock (New York, 1972), p. 246.

by the Moscow strike committee, these were the best-armed units in Moscow. Most witnesses believed the squads observed orders to protect railroad property from vandalism, but looting of freight occurred on a wide enough scale for some to charge that the detachments deliberately ignored or even participated in this.[38] A priest from suburban Perovo, however, complimented strikers on the Moscow-Kazan line on their deportment. "A few squad members came from questionable elements," he admitted, but the looting of goods and vodka was the fault of "peasants [who] came in large numbers on horses from the surrounding countryside."[39]

Most railroad terminals were situated away from the center of the street fighting, which kept railwaymen from participating in key battles; only the Moscow-Brest terminal, with the smallest railroad fighting squad, was accessible to the Presnia district, site of the bloodiest combat. But the railroad detachments played an important part in the fighting by running delegate trains that spread the strike to, and recruited additional fighters from, the surrounding industrial region. On the Moscow-Kazan line, such a train traveled for days under Ukhtomskii's stewardship. Moreover, railwaymen were central to several street battles outside Presnia, including the prolonged and ultimately unsuccessful struggle for control of Kalanchevskaia Square and the terminal of the Nicholas Railroad.[40]

From the first days of the strike crowds from the Moscow-Kazan and Moscow-Iaroslavl-Archangel lines spontaneously attacked the Nicholas Railroad terminal, which was occupied by troops. These initial assaults were unsuccessful, however, and on December 12 it was decided that the Kazan and Iaroslavl squads would launch a major "offensive." That afternoon reinforcements from the Liuberts and Kolomna stations of the Kazan road arrived and the attack began. The battle lasted two days and succeeded in stopping traffic on the Nicholas road. But the troops could not be dislodged from the terminal; the sorties launched by the insurgents were repulsed "by artillery fire."[41]

38. Kokhmanskii, pp. 123–24, 126, 166–67; Engelstein, p. 201.

39. Dymkov and Lipovetskii, p. 121.

40. Ibid., pp. 123–30. In 1925 one railroad fighter lamented the lack of attention paid to the battles fought by armed railroad workers in December (TsGAOR, f. 6865, d. 120, ll. 9–10). Engelstein mentions the Kalanchevskaia Square battle only in passing.

41. Sidorov, ed., vol. 1, p. 683; Dymkov and Lipovetskii, pp. 139–40; Gorchilin, pp. 62–65, 69–71.

It was still impossible, however, for the soldiers ensconced in the Nicholas terminal to counterattack across the square and invade the workers' strongholds in the Kazan and Iaroslavl shops and depot. After December 13, when the fighting squads began to run short of ammunition—they apparently did not know of two freight cars loaded with arms sitting in the Moscow-Kazan yards—the square grew quiet and the Nicholas road resumed operation. On December 15 the Semenovskii Guards arrived at the station. Their first objective was to seize control of the militant Moscow-Kazan terminal and shops. The *Kazantsy*, cut off from contact with the fighting in other districts and demoralized by the obvious lack of support from St. Petersburg, still fought tenaciously. They were hopelessly outnumbered and outgunned, however, especially since a trainload of partisans had just departed to search for ammunition and arms and to gather recruits from the line. The defenders of the Kazan terminal managed to escape when Ukhtomskii fired up a locomotive and, beneath a hail of bullets, drove a trainload of fighters out of the city to Perovo, where the men dispersed.[42]

A major cause of the Moscow defeat was the weak support the December strike found in St. Petersburg. With their leadership crippled by arrests, and faced with a mammoth garrison composed of the tsar's most loyal troops, the St. Petersburg workers could not initiate an uprising. Their strike eventually involved over 110,000 workers in more than 200 enterprises, but it never posed a real threat to the authorities. The movement started on December 8 at a meeting of what remained of the soviet executive committee and began to collapse as early as December 12. At the December 8 meeting a representative of the Railroad Union agreed to declare a railroad strike if the soviet decided on a general strike, but support for the walkout among St. Petersburg railwaymen was weak. The strike was most successful in the shops of the St. Petersburg–Warsaw and Baltic Railroads and, to a lesser degree, the Nicholas road. Administrative and operative personnel were less supportive, however, and, according to official reports, "all the railroads were functioning." Where the strike affected rail traffic, military crews kept trains moving, as on the St. Petersburg–Warsaw line.[43]

Of course, the most important failure of the December strike

42. Iakovlev, p. 192; Sidorov, ed., vol. 1, pp. 817–21.
43. Sidorov, ed., vol. 1, p. 459.

was the insurgents' inability to control the Nicholas Railroad. At this line's St. Petersburg terminus efforts were made to foment a walkout, but these were only partially successful. When word arrived on December 7 of the strike's start in Moscow, a special meeting of active workers and employees declared in the name of the Railroad Union that the line would "support the decision of the Moscow congress of representatives of all the railroads and declare a strike at noon on December 8." The strike did not begin, however, until after three P.M., when shop craftsmen walked out. There was virtually no support among administrative employees, and only slightly more among operations personnel. Even the craftsmen vacillated. On December 9, 700 men reported to work, but by afternoon only 156 remained. The strike began to collapse the next day, however, as about 1,000 craftsmen reported. By December 11 the walkout was over, although there was a brief skirmish with Cossacks at the workshops two days later.[44]

Some Social Democrats tried to blame the Railroad Union for the failure of the Nicholas Railroad to support the December strike, even charging the union with sabotage, but that was at best unfair. To be sure, the Railroad Union leaders tended to exaggerate their own influence—Pereverzev perhaps most of all—but the Bolsheviks were at least equally guilty of exaggerating the ability of the St. Petersburg workers to act. The Railroad Union had gained considerable influence at the St. Petersburg junction in November, but like all worker organizations in 1905 its structure there remained flimsy, and the union's strength in the capital could never compare with its influence in Moscow. Moreover, of the Moscow roads organized by the union, the evidence suggests that the Nicholas road was probably the least penetrated. Most likely, the Railroad Union leaders could not have sabotaged the strike on the Nicholas road even if they had tried. Far more critical than any negative role played by the Railroad Union was the swift and forceful military occupation of the Nicholas Railroad and its Moscow terminal by the government. Even though workers on the road did not join the strike on December 7 and 8, Dubasov doubted they could be kept at work without official intervention. He requested military train crews from St. Petersburg and secured the station and workshops with trusted units.[45]

44. Ibid., pp. 455, 488, 511.
45. Iakovlev, p. 157.

Yet even if the main factor was effective government action, it remains to be asked why the Nicholas workers did not join the strike at its start, as did railwaymen at the adjacent Kazan and Iaroslavl terminals, and as they had in October? Why this was so is not entirely clear, but at the heart of the problem was certainly the fact that, unlike the other major railroads terminating in Moscow, the Nicholas line did not have many workers based in the city: its main offices and workshops were in St. Petersburg. Most important, there were relatively few shop craftsmen and administrative staff, and most engine-drivers lived in St. Petersburg or elsewhere on the road, at Tver in particular. The Nicholas Railroad was thus not really a part of the Moscow network, but, in a certain sense, an "outsider." This may help explain why its Moscow terminal was so far out of tune with the militancy and organization of workers on other Moscow lines.

The December strike touched all parts of the Russian railroad network. Although transport did not come to a complete halt, on many roads the level of militancy reached a new peak. The Moscow-Kazan, Vladikavkaz, and Catherine Railroads were special hotbeds of rebellion. Although in late November the Railroad Union leadership cautioned against dissipating strength in partial strikes, on many roads the December strike continued local conflicts. On the Riga-Orel, Central Asian, Baltic, Pskov-Riga, South West, Kursk-Kharkov-Sevastopol, Kharkov-Nikolaev, Moscow-Vindau-Rybinsk, Warsaw-Vienna, South East, and Kiev-Poltava Railroads the general strike call came as local strikes were either in progress or had only recently ended.[46]

At many junctions, workshops, and stations on lines radiating from Moscow strikers wrenched power from local authorities, usually with little or no violence. Trainloads of agitators set out from the Moscow terminal of the Moscow-Kazan Railroad to recruit fighters and spread the strike. Trains were commandeered at the suburban Liuberts station. At the Perovo repair shops workers walked off on December 6. Looting took place at Nikolaevka on December 9. On December 13 the authorities learned of the ar-

---

46. For data on the dates and length of strikes on separate railroads in December, see TsGIA, f. 273, op. 12, d. 355, l. 208; Sidorov, ed., vol. 1, pp. 135–36; Krugliakov, "Professional'noe dvizhenie," pp. 121–26.

rival at Bykovo of some hundred strikers, who allegedly attacked the stationhouse with gunfire before returning to Moscow.[47]

After Moscow the main center of unrest on the Moscow-Kazan Railroad was the Ruzaevka depot in Penza province. Support for the strike here wavered at first owing to a lack of "energetic leadership," but on December 8 an engineer and a driver returned from Moscow to organize an effective strike committee—two administrators, two employees, eight engine-drivers, four telegraph operators, and a road foreman—and a fighting squad—five engine-drivers, two craftsmen, a clerk, and a student. The strikers took control of the entire town, holding regular daily meetings with local peasants. After the Moscow rising was suppressed, a central strike committee for the Moscow-Kazan line was established at Ruzaevka, continuing to function until the Semenovskii regiment placed its members under arrest on December 21.[48]

At the Kovrov workshops on the Moscow-Iaroslavl-Archangel Railroad fighting squads were organized and strikers held daily meetings addressed by revolutionary orators. Another hotbed of unrest on this line was Uroch', where craftsmen, conductors, employees, and several railroad officials voted to cease work on December 7, remaining out until the arrival of troops on December 15. An executive strike committee controlled the transit of all trains and telegraph communication, and a fighting squad was formed to guard and inspect trains.[49] The Kursk headquarters of the Moscow-Kiev-Voronezh Railroad voted to join the general strike on December 9, but shortly thereafter the entire leadership of the Railroad Union and of the delegate assembly meeting in Kursk were arrested. The Kursk employees and depot workers then focused on demanding their freedom. Several demonstrations were held, and surrounding stations sent telegrams, but when news arrived of the suppression of the Moscow rising, the strike collapsed.[50]

The delegate assembly of the Riazan-Ural Railroad was still meeting in Moscow when the events leading to the December 7

47. Sidorov, ed., vol. 1, pp. 680–81, 799.
48. TsGIA, f. 273, op. 12, d. 328, l. 447; Sidorov, ed., vol. 2, pp. 674–75; Dymkov and Lipovetskii, pp. 147–63.
49. Sidorov, ed., vol. 2, pp. 19, 231–33, 276–77.
50. Ibid., pp. 49–50, 337–38; Maruta, pp. 79–89.

strike call unfolded. On December 6 three delegates—an SR and two members of the Railroad Union—left to attend the Conference of Twenty-nine Railroads. On their return they informed the assembly of the decision to endorse a new strike call. The meeting voted to join the strike, although the Railroad Union faction opposed the vote as a "historic crime" and abstained from the election of a 21-member strike committee that followed. Departing Moscow by special train on December 7, the delegates returned to Saratov, pausing at stations along the way to agitate.[51]

The strike thus spread to places relatively untouched by previous strike activity, where individual leaders could still play critical parts. At Belev, for example, the strike call was initially ignored. After an unenthusiastic meeting on December 8, however, a minority of prostrike workers succeeded in calling a second meeting, where a popular agitator, the railroad engineer Petr Ragozin, back from the Moscow assembly, persuaded the men to walk out. Under the strong leadership of this "remarkable orator . . . with an iron will," the strikers took over the station, forcing the local police chief out of town. A similar situation arose at Kashira, where, under the leadership of the assistant stationmaster, the strikers held meetings at which they vowed to start their own people's government should the Moscow insurrection emerge victorious. The Riazan-Ural strike committee attempted to coordinate such activity from Saratov—where the strike, concentrated in the workshops, came under the leadership of the city soviet—but the entire movement was increasingly crippled by arrests. By the time the Riazan-Ural strike ended on December 21, only six members of the strike committee remained free.[52]

Outside Moscow the December strike was most effective—and most violent—in the south. The largest of the southern uprisings took place in Rostov-on-Don where, as so often in the labor history of this city, the workshops of the Vladikavkaz Railroad played a central role.[53] The Rostov organizing bureau received word of the

51. I. S. Sokolov, *1905 god na Riazansko-Ural'skoi zheleznoi doroge* (Saratov, 1925), pp. 49–50; N. Sushkin, "Oktiabr', noiabr', i dekabr' 1905 g. na Riazansko-Uralskoi zh. d.," *Katorga i ssylka*, 1930, no. 12: 156.

52. Sidorov, ed., vol. 2, pp. 206–7, 209–10; Sokolov, p. 52; D. A. Malinin, "Saratovskie zheleznodorozhniki v revoliutsii 1905–1907 gg.," *Uchenye zapiski Saratovskogo universiteta* 55 (1956): 146–48.

53. On the Rostov armed uprisings, see Sidorov, ed., vol. 2, pp. 430–84. For a secondary account, see Iakovlev, pp. 215–60.

strike call by telegraph on December 7. After "heated debate" they decided to call for a strike at midnight and to hold a meeting in the railroad shops the next day. Telegrams were dispatched to depots and stations calling for another delegate assembly to be convened in Rostov on December 11, although this meeting seems never to have taken place.[54] The bureau did not call for an insurrection, although Bolshevik members argued for this. That evening railwaymen began to walk off the job at various points on the road and at connecting stations of the South East and Catherine roads. The Rostov workshops struck on December 8. Initially, all was peaceful, but the next morning twelve leaders were arrested, only to be released later in the day. The authorities were not intimidated, however; troops occupied the railroad terminal and arrests continued. On December 12 martial law was decreed in Rostov.

Soviet and railroad strike leaders had met the previous evening in the dining area of the railroad shops to discuss the need to seize the railroad telegraph, which had not joined the walkout, and to consider arresting the mayor, the head of the Okhrana, and the police chief. Several fighting squads met simultaneously, and all the meetings came to a common conclusion: it was time to launch an armed rising. The principal target of the insurgency was to be the main terminal of the Vladikavkaz Railroad. On December 13 several groups of armed strikers attacked the terminal building, driving out the police. The authorities responded by shelling a meeting in the workshops, killing nine and injuring several more. Barricades then went up in the surrounding working-class Temernik district, later dubbed the "Rostov Presnia." These, too, were shelled by government artillery. Late in the evening soldiers managed to retake the railroad terminal, but on December 15 the railwaymen launched a second attack and again met with success. Fighting continued until December 20.

From the Rostov terminal agitational trains embarked for other stations, spreading the strike and the spirit of armed resistance. As in Rostov, shop craftsmen in Tikhoretskaia played a central part in the strike, as more than a thousand walked out on December 7, disarming city police and seizing arms and ammunition. On December 13 a squad of over seventy Tikhoretskaia strikers went to

54. TsGAOR, f. 6865, d. 70, l. 93.

Rostov to assist the insurgents. On December 16 a company of Cossacks refused orders to crush the Tikhoretskaia rebellion, which was not finally quelled until December 28.[55] Similar armed struggles took place at Mineral Waters, Kavkaz, Groznyi, Taganrog, Kotelnikov, and other stations. Formation of the "Novorossiisk Republic" was also greatly influenced by the turmoil on the Vladikavkaz Railroad.[56]

Probably the most extensive unrest on any provincial line occurred on the Catherine Railroad.[57] Like the Moscow-Kazan line, this road could only be subdued through the systematic application of military force. By late November the Catherine Railroad was already in considerable turmoil, with extensive power enjoyed by the standing leadership of the road's delegate assembly. The chair of that body, a forty-two-year-old employee named Vasilii Vasilevich Nauman, intercepted a telegram on December 3 from St. Petersburg informing the road management of the tsar's decree on strikes. He kept the information to himself and the road director only learned of the stiff new repressive powers he enjoyed from St. Petersburg newspapers on December 7. That day, however, a second telegram containing the strike call of the Conference of Twenty-nine Railroads was received. Nauman initially branded the strike a provocation, arguing that it was at best "untimely," but he communicated the news to the delegate assembly, which voted fifty-one to three on December 8 to join the walkout, a decision the chair reluctantly endorsed.[58] Simultaneously, an assembly of Ekaterinoslav factory delegates voted unanimously to go out. That evening representatives of both factions of Social Democrats, the Bund, and the

55. Ibid., ll. 226–27; Sidorov, ed., vol. 2, pp. 418–19.

56. TsGAOR, f. 6865, d. 70, ll. 227–34; Sidorov, ed., vol. 2, pp. 404–6, 417–20, 525–27, 545, 547, 549–52, 559, 572–640; Iakovlev, pp. 253–56, 261–81.

57. The rebellion on the Catherine Railroad generated extensive legal proceedings, which in turn left a rich legacy of source material to the historian. The 234-page indictment of the strikers is in TsGAOR, f. 6865, d. 78a. From the other side, the defense attorney in the case, S. S. Anisimov, published a book-length and station-by-station account based on court records, *Delo o vosstanii na Ekaterininskoi zh. d.* (Moscow, 1926). See also Sidorov, ed., vol. 3, pt. 1, pp. 33–164; I. A. Slavkin, "Vooruzhennoe vosstanie na Ekaterinoslavskoi zh. d. (Dekabr' 1905)," *Proletarskaia revoliutsiia*, 1925, no. 10 (45): 11–58; N. P. Donii, "Vooruzhennoe vosstanie na Ekaterinoslavshchine v dekabre 1905 godu," *Voprosy istorii*, 1955, no. 12: 19–32; and Iakovlev, pp. 285–343.

58. TsGAOR, f. 6865, d. 78a, ll. 17, 28.

SRs formed a citywide strike committee and an executive committee of railwaymen assembled as a branch of this unit. From this point leadership passed into the hands of a more militant and younger group of shop craftsmen, telegraph operators, and students.[59]

On December 8 a delegation of strikers arrived from Moscow, and the next morning workers walked out of the shops and depot, marching on the station, where they were joined by employees and operations workers. By evening the entire terminal complex was controlled by strikers, and a citywide strike committee established itself in the workshops. The strikers effectively ran the terminal for forty-eight hours, dispatching delegate trains and even collecting for the strike fund from the purses of stranded passengers. But on December 10 police and soldiers surrounded the station. By evening the terminal had been retaken, and the strike committee fled to Niznedneprovsk. This did not end the struggle in Ekaterinoslav, however. On December 11 a crowd of strikers was peacefully dispersed from the terminal plaza. The next day, according to police, a crowd of nearly 2,000, including "a significant number of railroad conductors and petty employees," gathered outside the railroad offices demanding permission to work. A meeting of engine-drivers and shop craftsmen, however, voted to continue the strike. On December 15 strikers showed up to receive their November wages, and many, following the dictates of the St. Petersburg soviet, demanded payment in gold. The next day martial law was declared.[60]

As one indictment later put it, starting in the first week of December, "actual power over the Catherine Railroad passed over to the delegate assembly of employees and workers." Insurrectionary activity took place at Iasinovataia, Avdeevka, Gorlovka, Nikitovka, Enakievo, Alchevskaia, Deval'tsevo, Iuzovo, Almaznaia, Chernukhino, Grishino, Chaplino, and some other stations, with the most significant confrontation at Gorlovka, where nearly 5,000 railroad and factory workers, miners, and local peasants clashed with Cossack troops.[61] Nearly everywhere strikers formed committees to run the railroad and kept in constant telegraph and rail communication with one another and the executive committee in Ekaterino-

59. Sidorov, ed., vol. 3, pt. 1, pp. 55–59.

60. Ibid., pp. 113–15.

61. Ibid., p. 160; On Gorlovka, see TsGAOR, f. 6865, d. 78a, ll. 72–99, and Anisimov, pp. 74–83.

slav and then Nizhnedneprovsk. Blue-collar workers and engine-drivers were most active at several stations, but local intellectuals and some railroad officials were involved too. At Iasinovataia, where delegates returning from Ekaterinoslav were initially met by workers hostile to the political orientation of the movement, the strike eventually came under the dynamic leadership of a male nurse in the public health section.[62] At most stations poorly armed fighting squads disarmed local police and protected railroad property from vandals. Station offices and waiting rooms were frequently scenes of "uninterrupted meetings" attended by striking railwaymen, townspeople, soldiers, and peasants.[63]

In Kharkov railwaymen—mainly shop craftsmen—on the Kursk-Kharkov-Sevastopol and Kharkov-Nikolaev Railroads struck on December 8 and participated in an armed uprising begun by factory metalworkers. Surrounding stations assisted the urban rebels by in effect blockading transit of the troops to the city. According to one official, the Kharkov-Nikolaev road "was in fact in the hands of the strikers."[64] Liubotin, a small town, but a key railroad junction with lines radiating in four directions, was an especially stubborn center of revolt. The strike here began on December 9, and within two days a Temporary Unified Administration of the Kharkov-Nikolaev Railroad had been formed by strikers to run the terminal. This group rather pretentiously declared itself at the head of a new revolutionary regime, the "Liubotin Republic," which lasted for several days. The railroad strikers arrested all railroad and government officials, taking control not only of the station, but of the entire town and surrounding settlements. On December 17 troops arrived and the uprising was suppressed with considerable bloodshed.[65]

The December strike also won support in the minority regions. A delegate assembly on the Transcaucasian Railroad was meeting in Baku when word arrived of the strike call on December 8. After a day's vacillation, the delegates voted to endorse the strike, and the next day the Tiflis shops and depot also went out. The strike soon spread to nearly all stations on the line, and order was not restored until Christmas. On the Riga-Orel Railroad the leaders were skep-

62. TsGAOR, f. 6865, d. 78a, ll. 34–55.
63. Sidorov, ed., vol. 3, pt. 1, p. 150.
64. Kramer, ed., pp. 243, 245; Sidorov, ed., vol. 3, pt. 1, p. 448.
65. On the "Liubotin Republic," see Sidorov, ed., vol. 3, pt. 1, pp. 412–41.

tical of winning support for a new walkout so soon after the failure of the late-November strike. Isolated from the rest of the country by army units sent to suppress the Baltic peasants, Riga's railwaymen did not launch an insurrection, although a railroad strike began on December 9 and became general on December 11. The movement was broken by arrests on December 17, however, and sputtered to a conclusion on December 20. In Poland the strike won the backing of railwaymen on the St. Petersburg–Warsaw, Warsaw-Vienna, and Vistula Railroads, but since by December tsarist Poland was occupied by a quarter of a million Russian soldiers, this support was weak, and traffic kept moving, though at a much reduced level, with the assistance of military crews. The situation was compounded as well by the lukewarm support given the December movement by the Polish Socialist party and the NKK.[66]

In October the railroad strike included in its ranks nearly all segments of the work force; especially in Moscow, administrative employees played a central part. As already noted, the December strike differed in its composition, reflecting changes that had occurred in the turbulent weeks separating the two walkouts. Now some white-collar railwaymen retreated from the movement and the center stage was occupied by the men of the repair shops and depots. On the Samara-Zlatoust Railroad officials noted that administrative and line employees joined the strike only under extreme pressure from agitators associated with Social Democratic shop craftsmen.[67] The changed composition was especially noticeable in the largest railroad centers. In Moscow the employees were at best lukewarm supporters of the uprising, while young railroad metalworkers joined fighting detachments in large numbers. At the Kiev offices of the South West Railroad, the great majority of employees continued to work during the December strike, which won full support only in the workshops.[68] At Paniutino on the Kursk-Kharkov-Sevastopol Railroad it was reported that "the disorders at this station were caused, it would seem, exclusively by lower-level

66. Henry F. Reichman, "Russian Railwaymen and the Revolution of 1905," Ph.D. diss., University of California, Berkeley, pp. 531–34.
67. TsGIA, f. 273, op. 12, d. 364, l. 494.
68. TsGAOR, f. 6865, d. 35, ll. 141–49.

workers at the depot: the craftsmen, workers, and apprentices, with the participation of a large number of outside agitators."[69]

It would be wrong, however, to conclude that employees, low-level administrators, and engineers were no longer represented. The summation offered in an official report on the strike on the Kursk-Kharkov-Sevastopol Railroad applies to most other lines: "The main participants in the strike were the skilled craftsmen . . . but there were also agents and other employees involved."[70] In the wake of the December strike thousands of railwaymen were dismissed from service and/or arrested. The authorities did not limit their attacks to those taking part in the December revolts, however, and the lists of workers and employees singled out sketch an approximate picture of the most active participants during the entire October-December period. A wide variety of occupations appear on the lists, but there are significant concentrations in key sectors. For instance, among a group of a hundred activists arrested on the militant Moscow-Kazan Railroad after December—a list excluding those who perished in the bloody repression following the December strike on that line—were thirty-one shop craftsmen, twenty-seven white-collar clerks and accountants, seventeen engine drivers, nine telegraph personnel, seven administrators, four in other occupations, and four whose position is unknown. Lists of those arrested or dismissed elsewhere offer a comparable picture.[71]

Especially at smaller stations unconnected to major workshops and depots, station personnel, telegraph operators, railroad medical personnel, stationmasters, and even some railroad engineers and administrators were active participants in the December strike. Even in some major cities such forces could still be represented in disproportionately large numbers on strike committees and in soviets. It would seem that many white-collar activists were swept up by the rising tide of struggle that surrounded them, even as their social base retreated somewhat from the battle. Others may have taken part in the strike and uprisings in the hope of moderating the growing extremism of blue-collar railwaymen and their revolution-

69. Sidorov, ed., vol. 3, pt. 1, p. 465.
70. Ibid., p. 468.
71. TsGAOR, f. 6865, d. 65, ll. 16–26. Additional lists of those arrested and/or dismissed are in TsGIA, f. 273, op. 12.

ary leaders—this, for instance, was the excuse offered by some railroad administrators and intellectuals, no doubt self-servingly, at their trial for participation in the fighting at Gorlovka.[72] Some elected delegates may also have been pressured into support for the movement: a government inspector sent to the Catherine Railroad reported that by late November many employee representatives were acting "not by conviction, but only out of fear."[73]

Engine-drivers emerged as an especially critical group in December, joining in strike leadership to an extent far out of proportion to their limited number. At some depots unconnected to major repair facilities, as at Mineral Waters on the Vladikavkaz Railroad, the drivers were the heart of the strike. At major junctions, however, they tended to act more as individuals than in a group. Since the engine-drivers were in the most advantageous position to affect train operations, all sections of the railroad work force and each group attempting to gain influence among railwaymen vigorously sought their support. During the first ten months of 1905 many engine-drivers participated in the railroad movement in close cooperation with privileged administrators and employees, reflecting their own rather prestigious and elite position. Drivers on the Moscow-Kazan road, for example, were central to the organization of the Railroad Union and several had been coopted onto its Central Bureau. As has been seen, however, the drivers were also linked to the industrial section of railroad labor, as many, especially among younger drivers, had been recruited from the ranks of shop craftsmen.

As militant class consciousness emerged among railroad personnel, a good number of individual cabmen—it is impossible to say whether they were a majority or not—became radicalized and began to link their fortunes with the proletarian movement rather than the strictly professional one. It does not seem to have been principally a case of drivers shifting their loyalty as an occupational group from the administrative to the industrial sections of the work force, but more one of individual drivers emerging as leaders and articulate advocates of the more revolutionary and class-conscious mood most prevalent among the shop craftsmen. By virtue not only of their pivotal position in the railroad economy but also of their

72. Reichman, "Russian Railwaymen," p. 527.
73. TsGIA, f. 273, op. 12, d. 350, l. 342.

greater experience and maturity and their higher level of educational achievement, individual engine-drivers could be embraced by craftsmen and other young militant railwaymen as effective spokesmen for their cause.

Individual "outside agitators"—students, railroad doctors, or local intellectuals, often associated with one of the socialist parties—could command similar respect. This was especially true at smaller stations and outlying junctions, where the December strike reproduced some characteristics seen in larger centers in October and even January. Where in Moscow, Rostov-on-Don, Ekaterinoslav, and other sites of insurrection the December movement was much more determined and stubborn, and the situation more polarized and violent than had been the case in October, at many small stations the previous pattern of a general popular outpouring, with mass meetings and a relatively peaceful transfer of power to local liberationists, was repeated anew. At such places the role of individual strike leaders could prove critical. Aleksei Poliakov, a teacher at a railroad technical academy, emerged from obscurity in December to become an effective organizer and chair of the strike committee at Dolgintsevo on the Catherine Railroad. At Gorlovka on the same line a Caucasian Menshevik, A. M. Zubarev, known also as Mark Kuznetsov, arrived in late November and quickly galvanized not only railwaymen but workers at the town's large machine building plant and miners.[74] At Belev on the Riazan-Ural Railroad the influence of the depot engineer, Petr Ragozin, was "despotic." On December 14 he addressed a mass meeting on the need to redistribute the country's wealth. Fired by his oratory, a crowd of railroad workers, townspeople, and peasants descended on the town's better stores and began looting. Ragozin rushed to the scene and called on the looters to stop. "Instantly, without protest, the crowd dispersed."[75]

The December events were not characterized by a qualitatively higher degree of organization than the October strike. Although on several lines there was significantly greater coordination between stations, practical strike leadership was still local. This can be attributed to three factors. First, in contrast to October, the regime

74. TsGIA, f. 273, op. 12, d. 350, l. 417; Reichman, "Russian Railwaymen," pp. 527–28.
75. Sidorov, ed., vol. 2, pp. 207–8.

did all in its power to defeat the workers, which placed additional burdens on the strikers. Second, in December the strikers did not control the railroad telegraph as thoroughly as they had two months earlier. Exhausted by their November effort, the telegraph operators were not as a group especially strong supporters of the December actions, although this varied from road to road. The government was, however, able to retain control of many key stations and, especially after the armed struggle began in Moscow, a number of important junctions and lines were cut off from communication with the rest of the country. A third factor was that although many more railwaymen had come forward to create and participate in organizations in November, most of these groups were still very primitive and their leaders untested. The South East Railroad was one of the best organized lines, but in December its "organizational structure . . . was still incomplete." Of thirty local committees on the road, only twenty could even claim an established command structure.[76]

On the national level what leadership there was came almost exclusively from the socialist parties. The Central Bureau of the Railroad Union again played an insignificant part—if, indeed, it played any role at all—once the strike began. The *Kazantsy*, its most militant members, seem to have been totally absorbed in the Moscow uprising. Other members were arrested almost immediately after the strike was declared. Although charges by Soviet historians that the Central Bureau engaged in "capitulationist strikebreaking activity" during the December risings seem unwarranted, some of its members do appear to have joined with a rump body of delegates from the Conference of Twenty-nine Railroads in calling for an end to the strike as early as December 12. The strikers ignored this directive, of course, and according to Minister of Internal Affairs Durnovo resistance continued "as stubbornly as at first."[77]

In October the railroad system completely shut down, but in December the strikers attempted to keep some trains moving to serve their own purposes, which placed a major burden on local strike organizations, whose leaders were often completely occupied with problems of traffic management. In a few places strike committees sought to fill strike coffers with fares collected from

76. *1905 god na Iugo-Vostochnykh zheleznykh dorogakh* (Moscow, 1925), p. 63.
77. Korablev et al., pp. 258–59; Sidorov, ed., vol. 1, p. 682.

stranded passengers willing to ride an unscheduled delegate train, although the strike declaration released by the Railroad Union and the Conference of Twenty-nine Railroads had promised only that "passengers trapped by the strike will be carried to the nearest large city." But the strikers mainly kept the lines open in an effort to maintain comradely relations with local peasants and soldiers, whose places in the revolutionary alliance now seemed especially critical in the face of the growing rift between the proletariat and some elements of the urban middle class. "We are not alone," the December strike call concluded, "the urban proletariat, the laboring peasantry, and the conscious parts of the army and fleet have already risen up for popular freedom, for land, and for liberty."[78]

In October many strike activists feared a peasant backlash to the breakdown of rail transport, but instead the strike helped spread the spirit of rebellion to the villages. By December the peasant movement was already ebbing, however, and the countryside was preparing for the hard Russian winter. Acting on the strike declaration's pledge to "take all measures for the transport of needed bread for the hungry peasants along with provisions for comrades out on the lines," railroad strikers tried to keep village stations supplied with necessities in order to win rural support, especially in the Volga region and parts of the south. In Saratov the city soviet and the strike committee of the Riazan-Ural Railroad pledged to keep bread shipments moving to nearby settlements. At Voronezh strikers on the South East Railroad distributed a proclamation in the surrounding countryside calling for "full freedom to the Russian people, [and] land to the peasants."[79] At rural stations railroad strikers worked especially hard to maintain friendly relations with the peasants. The "Liubotin Republic" was successful in part because of close ties linking the railroad workers with peasants of Old Liubotin village on the Sviatopolk-Mirsky estate. At Belev on the Riazan-Ural road strikers offered to sell confiscated freight to local peasants for as little as one-third of its indicated value.[80]

More important, however, were efforts to link up with rebellious soldiers. Mutinies had taken place in a number of garrisons in the fall, which encouraged the revolutionaries. In December, however,

78. Sidorov, ed., vol. 1, p. 130.
79. Ibid., vol. 1, p. 130; vol. 2, pp. 730, 304.
80. TsGAOR, f. 6865, d. 35, ll. 248–49; Ibid., vol. 2, p. 207.

few, if any, soldiers went over to the insurgents. Newly demobilized troops returning from the recently concluded hostilities in the Far East added a new and highly explosive element to the unrest, however, which had not been present two months earlier. The December 7 strike call promised to "take care of the returning troops from Manchuria; indeed, the delivery of these troops back to Russia will be swifter than under the government."[81]

This was easier said than done. Even under ordinary conditions the rapid return of a largely spiritless army would have strained the logistical capacities of the railroad system; under strike conditions there was chaos. In Samara "there were days when eight to ten troop trains arrived unexpectedly, but others when there wasn't one." With traffic moving inexorably from east to west, there was a growing imbalance in cars that simultaneously overcrowded lines to the west and left growing numbers of increasingly impatient soldiers stranded in the east. There were also shortages of fuel.[82] Even before the December strike began, the returning soldiers themselves had begun to add a new element of turmoil. As one striker at a small station on the Kharkov-Nikolaev Railroad later recalled:

Every day, troop train after troop train, they passed—tired, embittered, having lost all pretense of discipline. They destroyed station lamps, window glass, buffets, and even sacked the station canteen. And the officers, crestfallen and out of control, having forgotten all their past honor, hid like cowards behind the railroad cars or even took part in the brawl themselves, demanding vodka and food.[83]

Throughout the country, but overwhelmingly in the Urals and the south east, railroad strikers took control of trains carrying soldiers, dismissed the officers, and began to bring the men home as best they could. In Cheliabinsk nearly 5,000 soldiers were taken from the command of 29 officers and transported through town by strikers on the Perm Railroad. The troops wandered freely through the trains, entering the first-class cars, much to the chagrin of powerless railroad administrators and police. Six detachments of loyal troops had to be dispatched to restore order.[84]

81. Sidorov, ed., vol. 1, p. 130.
82. TsGIA, f. 273, op. 12, d. 364, l. 497; *1905 god na Iugo-Vostochnykh zheleznykh dorogakh*, pp. 70–72.
83. *1905 g. vo vospominaniiakh ego uchastnikov* (Rostov-on-Don, 1925), p. 63.
84. Sidorov, ed., vol. 2, pp. 830–34.

Ten

Repression and Retreat

The December rebellion was brutally suppressed. Even before Moscow had been pacified the government was planning to take back the railroads. On December 14 Nicholas II issued a lengthy decree introducing extraordinary measures to control the railroads and punish strikers.[1] Reinforcing the orders of December 2 and 3, the new directive let local authorities place entire lines under martial law. Special committees dominated by railroad police and the military took over railroad management. Workers disobedient to the new authorities were subject to immediate arrest for up to three months and fines of up to 500 rubles without trial. Labor assemblies were banned. Strikers were subject to immediate dismissal and agitators to prison terms. On February 9, 1906, Nemeshaev declared that "every railroad employee must be thoroughly imbued with the sense that any stoppage of railroad traffic is a heinous crime against the state and against all society and each of its members."[2]

After defeat of the Moscow insurrection the tsar dispatched "punitive expeditions" to pacify rebellious regions. The armed forces had already been employed since late November against the peasant movement in the Volga and Baltic regions, but now special regiments were outfitted to travel in armored trains along key railroad lines controlled by strikers. As the title "punitive expedition" suggested, these were designed to punish, not simply suppress. In

1. A. L. Sidorov, ed., *Vysshii pod'em revoliutsii 1905–1907 gg.: vooruzhennye vosstaniia, noiabr'–dekabr' 1905 god* (Moscow and Leningrad, 1955), vol. 1, pp. 152–55.
2. *Zhel.*, 139, February 20, 1906, pp. 3–5.

Moscow the Semenovskii Guards were sent along the Moscow-
Kazan Railroad under the command of General N. K. Riman with
orders to "make no arrests and act without mercy." Riman told his
men to destroy all buildings from which they were fired upon.[3]

From December 16 through 21 the Riman expedition wreaked
vengeance on strikers and bystanders almost indiscriminately.
Bloody confrontations—more massacres than battles—occurred at
Sortirovochnaia, Perovo, and Golutvin. The troops caught up with
Ukhtomskii in a tavern near the Liuberts station; he was before a
firing squad within hours.[4] According to General Riman's report, 68
individuals perished at the hands of the Semenovskii regiment, 8 at
Sortirovochnaia, 16 at Perovo, 14 at Liuberts, 3 at Ashitkovo, and
27 at Golutvin. Further investigation by a writer sympathetic to
the workers revealed that an additional 57 men perished at Perovo
and another 25 at Sortirovochnaia, raising the death toll to 150. Of
this group, just 2, Ukhtomskii and a railroad technician, were active participants in the Moscow revolt; 3 more, including the assistant stationmaster at Liuberts, aided the Moscow fighters from
outside; and another 16 were members of fighting detachments "organized exclusively for self-defense against hooliganism." The remaining 129 victims, including local factory workers, students, and
other strike supporters as well as railwaymen, were "killed without
reason." Among railroad workers, the overwhelming majority of
victims were shop craftsmen.[5]

A regiment was dispatched from Ekaterinoslav along the Catherine Railroad after martial law was declared on December 20. Some
stations on this line were already secured by Cossacks, but the
punitive force engaged in mopping-up, disarming, and arresting
railwaymen at Grishino, Avdeevka, Iasinovataia, and Lugansk. At
Paniutino on the Kursk-Kharkov-Sevastopol Railroad, where the
strike had largely proceeded peacefully, the arrival of troops triggered violence. In the Baltic provinces, where the punitive expedition under the command of General Orlov won an especially
savage reputation for its suppression of rebellious peasants and farm

3. V. Vladimirov, *Karatel'naia ekspeditsiia* (Moscow, 1906), p. 9; Sidorov, ed.,
vol. 1, p. 800.
4. Vladimirov, pp. 80–82.
5. Ibid., p. 61.

laborers, troops occupied the Riga-Orel Railroad; in Riga alone more than a hundred railwaymen were court-martialed.[6]

The ranks of the survivors were decimated by arrests and firings. Among those dismissed were all the leaders of the Railroad Union and virtually every delegate to the pension congress, including Orekhov, Elizarov, and Arkhangelskii. On January 27 the editors of *Zheleznodorozhnik* noted that each day saw

a rain of dispatches reporting the firing of agents from every department without appeal and even without explanation. . . . They fire with no investigation, no warning, taking no account of length of service or family situation. Scores of people have been thrown on the street only because their co-workers elected them delegates (at a time when management not only did not forbid this, but deemed such service an obligation). Others are dismissed for participation in the Railroad Union (freedom of unions!), but the majority are let go simply because the administration doesn't like them, or they don't know how to flatter, to bow and scrape.[7]

On the Vladikavkaz Railroad the Rostov, Tikhoretskaia, and Novorossiisk workshops were closed on January 1 and some 5,000 workers dismissed. Rehiring began on January 18 for a work force about 10 to 15 percent smaller. Rehirees were compelled to sign a statement pledging to submit to all orders from management and its foremen; to work under the pre-October wage schedule; not to demand a shorter work day, be late for work, or leave before the final whistle; to forego requests for housing subsidies; and to accept existing pay-books. Similar dismissals and rehirings took place elsewhere.[8]

Most of those dismissed eventually found work on other railroads or were rehired by their old lines after six to eighteen months. But many continued to congregate among the unemployed in major railroad centers, especially Moscow, St. Petersburg, and Saratov.[9] As late as November 1906 the press reported that more than 500 rail-

6. Sidorov, ed., vol. 3, pt. 1, pp. 117–18; 464–65; A. Paulish, "Zabastavochnoe dvizhenie na Rigo-Orlovskoi zh. d.," *Proletarskaia revoliutsiia*, 1925, no. 11 (46): 173. The largest and most famous of the punitive expeditions were mounted on the Siberian Railroad, which remained under military occupation until 1908.

7. *Zhel.*, 136, January 27, 1906, p. 3.

8. Ibid., 138, February 13, 1906, pp. 7–8, 12.

9. The fate of fired railwaymen is amply documented in TsGIA, f. 273, op. 12, d. 355, ll. 1–208. See also *Zhel.*, January–July 1906, passim.

road engineers dismissed for strike activity were seeking work in St. Petersburg. A great number came from the Siberian Railroad, where only two members of the pre-December corps of engineers remained with the road. According to one newspaper report, between the end of the general strike and midsummer 1907, 59,195 railwaymen were fired for strike activity, of whom 35,379 eventually found work again in the railroad system.[10]

Repressive measures effectively decapitated the railroad labor movement, a significant achievement, since the movement had been something of a hydra. During the December strike itself, the former Central Bureau of the Railroad Union disintegrated, its commanding figure, Pereverzev, fleeing eventually to Finland. Of far greater significance was the dispersal through arrest and dismissal of the various local leadership groups that had been so important in October and December. On March 4, 1906, the government released a set of "Temporary Regulations on Unions and Societies," which legalized trade unions for the first time and led to a blossoming of union groups in private industry. But the new law explicitly banned union participation in politics and the pursuit of goals that threatened the established order. Closely identified with the instigation of two national strikes and openly espousing political aims, the Railroad Union was effectively proscribed. Moreover, union groups were barred from unifying on a national or even regional basis, an especially serious barrier to the organization of railroad labor. According to the report of a September 1906 meeting on the Kharkov-Nikolaev Railroad, the Railroad Union was "completely destroyed after the December strike. All the more or less visible members were deported, arrested, or fired. Virtually not a single member of the central and regional committees remained untouched. The union was frozen, the terrorized railroad masses frightened into silence."[11]

Union activists sought to rebuild from underground. In late February 1906 an initiating group of ex-railroad employees, including

10. TsGIA, f. 273, op. 12, d. 347, l. 767; *Russkie vedomosti*, August 9, 1907, 181.

11. TsGAOR, f. 6865, d. 197, l. 18. On the legal union movement see Victoria E. Bonnell, *Roots of Rebellion: Workers' Politics and Organizations in St. Petersburg and Moscow, 1900–1914* (Berkeley and Los Angeles, 1983), pp. 194–349.

at least one former member of the Central Bureau, began, with the assistance of the Socialist Revolutionary Party, to organize a representative meeting. In mid April, delegates from twenty-one lines met secretly in a Moscow suburb with representatives of the socialist parties to reconstitute the Central Bureau. It was reported that several roads still counted more than a thousand members and none claimed fewer than three hundred, although these figures probably included people who had been arrested or dismissed from service. In May the new Central Bureau distributed a leaflet to Moscow railwaymen that boasted that although the union had "lost its best representatives," it was already "sprouting new shoots and growing more and more each day." Still, it was admitted, "many weak-spirited comrades are afraid to join us again." [12]

In August the Railroad Union managed to convene a conference to consider a new general strike in response to dismissal of the Duma in June. Attended by delegates from twenty-three roads, the Social Democratic and Socialist Revolutionary parties, the Duma labor group, the Polish Socialists, the Jewish Bund, and the postal-telegraph union, the meeting issued a general call to prepare for a new strike but avoided concrete proposals. As Pereverzev told the delegates, "At present we are a staff without an army, or, it would be more accurate to say, with the permanently diminishing remnants of an army." [13]

By autumn, however, junction committees were functioning in several regions. In Moscow leadership fell to the SR group on the Kazan line. In St. Petersburg and Kiev Social Democrats took the initiative. On September 15 sixteen delegates from stations on the Kharkov-Nikolaev Railroad gathered to reconstitute a local. The body claimed the support of 620 members, of whom 67 percent were shop craftsmen, 14 percent clerks and telegraph operators, and 12 percent engine-drivers and conductors. Thirty-eight percent were members of the Social Democratic party, 4 percent were SRs, and the remainder were unaffiliated. A month earlier a union com-

---

12. TsGIA, f. 229, op. 2, d. 1649, ll. 164–65; TsGAOR, f. 518, d. 35, ll. 28–31; f. 6865, d. 195b, l. 2.
13. Quoted in I. M. Pushkareva, *Zheleznodorozhniki Rossii v burzhuazno-demokraticheskikh revoliutsiiakh* (Moscow, 1975), p. 259. The conference resolution is in *1905: Vtoroi period revoliutsii* (Moscow, 1957), vol. 2, pt. 1, p. 67, and TsGAOR, f. 518, d. 35, l. 44.

mittee had been formed on the Kursk-Kharkov-Sevastopol Railroad, but under Socialist Revolutionary leadership. Relations between the two groups were increasingly hostile.[14]

The third congress of the Railroad Union convened in Tammerfors, Finland, on December 9–15, 1906. Thirty-five delegates, including five members of the new Central Bureau, claimed to represent nineteen roads with a total membership of 9,336. Eight lines, with an approximate membership of 6,000, were without representation. Few, if any, delegates had actually been elected, however, partly because of repression and partly owing to bitter factional fighting. Although on paper membership stood at double that of late 1905, the real level of activity remained low. The Central Bureau's ties with local groups were highly scattered and irregular. Most junction committees met infrequently and were concerned mainly with survival. As the delegates to the Kharkov-Nikolaev meeting had earlier acknowledged, "the striving for organization is paralyzed by repression and fear."[15]

This was also recognized by the authorities, who kept close tab on attempts to revive the railroad labor movement. In late September Moscow police reported that the Railroad Union posed "no serious threat to social order," being absorbed almost exclusively in fund-raising. They noted that the once-powerful Moscow junction committee had met no more than twice since January. After the December union congress the police reported that the union was crippled by "organizational inertia" and lagging enthusiasm. "Even on the Moscow-Kazan Railroad, this former revolutionary hotbed, a weakening of interest in criminal political organization can be noted."[16]

In fact, the Railroad Union's problems could be attributed to more than repression, and also stemmed from the shifting social basis of railroad activism after the October strike. A July 1907 government report claimed that the union had become not so much an organization of people in railroad work as one of former railwaymen and outside agitators.[17] More important, the regional committee of the Kharkov-Nikolaev road noted in August that enthusiasm for or-

14. TsGAOR, f. 6865, d. 198, ll. 4–7, 16–17; d. 197, l. 20; f. 518, d. 35, l. 50.
15. Pushkareva, *Zheleznodorozhniki*, p. 273; TsGAOR, f. 6865, d. 197, l. 22.
16. TsGAOR, f. 6865, d. 198, ll. 7, 25.
17. TsGIA, f. 229, op. 2, d. 1655, l. 71.

ganization remained strong among shop craftsmen, but had weakened among white-collar employees. The third congress concluded that "after the December events the center of gravity of the union began to shift from the ranks of the administrative employees to the workers and lower line agents." The delegates also found that organization could best be maintained not at the largest terminals but at the "most remote corners of the lines."[18]

The shifting political situation exacerbated the long-standing tension between the Railroad Union and Russian Social Democracy, especially as the Socialist Revolutionaries began to exert greater political and organizational influence within the union. In May the reconstituted Central Bureau issued a lengthy appeal to the socialist parties, including a thirteen-point program of cooperative action. The SRs quickly agreed to the proposed terms, but they were rejected by the Central Committee of the now reunited Social Democratic party.[19] The Marxists did not adopt a unified approach to the union, however. While the Central Committee ordered party members to work within the railroad organization in the hope of capturing its leadership, the Moscow Committee angrily withdrew from the union, organizing instead another "purely professional"—that is, strictly economic—union, which claimed more than 300 members by mid 1906. For the remainder of 1906, Social Democrats, Socialist Revolutionaries, and independent union activists jockeyed for position within the sputtering railroad labor movement. In Moscow the two separate unions vied for influence, while in St. Petersburg and on the South West Railroad the Social Democrats won control of the Railroad Union apparatus. Elsewhere, the organization was bitterly divided.[20]

Everywhere, however, the Social Democrats offered the same by now familiar critique of the Central Bureau. *Golos zheleznodorozhnika*, the short-lived newspaper of the Moscow Social Democratic union, complained that the Railroad Union had not been rebuilt on the basis of a democratically elected congress. In April the Social

18. TsGAOR, f. 6865, d. 197, l. 5; f. 518, d. 35, ll. 28–29.
19. TsGAOR, f. 518, d. 35, ll. 35–43.
20. V. Boshko, "Zheleznodorozhnyi soiuz i sotsialisticheskie partii v 1905–10 gg.," *Zheleznodorozhnik* [Postrevolutionary trade union organ], 1927, no. 1, pp. 52–53; "Vospominaniia uchastnikov pervoi Russkoi revoliutsii," *Voprosy istorii*, 1955, no. 12: 33–44.

Democratic paper *Volna* argued that the national union's failure to survive the post-December repressions stemmed from organizational flabbiness and lack of internal democracy. More critical, however, was the continued emphasis on the achievement of a broadly democratic political program by means of a vaguely defined general strike, which seemed to spread a leftist veneer over essentially liberal goals. Once again the Social Democrats were careful to distinguish trade unionist, reformist politics from revolutionary socialism, stressing that the Central Bureau and its Socialist Revolutionary allies were shackling railroad workers to the former.

Trade unions, the Social Democrats argued, should not espouse a political program; the political struggle for socialism could not be waged on a professional basis, as this would mean substituting the politics of separate industries for the politics of the working class as a whole. Such a program must inevitably lower the level of worker politics to that of the reformist bourgeoisie. Instead, unions should concentrate on defending workers' economic interests and leave political agitation—revolutionary socialist agitation—to the party. The Social Democratic critique did not lack validity. Even *Zheleznodorozhnik* acknowledged that the Railroad Union had declined while other unions were growing, in part because it still stubbornly refused to take on the proper role of a union, instead reducing its entire program of action to the political general strike.[21]

The conflict came to a head at the third congress, where the delegates debated the respective merits of "professional" and "professional-political" organization. The result was a foregone conclusion, however, since the meeting was not democratically built, and the organizers were able to limit the Social Democratic voting presence to the St. Petersburg contingent. The Central Bureau's approach was endorsed by a vote of sixteen to one, with two abstentions.[22] With the movement ebbing and the social base of activism shifting to precisely those sections of the railroad proletariat most open to direct Social Democratic appeals, the Marxist faction had little reason to continue the fight. In early February 1907

21. TsGAOR, f. 518, d. 35, l. 46; *Volna*, 5, April 30, 1906, p. 2; *Zhel.*, 190, March 6, 1907, p. 5. For the Central Bureau's response, see "Sotsial demokraty i VZhS," *Zheleznodorozhnyi soiuz*, April 1907, pp. 3–6.
22. TsGAOR, f. 518, d. 35, l. 29; Boshko, p. 53.

a conference of delegates from party railroad committees in St. Petersburg, Moscow, Kharkov, Ekaterinoslav, Kiev, Voronezh, and Warsaw decided to withdraw from the Railroad Union:

In its time the All-Russian Railroad Union played a tremendous political role, but now it is in its final days. And this is not just the result of repression. Despite all the malicious designs of the reaction, unions in other spheres of production are developing slowly but surely. . . . It is quite a different story with the Railroad Union. As an organ of the professional movement it plays an insignificant role. It involves only the upper reaches of the huge railroad army, who have joined it as a general democratic organization, consumed by political ambitions. As a class organization of the masses of the railroad proletariat fighting to achieve the goals of the professional struggle, it hardly exists.[23]

The criticism was perhaps overdrawn; certainly the failure of railroad labor militancy after 1905 was attributable more to repression than to the failures of union leadership. Still, after the Social Democratic exit the Railroad Union degenerated rapidly into a relatively insignificant agency of Socialist Revolutionary politics, and by 1908 it had ceased to exist. The Social Democrats were no more successful than their rivals, however, and their "professional" unions also faded quickly into oblivion.

During the first half of 1907 railroad organizing received a temporary boost from the upsurge of oppositional activity surrounding the sessions of the second state Duma. Many railwaymen had joined with other oppositionists in boycotting the elections to the first Duma, but they entered the second electoral campaign with almost universal enthusiasm, encouraged to vote for "socialist" candidates by the Railroad Union.[24] The electoral sympathies of railwaymen varied, however. In elections to city electoral assemblies, it seems, shop craftsmen tended to vote for socialists, especially Social Democrats, but white-collar elements leaned toward more moderate forces, the Trudoviki or the Kadets. Railroad electors on the Moscow-Kiev-Voronezh Railroad in Kursk selected twelve office employees and an engine-driver, all Kadets, and voters on the Riazan-Ural Railroad in Saratov chose twenty Trudoviki and a single Kadet. On the Catherine Railroad in Ekaterinoslav, however,

23. *Novyi luch*, 5, February 24, 1907, p. 4.
24. TsGAOR, f. 6865, d. 198, l. 33.

the slate was dominated by Social Democrats, about equally divided between shop craftsmen and employees.[25]

Among the deputies to the second Duma were seven railwaymen, both administrative personnel and workers. Although none had been visibly active in the organizations and movements of 1905, they quickly formed an informal bureau to address the concerns of railroad labor. The intent was to gather materials that could serve as a basis for putting the rights of workers on a firm legal footing. The railroad deputies also tried to oversee the budget of the Ministry of Communications, but with little success. The delegates soon became an important sounding board for complaints against management and for the lodging of appeals by those subject to repression. As union organization and radical political consciousness both continued to wane, the Duma group began to emerge as a legitimate representative of railroad worker interests.[26] The Stolypin "coup d'etat" of June 3, 1907, put an end to this, however. The long-overdue legal redefinition of the rights and responsibilities of railroad labor would come without the participation of railroad workers or their elected representatives.

Defeat of the railroad revolution enabled the Ministry of Communications to address the labor problems that had troubled management before the revolutionary upsurge. With Nemeshaev's appointment, the ministry took charge of preparing a legislative reform package, including yet another labor charter, a disciplinary code, and "norms of work and rest." On November 30, 1905, selected officials in the capital region were invited to discuss the proposals. Nemeshaev toured several key lines between January 19 and 31, 1906. In his travel journal he attributed unrest to "the confusion of higher railroad officials and their isolation from lower personnel" and vowed to continue pushing reform efforts.[27] But these were overshadowed by repression. "Behind the noise of recent events," wrote a *Zheleznodorozhnik* commentator in late January, "the Ministry of Communications and the new minister have been

25. TsGIA, f. 229, op. 2, d. 1654, ll. 20–29.

26. *Rus'*, 60, March 1, 1907; *Zheleznodorozhnyi soiuz*, April 1907, pp. 1–3, 17–22.

27. TsGIA, f. 273, op. 12, d. 408, ll. 34–38; f. 229, op. 2, d. 1647, l. 79; d. 1649, ll. 111–13; *Zhel.*, 139, February 20, 1906, pp. 3–5.

almost completely forgotten. Whether they are working, creating some beneficial projects, while [Minister of Internal Affairs] Durnovo introduces 'pacification' no one knows, and I would hardly be mistaken to say, no one cares."[28]

On February 25, dismissing last-minute objections from private railroads, Nemeshaev presented his three-part program to the Council of Ministers. The new charter, he explained, would apply to all state and private railroad employees except elected officers of private lines, shop craftsmen, daily workers, and employees of contractors. Those covered were split into permanent and provisional staff. The latter, defined as those with less than two years' service, would enjoy fewer rights. The work force was further divided into four categories: locomotive crews, conductors, station and line employees directly involved in moving trains, and those not involved in movement. Each category would have differing rights and responsibilities. The accompanying disciplinary rules established local disciplinary commissions, general disciplinary hearing boards under each road, and, as a court of last appeal, a disciplinary council directly under the ministry. In view of differing regional conditions, the norms of work and rest set only general guidelines. Nemeshaev urged his fellow ministers to enact the entire program, especially the charter, immediately, and not to leave it to the state Duma, where it would surely receive low priority.[29]

On March 16, however, the minister of finance sent Nemeshaev a lengthy memo attacking the proposals and supporting the private roads in their efforts to be exempted. The next day the council decided to refer the charter to the Duma and to refer the work norms to yet another interdepartmental commission. Pending approval by the Ministry of Justice, however, it was agreed to accept the disciplinary rules. This was essentially meaningless, though, since the overwhelming majority of roads remained officially in a state of siege superseding all usual disciplinary procedures.[30]

The next month, with Witte's replacement by Goremykin, Nemeshaev resigned to return to the South West road. His replacement was General Schaufus. The idea of a railroad labor charter had thus

28. *Zhel.*, 136, January 27, 1906, p. 1.
29. TsGIA, f. 273, op. 12, d. 408, ll. 241–71.
30. Ibid., ll. 266, 279–318.

once again been smothered by the bureaucracy. But this reform effort was also frustrated by the limited aspirations of its principal champion. Nemeshaev's reforms were doomed because they were destined to run headlong into the aspirations of railwaymen on one side and the autocratic system's disinclination and inability to delegate power on the other, a disinclination shared to a great extent by the reform element in the Ministry of Communications. It is little surprise that in the end the reform-minded Nemeshaev was perceived as a mere puppet of the police.[31]

After 1905 the Ministry of Communications drifted steadily toward police-military "solutions" of the labor question. In 1907 Schaufus succeeded in gaining approval for yet another version of the long-sought charter, prepared now by a commission chaired by Dumitrashko. But few even took note of its passage, and those who did complained that it "only introduces a series of new repressive measures." Indeed, as late as 1912 a Menshevik member of the former railroad bureau of the second Duma could still write that "in actuality no charter exists—only orders, circulars, norms, temporary rules, etc."[32]

More characteristic of Schaufus's reign were his abortive efforts in 1906 to claim dictatorial powers over the railroads. Although to some extent this was an attempt by the ministry to regain control from the police, whose representatives were in 1906 the real power on most lines, its antidemocratic implications remained consistent with general policy trends. Vicious repression continued long after actual pacification. The extraordinary antistrike measures of December 1905 remained in force through World War I. In early 1908 Prime Minister Petr Stolypin brought 184 December insurgents from the Catherine Railroad to military court, beginning a series of much-publicized courts-martial of railroad activists, which continued into 1911.[33]

31. When Nemeshaev stepped down, his former supporters at *Zheleznodorozhnik* wrote that his tenure had been "marked by such violence, such illegality and tyranny, as could not even be scented in 'preconstitutional' times" and asked rhetorically, "Who can separate the guilt of Nemeshaev from that of Durnovo?" (*Zhel.*, 150, May 13, 1906, p. 2).

32. *Zhel.*, 200, May 16, 1907, pp. 2–3; V. Dmitriev "Byt sluzhashchikh i rabochikh na zheleznykh dorogakh," *Sovremennyi mir*, 1912, no. 1, p. 282.

33. *Zhel.*, 155, June 20, 1906, p. 5; N. Rostov, "Zheleznodorozhniki v pervoi revoliutsii," *Proletariat v revoliutsii 1905–1907 gg.* (Moscow, 1930), p. 175; S. S. Anisimov, *Delo o vosstanii na Ekaterininskoi zh. d.* (Moscow, 1926).

Beginning in 1907 the ministry began to consider a number of projects that to one degree or another involved the "militarization" of railroad work. Although the most extreme proposals were rejected, by 1914 a repressive, quasi-military approach was in command. The notion of militarization of railroad transport is inextricably tied to the name of General A. A. von Vendrikh, who first formulated the concept as a solution to labor fluidity and indiscipline. Vendrikh, a close associate of such leading conservatives as Krivoshein and Durnovo, and an early mentor of Schaufus's, played a leading role in organizing the punitive expeditions. In 1907 he devised a scheme whereby special "railroad operational corps" of armed detachments, serving under separate military discipline and command, would work alongside civilian railroad workers. These would be formed mainly from military men already in railroad service and reserve junior officers, though active-duty soldiers could volunteer as well. After a trial period in which the system would operate only on the major roads serving the two capitals, it would be extended to the empire as a whole. Vendrikh eventually foresaw the corps—with himself as commander—encompassing nearly the entire permanent staff of the railroad network.[34] Although the tsar later endorsed the proposal, the Council of Ministers concluded that the plan would be too costly, result in "a hostile division of power in the Ministry of Communications, and would inevitably lead to a complicated collision with the military."[35] The general was forced out, but in the years that followed the spirit, if not the letter, of his concept gained ascendancy.

At the start of 1909 the former head of the main prison administration of the Department of Police, S. V. Rukhlov, replaced Schaufus. Rukhlov's ministry, which lasted until 1915, saw the triumph of police methods and of de facto militarization. In 1909 he promulgated "Special Rules for the Struggle with Railroad Strikes" that introduced compulsory registration with the police of all railroad job applicants. In 1910 he created "flying squads" of railroad troops for dispatch at the request of civil authorities. In March 1913 Rukhlov proposed a new "Code for Railroad Service," requir-

34. TsGIA, f. 273, op. 12, d. 725, l. 385; f. 229, op. 4, d. 1220, ll. 1–6. On "militarization" and post-1905 policy in general, see Pushkareva, *Zheleznodorozhniki*, pp. 279–94.
35. Pushkareva, *Zheleznodorozhniki*, pp. 285–86.

ing loyalty oaths for railroad employees and automatic dismissal for membership in "antigovernment organizations and parties." Rukhlov encouraged patriotic and religious propaganda on the roads and in shops and depots, and in December 1909 he banned hiring of "Jews, Catholics, Lutherans, and persons of Polish and German origin."[36]

Post-1905 repression allowed the ministry to increase productivity and thus bring to a virtual halt the previously uncontrolled expansion of the work force, but the composition of railroad labor changed as well. Though in 1914 the work force was not very much larger than it had been in 1905 (it had grown by 64,000), nearly half the staff had begun work after 1907. Many recruits were former military men. In December 1909 the ministry adopted rules for "increasing the military element in the ranks of railroad employees," which among other things offered bonuses for employees who had served in the armed forces. As a result, by 1911 nearly a third of all those covered by the pension fund were veterans, their number rising from 89,000 in 1908 to 123,000 in 1911.[37]

In short, Rukhlov's program put into practice many of Vendrikh's notions. The new minister sought formal recognition of this in October 1911 by introducing a militarization proposal that met past criticism by eliminating Vendrikh's separate command structure and moderating his ambitious goals for expansion. The project was not implemented, however, and formal militarization after 1914 took a different form.[38]

Such policies enabled railroad management to make progress in the rationalization of administration, but largely at the expense of labor. Improvements in wages, hours, and benefits were soon lost to inflation and the steady restructuring of labor relations along authoritarian lines. Still, the combination of repressive pacification and reactionary reform meant that the Russian railroads, locus of perhaps the most militant and extreme opposition to the regime in 1905, would remain largely untouched by strikes until after the February Revolution of 1917. Even the prewar labor upsurge of

36. Ibid., p. 289; TsGIA, f. 273, op. 12, d. 483, ll. 55–62; f. 229, op. 4, d. 1176, ll. 1–2.
37. Ibid., pp. 289, 290.
38. TsGIA, f. 229, op. 4, d. 1220, ll. 1–2.

1912–14, which, many contend, again brought urban Russia to the brink of revolution, found only modest support among railwaymen. If the failure of a directionless and confused approach to railroad labor contributed to the onset of revolution in 1905, however, the resort to militarism and repression in the years that followed ultimately yielded the same result.[39]

39. On the railroad workers in 1917, see William G. Rosenberg, "The Democratization of Russia's Railroads," *American Historical Review* 86 (1981): 983–1008, and P. F. Metel'kov, *Zheleznodorozhniki v revoliutsii. Fevral' 1917–iiun' 1918 g.* (Leningrad, 1970).

Conclusion

This study has examined the development, structure, and condition of railroad labor in tsarist Russia and probed the complex relationship that emerged between professional mobilization and nascent political class consciousness among railroad workers in 1905. As a result, accepted images of the prerevolutionary Russian working class and of the 1905 revolution have been refined and modified. The experience of the railroad workers suggests, first, that important segments of the Russian working class, if not the class as a whole, lived and struggled neither as displaced peasants nor as stereotypically "mature" proletarians. Rather, their actions and ideas reflected a broad variety of experiences and multifaceted links with other social groups, including administrative and professional elements. The ideas of the oppositional intelligentsia entered the working class not only through the concerted efforts of activists but also across the hazy border separating blue- and white-collar work.

The existence within the railroad work force of distinct administrative and industrial groupings did much to shape labor unrest. Interchange between white-collar employees and shop craftsmen, carried out through a variety of channels, encouraged mobilization on a professional basis. Initially, the industrial section was concerned with more classically "economic" issues, and it fell largely to white-collar employees to raise political demands. In turn, craftsmen taught the administrative element how to strike. For much of 1905 the differing segments of the railroad work force jointly fueled one another's radicalization and politicization. However, the kind

of politics to which each group was in the end attracted differed
considerably.

The effects of managerial efforts to rationalize an administratively chaotic and organizationally archaic system were one common concern that linked differing kinds of railroad workers. The
transformation of the factory order in the repair shops was not
atypical of international trends in labor organization. But rationalizing efforts also had their counterpart in less clearly industrial
spheres of railroad employment. Previously privileged skilled workers found both their economic position and their control over the
work process under steady assault. Engine-drivers in particular
played a critical part in the revolutionary process owing to the
marked deterioration before 1905 of their hitherto privileged position and their unique situation "midway" between the administrative and industrial sections of the work force.

"Worker control" was *not* the central issue on the railroads in
1905—indeed, the story of the year is mainly of how workers
moved beyond syndicalist concerns and sought political solutions.
Still, the changing experience of work and related shifts in rewards
and status were fundamental to the formulation of political goals.
Some railwaymen sought in different ways to preserve or restore
the status that railroading had seemed to enjoy in the nineteenth
century, but others saw emerging a railroad world not fundamentally distinguishable from other spheres of industry. The first group
was thus drawn to professional organizing within the "railroad family," while the second, no less concerned with economic issues,
gravitated toward unity with other industrial groups.

The railroad network has frequently been seen by historians
as an important mechanism through which change spread slowly
outward from the two central metropolises of St. Petersburg and
Moscow. Similarly, it is generally assumed—and was assumed by
contemporaries—that the railroads also spread revolutionary activity outward from the capitals. Such dissemination of oppositional sentiment and organization surely occurred, but a look at the
railroad labor movement of 1905 also suggests that perhaps the un-
derstandable concentration of historians on the labor movement in
the two biggest industrial centers has somewhat distorted the picture of the Russian revolutionary process as a whole. For if the rail-

roads carried revolutionary fervor to the provinces, they also provided a route along which provincial radicalism reached the center.

Even before 1905 the most militant railroad strikes took place in southern Russia. St. Petersburg railwaymen were never as militant or as politically radical as strikers in several less sophisticated cities. To be sure, railroad unrest was naturally concentrated in the Moscow junction, which became the most critical organizing center. But even Moscow was not always in the vanguard of struggle. In January 1905 strikers on the Riazan-Ural line in Saratov raised the first explicitly political demands. Radicals from this road and from Kharkov and Rostov-on-Don were critical in pushing the September pension congress leftward, which in turn accelerated unrest on the lines. During the final three turbulent months of the year the radicalization of provincial roads often occurred independently of developments at the center. On several distant lines the level of militancy was significantly higher, and the extent of the gulf between moderates and radicals significantly wider, than in the capitals.

The developing tension of the weeks following the October manifesto cannot be fully understood without reference to the radicalizing pressure exerted by the provinces on the capitals, pressure communicated mainly along the railroads. On individual roads the initial spread of unrest and organization from urban centers outward was sometimes followed by a phase in which radicalized line workers united with mainly Social Democratic shop craftsmen against increasingly moderate urban employees and officials. This was, for instance, the case on the Vladikavkaz Railroad. The pattern was partially reflected in the national picture, as provincial activism begun under the influence and stimulus of events in St. Petersburg and Moscow took on an increasingly socialist cast, strengthening in turn the influence of the far left in the capitals.

Most Russian railroads were owned and operated by the state. But this in itself did not politicize economic unrest. In fact, even before the revolution an important element of the state bureaucracy was already pressing for railroad labor reform and for improvements in the economic situation of many railwaymen. Although conditions were neither qualitatively nor uniformly worse on the private roads, private managers were vigorous and uncompromising opponents of concessions to strikers, thus frequently exacerbating tension on those lines. Many of the most militant hotbeds in 1905 were private railroads: the Moscow-Kazan, Vladikavkaz, Riazan-Ural, and South East Railroads.

Railroad strikers themselves did not make an issue of the distinction between government and private enterprise, however, and for good reason: there was no fundamental conflict of interest between the Ministry of Communications and private railroad entrepreneurs. For one thing, policies recommended by the private lines frequently won out over the reformist proposals of government bureaucrats. This was principally because reformist sentiment was both too weak and too limited in its challenge to the status quo. Systematizing officials were confronted by such extensive use of arbitrary authority that in the end they could not help but unite with the sentiment of private managers that repressive order was an essential prerequisite to any potentially disruptive restructuring of labor relations. The economic interests of railroad administrators—state and private—were at one with the political position of the government.

In fact, the distinction between "politics" and "economics" was by no means necessarily so great—or so critical—among workers either. More often than not the conflict between political and economic struggle was as much imagined as real. For workers the central question was not really "politics or economics?" but "*whose* politics?" The emerging radicalism of 1905 rested upon a firmament of spontaneous unrest, but only relatively small groups of activists—political, if not always occupational, "outsiders"—could give direction to the movement by articulating coherent political alternatives. Lenin was thus largely correct when he argued that political consciousness had to come from without.

Still, divisions among the workers that emerged in the course of the strike movement underlay political differences. It was not so much that the demands raised by different groups within the work force differed, but that political demands served professional organizing for some, whereas for others occupational concerns became secondary to political change itself. By December 1905 there were, essentially, two diverging movements of railwaymen, which cooperated with increasing difficulty. One movement, though continu-

ing to espouse political goals, did so in the context of liberal profes-
sionalism. It was based on the administrative hierarchy. In a sense
this movement looked backward to that period in Russian railroading when the railroad enterprise itself seemed to make of the railwaymen a special group. The other movement rejected the notion
of the "railroad family"; its socialist appeal was increasingly to an
emerging consciousness of class among those, especially blue-collar
shop craftsmen, who were coming to see themselves less as railwaymen than as members of the working class.

To be sure, the conflict was still almost inchoate and mediated by
scores of particularities, and it was defined only hazily by social
categories. But if the 1905 revolution seemed to polarize the broadest social coalition against the regime, at least among railroad workers, within that coalition the outlines of a second polarization—and
of a second, more radical, revolution—could already be discerned.

Bibliography of Sources Cited

I. Archives

Tsentral'nyi gosudarstvennyi arkhiv oktiabr'skoi revoliutsii (TsGAOR) [Central State Archive of the October Revolution, Moscow]
fond 518, Soiuz Soiuzov [Union of Unions]
  delo 35—Ob organizatsii i deiatel'nosti Vserossiskogo zheleznodoro-zhnogo soiuza [On the Organization and Activity of the All-Russian Railroad Union]
fond 6865, Kommissiia po istorii professional'nogo dvizheniia v Rossii. Istprof pri TsK Soiuza zheleznodorozhnikov (Istproftran) [Commission on the History of the Trade Union Movement in Russia. Section Under the Central Committee of the Union of Railwaymen]
  delo 23—Kopii dokumentov iz del arkhiva (fond Moskovskogo okhran-nogo otdeleniia) o stachechnoi dvizhenii zheleznodorozhnikov Mos-kovskikh zh. d., 1892–1894 gg. [Moscow Okhrana Documents on the Strike Movement of Moscow Railwaymen, 1892–94]
  delo 28a—Vypiski iz del (arkhiva byvshego Ministerstva putei soobsh-cheniia) s khronologicheskimi svedeniiami [Excerpts from the Ar-chive of the Ministry of Communications]
  delo 29a—Sbornik iz Istproftrana po rabochemu dvizheniiu na zh. d. do 1905 g. [Collection on the Labor Question on the Railroads Be-fore 1905]
  delo 30—Sbornik N. Biryshkova i drugikh po istorii VZhS s 1895 g. po 1923 g. (ne polnost'iu) [Collection of N. Biryshkov and Others on the History of the Railroad Union, 1895–1923]
  delo 31—Vospominaniia Gleshenko, Gorbunova i Lishevich o pod-pol'noi rabote sredi zheleznodorozhnikov Iugo-Zapadnykh zh. d. (1904–1909) [Memoirs of Gleshenko, Gorbunov, and Lishevich on Underground Work on the South West Railroad (1904–9)]

delo 34—Vospominaniia A. F. Gorovuvena ob usloviiakh truda i byta zheleznodorozhnikov (1880–1917 gg.) [Memoir of A. F. Gorovuven on Working and Living Conditions of Railwaymen, 1880–1917]

delo 35—Materialy po istorii revoliutsionno-professional'nogo dvizheniia na zh. d. Ukrainy 1900–07 gg. [Materials on the History of the Revolutionary Union Movement on the Ukrainian Railroads, 1900–1907]

delo 36b—Vospominaniia N. Leshava o professional'nom dvizhenii i revoliutsionnoi bor'be zheleznodorozhnogo proletariata Zakavkaz'ia v 1904–1917 gg. [Memoirs of N. Leshav on the Movement of the Railroad Proletariat of Transcaucasia]

delo 37—Vospominaniia M. I. Markelova i Lisovtsy o rabote v soiuznykh organizatsiiakh Ekaterininskoi zh. d. v 1904–17 gg. [Memoirs of Markelov and Lisovets on Work in Union Organizations on the Catherine Railroad, 1904–17]

delo 38a—Vospominaniia Mironova o rabochem dvizhenii na stantsii Tambov Riazano-Ural'skoi zh. d. [Memoir of Mironov on the Workers' Movement at Tambov Station, Riazan-Ural Railroad]

delo 39a—Vospominaniia I. T. Pliukhina [Memoir of I. T. Pliukhin]

delo 39b—Obzor D. Prokudina-Gorskogo po revoliutsionnomu dvizheniiu na Moskovsko-Kurskoi zh. d. c 1878 g. do 1906 g. [Survey of the Revolutionary Movement on the Moscow-Kursk Railroad, 1878–1906, by D. Prokudin-Gorskii]

delo 44—Vospominaniia P. S. Solomko o zhurnale "Zheleznodorozhnik" i drugikh zheleznodorozhnykh zhurnalakh c 1900 g. do 1914 g. [Memoir of P. S. Solomko on the Journal *Zheleznodorozhnik* and Other Railroad Journals, 1900–1914]

delo 45—Obzor G. Khudiaka professional'no-revoliutsionnogo dvizheniia na Iuzhnykh zh. d. c 1869 g. po 1904 g. [Survey of the Movement on the Southern Railroads, 1869–1904, by G. Khudiak]

delo 49—Istoricheskii ocherk o vozniknovenii zh. d. transporta v Rossii, rabochem dvizhenii na transporte i organizatsii profsoiuza zheleznodorozhnikov v 1836–1917 gg. [Historical Essay on the Beginnings of Railroad Transport in Russia, the Labor Movement in Transport, and the Organization of Unions of Railwaymen, 1836–1917]

delo 59—Doklad Tsentral'nogo Biuro VZhS III Vserossiiskomu s'ezdu o svoei deiatel'nosti c iiulia 1905 po dekabria 1906. [Report of the Central Bureau to the Railroad Union's Third Congress]

delo 63—Kopii dokumentov iz del arkhiva departmenta politsii (1905–07) [Documents from the Archive of the Department of Police]

delo 65—Untitled. Assorted documents on suppression of strikes after December 1905 from the archive of the Moscow Okhrana

dela 70, 71—Kopii dokumentov iz del Tsentrarkhiva SSR Gruzii (fond
b. kantseliarii zaveduiushego politsiei na Kavkaze) i Kubanskogo
okruzhnogo arkhivnogo biuro (fond b. Novocherkaskoi sudebnoi
palaty) o zabastovochnom i rabochem dvizhenii sredi zheleznodorozhnikov Vladikvkazskoi zh. d. v 1905–1906 g. [Documents from
Georgian Police Archive and Kuban Judicial Archive on Strike
Movement on Vladikavkaz Railroad, 1905–6]

delo 78a—Obvinitel'nye akty po dely rabochikh i sluzhashchikh Ekaterininskoi zh. d. uchastnikov v dekabr'skoi zabastovki 1905 g. [In-
dictments of December Strikers on Catherine Railroad]

delo 93—Untitled. Material on electoral meeting for pension congress
on Transcaucasian Railroad.

delo 96—Untitled. Newspaper clippings on the Kushka incident.

delo 99—Untitled. Newspaper clippings on strike demands.

dela 111, 112, 115, 118, 119—Untitled. Assorted newspaper clippings.

delo 120—Stenogramm vechera vospominanii uchastnikov sobytii
1905 goda [Stenographic Record of an Evening of Reminiscences by
Participants in the Events of 1905]

delo 122—Vospominaniia Akimova, Arkharova, Golubenkova i Ovodova
o revoliutsionnykh sobytiiakh na Nizhegorodskoi zh. d. v 1905 g.
[Memoirs of Akimov, Arkharov, Golubenkov, and Ovodov on the
Revolutionary Events on the Nizhegorod Railroad in 1905]

delo 127—Vospominaniia V. Borzina, Voznesenskogo, A. Gorbunova,
Evgen'eva, G. Krasil'nikova, Stepanova, D. Filitova, i Chernosvitova
o zabastovochnom i rabochem dvizhenii na Moskovsko-Kurskoi zh.
d. v 1905 g. [Memoirs on Strike and Workers Movement on the
Moscow-Kursk Railroad in 1905]

delo 128a—Vospominaniia G. Bykolovicha i V. Ia. Tatarinskogo o zabastovkakh rabochikh i sluzhashchikh Moskovsko-Kazanskoi zh. d. v
1905 g. [Memoirs of G. Bykolovich and V. Ia. Tatarinskii on Strikes
of Workers and Employees on the Moscow-Kazan Railroad]

delo 194—Kopii dokumentov iz del Gosarkhiva RSFSR (fond Moskovskogo okhrannogo otdeleniia) o VZhS, o rabochem i professional'nom dvizhenii, ob areste chlenov VZhS i po drugim voprosam
1906–1907 gg. [Documents from the Moscow Okhrana 1906–7]

delo 195—Untitled. Contains 1906 Railroad Union leaflets.

delo 197—Protocol IV–V s'ezda raionnykh deputatov Khar'kovo-
Nikolaevskoi zh. d., i doklady o deiatel'nosti ispolnitel'nogo komiteta
"Soiuza zh. d." [Protocols of the Fourth and Fifth Congresses of
District Deputies of the Kharkov-Nikolaev Railroad and Reports on
the Activity of the Executive Committee of the "Railroad Union"]

delo 198—Kopii dokumentov iz del arkhiva b. departmenta politsii za

1906 g. o zabastovochnoi dvizhenii na zh. d. [Documents from the Archive of the Department of Police for 1906 on the Railroad Strike Movement]

delo 199—Kopii dokumentov iz del arkhiva Moskovskogo gubernskogo zhandarmskogo upravleniia za 1906 g. o stachkakh i zabastovkakh na zh. d. [Documents from the Archive of the Moscow Guberniia Gendarme Administration for 1906 on Strikes]

Tsentral'nyi gosudarstvennyi istoricheskii arkhiv v Leningrade (TsGIA) [Central State Historical Archive, Leningrad]

fond 229, Ministerstvo putei soobshcheniia. Kantseliariia ministerstva [Ministry of Communications. Chancellery]

Opis' 2:

dela 1645, 1647, 1654, 1655—Po raznym voprosam [On Various Questions]

dela 1649, 1650, 1651, 1652—Po voprosam o zabastovkakh i bezporiadkakh, 1906 g. [On Strikes and Disorders, 1906]

Opis' 4:

delo 925—Po proektu Polozheniia o zheleznodorozhnykh sluzhashchikh [On the Proposed Charter for Railroad Employees]

fond 273, Ministerstvo putei soobshcheniia. Upravlenie zheleznykh dorog [Ministry of Communications. Administration of Railroads]

Opis' 8:

dela 126, 129, 132, 133, 138, 148–9, 155, 159, 160—Vrachebnosanitarnye otchety [Public Health Reports—each *delo* a different railroad line. In order: Catherine, Transcaucasian, Moscow-Kursk, Nicholas, Riga-Orel, South West, Vladikavkaz, and Moscow-Kazan Railroads]

delo 180—Ob uluchenii vrachebnoi chasti [On Improvement of the Public Health Section]

Opis' 12:

delo 45—Sekretnaia perepiska o zabastovkakh, 1899–1900 gg. [Secret Correspondence on Strikes, 1899–1900]

delo 46—Sekretnaia perepiska o zabastovkakh, 1903 g. [Secret Correspondence on Strikes, 1903]

delo 107—O normakh raboty i otdykha, 1900–1903 gg. [On Norms of Work and Rest, 1900–1903]

delo 226—Sekretnaia perepiska o zabastovkakh, 1902 g. [Secret Correspondence on Strikes, 1902]

delo 295—Po zaiavleniiu rabochikh tovarstantsii 'Vilno' S. Peterburg-Varshavskoi zh. d. i drugikh o tiazhelykh usloviiakh truda i byta [On the Complaint of Workers at the Vilno Freight Station of the St. Petersburg–Warsaw Railroad and Other Items on Difficult Working and Living Conditions]

dela 316, 322, 325, 328, 330, 332, 335, 343, 345, 347, 350, 364, 367, 371, 373, 375, 377—Sekretnaia perepiska o zabastovkakh, 1905 g. [Secret Correspondence on Strikes, 1905—each *delo* a different railroad line. In order: Nicholas, Transcaucasian, Riazan-Ural, Moscow-Kazan, Libau-Romny, Moscow-Kursk, Riga-Orel, Moscow-Brest, South West, Siberian, Catherine, Samara-Zlatoust, Trans-Baikal, Moscow-Iaroslavl-Archangel, Vladikavkaz, Kursk-Kharkov-Sevastopol, and South East Railroads]

dela 354, 354a, 355—Po obshchemu voprosu o zabastovkakh sluzhashchikh i rabochikh, 1905 g. [General Questions on Strikes of Employees and Workers, 1905]

delo 361—So Svedeniiami o vremennykh pravilakh dlia vybornykh ot rabochikh [Information on the Temporary Rules for Election of Delegates from the Workers]

delo 407—Po voprosu ob assignovanii kreditov na uluchenie byta sluzhashchikh i rabochikh [On Assigning Credits to Improving the Conditions of Employees and Workers]

delo 408—S proektom polozheniia o zh. d. sluzhashchikh [On the Proposed Charter for Railroad Employees]

delo 430—Po voprosu o rasprostranenii na masterovykh i rabochikh prav shtatnykh sluzhashchikh [On Assigning Rights of Staff Employees to Craftsmen]

dela 467, 468—Po primeneniiu k zheleznym dorogam trebovanii tsirkuliari Soveta Ministrov ot 14/IX/06 ob uchastii sluzhashchikh v soiuzakh, partiiakh i obschestvakh [On the Relevance to the Railroads of the Council of Ministers Circular of September 14, 1906 on Participation of Employees in Unions, Parties, and Societies]

fond 1162, Gosudarstvennyi sovet [State Council]
Opis' 6:

delo 188—O sluzhbe chlena gosudarstvennogo soveta Dumitrashko [On the State Service of Member of State Council Dumitrashko]

delo 357—O sluzhbe chlena gosudarstvennogo soveta Nemeshaeva [On the State Service of Member of State Council Nemeshaev]

delo 602—O sluzhbe chlena gosudarstvennogo soveta General'-leitenanta Shaufusa [On the State Service of Member of State Council Lieut.-Gen. Schaufus]

II. Government Publications

Abbreviations used in notes are given in brackets.

Ministerstvo putei soobshcheniia. Otdel statistiki. *Statisticheskii sbornik*, no. 89, St. Petersburg, 1907.

Ministerstvo putei soobshcheniia. Pensionnaia kassa. *Statistika sluzhash-*

chikh na kazennykh zheleznykh dorog uchastnikov pensionnoi kassy.
St. Petersburg, 1896–1903. [*Statistika*]
Ministerstvo putei soobshcheniia. Upravlenie zheleznykh dorog. "Ob izmenenii i dopolnenii Polozheniia o pensionnoi kasse sluzhashchikh na kazennykh zh. d.," no. 9302, 1902.
Ministerstvo putei soobshcheniia. Vrachebno-sanitarnaia chast'. *Otchety o vrachebno-sanitarnom sostoiianii eksploatiruemykh zheleznykh dorog za 1903–1907 gg.* St. Petersburg, 1905–9. [*Vrach-san otchet*]

III. Books, Articles, and Unpublished Works

Ainzaft, S. S. *Pervyi etap professional'nogo dvizheniia v Rossii. (1905– 1907 gg.).* Moscow, 1925.
Akademiia nauk SSSR. Institut istorii. *Revoliutsiia 1905–1907 gg. v Rossii. Dokumenty i materialy.* Moscow, 1955–61. Individual volumes cited and listed individually under editor.
Al'manakh sovremennykh Russkikh gosudarstvennykh deiatelei. St. Petersburg, 1897.
Amvrosii (pseud.). *Pravda o Rostovskikh sobytiiakh.* Stuttgart, 1903.
Anisimov, S. S. *Delo o vosstanii na Ekaterininskoe zh. d.* Moscow, 1926.
Antoshkin, D. *Ocherk dvizheniia sluzhashchikh v Rossii (so vtoroi poloviny XIX v.).* Moscow, 1921.
Anweiler, Oskar. *The Soviets.* New York, 1973.
Arkomed, S. T. *Rabochee dvizhenie i sotsial-demokratiia na Kavkaze (s 80-kh gg. po 1903 g.).* Moscow, 1923.
Belinskii, E. F. "Formirovanie zheleznodorozhnogo proletariata na Ukraine vo vtoroi polovine XIX v." Kandidat diss., Kiev, 1965.
Bonnell, Victoria E. *Roots of Rebellion: Workers' Politics and Organizations in St. Petersburg and Moscow, 1900–1914.* Berkeley and Los Angeles, 1983.
———, ed. *The Russian Worker: Life and Labor Under the Tsarist Regime.* Berkeley and Los Angeles, 1983.
Boshko, V. "Zheleznodorozhnyi soiuz i sotsialisticheskie partii v 1905–10 gg." *Zheleznodorozhnik,* 1927, no. 1: 52–59.
Caron, François. "Essai d'analyse historique d'une psychologie du travail: Les Mécaniciens et chauffers de locomotives du reseau du Nord de 1850 a 1910." *Le Mouvement social* 50 (January–March, 1965): 3–40.
Chaumel, Guy. *Histoire des cheminots et de leurs syndicats.* Paris, 1948.
Chernomordik, S. I., ed. *Piatyi god.* 2 vols. Moscow, 1925.
Cronin, James E., and Carmen Sirianni, eds. *Work, Community and Power.* Philadelphia, 1983.
Danilov, I. Kh., and P. G. Sdobnev, eds. *Zheleznodorozhniki v 1905 godu.* Moscow, 1940.

Demochkin, N. N. *Sovety 1905 goda—organy revoliutsionnoi vlasti.* Moscow, 1963.

Denkovskii, G. M., I. M. Raschetnova, and M. S. Semenova. "1905 god v Saratove." *Istoricheskie zapiski* 54 (1955): 74–104.

Dmitriev, V. "Byt sluzhashchikh i rabochikh na zheleznykh dorogakh." *Sovremennyi mir*, January 1912, no. 1: 281–302.

Donii, N. P. "Vooruzhennoe vosstanie na Ekaterinoslavshchine v dekabre 1905 godu." *Voprosy istorii*, 1955, no. 12: 19–32.

Dymkov, M. K., and D. Ia. Lipovetskii, eds. *1905 god na Kazanke. Sbornik.* Moscow, 1925.

El'nitskii, A. E. *Istoriia rabochego dvizheniia v Rossii.* Moscow, 1924.

Engelstein, Laura. *Moscow 1905: Working-Class Organization and Political Conflict.* Stanford, Calif., 1982.

Erman, L. K. *Intelligentsiia v pervoi Russkoi revoliutsii.* Moscow, 1966.

———. "Uchastie intelligentsii v oktiabr'skoi politicheskoi stachke." *Istoricheskie zapiski* 49 (1954): 352–90.

Fain, B. "Zheleznodorozhniki v revoliutsii 1905 goda." *Zheleznodorozhnik,* 1930, no. 6: 17.

Finkelshtein, L. M. "Liubotinskaia respublika." *Proletarskaia revoliutsiia*, 1925, no. 12 (47): 178–93.

Freeze, Gregory L. "The *Soslovie* (Estate) Paradigm and Russian Social History." *American Historical Review* 91 (1986): 11–36.

Frieden, Nancy. *Russian Physicians in an Era of Reform and Revolution, 1856–1905.* Princeton, N.J., 1981.

Garvi, P. A. *Vospominaniia sotsial demokrata.* New York, 1946.

Giddens, Anthony. *The Class Structure of the Advanced Societies.* New York, 1975.

Gindin, I. F. *Gosudarstvennyi bank i ekonomicheskaia politika tsarskogo pravitel'stva, 1861–1892.* Moscow, 1960.

Glickman, Rose L. *Russian Factory Women: Workplace and Society, 1880–1914.* Berkeley and Los Angeles, 1984.

Goncharov, K. V. *O venercheskikh bolezniakh v S. Peterburge.* St. Petersburg, 1910.

Gorchilin, A. *1905 god na Kazanke. Vospominaniia podpol'shchika.* Moscow, 1934.

Gudvan, A. M. *Ocherki po istorii dvizheniia sluzhashchikh v Rossii. Chast' 1: Do revoliutsii 1905 goda.* Moscow, 1925.

Guliev, A. N. "Stachka bakinskikh rabochikh v dekabre 1904 goda." *Voprosy istorii*, 1954, no. 12: 26–38.

Gurvich, S. "Rostovskoe vooruzhennoe vosstanie 1905 g." *Proletarskaia revoliutsiia*, 1925, no. 12 (47): 165–77.

Harding, Neil. *Lenin's Political Thought.* Vol. 1. London, 1977.

Haywood, Richard Mowbray. *The Beginnings of Railway Development in*

Russia in the Reign of Nicholas I, 1835–1842. Durham, N.C., 1969.

Hogan, Heather. "Industrial Rationalization and the Roots of Labor Militance in the St. Petersburg Metalworking Industry, 1901–1914." *Russian Review* 42, no. 2 (1983): 163–90.

———. "Labor and Management in Conflict: The St. Petersburg Metal Working Industry, 1900–1914." Ph.D. diss., University of Michigan, 1979.

Iakovlev, A. F. *Ekonomicheskie krizisy v Rossii.* Moscow, 1955.

Iakovlev, N. N. *Vooruzhennye vosstaniia v dekabre 1905 g.* Moscow, 1957.

Iaroslavskii, E. M. *Vooruzhennoe vosstanie: dekabr'skoe vosstanie.* Vol. 3, pt. 2 of Pokrovskii, *1905,* listed below.

Ionova, G. I. "Rabochee dvizhenie v Rossii v period revoliutsionnoi situatsii, 1859–1861 gg." In *Iz istorii rabochego klassa i revoliutsionnogo dvizheniia,* edited by M. V. Nechkina et al. Moscow, 1958.

Ivanov, L. M., et al., eds. *Rossiiskii proletariat: oblik, bor'ba, gegemoniia.* Moscow, 1970.

Ivanov, L. M., ed. *Vserossiiskaia politicheskaia stachka v oktiabre 1905 goda.* 2 vols. Moscow and Leningrad, 1955–57.

Johnson, Robert Eugene. *Peasant and Proletarian: The Working Class of Moscow in the Late Nineteenth Century.* New Brunswick, N.J., 1979.

"K istorii 'Krovavogo Voskresenia' v Peterburge." *Krasnyi arkhiv* 68 (1935): 39–64.

Kats A., and Iu. Milonov, eds. *1905: professional'noe dvizhenie.* Moscow and Leningrad, 1926.

Keenan, E. L. "Remarques sur l'histoire du mouvement révolutionnaire à Bakou (1904–1905)." *Cahiers du monde Russe et sovietique* 3, no. 2 (1962): 225–60.

Khoshtaria, E. V. *Ocherki sotsial'no-ekonomicheskoi istorii Gruzii: Promyshlennost', goroda, rabochii klass, XIX–nachalo XX v..* Tbilisi, 1974.

Kingsford, Peter. *Victorian Railwaymen: The Emergence and Growth of Railway Labor, 1830–1870.* London, 1970.

Kir'ianov, Iu. I. *Zhiznennyi uroven' rabochikh Rossii (konets XIX–nachalo XX v.).* Moscow, 1979.

Kislinskii, N. A. *Nasha zheleznodorozhnaia politika po dokumentam arkhiva komiteta ministrov.* St. Petersburg, 1902.

Kocka, Jürgen. *White-Collar Workers in America, 1890–1940.* Translated by Maura Kealey. London and Beverly Hills, Calif., 1980.

Koenker, Diane. "Collective Action and Collective Violence in The Russian Labor Movement." *Slavic Review* 41, no. 3 (1982): 443–48.

———. *Moscow Workers and the 1917 Revolution.* Princeton, N.J., 1981.

Kokhmanskii, P. V., ed. *Moskva v dekabre 1905 g.* Moscow, 1906.

Kolokolnikov, P., and S. Rapoport, eds. *1905–1907 gg. v professional'nom dvizhenii: I i II Vserossiiskie konferentsii professional'nykh soiuzov.* Moscow, 1925.

Korablev, Iu. O., et al. *Revoliutsiia 1905–1907 gg. v Rossii.* Moscow, 1975.

Kostomarov, G. D., ed. *1905 v Moskve.* Moscow, 1955.

Kramarov, G. "Dekabr'skoe vosstanie v Rostove-na-Donu 1905 g." *Proletarskaia revoliutsiia,* 1923, no. 2 (14): 310–25.

Kramer, S., ed. *1905 god v Kharkove.* Kharkov, 1925.

Krugliakov, B. "Professional'noe dvizhenie zheleznodorozhnikov v 1905–1907 gg." *Krasnaia letopis'* 18 (1926): 76–103.

———. "Zabastovki sredi zheleznodorozhnikov v nachale 1905 godu v Peterburge." *Krasnaia letopis'* 12 (1925): 57–66.

Kruze, E. E. *Polozhenie rabochego klassa Rossii v 1900–1914 gg.* Leningrad, 1976.

Lediaeva, S. D. *Istoriia zheleznodorozhnoi leksiki v Russkom iazyke XIX veka.* Kishinev, 1973.

Lenin, V. I. *Collected Works,* 45 vols. Moscow, 1961–66.

Lewis, Richard Donald. "The Labor Movement in Russian Poland in the Revolution of 1905–1907." Ph.D. diss., University of California, Berkeley, 1971.

Liadov, M. N. *Iz zhizni partii v 1905–1907 gg.* Moscow, 1956.

Liashchenko, Petr. *History of the National Economy of Russia.* New York, 1949.

———. *Istoriia narodnogo khoziastva Rossii.* Vol. 2. Leningrad, 1948.

Licht, Walter. *Working for the Railroad: The Organization of Work in the Nineteenth Century.* Princeton, N.J., 1983.

Lincoln, W. Bruce. *In War's Dark Shadow.* New York, 1983.

Listovki Moskovskikh bol'shevikov v period pervoi Russkoi revoliutsii. Moscow, 1955.

Lopukhin, A. "Zapiska direktora departmenta politsii Lopukhina o stachkakh v iule 1903 g. v Odesse, Kieve, i Nikolaeve." *Krasnaia letopis'* 4 (1922): 382–95.

Los', F. E., ed. *Revoliutsiia 1905–1907 gg. na Ukraine.* Kiev, 1955.

M. B. [M. Bogdanov]. *Ocherki po istorii zheleznodorozhnykh zabastovok v Rossii.* Moscow, 1906.

McKay, John P. *Pioneers for Profit.* Chicago, 1970.

McKenna, Frank. "Victorian Railway Workers." *History Workshop Journal* 1 (1976): 26–73.

Maevskii, E. "Obshchaia kartina dvizheniia." In *Obshchestvennoe dvizhenie v Rossii v nachale XX veka,* edited by Iu. Martov et al. St. Petersburg, 1909–14.

Maglakelidze, S., and A. Iovidze, eds. *Revoliutsiia 1905–1907 gg. v Gruzii. Sbornik dokumentov*. Tbilisi, 1956.

Maiskie dni v Kharkove. Geneva, 1901.

Malinin, D. A. "Saratovskie zheleznodorozhniki v revoliutsii 1905–1907 gg." *Uchenye zapiski Saratovskogo universiteta* 55 (1956): 124–54.

Manning, Roberta Thompson. *The Crisis of the Old Order in Russia: Gentry and Government*. Princeton, N.J., 1982.

Martov, Iu., et al., eds. *Obshchestvennye dvizheniia v Rossii v nachale XX-go veka*. St. Petersburg, 1909.

Maruta, Ivan. *Ocherki po istorii revoliutsionnogo professional'nogo dvizheniia na Moskovsko-kievo-voronezhskoi zh. d. Vypusk pervyi. 1905 g*. Kursk, 1925.

Masliev, I. "Krasnodarskie zheleznodorozhniki v 1905 godu." *Proletarskaia revoliutsiia*, 1926, no. 6 (53): 159–80.

Materialy po professional'nomu dvizheniiu rabochikh. Vol. 1. St. Petersburg, 1906.

Metel'kov, P. F. *Zheleznodorozhniki v revoliutsii. Fevral' 1917–iiun' 1918 g*. Leningrad, 1970.

Mil'man, E. M. "Formirovanie kadrov zheleznodorozhnogo proletariata Urala vo vtoroi polovine XIX veka." *Iz istorii rabochego klassa Urala. Sbornik statei*. Perm, 1961.

Mints, L. E. "Statistika chislennosti i sostava rabochei sily na zheleznodorozhnom transporte v Rossii." Akademiia nauk SSSR. *Ocherki po istorii statistiki SSSR (Sbornik tretii)*. Moscow, 1960.

Mitskevich, S. I. *Revoliutsionnaia Moskva*. Moscow, 1940.

Montgomery, David. *Workers' Control in America*. New York, 1979.

Moskovskoe dekabr'skoe vooruzhennoe vosstanie 1905 g. Sbornik materialov, vospominanii i dokumentov. Moscow, 1940.

Moskovskoe vooruzhennoe vosstanie po dannym obvinitel'nykh aktov i sudebnykh protokolov. Vol. 1. Moscow, 1906.

Nevskii, V. I. "Dekabr'skaia zabastovka 1904 g. v Baku." *Proletarskaia revoliutsiia*, 1924, no. 2 (25): 46–84.

———. "Ianvarskie dni 1905 g. na Kavkaze." *Proletarskaia revoliutsiia*, 1924, no. 4 (28): 40–53.

———. "Ianvarskie dni 1905 g. v Moskve." *Krasnaia letopis'* 2–3 (1922): 7–26.

———. "Ianvarskie dni 1905 g. v provintsii." *Krasnaia letopis'* 4 (1922): 52–132.

———. *Rabochee dvizhenie v ianvarskie dni 1905 goda*. Moscow, 1930.

1905 god na Moskovsko-Kurskoi-Nizhegorodskoi i Muromskoi zh. d.. Moscow, 1931.

1905 god na Iugo-Vostochnykh zheleznykh dorogakh. Moscow, 1925.

1905 god vo vospominaniiakh ego uchastnikov. Rostov-on-Don, 1925.

1905–1907 gody na Donu. Sbornik dokumentov. Rostov-on-Don, 1955.

Nosar', Georgii S. "Istoriia soveta rabochikh deputatov." *Istoriia soveta rabochikh deputatov S. Peterburga.* St. Petersburg, 1906.

Obshcheprofessional'nye organy 1905–1907 gg. Vypusk 1: Moskovskie zhurnaly 1905 goda "Biulleten' Muzeia sodeistviia trudu" i "Materialy po professional'nomu dvizheniiu rabochikh". Moscow, 1926.

Olkhovaia, L. V. "Rabochaia kooperatsiia kak forma organizatsii proletariata." In *Rossiisskii proletariat: oblik, bor'ba, gegemoniia,* edited by L. M. Ivanov. Moscow, 1970.

Paulish, A. "Zabastavochnoe dvizhenie na Rigo-Orlovskoi zh. d." *Proletarskaia revoliutsiia* 1925, no. 11 (46): 152–73.

Pazhitnov, K. A. *Polozhenie rabochego klassa v Rossii.* St. Petersburg, 1906.

Perepis' Moskvy 1902 goda. Chast' 1: Naselenie. Vyp. 2. Moscow, 1906.

Pereverzev, V. N. "Pervyi vserossiiskii zheleznodorozhnyi soiuz 1905 goda." *Byloe,* 1925, no. 4 (32): 36–69.

Pervaia Russkaia revoliutsiia: ukazatel' literatury. Moscow, 1930.

Pervoe maia v tsarskoi Rossii, 1890–1916 gg. Sbornik dokumentov. Moscow, 1939.

Piaskovskii, A. V. *Revoliutsiia 1905–1907 gg. v Rossii.* Moscow, 1966.

Pokrovskii, M. N., ed. *1905: Istoriia revoliutsionnogo dvizheniia v otdel'nykh ocherkakh.* 3 vols. Moscow, 1925–27.

———. *Russkaia istoriia v samom szhatom ocherke* in *Izbrannye proizvedeniia.* Vol. 3. Moscow, 1962.

Portal, Roger. "The Industrialization of Russia." In *The Cambridge Economic History of Europe.* Vol. 6, pt. 2. Cambridge, 1966.

Posse, V. A. *Vseobshchye stachki.* Geneva, 1903.

Protokoly zasedaniia 4-go soveshchaniia s'ezda zheleznodorozhnykh vrachei. St. Petersburg, 1909.

Pushkareva, I. M. "Zarabotnaia plata zheleznodorozhnikov nakanune revoliutsii 1905–1907 gg." *Istoriia SSSR,* 1957, no. 3: 159–73.

———. "Zheleznodorozhniki Rossii—uchastniki oktiabr'skoi politicheskoi stachki." *Voprosy istorii,* 1958, no. 12: 152–69.

———. *Zheleznodorozhniki Rossii v burzhuazno-demokraticheskikh revoliutsiiakh.* Moscow, 1975.

Rabochee dvizhenie v Ekaterinoslave. Geneva, 1900.

Rabochee dvizhenie v Kharkove. Geneva, 1900.

Rabochee dvizhenie v Rossii v 1901–1904 gg. Sbornik dokumentov. Leningrad, 1975.

Rabochee dvizhenie v Rossii v XIX veke. Sbornik dokumentov i materialov. 4 vols. Moscow and Leningrad, 1950–63.

Rashin, A. G. *Formirovanie rabochego klassa v Rossii.* Moscow, 1958.

Reichman, Henry. "The Rostov General Strike of 1902." *Russian History* 9, pt. 1 (1982): 67–85.

———. "Russian Railwaymen and the Revolution of 1905." Ph.D. diss., University of California, Berkeley, 1977.

———. "Tsarist Labor Policy and the Railroads, 1885–1914." *Russian Review* 42, no. 1 (1983): 51–72.

Rikhter, I. I. *Lichnyi sostav Russkikh zheleznykh dorog.* St. Petersburg, 1900.

Robbins, Richard G., Jr. *Famine in Russia, 1891–1892.* New York, 1975.

Rogger, Hans. "*Amerikanizm* and the Economic Development of Russia." *Comparative Studies in Society and History* 23, no. 3 (1981): 382–420.

Romanov, V. "Dvizhenie sredi sluzhashchikh i rabochikh Russkikh zh. d. v 1905 g." *Obrazovanie,* 1906, no. 10: 25–64; no. 11a: 17–47; 1907, no. 6a: 24–53; no. 7: 64–88.

Rosenberg, William G. "The Democratization of Russia's Railroads in 1917." *American Historical Review* 86 (December 1981): 983–1008.

Rostov, N. *Prolog pervoi revoliutsii. Zheleznodorozhniki i pervaia vseobshchaia zabastovka v 1903 godu.* Moscow, 1928.

———. *Zheleznodorozhniki v revoliutsionnom dvizhenii 1905 g.* Moscow and Leningrad, 1926.

———. "Zheleznodorozhniki v pervoi revoliutsii." *Proletariat v revoliutsii 1905–1907 gg.* Moscow, 1930.

Sablinsky, Walter. "The All-Russian Railroad Union and the Beginning of the General Strike in October, 1905." In *Revolution and Politics in Russia,* edited by Alexander and Janet Rabinowitch, with Ladis K. D. Kristof. Bloomington, Ind., 1972.

———. *The Road to Bloody Sunday.* Princeton, N.J., 1976.

Sankt-Peterburg po perepisi 15 dekabria 1900 g. Vyp. 2. St. Petersburg, 1903.

Schivelbusch, Wolfgang. *The Railway Journey: Trains and Travel in the 19th Century.* Translated by Anselm Hollo. New York, 1979.

Schneiderman, Jeremiah. *Sergei Zubatov and Revolutionary Marxism: The Struggle for the Working Class in Tsarist Russia.* Ithaca, N.Y., 1976.

Schwarz, Solomon M. *The Russian Revolution of 1905: The Workers' Movement and the Formation of Bolshevism and Menshevism.* Chicago, 1967.

Semanov, S. N. *Peterburgskie rabochie nakanune pervoi Russkoi revoliutsii.* Moscow and Leningrad, 1966.

Semenov, M. I. "1905 god v Saratovskoi gubernii." *Proletarskaia revoliutsiia,* 1926, no. 3 (50): 197–217.

Shestakov, A. V. "Zheleznodorozhniki Moskovskogo uzla v revoliutsii

1905 g." *Partiinyi rabotnik zheleznodorozhnogo transporta*, 1940, no. 3–4: 277.

Shigabudinov, M. Sh. *Bor'ba rabochikh severnogo kavkaza nakanune i v period revoliutsii 1905–1907 gg.* Makhachkala, 1964.

Shuster, U. A. *Peterburgskie rabochie v 1905–1907 gg.* Leningrad, 1976.

Sidorov, A. L., ed. *Vysshii pod'em revoliutsii 1905–1907 gg. Vooruzhennye vosstaniia, noiabr'-dekabr' 1905 god.* 4 vols. Moscow and Leningrad, 1955–57.

Slavkin, I. A. "Vooruzhennoe vosstanie na Ekaterinoslavskoi zh. d. (dekabr' 1905)." *Proletarskaia revoliutsiia*, 1925, no. 10 (45): 11–58.

Sokolov, I. S. *1905 god na Riazansko-Ural'skoi zheleznoi doroge.* Saratov, 1925.

Solov'eva, A. M. *Zheleznodorozhnyi transport Rossii vo vtoroi polovine XIX v.* Moscow, 1975.

Spiridonov, I. V. *Vserossiiskaia politicheskaia stachka v oktiabre 1905 g.* Moscow, 1955.

"Stachka rabochikh zheleznodorozhnykh masterskikh v Tiflise (1900 g.)." *Krasnyi arkhiv* 94 (1939): 32–63.

"Stachka zheleznodorozhnykh rabochikh v g. Rostove-na-D. v 1894 g. (rasskaz rabochego-ochevidtsa)." *Byloe* 18 (1921): 124–27.

Stanchinskii, A. "Rostovskaia stachka v 1902 godu." *Proletarskaia revoliutsiia*, 1927, no. 12 (71): 141–70.

Stein, Margot B. "The Meaning of Skill: The Case of the French Engine-Drivers, 1837–1917." *Politics and Society* 8 (1978): 399–427.

Stromquist, Shelton. "Enginemen and Shopmen: Technological Change and the Organization of Labor in an Era of Railroad Expansion." *Labor History* 24 (1983): 485–99.

Strumilin, S. G. "Zheleznodorozhnyi transport," *Izbrannye proizvedeniia.* Vol. 1. Moscow, 1964.

Surh, Gerald Dennis. "Petersburg Workers in 1905: Strikes, Workplace Democracy, and the Revolution." Ph.D. diss., University of California, Berkeley, 1979.

―――. "Petersburg's First Mass Labor Organization: The Assembly of Russian Workers and Father Gapon," *Russian Review*, part 1, 40, no. 3 (1981): 241–62; part 2, 40, no. 4 (1981): 412–41.

Sushkin, N. "Oktiabr', noiabr', i dekabr' 1905 g. na Riazansko-Ural'skoi zh. d. (Vospominaniia)." *Katorga i ssylka*, 1930, no. 12: 145–59.

"Svedeniia o volneniiakh rabochikh proiskhodivshikh v iule i avguste 1903 goda." *Krasnyi arkhiv* 88 (1938): 76–122.

Titok, V. A. "Formirovanie i revoliutsionnaia bor'ba zheleznodorozhnogo proletariata Belorussii vo vtoroi polovine XIX v. nachale XX veka." Kandidat diss., Minsk, 1966.

Tokarev, S. "Volneniia rabochikh na postroikakh zheleznykh dorog v 1859–1860 godakh." *Voprosy istorii*, 1949, no. 1: 88–92.

Tregubov, S. L. *Opyt izucheniia v sanitarnom otnoshenii byta zheleznodo-rozhnykh sluzhashchikh v predelakh Kursko-Kharkovo-Sevastopol'-skogo zh. d.* Kharkov, 1904.

Trotsky, Leon. *1905*. Translated by Anya Bostock. New York, 1972.

Trusova, N. S., ed. *Nachalo pervoi revoliutsii, ianvar'–mart, 1905 god*. Moscow, 1955.

Trusova, N. S., ed. *Revoliutsionnoe dvizhenie v Rossii vesnoi i letom 1905 goda, aprel'–sentiabr'*. 2 vols. Moscow, 1955–57.

Tugan-Baranovsky, M. I. *The Russian Factory in the Nineteenth Century*. Translated by Arthur Levin and Claora S. Levin, under the supervision of Gregory Grossman. Homewood, Ill., 1970.

Tutaev, David, ed. *The Alliluyev Memoirs*. London, 1968.

Ushakov, A. V. *Revoliutsionnoe dvizhenie demokraticheskoi intelligentsii v Rossii 1895–1904*. Moscow, 1976.

Vasiliev, G. A. *Iz revoliutsionnogo proshlogo*. Ulan-Ude, 1968.

Vasiliev-Iuzhin, M. I. *Moskovskii sovet rabochikh deputatov v 1905 g.* Moscow, 1925.

Vladimirov, V. *Karatel'naia ekspeditsiia*. Moscow, 1906.

Volin, M. S., et al., eds. *Rabochii klass Rossii ot zarozhdeniia do nachala XX v.* Moscow, 1983.

Volkovicher, I. "Pervomaiskii prazdnik v 1905 g." *Proletarskaia revoliut-siia*, 1925, no. 3 (38): 82–117.

Von Laue, Theodore H. "Factory Inspection Under the 'Witte System': 1892–1903." *American Slavic and East European Review* 19 (1960): 347–62.

———. "Russian Labor Between Field and Factory, 1892–1903." *California Slavic Studies*, no. 3 (1964): 33–66.

———. "Russian Peasants in the Factory, 1892–1904." *Journal of Economic History* 21 (1961): 61–80.

———. *Sergei Witte and the Industrialization of Russia*. New York, 1963.

———. "Tsarist Labor Policy, 1895–1903." *Journal of Modern History* 34 (1962): 135–45.

Von Raaben, B. A. *Sbornik pravitel'stvennykh rasporiazhenii otnosia-shchikh do sluzhby podvizhnogo sostava i tiagi zh. d. so vremeni obra-zovaniia Ministerstva putei soobshcheniia po 1-omu ianvaria 1914 goda*. Petrograd, 1915.

Vorovskii, V. V. *Izbrannye proizvedeniia o pervoi Russkoi revoliutsii*. Moscow, 1955.

"Vospominaniia uchastnikov pervoi Russkoi revoliutsii." *Voprosy istorii*, 1955, no. 12: 33–44.

Vseobshchaia stachka na iuge Rossii v 1903 godu. Sbornik dokumentov. Moscow, 1938.

Vtoroi period revoliutsii: 1906–1907 gg. 4 vols. Moscow, 1957.

Westwood, J. N. *A History of Russian Railways.* London, 1964.

Wildman, Allan. *The Making of a Workers' Revolution.* Chicago, 1967.

Witte, Sergei I. *Vospominaniia.* 3 vols. Moscow, 1960.

Yaney, George L. *The Systematization of Russian Government: Social Evolution in the Domestic Administration of Imperial Russia, 1711–1905.* Urbana, Ill., 1973.

"Zabastovka v Kharkove na Mae 1, 1900 g." *Krasnyi arkhiv* 93 (1939): 189–207.

Zaionchkovskii, P. A. *Samoderzhavie i Russkaia armiia na rubezhe XIX–XX stoletii, 1881–1903.* Moscow, 1973.

Zheleznodorozhniki i revoliutsiia. Moscow and Leningrad, 1925.

Zheleznodorozhniki v 1905 g. (ocherki iz istorii soiuza). Moscow, 1922.

Zola, Emile. *La Bête humaine.* Translated by Leonard Tancock. New York, 1977.

IV. Periodicals

Birzhevye vedomosti (Bir. ved.)
Golos zhizni
Iskra
Krasnaia letopis'
Krasnyi arkhiv
London Times
Nachalo
Nasha zhizn'
Novaia zhizn'
Novoe vremia
Novyi luch
Osvobozhdenie
Pravo
Privolzhskii krai (Privol. kr.)
Proletarii
Revoliutsionnaia Rossiia
Russkie vedomosti
Russkoe slovo
Soiuz potrebiteli
Vecherniaia pochta (Vech. poch.)
Vestnik ministerstva putei soobshcheniia (VMPS)
Volna

Vpered
Zheleznodorozhnaia nedelia (ZhN)
Zheleznodorozhnik (Zhel.)
Zheleznodorozhnoe delo (ZhD)
Zheleznodorozhnyi soiuz

Index

Accidents, 35–36; casualties in, 95; and hours of work, 29, 92, 94

Accountants. *See* Employees

Administration of Railroads, 93, 208, 228; organization of, 24; on strikes in 1899–1903, 127. *See also* Ministry of Communications

Administrative Department, 48, 87

Age distribution of railroad labor, 57–58

All-Russian Union of Railroad Employees and Workers, 9, 159–68, 175–81; after 1905, 294–99; Central Bureau of, 160–61, 167–68; congresses of, 165–68, 178–80, 296; and "days of freedom," 240–41; and December general strike, 265–69, 288, 289; and Kushka incident, 263; local sections of, 176–77, 244, 246, 247, 276, 279; and October general strike, 194–205, 214–18, 221–22; origins of, 151, 163–64; and pension congress, 189; and Poland, 178–81; and postal-telegraph strike, 261–62; program of, 164–67; repression of, 265, 293; and Social Democrats, 164, 168, 169–74, 175, 178–81, 241–43, 244–45, 297–99; Soviet historians on, 160, 162; split in, 181, 253; and strike committees, 238. *See also* Central Bureau; *under individual railroads*

Alliluyev, Sergei, 89, 90

Amerikanizm, 62

Amnesty, demand for, 221

Anarchists, 245

Andreev, P., 71–72, 93

Arkhangelskii, A. M., 191, 192, 216, 293

Artels, 61, 69

Assembly of Russian Factory Workers, 135, 136

Authority, abuses of, 32–33

Bakliukov, Nikanor N., 250–51

Baku, general strikes in, 132, 134. *See also* Transcaucasian Railroad

Baltic Railroad, 42, 86, 244, 253; strikes on, 136, 208, 222–23, 260, 275

Baranov Commission, 22, 29, 39, 99

Bednov, I. I.: on Central Bureau, 167; and December general strike, 273; and October general strike, 198, 201, 203; on Social Democrats and the Railroad Union, 174, 242

Belev, December strike in, 279, 287. *See also* Catherine Railroad

Belorussia, recruitment of railroad labor in, 44. *See also* Libau-Romny Railroad; Riga-Orel Railroad

Black Hundreds, 225, 245, 248

Bloch, Jan, 21

Bloody Sunday, 1, 135

Bogdanov, M. I., 167, 201

Bolsheviks, 4, 9; and December general strike, 264, 267–68; and October general strike, 196–205, 208; in Saratov, 141, 172; and trade unions, 169–74, 178–81, 239. *See also* Lenin, V. I.; Social Democrats

Bonnell, Victoria E., 2n, 10n, 209, 232

Bonus payments and subsidies, 82–85

Borisov, M., 172–73

Brakemen, 67

Bulygin Duma, 186, 196

Bunge, N. K., 22, 227

Bureaucracy, 23

Capital investment in railroading, 19
Catherine Railroad, 18; and December
    general strike, 281–83, 286, 287; and
    Duma elections, 299; and October gen-
    eral strike, 211; between October and
    December strikes, 225, 230, 233, 235,
    239, 247, 260; repression on, 292, 302;
    strikes on, 123, 137, 147, 183; wages,
    hours, and conditions on, 80, 83, 94,
    104
Catholics in railroading, 44
Central Asian Railroad, 215, 262–63
Central Bureau (Railroad Union): charac-
    ter and selection of, 161, 167–68; and
    December general strike, 265, 269,
    287; and Kushka incident, 263; and
    Moscow strike committee, 207; and
    October general strike, 162, 195–203,
    214–18, 221; opens public office, 240;
    and pension congress, 189; and postal-
    telegraph strike, 261–62; and Social
    Democrats, 241–43. *See also* All-
    Russian Union of Railroad Employees
    and Workers; Pereverzev, V. N.
Charter. *See* General Charter of 1885;
    Labor charter
Class consciousness, 2, 7–8, 256–57,
    286–87, 307
Class struggle, appeal of, 232
Clerks. *See* Employees
Conditions of work. *See* Hours and work-
    ing conditions
Conductors, 29, 48, 67–68, 82, 92–93
Conference of Delegates from Twenty-
    nine Railroads, 267–69, 279, 281, 288,
    289
Consumer cooperatives, 30, 104–5, 251
Council for Railroad Affairs, 24
Council of Ministers, 227
Council of Representatives of Five Pro-
    fessions, 197
Couplers, 48
Courteous treatment, demand for, 33
Craftsmen (*masterovye*), 58–64; and De-
    cember general strike, 284–86; and
    employees, 307–8; and pension con-
    gress, 191; and Railroad Union after
    1905, 297; and Social Democrats, 238;
    and strike committees, 234; wages of,
    78–82. *See also* Workshops and depots
Crimean War, 19

Daily workers, 50
"Days of freedom," 229–32, 240–41
December general strike: features of,
    269–71, 284–90; in Moscow, 271–75,

277; origins of, 259–69; on provincial
    railroads, 277–84; in St. Petersburg,
    275–77. *See also under individual
    railroads*
Delegate assemblies, 243–48
Delegate trains, 235–37
Demands: for courteous treatment, 33;
    economic, 4–5; in January-February
    1905, 139, 143–44, 153–54; of October
    general strike, 201, 216–19; political,
    3, 3n, 4; of strikes before 1905, 127
Department of Engines and Rolling Stock,
    48, 79, 87
Department of Track Maintenance and
    Construction, 49, 82, 87
Department of Traffic Management, 48, 87
Diet of railroad workers, 104–6
Doctors: on dangers of railroad labor, 94–
    95; experience and dedication of, 102;
    number in public health section, 100.
    See also Public health section
Drinking among railroad workers, 114
Dubasov, F. V., 271, 272, 276
Duma, second, 299
Dumitrashko, Petr N., 39, 146, 187, 192,
    227, 302
Durnovo, P. N., 264, 288, 303

Education of railroad workers, 115–16
Ekaterinoslav, 18, 133, 211, 234, 281–82.
    See also Catherine Railroad
Elders. See *Starosty, vybornye*
Elizarov, Mark, 192, 244, 293
Employees (*sluzhashchie*), 51–58; and
    craftsmen, 307–8; in January-February
    1905, 151; and October and December
    general strikes, 234, 284–86; and Rail-
    road Union after 1905, 297; social ori-
    gins of, 45; wages, hours, and condi-
    tions of, 77, 89, 108
Engelstein, Laura, 160n, 206, 242n
Engine-drivers, 15, 48, 65–67, 308; and
    December general strike, 286–87; and
    October general strike, 234; social ori-
    gins of, 44, 45; on Vladikavkaz Rail-
    road, 249–51; wages and hours of, 29,
    75–77, 84, 93–94
Engineers, 21
England. *See* Great Britain

Factory inspectors, 27
Families of railroad workers, 109–10
Famine of 1891–92, 23, 99
Fighting detachments, 273–74
Fines, 83–84
First All-Russian Delegate Congress of

Railroad Employees. *See* Pension congress
Foreign investment in railroading, 20
Foreign labor in railroading, 20–21
Foremen, hostility to, 124
France, railroading in, 6n, 26n, 65n–66n

Gapon, Father Georgii, 135
Gendarmes. *See* Police, railroad
General Charter of 1885, 28
Germany, railroading in, 36
Giddens, Anthony, 4n
Gorchilin, Aleksandr (Grenadier), 199, 200, 203, 204, 221–22, 273
Government policy. *See* Labor policy
Greasemen, 48
Great Britain, railroading in, 5n, 26n, 31n, 83n

Harding, Neil, 170n
Health of railroad labor, 103–4. *See also* Doctors; Public health section
Historians, Soviet, 44, 45, 160, 162, 202, 288
Hogan, Heather, 62n
Holidays, 90–91
Hospitals, number in public health section, 100
Hours and working conditions, 89–96; of clerks, 89; of conductors, 92–93; of engine-drivers, 93–95; legal limits on, 29; of stationmasters, 57; of switchmen, 92; of telegraph operators, 89–90; in workshops and depots, 90–91, 96. *See also under individual railroads*
Housing, 106–9; of repair crews, 69; subsidies for, 82–83

Iastrzhembskii, S. N., 39
Imperial Russian Technical Society, 102, 163
Inflation, 85–87
Iskra, 169, 179
Ivanov, F. M., 128–29
Ivanovo-Voznesensk, June strike in, 182

Jewish Bund, Railroad Union and, 178
Jews, 43, 127, 225, 245, 304
Johnson, Robert Eugene, 2n, 10n, 44, 109

Kalanchevskaia Square, 17, 200, 274–75
Kazantsev, Petr Nikolaevich, 142, 152, 176
Kharkov, 18; December general strike in, 283; June strike in, 183; May Day 1900

in, 129; November general strike in, 262; October general strike in, 210–11, 234; Social Democratic union in, 165. *See also* Kursk-Kharkov-Sevastopol Railroad; Kharkov-Nikolaev Railroad
Kharkov-Nikolaev Railroad, 37; after 1905, 294, 295; and December general strike, 283, 290; delegate assembly on, 245; delegate train on, 236n; and October general strike, 210–11, 237; and pension congress, 190, 193, 194; piece rates on, 81; post-October mood on, 231
Khilkov, Prince Mikhail I.: biography of, 39; in January-March 1905, 146, 149, 157, 158; and November 4, 1902, meeting, 131; and October general strike, 201, 216; and pension congress, 187; resigns, 227
Kiev, 18, 59; housing in, 108–9; inflation in, 87; 1903 general strike in, 132; November general strike in, 262; October general strike in, 212. *See also* Moscow-Kiev-Voronezh Railroad; South West Railroad
Kir'ianov, Iu. I., 2n
Kocka, Jurgen, 54n
Koenker, Diane, 10n
Konotop, 61, 133, 212, 235, 254. *See also* Moscow-Kiev-Voronezh Railroad
Kotliarenko, D. M., 200, 204, 240, 242, 273
Krasin, G. B., 167, 168
Krasnoiarsk, 18
Kuropatkin, General A. I., 131
Kursk-Kharkov-Sevastopol Railroad, 18; conditions on, 36, 69n, 91, 105–6, 114, 117; and December general strike, 283, 284–85; delegate assembly on, 245; delegate train on, 235; after 1905, 296; and October general strike, 210–11, 225; and pension congress, 190; repression on, 292; strikes on, 126n, 129–30, 145, 183; wages and hours on, 80, 84, 93
Kushka incident, 262–63, 265
Kuznetsov, Mark, 287

Labor charter, 39, 227, 301–2
Labor legislation, 27
Labor policy, 26–31, 34, 39, 227, 300–304
Labor turnover, 36–37, 44
Leisure of railroad workers, 114
Lenin, V. I., 1, 3, 130, 310; on trade unionism, 170–73
Liadov, M. N., 268

Liakhin, A., 128–29
Liakhovskii, Dr. Ia., 193
Libau-Romny Railroad, 18, 43–44, 177, 221, 261
Liberals and Railroad Union, 175, 241
Libraries and readings rooms, 30, 117–18, 251
Literacy, 115
Lithuanians in railroading, 43
Liubitch, I. (Sammer), 267
Liubotin, October congress in, 245
Liubotin Republic, 283, 289
Locomotive crews. *See* Engine-drivers
Lodz, June strike in, 182
Lodz Railroad, 177
Lopukhin, A., 141

Mandelshtam, N. N., 174–75, 199n, 204
March 29 circular, 158, 159
Martial law, 149, 264
Masal'skii, A. I., 255
Masterovye. See Craftsmen
May Day, 129–30, 182
Mensheviks, 169, 207, 208, 242n, 268
Metalworkers, 59. *See also* Craftsmen; Workshops and depots
Midwives, number in public health section, 100
Military, influence in railroading of, 26, 303–4
Mineral Waters, 43, 65, 184–85, 250–51, 286
Ministry of Communications, 21; bureaucracy and reform in, 25; compared to family, 26; and education, 115; in January-February 1905, 146; and labor policy, 26–31; after 1905, 300–304; October general strike in offices of, 208; organization of, 24; and railroad police, 34. *See also* Administration of Railroads; Khilkov, Prince Mikhail I.; Labor policy; Nemeshaev, Klavdii S.
Ministry of Finance, 24, 27
Ministry of Internal Affairs, 34
Mitskevich, S. I., 202, 204
Montgomery, David, 62
Moscow: December general strike in, 267–69, 271–75, 277; housing in, 108; as hub of railroad system, 17; in January-February 1905, 137, 145; October general strike in, 206–7, 210; Riazan-Ural delegate assembly in, 245–47; September strikes in, 194–95. *See also* Moscow-Brest Railroad; Moscow-Iaroslavl-Archangel Railroad; Moscow-Kazan Railroad; Moscow-Kursk Railroad; Nicholas Railroad

Moscow-Brest Railroad, 17, 27; accidents on, 36; arrests on, 264; called Menshevik citadel, 169; and December general strike, 273, 274; in January-February 1905, 137, 145; and Railroad Union, 177, 180; September strike on, 195; Social Democratic union on, 242; wages and conditions on, 79, 104, 113
Moscow-Iaroslavl-Archangel Railroad, 17, 27; and December general strike, 266, 273, 274–75, 278; and October general strike, 195, 198, 200, 219; and Railroad Union, 177, 180
Moscow-Kazan Railroad, 17, 28; conditions on, 83, 90, 91, 100, 109; and December general strike, 272–75, 278, 285; in January-February 1905, 137, 147, 149, 150; July strike on, 183; management and labor relations on, 156, 226, 230; after 1905, 296; and October general strike, 195, 198–200, 202–3, 222; organizing on, 128, 133, 155n, 233; pension fund on, 189; petitions on, 152; punitive expedition on, 292; and Railroad Union, 176, 177, 286; Social Democratic union on, 242; strikes before 1905, 126–27
Moscow-Kiev-Voronezh Railroad, 17, 61; conditions on, 86, 91, 94, 116, 118; and December general strike, 273, 278; and Duma elections, 299; and October general strike, 211–12, 223; organizing on, 235, 236, 253–55; and Railroad Union, 177; strikes on, 130, 147; wages on, 75, 89. *See also* Konotop
Moscow-Kursk Railroad, 17, 55, 195; accidents on, 94; conditions on, 95; consumer cooperative on, 105; and December general strike, 273; delegate elections on, 155n; education on, 116; in January-February 1905, 137, 138, 147; before 1905, 126n, 128, 133; and October general strike, 201, 222; piece rates on, 80; and Railroad Union, 176, 177, 180, 240, 241
Moscow-Vindau-Rybinsk Railroad, 32, 261; and December general strike, 273; delegate assembly on, 244; in January-February 1905, 136, 145; and Kushka incident, 263; and October general strike, 208; and pension congress, 189; and Railroad Union, 177, 180
Museum for Assistance to Labor, 133, 151, 264; and Railroad Union, 163–64, 165
Mutinies, 289

Nachalo, 226
Nametnichenko, K. D., 167, 168, 241
Narodowe Kolo Kolejanzy (NKK), 180,
    214, 284
Nasha zhizn', 193
Nationality of railwaymen, 43–44
Nauman, V. V., 281
Nazarevich, B. F., 247
Nemeshaev, Klavdii S.: as director of
    South West Railroad, 30–31, 87, 108,
    133, 148, 181; and labor policy, 38, 40,
    131, 228, 300–301; as Minister of Com-
    munications, 227, 260, 263, 264, 291,
    302; replaced by Schaufus, 301
Nicholas Railroad, 17, 19, 27, 36; acci-
    dents on, 36; construction of, 16; and
    December general strike, 273, 274–77;
    female labor on, 42; health and diet of
    workers on, 102, 104, 111, 112; housing
    subsidy on, 83; and Kushka incident,
    263; and October general strike, 198,
    201, 207, 208, 222; and pension con-
    gress, 193; strikes on, 124, 130, 136,
    147, 260; turnover on, 67; wages on,
    74, 79–80
Nizhnedneprovsk, October general strike
    in, 211
Nosar', G. S., 209, 263
Nurses, number in public health section,
    100

October general strike, 198–223; de-
    mands of, 216–19; and mass organiz-
    ing, 229–37; in Moscow, 198–205,
    206–7; origins of, 194–205; and pen-
    sion congress, 195, 207–8, 216, 218–
    19, 223; on provincial railroads, 210–
    14; and Railroad Union, 194–205,
    215–16, 217–18, 221–22; in St. Peters-
    burg, 207–10; spread of, 205
October manifesto, 220–21, 224; divides
    Railroad Union, 241
Odessa, 59, 61, 132, 182, 220. *See also*
    South West Railroad
Orekhov, M. D.: and pension congress,
    191, 192, 193, 216; and Railroad
    Union, 179; and Riazan-Ural Railroad,
    246, 293
Orenburg-Tashkent Railroad, 165, 180,
    260
Organizing: during December general
    strike, 287–89; after October general
    strike, 233–37. *See also* Delegate as-
    semblies; Delegate trains; Strike com-
    mittees
Outside agitators, 287

Party unions. *See* Unions, Social
    Democratic
Paternalism, 31
Paulish, Aleksandr, 234n
Pavlovskii, A. A., 80, 105–6, 115
Pay-books, 28–29
Peasants: and December general strike,
    289; and delegate trains, 236–37; dis-
    turbances among, 225, 265; and rail-
    road labor, 44–47
Pechkovskii, N. K., 198, 201, 273
Pension congress, 187–94; delegates
    fired, 293; and mass movement, 196,
    244; and October general strike, 195,
    207–8, 216, 218–19, 223
Pension funds, 30, 83, 154, 187–89
Pereverzev, V. N., 164; arrested, 201,
    271; and Central Bureau, 167; and
    Conference of Twenty-nine Railroads,
    268; drafts Railroad Union program,
    165–66; after 1905, 295; on October
    general strike, 196, 200, 204; on Rail-
    road Union, 174, 181, 240, 242, 276
Perm-Tiumen Railroad, 118, 128, 290
Permanent staff, number and definition
    of, 49
Piece rates, 79–81
Plehve, V. K. von, 131, 134
Pogroms, 225, 245. *See also* Jews
Pokotilov, A. D., 37, 192
Pokotilov Commission. *See* Pension
    congress
Pokrovskii, M. N., 193n
Poland, railroad strikes in, 138–39, 149,
    214, 260, 284
Poles in railroading, 43
Polessky Railroad, 145, 177, 193, 261
Poliakov, Aleksei, 287
Poliakov, Samuel, 21
Police, railroad, 34, 226
Polish Socialist Party, 138, 177, 178, 180,
    284
Popechitelstvo, 117–18. *See also* "So-
    briety" programs
Postal-telegraph strike, 261–63
Potemkin, mutiny on, 182
Productivity, 36
Professional, usage defined, 6
Profitability of railroads, 34
Program of Railroad Union, 165–67
Proletariat, heterogeneity of, 2
Public health section, 30, 99–103; de-
    mand for change in, 153; and maternity
    care, 110; on trauma, 95–96
Punitive expeditions, 291–93
Pushkareva, I. M., 6n, 17n, 46–47, 235;
    on Railroad Union in Soviet histo-

Pushkareva, I. M. (*continued*)
riography, 202n; on strikes, 123, 124, 181; on wages and incomes, 74, 74n, 79n

Radtsig, Aleksandr, 37
Ragozin, Petr, 279, 287
"Railroad kings," 21
Railroad labor: in administration and communications, 51–58; classified by department, 47–49; classified by division of labor, 50; conditions of, 103; deteriorating economic position of, 85–89; in 1917, 6n, 305n; in railroad operations, 64–68; statistics 1860–1905, 16–17. *See also* Craftsmen; Employees; Engine-drivers; Hours and working conditions; Labor policy; Wages and income; Workshops and depots; *under individual occupations; under individual railroads*
Railroads in Russia: construction, 15–16, 19–26; and the military, 26, 303–4; and spread of strikes, 6; and tsarist state, 19–26. *See also under individual railroads*
Railroad Union. *See* All-Russian Union of Railroad Employees and Workers
Railwayman, use of word in Russian, 6
Rashin, A. G., 47
Reizman, Solomon, 249
Repair crews, recruitment and composition of, 69
Reutern, Mikhail, 15
Riazan-Ural Railroad, 18, 32; and December general strike, 273, 278–79, 287, 289; delegate assembly on, 245–47; and Duma elections, 299; early strikes on, 130; in February 1905, 147; fines on, 84; health care on, 101n; January 1905 strike on, 140–44; and Kushka incident, 263; leisure on, 114, 118; and October general strike, 213, 222, 223, 234; and pension congress, 190–91, 193; piece rates on, 81; and Railroad Union, 176–77; Social Democratic union on, 172
Riga, 18, 108, 174. *See also* Riga-Orel Railroad
Riga-Orel Railroad, 18; conditions on, 95, 100, 108; and December general strike, 283–84; and October manifesto, 222; and pension congress, 190; piece rates on, 81; and Railroad Union, 177, 180; repression on, 293; strikes on, 139, 147, 183n, 234n, 265

Rikhter, I. I., 38, 40, 45
Riman, General N. K., 292
Road and crossing guards, recruitment and personnel, 69
Romanov, V., 31, 158, 167, 168, 203
Rosenberg, William G., 6n, 310n
Rostov-on-Don, 18, 59; December general strike in, 279–81; 1894 strike in, 125n; 1902 general strike in, 63, 130, 206. *See also* Vladikavkaz Railroad
Rukhlov, S. V., 303–4
Russo-Japanese War, 133–34
Russo-Turkish War, 21, 26
Ruzaevka, December strike in, 278. *See also* Moscow-Kazan Railroad

Sablinksy, Walter: on October general strike, 197n, 202n, 203, 205n, 216n; on Railroad Union, 160n
St. Petersburg: December general strike in, 275–76; delegate assemblies in, 244; housing in, 108; in January 1905, 134–35, 136–37; October general strike in, 207–10, 222–23; as regional junction, 18; September strikes in, 194; venereal disease in, 111, 112. *See also* Baltic Railroad; Nicholas Railroad; Pension congress; St. Petersburg–Warsaw Railroad
St. Petersburg–Warsaw Railroad: and December general strike, 275; delegate assembly on, 244; early strikes on, 130; in January 1905, 136; and Kushka incident, 263; in November 1905, 260, 265; and October general strike, 208, 214; wages and conditions on, 33, 77
St. Petersburg Railroad Club, 191
Samara, 86, 176, 231, 290. *See also* Samara-Zlatoust Railroad
Samara-Zlatoust Railroad: delegate train on, 235; and eight-hour day, 260; housing on, 106, 108; inflation on, 86; and Kushka incident, 263; libraries and consumer cooperatives on, 105n, 118; strikes on, 138, 147, 183, 212, 234, 284
Saratov, 18, 140–44, 174, 213, 222, 289. *See also* Riazan-Ural Railroad
Schaufus, Lieutenant General Nikolai K., 146, 227, 301–3
Schivelbusch, Wolfgang, 65
Semenovskii Guards, 272, 278, 292
Serfdom, railroad work compared to, 32
Serfs, in railroad construction, 123
Shestakov, A. V., 202
Shingarev, I. L., 145, 152, 177, 256
Shlikhter, A. G., 98, 251, 252; and Rail-

road Union, 168, 176, 178; and South
West Railroad, 148, 152, 181, 212
Shvedov, Ivan, 247–49
Siberian Railroad, 18; accidents on, 36;
early strikes on, 130; health care on,
101; and Kushka incident, 263; libraries
on, 118; repression on, 293n, 294; So-
cial Democratic union on, 174; wages
on, 74, 85
Signalmen, 48, 87, 92
Skupevsky, Bronislaw, 192
"Sobriety" programs, 30. *See also*
Popechitelstvo
Social Democrats: appeal of, 232; gains in
November by, 257; and liberals, 239; in
Mineral Waters, 250; and October gen-
eral strike, 196–205, 238; and Railroad
Union, 164, 168, 169–74, 175, 178–81,
241–43, 244–45, 297–99; on Riazan-
Ural Railroad, 246; in Saratov, 140; on
South West Railroad, 148. *See also* Bol-
sheviks; Mensheviks; Unions, Social
Democratic
Socialist Revolutionaries, 9, 140, 148,
204, 257, 268; in Mineral Waters, 250;
on Moscow-Kazan Railroad, 198–99,
200; and Railroad Union, 164, 175,
178, 241, 244–45, 295, 297, 299; on
Riazan-Ural Railroad, 246
Sokolov, L. G., 263
South East Railroad, 18; and December
general strike, 288, 289; and Kushka
incident, 263; and October general
strike, 212–13; organizing on, 235,
238, 255–56; and Railroad Union, 176,
177; strikes on, 124, 130, 145, 147; telegraph operators on, 157; wages on, 75
South West Railroad, 18, 56, 61, 67; accidents on, 35; benefits on, 30–31, 116,
117, 118; housing on, 107, 108–9; inflation on, 87; and Kushka incident, 263;
after 1905, 297; organizing on, 235,
251–52; and pension congress, 190;
and Railroad Union, 176, 180; strikes
on, 124, 132, 148, 157, 212, 262, 284;
wages and incomes on, 72, 73, 77, 78,
80, 84
Soviet historians. *See* Historians, Soviet
Soviet of Workers' Deputies, St. Petersburg, 208–9, 223
Soviets, railroad workers and, 238
Starosty, vybornye, 146, 154–56
State Council, 187
Stationmasters, 45, 48, 56–57; and
strikes, 237, 285; wages and hours of,
77, 89

Stavskii, I. I., 163
Stokers, 48
Stolypin, Petr, 141, 245, 300, 302
Strike committees, 233–35. *See also* De-
cember general strike; October general
strike; Strikes
Strikes: in February 1905, 145–51; in
January 1905, 135–44; before 1905,
123–34; in November 1905, 259; in
September 1905, 194–96; in spring and
summer 1905, 182–85. *See also* De-
cember general strike; October general
strike; *under individual railraods*
Strumilin, S. G., 85
Surh, Gerald, 61
Sushkin, G. G., 246, 247
Switchmen, 48, 68; hours of, 29, 92; and
labor turnover, 37; wages and incomes
of, 77, 87
Syn otechestva, 128
Syzran'-Viazma Railroad, 147, 180, 212

Tambov-Ural Railroad, 142, 147
Tatarinskii, V. Ia., 273
Taylorism, 61–62
Tbilisi. *See* Tiflis
Telegraph Department, 49
Telegraph operators, 49, 57–58; condi-
tions of, 113–14; health of, 90, 113;
hours of, 89; in 1905, 157, 285, 288; so-
cial origins of, 45; women as, 42
Telegul crash, 35
Temporary workers, 49
Thompson, E. P., 7
Tiflis, 18, 43, 59, 132, 139–40. *See also*
Transcaucasian Railroad
Trade unions. *See* All-Russian Union of
Railroad Employees and Workers;
Union organizing; Unions, Social
Democratic
Train handlers, 48
Trans-Baikal Railroad, 36, 74, 85, 174
Transcaucasian Railroad, 18, 43; accidents
on, 94; and December general strike,
283; health care on, 100, 112; and Oc-
tober general strike, 214, 223; and pen-
sion congress, 190; Social Democratic
union on, 174; strikes on, 129, 132,
133, 139–40, 182; wages and hours on,
75, 77, 81–82, 89, 90
Trauma, 96, 103
Tregubov, Dr. S. L., 114
Trotsky, Leon, 6n, 136, 209
Tsarskoe Selo, first railroad line to, 16
Tsimoshenko, G. O., 193
Tsvetkov, A. A., 194

Turkish War of 1877. *See* Russo-Turkish War
Turnover, labor, 36–37, 44

Ukhtomskii, A. V., 65n; death of, 292; and December general strike, 272, 273, 274; and October general strike, 198, 201
Ukraine: formation of railroad work force in, 44; 1903 strikes in, 133; pogroms in, 225. *See also* Kharkov; Kharkov-Nikolaev Railroad; Kiev; Kursk-Kharkov-Sevastopol Railroad; Moscow-Kiev-Voronezh Railroad; South West Railroad
Unemployment, 293–94
Union of Postal and Telegraph Employees, 261
Union of Unions, 207
Union organizing, early efforts at, 163
Unions, growth after October general strike, 240. *See also* All-Russian Union of Railroad Employees and Workers
Unions, Social Democratic, 165, 173–74, 176, 242–43, 297, 299
United States: organization of factory work in, 62; railroad labor in, 6n, 37, 66n, 68, 83n, 90, 107, 114n, 188n; railroads in, 16, 31n, 35
Urals, recruitment of railroad labor in, 45n

Vasil'chenko, S. F., 63
Vendrikh, A. A. von, 23, 303–4
Venereal diseases, 111–13
Vilna, Railroad Union meeting in, 177–78, 179
Vistula Railroad, 138, 149, 177, 190, 284
Vladikavkaz Railroad, 18, 23, 29, 43, 56, 65, 83, 113, 125n, 134, 293; and December general strike, 279–81, 286; in January-February 1905, 140, 147, 150; July strike on, 178, 183–85, 186–87; and Kushka incident, 263; and October general strike, 214, 219; organizing on, 128, 163, 238, 247–51; and pension congress, 193, 194; and Rostov general strike, 130
Volkov, Efim, 254, 255

Voronezh, 18, 145, 163. *See also* South East Railroad
Vorovskii, V. V., 171–72
Vyshnegradskii, I. A., 21

Wages and income, 37, 73–89; change over time, 85–89; of craftsmen, 78–82, 87–89; of engine-drivers, 84–85. *See also under individual railroads*
Warsaw-Vienna Railroad, 74, 75, 187; in 1905, 138, 149, 214, 284; and Railroad Union, 177
What Is to Be Done?, 170
White-collar work. *See* Employees
Witte, Sergei I., 15, 21, 22, 39, 131; in 1905, 148, 216, 220, 224, 227; replaced by Goremykin, 301
Women in railroading, 42–43
Working conditions. *See* Hours and working conditions
Workshops and depots, 48, 60; hours and conditions in, 90–91, 96; and labor legislation, 27; literacy in, 115; nature of work in, 58–64; politics in, 257; wages and incomes in, 78–82, 87–89. *See also* Craftsmen; *under individual railroads*

Yaney, George L., 25n, 28n
Youth: effect of October general strike on, 231; of telegraph operators, 57–58

Zemstvo, 1, 54, 101, 141
Zheleznodorozhnaia nedelia, 38–39, 46, 56, 93
Zheleznodorozhnik, 38–39, 266; on delegate assemblies, 155; on March 29 circular, 158; on Nemeshaev, 227, 228, 300–301, 302n; on pensions and pension congress, 190, 192, 193; on railroad doctors, 101; on Railroad Union, 298; on repression, 293; on Russo-Japanese War, 133; on stationmasters, 56
Zheleznodorozhnoe delo, 38, 42, 90
Zhmerinka, delegate assembly in, 252. *See also* South West Railroad
Zubarev, A. M., 287
Zubatovism, 132–33, 164